Praise for Myths of Sport Performance

Have your ever wondered why, despite training hard, you don't achieve the expected results? Do you believe in most of the "stories" they tell you about issues that affect your sport performance? Behind every elite or recreational athlete, there is a mountain of information, but also a cloud of myth that can sabotage your progress. In this book, the most common beliefs are dismantled and offer science based tools to put an end to this cloud of myths and optimize and improve your health and, therefore, your performance.

Dr Cristina Salazer Ramirez, expert sport science Doctor, Master Skyrunning World Champion.

A brilliant, paradigm-shifting book written by genuine experts in sport. I'm delighted to see the generic cr*p that is 'received wisdom' around training being challenged and corrected for the benefit of athletes and coaches. A fascinating read!

Dr Emma Pooley, Olympic medallist and world champion cyclist.

In a world of hearsay and amateur traditions, this book will go some way in smashing myths that have long been held as gospel. It is a remedy to the phrase 'we have always done it that way', founded in scientific research and cross sport thinking.

Kevin Pickard, Development Director, AP Race.

Whether you are a psychologist, coach or academic, The Myths of Sport Performance will offer you insights to improve your practice. If you are a practitioner psychologist, the book offers compelling arguments and great studies to back up points you might be discussing with athletes. If you are a coach, it offers great advice for how to get the best from your athletes. If you are coming from an academic approach, the book brings to light the many contradictions that exist within 'well established' disciplines of study so you can assess with a more questioning mindset.

Dr Josephine Perry, Sport Psychologist.

Myths of Sport Performance

Myths of Sport Performance

Dr Amy Whitehead and Jenny Coe

SEQUOIA BOOKS

Every possible effort has been made to ensure that the information contained in this book is accurate at the time of going to press. The publishers and author(s) cannot accept responsibility for any errors and omissions, however caused. No responsibility for loss or damage occasioned to any person acting, or refraining from action, as a result of the material contained in this publication can be accepted by the editor, the publisher or the author.

First published in 2024 by Sequoia Books

Apart from fair dealing for the purposes of research or private study, or criticism or review, as permitted under the Copyright, Designs and Patents act 1988, this publication may only be reproduced, stored or transmitted, in any form or by any means, with the prior permission in writing of the publisher, or in the case of reprographic reproduction in accordance with the terms and licenses issued by the CLA. Enquiries concerning reproduction outside these terms should be sent to the publisher using the details on the website www.sequoia-books.com

©Amy Whitehead & Jenny Coe

The right of Amy Whitehead & Jenny Coe to be identified as Editors of this work has been asserted in accordance with the Copyright, Designs and Patents act 1988.

ISBN
Print: 9781914110382
EPUB: 9781914110399

A CIP record for this book is available from the British Library

Library of Congress Cataloguing-In-Publication Data

Name: Amy Whitehead & Jenny Coe
Title: Myths of Sport Performance
Description: 1st Edition, Sequoia Books UK 2024
Print: 9781914110382
EPUB: 9781914110399

Library of Congress Control Number: 2024916477

Printed and bound by CPI Group (UK) Ltd, Croydon, CR0 4YY

Contents

Contributors ix
Myths of Sport Performance xi
Edited by Dr Amy E. Whitehead and Jenny Coe

1 Knowing Stuff: Myths, Science and Reality 1
  Christopher R. Matthews

2 Winning Matters Most in Elite Sport 17
  Elliott Newell, Cath Bishop, Laurence Halsted and Katie Mobed

3 The Myth of the Zombie: Why Automaticity Is Insufficient for
  (Aspiring) Elite Athletes 35
  Henrik Herrebrøden

4 Busting Myths: Navigating Pregnancy as an Elite Athlete 46
  *Melanie J Hayman, Margie H Davenport, Nicola Bullock
  and Amy E. Whitehead*

5 'All Feedback Is Beneficial': A Deconstruction of Feedback 61
  Ross Corbett, Mark Partington, Lisa Ryan and Ed Cope

6 The Myth of 'Periodization' 77
  James Steele, James Fisher, Jeremy Loenneke and Samuel Buckner

7 The Myth That Being a Good Mother and an Elite Athlete Are
  Not Compatible 97
  Kelly Massey and Amy E. Whitehead

8 Stretching the Truth: A Critical Examination of Stretching for Athletes 105
  Tim Pigott

CONTENTS

9	Distinguishing the Truths from the Myths: The Dual-Axis Framework *Philip E. Kearney, Frank Nugent and Andrew Harrison*	125
10	Smoke and Mirrors: The Superficial Rise of Women's Sport *Alex Lascu*	144
11	Physical Fatigue in Football: A Challenge to the Importance of Fatigue in Determining Performance in Football Match Play *Liam Anderson, Thomas Brownlee, Barry Drust and Matej Varjan*	155
12	Seeking Clarity on Psychological Safety: Tackling Myths and Misconceptions in Competitive Sport *Michael Cooke, Kyle Paradis, Lee Ann Sharp, David Woods and Mustafa Sarkar*	169
13	Harnessing the Power of Attention: Exploring 'Focus of Attention' Theories, Practice and Myths *Marianne Davies, Robin Owen, Victoria M. Gottwald, and Harjiv Singh*	182
14	Menstrual Cycle Myths *Jacky J. Forsyth*	195
15	Challenging the Myths of High Performance in Esports *Laura Swettenham, Kabir Bubna and Matthew Watson*	211
16	Think Using Electronics before Bed and Only Getting Five Hours of Sleep Is OK? We Bust These Athlete Sleep Myths *Kathleen Miles, Stephanie Shell and Dean Miller*	227
17	Leadership: A Title Bestowed from Above; a Position of Awarded Power. Truth or Myth? *Jane Booth*	241
18	'If You Want to Go Fast Go Alone. If You Want to Go Far, Go Together' – Engaging Productively with a Coach Developer *Andrew Bradshaw*	257

Contributors

Liam Anderson University of Birmingham, United Kingdom
Cath Bishop Olympian, Coach, Author, United Kingdom
Andrew Bradshaw Coach Development Consultant, United Kingdom
Jane Booth Opus 29 Consultancy, United Kingdom
Thomas Brownlee University of Birmingham, United Kingdom
Kabir Bubna The International Federation of Esports Coaches (IFoEC), United Kingdom
Samuel Buckner University of South Florida, USA
Nicola Bullock Australian Institute of Sport, Australia
Michael Cooke Ulster University, Northern Ireland
Ed Cope University, Loughborough, United Kingdom
Ross Corbett Loughborough University, United Kingdom; Edge Hill University, United Kingdom
Margie H. Davenport University of Alberta, Canada
Marianne Davies Sheffield Hallam University, United Kingdom; UK Coaching, United Kingdom
Barry Drust University of Birmingham, United Kingdom
James Fisher Solent University, United Kingdom
Jacky J. Forsyth Staffordshire University, United Kingdom
Victoria M. Gottwald Bangor University, United Kingdom
Laurence Halsted True Athlete Project, United Kingdom
Andrew Harrison University of Limerick, Ireland
Melanie J. Hayman CQ University, Australia
Henrik Herrebrøden Kristiania University College, Norway
Philip E. Kearney University of Limerick, Ireland
Alex Lascu University of Canberra, Australia
Jeremy Loenneke University of Mississippi, USA

CONTRIBUTORS

Kelly Massey Liverpool John Moores University, United Kingdom
Christopher R. Matthews Nottingham Trent University, United Kingdom
Katie Mobed The Prime Clinic, United Kingdom
Kathleen Miles The Australian National University, Australia
Dean Miller CQ University, Australia
Elliott Newell The Thrive Academy, United Kingdom
Frank J. Nugent University of Limerick, Ireland
Robin Owen Liverpool Hope University, United Kingdom
Kyle Paradis Ulster University, Northern Ireland
Mark Partington Edge Hill University, United Kingdom
Tim Pigott Salford University, United Kingdom; Health and Performance 3
Lisa Ryan Atlantic Technological University Galway City, Ireland
Mustafa Sarkar Nottingham Trent University, United Kingdom
Lee Ann Sharp Ulster University, Northern Ireland
Stephanie Shell Australian Institute of Sport, Australia
Harjiv Singh Orlando Magic Basketball Club, FL, USA
James Steele Solent University, United Kingdom
Laura Swettenham Liverpool John Moores University, United Kingdom
Matej Varjan Charles University, Czech Republic
Matthew Watson The International Federation of Esports Coaches (IFoEC), United Kingdom; German Sport University Cologne, Germany
David Woods Ulster University, Northern Ireland
Amy E. Whitehead Liverpool John Moores University, United Kingdom

Myths of Sport Performance

Edited by Dr Amy E. Whitehead and Jenny Coe

Introduction

Does winning really matter? Is stretching important? Do skills just become automatic? These are just a few of the many myths that this book aims to challenge.

Welcome to *Myths of Sport Performance*. Following the great success of the *Myths of Sport Coaching* and the feedback from many organizations, practitioners and academics in the field that there are so many more myths to bust, we decided to carry on with the series. However, as with the previous book, we realized that these myths expand beyond just coaching and coaches, and impact sport performance as a wider concept. Hence, *Myths of Sport Performance*. This informative and enlightening book showcases valuable contributions from talented authors worldwide, covering a diverse range of sports.

Sport and performance are multidisciplinary in nature, made up of a myriad of sciences and philosophies, with the aim (the majority of the time) of improving performance, well-being and health. This book aims to provide readers with the multidisciplinary team (MDT) perspectives of sport and performance, from the physiological, psychological, pedagogical, sociological and even philosophical areas. Think of this book as your pocket 'MDT'.

As both practitioners and academics, we (Amy and Jen) are constantly striving to connect research with practice. As the Player Care & Wellbeing lead for the Women's Professional Game (football), Jen is always seeking to answer questions that can improve the well-being of athletes along with supporting the clubs and their staff to look through this performance wellbeing lens. As an associate professor of Sport Psychology and Coaching, and an applied sport and exercise psychologist, Amy believes that it is vital to understand how the sciences interlink, and how this all plays into and impacts the psychology of the clients she works with. Hence our thirst for knowledge, especially knowledge that challenges ideas and concepts that we *think* we already know.

Certainly, this book is underpinned by science, but we also invited authors to bring their own personal experiences to the chapters. That's why we invited not just experts within academia but also those with vast experience working on the ground in sport and performance. This includes lead sport scientists working in national institutes of sport, physiotherapists, sport and exercise psychologists, and high-performance consultants. It is important to us that this book is read and enjoyed by practitioners in the field of sport, and therefore is informed by those successfully working in these areas. As a consequence, we give no apologies for the varied styles and ever so slight structure differences within each chapter.

What actually is a myth and how do they come to exist? We start the book with a chapter that aims to consider and answer this exact question. Following this, the book covers physiology-related myths such as fatigue within football, stretching and training amongst pregnant athletes and psychosocial-related chapters such as how gender equality is (or is not) improving within sport and how female athletes negotiate their identity during pregnancy. We also bring you chapters that consider multidisciplinary perspectives, such as myths around sleep, and the physiological, psychological and technological considerations that are needed when studying such a complex topic.

Whatever area of sport you work, participate or have an interest in, this book provides both the research underpinnings and practical considerations for you to be able to apply to your own environment and context. The aim of this book is to become a vehicle for conversation and where it needs to influence change. Whether you just become more aware of a specific topic or you actually change your practice as a result, we hope you enjoy reading as much as we enjoyed putting together.

Finally, we would like to thank all of the exceptional authors for their contribution to this book. Without them, their knowledge, enthusiasm and motivation to contribute their chapter, this book would not be possible. Please check out the QR codes within each chapter to learn a little bit about the chapter authors, ask further questions or just reach out to give them a virtual high five for their fantastic work.

Enjoy! Amy & Jen.

1 Knowing Stuff

Myths, Science and Reality

Christopher R. Matthews

I love a good myth, me. I think many of us do – if that wasn't the case, they wouldn't hold such a central place in human societies both cross-culturally and historically. They're vital to how many people make sense of their worlds. And, in that respect, as a means of guiding future actions, shaping interpretations and helping produce understanding, myths have much in common with religion, fables, traditions, legislation, social norms and, crucially for the topic of this chapter, scientific theory. Of course, we can argue around the rightness or wrongness of all these ways of knowing stuff about the world around us, but that wouldn't change the fact of their importance. I want to lean into those similarities in this chapter by considering what a myth is, how scientific theories can have mythical dimensions and how both relate to reality. My goal is to think more deeply about how we know stuff.

If you're like me and you didn't get access to much philosophy during your schooling, this might take a bit of work to get your head around. We're going to try to understand what it means to understand.[1] We'll need to consider some different examples of the ways that people know stuff, so that we can be clearer about the qualities that each might possess in relation to our understanding of myths and reality. And we must also get a better grasp of the social interactions and cultural processes which are the foundations on which myths, science and our knowledge of reality are built. Please bear with me while I start by taking what might feel like a detour.

Understanding human understanding

Hermes was a Greek god. He's a 'real' myth in the same way as Santa is (more about him later). But also, the legacy of Hermes is embedded in our use of language in various phrases and words such as hermetically sealed, hermaphrodite and, specifically of interest here, *hermeneutics* – that is, theories of interpretation.

Hermes, amongst other things, was the mediator between gods and mortals; he was known as the 'messenger of the gods'. And the story goes that he was the inventor of language – which is the main medium[2] by which we pass messages to each other (communicate) and understand something about the world. Now, as with most Greek gods, Hermes was a bit tricksy – he'd enjoy the disquiet and confusion that his messages might cause. You see, as a mediator Hermes could distort or twist the meaning of messages he'd been instructed to pass on. And it is the same with language and speech, for words – especially when used in combination with body language, emotion and tone of voice – are seldom black and white; *their meaning requires interpretation.*[3]

Unfortunately for those of us who build a career out of trying to understand the world scientifically, no word or idea can exist outside of this interpretative process. And this mediation via interpretation is fundamental to our ability to (mis)understand something. Our knowing of stuff is both built (enabled) and made problematic (constrained) within this process. Hermeneutics can be thought of as the methodology for that process – how we go about trying to conceptually grasp something about something.

Now, the 'something' we're trying to understand might be an object like a rock, so let's think a bit about the hermeneutic process connected to this.[4] To understand a rock we'll first need the word 'rock' as a kind of symbolic placeholder which we can use to stand in for a material rock when there isn't one in front of us. So I can write about a 'rock' and be confident that you'll know roughly what I mean. What follows might sound basic, but it's important – the word 'rock' is not the same as a rock. Both can become objects of our attention, but one is formally symbolic of the other. It's actually quite common for people (including scientists) to grasp this intellectually but for it to not follow through into their practical interaction with ideas (more on this later). For most of us going through daily life there is so much resonance between what we think a rock is, that the fact the word 'rock' and the thing 'rock' are not the same doesn't really matter. I might say 'look at that rock', and you cast your eyes to the floor, ignore the empty crisp packet, the chewing gum, my shoes and see the rock – a *seemingly* simple hermeneutic process which results in a *seemingly* clear understanding of the world that is shared between the two of us.[5]

But I couldn't go into a builders' merchant and simply ask for 'some rocks' and expect to be understood without follow-up questions. This is because in that trade there's far more nuance and complexity around what rocks (stones, sand, concrete, etc. – I think they'd term them 'aggregates') are and their associated properties (e.g. their hardness and greyish-brownness). In order to gain some clarity, and avoid misunderstanding, the builders merchant would probably ask something like 'What type o' rocks ya after, mate? What job ya doin'?' Here, our hermeneutic exercise becomes a bit more involved. I might need help understanding what I mean, and the correct terms to use, but we'll probably get there in the end.

This is a simplified version of what we can call a *single hermeneutic* – the process of me, you and the builders merchant understanding something of the object 'rock'. Here, we have aligned our ideas about an object sufficiently for us to move forward pragmatically. If we speak the same language and have grown up in broadly similar cultures, we can usually be confident that this shared understanding happens in common-or-garden circumstances. And when it doesn't proceed as normal, the breakdown in the process tends to be clear. If I was waiting for you at the pub, and you didn't turn up, it might be because we'd confused the meaning of the question 'fancy a pint in the local?' In this instance, our misinterpretation of each other resulted in a clear breakdown in the effectiveness of our language to match up with everyday activities. The resonance between our interpretation of the world and our actual worlds dropped importantly out of sync. Usually we would consider where the mistake happened and work to ensure we didn't do it again – our understanding of the world would increase. For example, I live in Beeston (a town in England), we have a few great local pubs and so in reply to my request of 'Fancy a pint in the local?' You could be sat in The Crown pub while I was actually sat in The Vic pub, so I needed to be clearer about which 'local' I was suggesting.

Where this gets 'fun' is when there's a *double hermeneutic*. This is when we move from trying to share understanding of objects (rocks/pubs) to trying to share understanding of subjects (or a group of subjects). In this usage of the term, a subject is a thinking person who can reflectively change their thoughts and actions. These subjects (me, you, them, us) can become our objects of study (we objectify ourselves by turning our intellectual attention towards ourselves and others), as is the case when I conduct a social science project. But, importantly, in such research, our participants aren't passive (like rocks) in this process. Not only do they often predict what we're trying to find out and might change their behaviours or answers to questions, but they're also not simply receivers of our findings about them.

So if I ask a person who holds racist views if they're racist, they will often be culturally savvy enough to recognize they shouldn't disclose this information in most situations. And if I were to report findings that a certain group does have racist views, that group will often take note of those claims and do better in the future at concealing or perhaps changing those views. We are, then, thinking beings/things, who, when we conduct research ourselves, are researching other thinking beings/things – the *double hermeneutic*.[6] Unlike rocks and pubs which have objective features that don't change in response to our research findings, the objective features of subjects can and do change as a result of our interactions with them and we, as researchers, are inevitably a part of that change.[7]

In contrast to the complexity of other scholars writing on this topic, I've deliberately framed this hermeneutic stuff as a rather unproblematic process, but think of what it's like for kids to learn how to know stuff – it takes years, it's full of setbacks, misplaced assumptions and misunderstandings. And it's not much different with adults. The complexities of interactional relations, historical, social and cultural differences, and the nuances of (especially technical) terminology all combine to shape the communication of our ideas about things. The result is that our attempts to understand each other and the things around us are likely to skew, conceal and obfuscate as well as define, reveal and clarify – *just like Hermes would have wanted*.

'But Chris, what's all this got to do with myths?'

Good question. As I described at the start of the chapter, myths, like religion, fables, traditions, legislation, social norms and scientific theories, are all ways in which we might understand something about the world. They're central features of our hermeneutic. What I've been establishing above is that our way of knowing stuff is what we can call 'concept-dependent'. That is, you can't understand a thing without some form of conception of that thing.[8] And such concepts are developed over time through social interactions with each other and the world around us. Therefore, classical myths, like that of Prometheus and the modern reworking of such a myth in a film like *Bladerunner 2049*, can provide us with different ways of thinking about and objectifying situations we might find ourselves within.

Myths can, then, be thought of as ideas that we use to understand something about the world. They're stories that give us certain ways of thinking about certain things. And, as such, they can help us pick a course of action and navigate our way in the world. We know that a myth is mythical in that it's not an attempt to empirically represent something of past events in the world, but that doesn't change its potential utility for us.

This separation from reality might lead some to think of myths as the opposite of scientific theories which, by definition, are attempts to say something truthful[9] about the world. But when considering theories in the way I'm about to highlight here, they can be found to occupy a functionally similar category – that of potentially useful hermeneutics. This is because a theory is also a way of understanding something about the world. Of course, there are important differences in the process of developing and substantiating theories, and they should have very different properties from myths in how they align with the objects they help us understand, but that doesn't change the potential similarities. We shouldn't, then, think of myths and science as simple opposites, and if we do we're liable to miss the very important utility of myths and over-estimate, perhaps even fetishize,[10] a scientific approach to understanding the world. And if we do fall into the trap of mythologizing elements of science, we're actively stripping away the inherent doubt that should differentiate it from how we consider myths (more about this below).

What I'm trying to do here is unpack the way that simplistic either/or thinking can lead to false dichotomies.[11] This is because when we think in such binary ways we tend to create a caricature of the world, and this limits our understanding of it. In that regard, it would be unscientific not to appreciate, account for and attempt to understand the ways that our theories might have accrued some mythical qualities. And at the same time this can also help us to grasp how myths, despite their apparent disconnection from the empirical world, can be pragmatic, useful and support us in understanding important elements of our reality. Or, as I put it elsewhere,[12] the scientist, rather than simply being the dispeller of myths, should also be the explorer of myths and mythical ways of thinking – let's give that a go.

Knowing stuff – real myths, myths made real and the mythically real

Although I hope I've made some of these abstract and philosophical points come to life with a few examples, now it's important to lock these ideas down even further. In what follows, I'll move along a continuum with myths at one end and the most accurate portrayal of reality at the other. This will show some of the key moments within the greyscale that sit between our most mythical and realist forms of knowing. Something to look out for as you proceed through these cases is the way in which social actors and their interactions are central to the ideas I'm outlining. It's within a focus on these people making myths and reality that we're able to trace how we develop our understanding of the world: this is a point I return to towards the end of the chapter before concluding with a final thought.

A real myth – Santa

I, like many people in the UK and other parts of the world, grew up believing in Santa. As an adult, I recognize that Santa is a fictitious story that is tied to Pagan and Christian traditions. Most people I know who perpetuate this myth do so knowing full well that it has no connection to reality in terms of there actually being an overweight, red-cheeked, white-bearded man who flies around the globe in a sleigh pulled by magic reindeers and delivers children's Christmas presents. Those who do believe in Santa are invariably children who are taught the story by family, friends and perhaps even school teachers.[13] And then there are those children who are slightly older who start to figure out the empirical impossibility of Santa, but still kinda believe, and play along, 'just in case'. This myth is largely harmless fun and can help parents teach important lessons around appropriate behaviours and their association with various rewards. In that regard, the story holds utility in helping young people grasp important moralistic ideas as a part of learning to conform to culturally normative standards.

In such utility, we can find something of the reality in the myth of Santa. While we know there is no material object we could point out as the 'real' Santa, we also know the very real importance of children being able to understand 'good' behaviour and how to manage and moderate their 'bad' behaviours. This story, with its complete disconnection from empirical reality, can then be a useful way of understanding something about the world. And via this process, the myth of Santa has very real outcomes for shaping the thoughts and behaviours of young people. And it is here, to paraphrase the Thomas theorem,[14] that myths become real in their consequences for the lives of those who live them out. There is, then, a social reality to Santa as it's a story, a symbolic placeholder (like the idea of a rock), that many of us use to help young people navigate certain realities about the world they're growing up within.

This is then a *real myth* in that most of us would understand it as existing with zero link to empirical reality in any simple sense. But even here, in a genuinely mythical idea, we can see how the reality we experience is shaped in terms of the moral ordering of life that the myth helps us construct.

A myth made real – testosterone is the 'male hormone'

My academic journey has taken a rather winding path, so even though I trained as a sociologist, I didn't really focus on that topic until my postgrad studies (in my late 20s). This means that when I was first reading sociology, I used to draw on subjects like biology and geography as frames of reference without knowing it. These academic disciplines provided ways of seeing the world that I was relatively comfortable with from my schooling. The biological side of this meant that, like most people, I understood something about hormones as important in relation to the different attributes that are assigned to men and women: broadly speaking, testosterone was the 'male hormone' and oestrogen was the female equivalent.

There is a reality to this. When taken as an aggregate across the population, men tend to have a higher level of testosterone than women. But to simply extract from that broad finding that testosterone in some essential sense equals 'maleness' is daft. It neglects the complexity of human biology in general, more specifically that women also produce and need testosterone, and that many men have naturally low levels of the hormone. It's also overly simplistic to associate raised testosterone with an increase in 'male-like' behaviours, whatever that might mean. Years of social science have repeatedly undermined such reductive and sexist understandings of sex and gender.[15]

Now, within the boxing gym where I conducted my PhD research, these simplified stories were taken as a plain fact of life. The men I trained and sparred with would regularly use such ideas to explain the joy and excitement they gained from boxing. There was a neat teleological match here between our homosocial environment, where women seldom stepped foot, and the men's recourse to biological interpretations of life – *being men doing 'manly' stuff with men proved they were men doing manly stuff*. And, therefore, it was self-evident to them that their (our) biological bodies explained why we loved punching each other so much.

Of course, the boxers didn't have a clue what their testosterone levels were, or much of an idea about the endocrine system or associated biological processes. But when you already know something to be the case (i.e. testosterone = male), evidence isn't something you really need. So, with their uninformed but very confident (mis)understandings of hormones, they happily claimed stuff like:

> It's testosterone ain't it, 'ave you ever seen any of those lot [motions toward the bodybuilders] when they're on 'roid rage? F******'ell if you wanna know about the power of that shit just go into town with 'em when they're on it, mate, they're

mental! So they've loads of it in 'em in an unnatural way and it fucks 'em up, but even in a normal way if you 'ave naturally high testosterone then that will make you aggressive at times. (Gary in Matthews, 2015)

Of course, as a sociologist in training, I wasn't looking for biological explanations for the behaviours that Gary referred to as 'aggression'. I was much more interested in the ways that ideas and social interactions were formative of social life.[16] And these interactions inside and around the ring were framed by pseudo-biological accounts around what it meant to be a man. It was in this process of framing that the myth of the 'male hormone' came to be made real.

Via the socially learned training associated with boxing, in a social space that has been traditionally coded as a male preserve,[17] these men could unproblematically experience their behaviours as an outlet of their natural maleness. And here, the association between men and testosterone could be turned into a largely uncontested reality about what it meant to be a man. The myth of testosterone as the 'male hormone' was made true for these men as they punched, grunted, sweated and grimaced, and slumped over each other knackered after training.

If you squint really hard some scientific papers can be read to support the myth, but, more importantly, when this idea is uncritically taken on by people it can be used to support a mythical reading of the world. In this sense, 'science' is caricatured and stripped of its complexity. It can then be used in an unscientific way – divorced from the essential attitude of doubt which should demarcate our approach to using scientific methodologies – to shore up a myth. And here again we see, within the consequences of this idea shaping men's beliefs about themselves and their behaviours, *a myth made real* – if we think ourselves to be naturally aggressive, don't be surprised if we act aggressively and place the blame for this on our nature.

Real science as myth-making – the hegemony of hegemonic masculinity

In the last example, I've shown how myths can be alluring and then become part of their own reproduction and symbolic substantiation. Now, even though there might be a kernel of science in this idea of the 'male hormone', we wouldn't consider it to be scientific when it's used as it was in the boxing club. We'd mark students down who wrote in such simplistic ways, and if an academic conducted research with such poorly constructed ideas, they'd struggle to get funding or publish in reputable journals. This is part of the social processes that those of us who claim to be scientists conform to as we seek to get on in our careers. However, a similar thing can happen in relation to peer-reviewed publications. Let me give an example.

In my first post-doc role, I worked as a researcher on a project evaluating a men's health programme. During that time, I read loads of work on masculinity and became well-versed in the broad theoretical ideas that dominated that literature. Much of this work employed Raewyn Connell's various discussions of 'hegemonic masculinity theory'.[18] This is a very useful and well-considered approach to understanding certain men's social power, but it also highlights how men's position in society can be damaging in various ways, not least to their health.

These theoretical ideas dominated much of the research on men, to the point where Jeff Hearn (2004) wrote a paper in which he noted something of the hegemony of hegemonic masculinity. Jeff argued that the concept of hegemonic masculinity had become so engrained in much scholarship that some scholars were interpreting the world such that this theoretical idea had lost a robust connection to empirical observations, as well as neglecting the broader hegemony concerning the social category of men. Specifically, the idea of hegemonic masculinity had begun to cast a conceptual shadow over the hegemony of the social category of men within gender hegemony. That is, Connell's conception of masculinity had begun to stand in for the behaviours of actual men. I don't have the space in this chapter to substantiate Jeff's work fully, but these ideas informed my thinking in various ways during my work on men's health and beyond.

What became increasingly apparent was that the object of study (men and their behaviours) moved into the background as the theoretical idea about masculinity was foregrounded. In some key literature on men's health, this manifests as an absence of the richness and contradictions of men's lives and relationships to health. In such cases, the scholars' use of theory was actively reducing the alignment between empirical observations and our scientific understanding.[19] My realization that this was happening in leading academic journals at the hand of relatively well-known academics has always stuck with me. It was something of a watershed moment. Later I expanded upon this idea through my discussion of 'theoretical determinism' – which is when a scholar is so captivated by their interpretation of the world that they see it playing out unproblematically despite evidence to the contrary.[20] In such cases, the scholars' commitment to a particular interpretative/hermeneutic lens means they won't/can't see such counter-evidence, or they find ways of making it align with their 'pet' theory. When this happens, there is no way in which their ideas could be incorrect, they become unfalsifiable, and it is at this point that the scientific endeavour collapses and theory begets theory.[21]

This is an example, then, of how real science – that which is taken to have met the academic standards required to be published – can contain clear mythical dimensions. In this case, the 'myth' was a scientific theory, and the myth-making process took these ideas and implanted them into the lives and experiences of men. And, if one were to read that work uncritically, those findings, which I argue are importantly divorced from reality, would be taken to be a robust and legitimate knowledge of stuff – *real science as myth-making*.

The mythically real – the 'perfect' measurement

The research I've just described in the previous example certainly has different academic standards, aims and achievements to those which some would simplistically refer to as 'hard science'. Within such disciplines, where experimentation and randomized control trials are taken to be the gold standard, scholars design their work with the *aim* of preventing these sorts of wonky interpretations and theoretical determinism. And in this way, scholars who do mechanical engineering, chemistry, rocket science and the like would rightfully point to the potential inherent in their approach for the alignment between their ideas and the real world to be checked and so verified or disproved.

In this regard, physics can claim to be the most accurate science in that its theoretical predictions match up with measurements to a degree which is unparalleled by other ways of knowing the world.[22] Take the 'electron magnet moment' (whatever that is), which Wikipedia tells me has been measured to within an accuracy of 1.7×10^{-13} relative to the 'Bohr magneton' (whatever that is).[23] I think that's within 1.700000000000000 of something, which I guess is pretty close to perfect. But at the same time as being really accurate when compared to other experimental knowledge, it also shows one of the fundamental issues at hand here: that no matter how close physicists get to perfect, they can never actually get there. That's because there's always a separation between their ideas of the world (the concept-dependent understanding that they use to make predictions) and their measurement of the real world. Put another way, the notion of producing perfect knowledge is a myth – and most scientists will happily acknowledge this as a foundational principle of their work.

Yet, this isn't how science is often viewed beyond the realms of academic life. Rather, scientific evidence and explanations of the world are often afforded a reverence in everyday discourse which can seem to have much in common with mythical ways of thinking. And, when this happens, 'science' is often used in a way that aims to shut down counter-evidence, debate and discussion. This is inherently anti-scientific. You see, if we can choose to take an idea from a myth and use it as a way to pragmatically frame a part of our lives, we do not need to doubt the myth, because we know by definition it is disconnected from empirical reality. But when science is mythically believed as definitive, without contestation, and some form of pure, absolute way of knowing stuff, it takes on some of the power of a myth to circumvent doubt. This is then *the mythically real*. It is only in our inherent doubting of scientific evidence that we can hold on to the fundamental difference between a scientific and mythical framing of reality.

What's scientific about good science?

In *What Is Sociology?* (1978) Norbert Elias discusses one of August Comte's contributions to the historical analysis of knowledge where he outlines the theological/mystical roots of the scientific method. Here our rational (scientific, logical, empirical) ways of knowing are firmly rooted in irrational (religious, mythical, magical) understandings of the world. Ludwik Fleck's classic analysis in *Genesis and Development of a Scientific Fact* shows numerous ways in which 'established scientific facts are undeniably linked in their development, to pre-scientific, somewhat hazy, related proto-ideas or pre-ideas' (1979 [1935], 23).

Perhaps you'll imagine this doesn't matter as we've now fully cut these links by removing the irrational from our best scientific theories. Yet, the legacy of these origins still works in various ways to frame science. For example, there's no inconsequential alignment between the worship of an all-knowing god with *his* divine laws and (often caricatured) positivistic scientific methods with their dogmatic search for conclusive truth and natural laws. Sandra Harding's (1991, 1992) work on standpoint epistemologies helps us to see how the historical development of Western society shapes the very structure of how science is done, by whom, with what goals and in which contexts.[24] Harding and colleagues would argue, then, that these verifiable scientific realities are made possible by, and are saturated in, the legacy of their historical patriarchal development. And, science, then, is not some pure connection to empirical reality but, rather, is a socially produced framework that fundamentally shapes the ways in which knowledge is produced and considered to be valid.

Now, when science is done properly, such critiques are taken on board and can inform the ways in which scholarly knowledge is doubted, refuted and advanced. The training we undergo during our graduate and post-graduate degrees should help us develop this sceptical approach. And as we design our own studies, analyse data and produce findings, the hallmarks of doing 'good science' should help us make limited but, in important ways, confident statements about what we think we know.[25] It is within this process, when it's effective, that the idea of science as having a mythical dimension loses some of its analytical purchase. This is because there is a resonance between theory, data and evidence which makes scientific ideas importantly different from other ways of knowing stuff.

Yet, by considering science in the way I have here, we are well-placed to see the processes of historical development and social interaction that shape how we interpret the world. It is within the tracing of this myth and reality-making that we can grasp the strengths and weaknesses of our ways of understanding. When we consider the examples above as evidence that the mythical and the real exist on a hermeneutic continuum, rather than as simple opposites, we can see how rational and irrational ways of knowing stuff can be intertwined, sometimes confused and often misunderstood.

A final thought

The main thing I'd like you to take away from this chapter is that myths and science are both ways in which we can know and understand stuff. And when considered in this way, despite very different relationships to the empirical world, they are in fact similar, overlap and can in certain cases perform the same function. Specifically then, we should reconsider both as connected to our concept-dependent understanding of the world and avoid the trap of lazily assuming they are *necessarily* different.

Fleck reminds us that 'a fact always occurs in the context of the history of thought' (1979 [1935], 95). Whether this 'fact' is one whose connection to reality meets the standards of what is claimed to be science doesn't change this crucial part of how we humans come to know stuff. Our job as scholars is to account for this while also appreciating the foundational characteristics that separate our scientific knowledge from other ways of understanding the world. You see, a property of a myth is that it doesn't need to be doubted, because we already know it isn't an empirically valid observation of the world. But as scientists who do make claims to know something truthful of the world, it is incumbent on us and those who use our ideas to maintain the scepticism which is inherent to our claims about evidence and the knowledge we produce. And this means appreciating that any claim to absolute knowledge and indisputable truth is necessarily a real myth, just like Santa.

My argument here shouldn't be confused with hackneyed and simplified postmodern accounts of knowledge as 'all relative'.[26] Rather, my goal in thinking about the important functional similarities between how we understand the world in mythical or scientific/realist methodologies is to help us think more critically about both. That is to understand the characteristics of scientism and scientific ways of knowing, and their limits, while also appreciating some of the profound positives that can accompany myths and mythical thinking (although I am aware I haven't focused much on the latter[27]).

I hope you'll see how science can fall into myth-making but, more importantly, is not some pure connection to empirical reality. It is, like other ways of knowing stuff, fundamentally enabled and constrained by the nature of human understanding – just like Hermes, it might reveal as well as conceal, clarify as well as confuse, and enlighten as well as cast in shadow. And when we explore this process and accept its consequences for our understanding, we're better able to hold on to what makes good science scientific. This should result in a sceptical approach that helps us maintain the contingent doubt which sits at the foundation of what we do profess to confidently know about the world.

Acknowledgements

Thanks to Thomas Basbøll, Matt Shaw, James Steele and the editors for their comments about an earlier version of this chapter. And to all PhD students I advise, if it wasn't for you lot I wouldn't have bothered to think and write in these ways, and in encouraging me to do so, you've made me understand the world better and become a better teacher.

Notes

1. This is a key dimension of 'epistemology', which can be thought of as the study of knowledge and understanding. What we'll do in the following is considering ideas which are philosophical in nature, but without *some* of the theoretical baggage that can put people off, I call this way of working 'philosophy by stealth'. It's important that you realize you're doing this as it might give you the confidence needed to tackle such ways of thinking in a more direct fashion in future. Oh, and a quick note on footnotes, I love (over)using them, as you'll see.
2. We're briefly studying some 'classics' in this section. If you're new to stuff like this, it might be worth looking on Wikipedia for a discussion of the Latin origins of 'medium', 'mediator' and so on. I remember becoming obsessed with etymology (the study of the origins

of words) some years ago, and ever since my understanding of language and ideas has flourished. If like me, your early schooling didn't do a great job of helping you understand stuff like this, I think it's worth investing some time in it.

3   In Ch.1 of *Doing Immersive Research Vol.1* (Matthews, 2021), I talk about this in relation to my own distrust of language. Specifically, because of my troubles with reading and writing I've never trusted words – I've often found the words people say in person or in writing to be capricious and slippery.

4   If you're a total nerd like me, you might like to think about how we're objectifying the process of discussing the objectification of a rock, and, in this footnote, I've objectified us doing that objectifying. This process continues into a madness of infinite regression.

5   If you think though the years of learning which this requires and the assumptions that it builds upon, this seeming simplicity quickly evaporates: How did you know to look down and not up to the sky? Why didn't you confuse the chewing gum with the rock? How did you even understand the sentence in that first place? And how did those words even come to stand for those things?

6   And this is but one of the reasons why 'soft' social science is much more challenging than the apparently 'hard' natural sciences.

7   Or, as Cicourel has it, social scientists have a particular problem in that 'the very conditions of their research constitute an important complex variable for what passes as the findings of their investigations. … The activities of the investigator play a crucial role in the data obtained' (1964, 39). For more on this, I suggest Giddens' *New Rules of Sociological Method: Second Edition* (1993) and Andrew Sayers' *Method in Social Science: Revised Second Edition* (1992).

8   If you're new to this sort of thinking, it's worth doing a quick thought experiment here – try to think of something, anything, without a pre-existing idea or without words which symbolize that thing and the other things associated with it. Even the notion of a 'thing', which could mean *anything*, requires a word to be considered as a thing.

9   For no matter how many qualifications and caveats we might put around the word 'true', this is what we do when we do science: we try to find some truthful – and, importantly, falsifiable –understanding of the world.

10 As is the case in 'scientism' whereby people have such an unthinking and unwavering dedication to a scientific world view that they become the very thing they critique – a zealot whose own knowledge of the world is undermined because of their beliefs.

11 My thinking in this regard owes much to Norbert Elias (*What Is Sociology?*, 1978; *Society of Individuals*, 1991), Richard Bernstein (*Beyond Objectivism and Relativism: Science, Hermeneutics, and Praxis*, 2011), Andrew Sayer (*Why Things Matter to People: Social Science, Values and Ethical Life*, 2011), Nick Crossley (*Intersubjectivity: The Fabric of Social Becoming*, 1996; *The Social Body: Habit, Identity and Desire*, 2014) and many others whose work engages with the philosophy of social sciences. Much of this work is challenging on first read, especially if like me you didn't follow a 'traditional' path into higher education, but I'm adamant that grasping these ideas is fundamental to doing good science. I strongly recommend these books to scholars who can take time away from the grind of writing papers and funding applications.

12 See Matthews et al. (2022).

13 I'm never quite sure how I feel about teachers passing on such fictions. It makes me nervous about their power to instil children with knowledge which we know to be false.

14 Simply put, and there is more complexity in the work than this. Dorothy and William Thomas argued in 1928 that if a person defines a situation as real, those situations become real in their consequences.

15 For good books on this topic, see Judith Lorber – *Paradoxes of Sex* (1994); John Hoberman, *Testosterone Dreams* (2005); Thomas Laqueur – *Making Sex* (1992); Martha McCaughey – *The Caveman Mystique: Pop-Darwinism and the Debates over Sex and Violence* (2008); Carolyn Merchant – *Death of Nature: Women, Ecology and the Scientific Revolution* (1980); and Nelly Oudshroon – *Beyond the Natural Body: An Archaeology of Sex Hormones* (1994).

16 These were my theoretical and philosophical assumptions, my concept-dependent understanding of the world. And they, like any ideas, shaped the data I collected and the work I produced. But there is a more robust alignment between the stories I use to frame observations and that of my participants, and this is why I claim my work to be 'scientific'. More on this below.

17 The idea of sport as a 'male preserve' can be traced to Sheard and Dunning's (1973) work on rugby. You can see my more recent discussions of this in Matthews (2018) and Matthews and Channon (2020).

18 There's a lot of places to find Connell's ideas in academic papers, but in terms of books, *Masculinities* (2020) and *Gender and Power: Society, the Person and Sexual Politics* (1987) are both good starting points. I strongly suggest you also read critiques of this work. More broadly, hegemony theory is a way of trying to understand the social power and control that certain people and groups might have. In particular, some people will consent to this social control in various implicit and explicit ways. Antonio Gramsci's *Prison Notebooks* is the origin of these ideas, and they're very useful for developing an analysis of social life.

19 See Matthews (2015).

20 See Ch. 4 of *Doing Immersive Research Vol. 1* (Matthews, 2021).

21 See p. 37 of *Doing Immersive Research Vol. 1* (Matthews, 2021), where I make this case in relation to my own problematic relationship with social theory.

22 This level of accuracy has even been a cause of concern for some scholars. If you do a search on Google Scholar for the following phrase 'the unreasonable effectiveness of physics', you'll see a number of papers that attempt to account for this.

23 My dear friend Max Cooper opened my eyes this to this area of science. We've shared many a road trip where we nerded out about such issues in various states of sobriety. If you can find people who are equally as nerdy as you, do what you can to hold on to them and embrace that side of your friendship.

24 Also, see Joey Sprague's (2005) *Feminist Methodologies for Critical Researchers: Bridging Differences* and *Doing Immersive Research Vol. 1*, p. 114 where I discuss this in more detail.

25 I discuss this in detail in pages 152–163 of *Doing Immersive Research Vol. 1*.

26 Gosh, what a boring trope that is – please see Richard Bernstein's (1983) *Beyond Objectivism and Relativism* and Rob Stones's (1996) *Towards a Past-Modern Sociology* for two excellent books that do away with such daft ideas.

27 Myth and stories aren't inherently positive or negative. Our job is to consider their content and how it relates to the lives people live, so while I'm sure there can be 'positive' myths, that is, stories that help people flourish and/or avoid suffering in some manner, there are also myths that can have a negative impact on our lives. Think for example of the fact

that many of us are brought up watching and learning about a hero's journey. But life isn't a hero story, so when it comes to our stories, which are most likely about community, connections and collaboration, rather than individual success, we can expect some people to feel de-centred and lacking in control, when in fact they never were the centre, and we only have a limited amount of control over our lives. The stories we tell and the myths we believe are important for the lives we lead. While those stories do not match the realities of life, they will continue to set some people up for an apparent, but equally mythical, feeling of failure.

References

Cicourel, A.V. (1964) *Method and Measurement in Sociology*. New York, Free Press.

Elias, N. (1978) *What Is Sociology?* University College Dublin Press.

Fleck, L. (1935 [1979]) *Genesis and Development of a Scientific Fact*. Chicago, The University of Chicago Press.

Harding, S. (1991) *Whose Science? Whose Knowledge? Thinking form Women's Live*. Milton Keynes, Open University Press.

Harding, S. (1992) Rethinking Standpoint Epistemology: What is 'Strong Objectivity?' *The Centennial Review*, 36(3), 437–470.

Hearn, J. (2004) From Hegemonic Masculinity to the Hegemony of Men. *Feminist Theory*, 5(1), 49–72.

Matthews, C.R. (2015) The Appropriation of Hegemonic Masculinity within Selected Research on Men's Health. *International Journal for Masculinity Studies*, 11(1), 3–18.

Matthews, C.R. (2016) The Tyranny of the Male Preserve. *Gender and Society*, 30(2), 312–333.

Matthews, C.R. (2021) *Doing Immersive Research Volume I*. Beeston, CRM Publishing.

Matthews, C.R. and Channon, A. (2020) The 'Male Preserve' Thesis, Sporting Culture, and Men's Power. In Gottzén, L., Mellström, U. and Shefer, T. (eds.), *Routledge Handbook of Masculinity Studies*. London, Routledge.

Matthews, C.R., Hurrell, A., Oliver, T.B. and Channon, A. (2022) Boxing, Myths and Reality Building in Sport for Development Programmes. *International Review for the Sociology of Sport*, ISSN 1012–6902.

2 Winning Matters Most in Elite Sport

*Elliott Newell, Cath Bishop,
Laurence Halsted and Katie Mobed*

It's early August 2012 in London, UK. Team GB are enjoying an incredible home Olympic Games in the capital. The event so far has yielded some outstanding performances and memorable sporting moments. Tim Baillie and Etienne Stott have delivered a run of supreme skill to become GB's first canoe slalom Olympic Champions, 0.36 seconds ahead of compatriots David Florence and Richard Hounslow. From a stunning 1-2 on the white-water rapids to an exhilarating time trial on the roads of south-west London, Bradley Wiggins storms to Gold, to be joined on the podium by compatriot Chris Froome in Bronze. More history is made at Lake Eton Dorney, as Helen Glover and Heather Stanning became Team GB's first-ever female rowing Olympic Champions. This was followed by a dream-come-true moment for Dame Katherine Grainger who, after Silver medals at the previous three Olympic Games, finally won Gold with partner Anna Watkins in the double sculls.

Glorious blue skies. The British national anthem is at full volume in sporting venues across the country. New heroes emerging, committed to inspiring a generation. Does it get any better?

Apparently so.

On Saturday 4th August, Team GB won an unbelievable seven Gold medals. On the river, the men's coxless (rowing) four beat arch-rivals Australia in front of a sell-out crowd of 30,000 cheering fans. Then came the women's double sculls with Kat Copeland and Sophie Hosking crossing the line in first place. Few will forget Kat's face, moving from absolute shock to utter joy as she exclaimed to her partner: 'We won the Olympics!' Success continued in the Velodrome as Dani King, Laura Trott and Joanna Rowsell won Gold in the women's team pursuit. A few hours to catch our breath before we turned our attention to the Olympic Stadium for the athletics. In a mind-blowing 48 minutes, Team GB won Gold in the women's heptathlon, men's long jump and men's 10,000 m. Dame Jessica Ennis, Greg Rutherford and Sir Mo Farah played their role in what became known as 'Super Saturday'.

Winning is great, isn't it? The joy and euphoria. The inspiring sense that anything is possible, and if these heroes can achieve their dreams, perhaps I can too. Implicit within this perspective is the mindset that no sacrifice is too great for the reward of coming first and having a medal hung around your neck. In the words of three-time Olympic champion Pete Reed: 'The hours we do, the pain. It's all worth it at the end' (BBC, 2012).

But is it always worth it?

As a society we can, and in many cases do, look upon winning – defined as finishing first – as something that is inherently good. However, when you dig a little deeper into the human stories behind the medals, you soon discover that not all Gold medals are cherished, not all winners are fulfilled and not all champions are positive role models. While the medals count equally in the medal table, the human value that they represent varies widely. It is this value that we want to explore and understand better in this chapter as we reflect on the myth that winning is inherently good and what matters most in elite sport.

The challenges with a 'winning matters most' mentality

We (the authors) are in the privileged position to work with a range of athletes, coaches and leaders across multiple sports in high-performance environments. The drive to win is important to the players and staff as part of their performance aspirations, as well as to the clubs and programmes as part of their reputation, legacy and financial stability. We write this chapter to offer a perspective on what the topic of winning (and the pursuit of winning) looks, sounds and feels like 'on the ground' and how we might better shape it for the future. To tell this story, we will refer to a number of anecdotes taken from the lived experiences of elite athletes, combined with research insight where appropriate.

Winning isn't always something to celebrate

One obvious situation when winning isn't something to celebrate is when an individual or organisation has violated the rules or spirit of competition, such as when 'winners' have had their titles stripped due to doping offences.

Less obvious can be those occasions when the winners themselves don't feel joy, pride or satisfaction when they win. Indeed, one of the reasons we challenge the myth that winning matters most is because there are multiple examples of winners who are not fulfilled by the achievement. Huge numbers of highly successful athletes have shared their experiences of this, including Jonny Wilkinson, Michael Phelps, Victoria Pendleton and Andrew Strauss. Andre Agassi (2009) went as far as to say in his autobiography 'Winning changes nothing'.

If the moment of winning, or the later reflection on the win, represents a negative or unfulfilling experience, then we have to question the value of it and explore how this could be improved for future athletes. While such concerning experiences exist, it's hard to assert that winning is what matters most.

The costs of winning

Amy Tinkler (British Artistic Gymnast) reflected on her Olympic career in which she won bronze at the 2016 Rio Olympics by saying,

> *The medal wasn't worth it. I would give up my whole Olympic experience to have never gone through this, and for any other gymnast to not. Nothing is worth what I have been through and what I am still dealing with.*
>
> (The Sunday Times, 2020)

It's important to understand the costs that can come from an approach that considers winning as the thing that matters most in elite sport. To achieve such tough and remarkable things comes at some form of cost. The question for all of us to consider is, what is the cost worth paying to win?

We understand that pursuing excellence is highly challenging and comes with a number of stressors and risks related to both mental and physical health and well-being (e.g. Baldock et al., 2022; Gallo et al., 2020; Mountjoy et al., 2014; Prior, Papathomas and Rhind, 2022). In recent years, we have seen an increase in the number of athletes citing the negative impact the pursuit of winning has had on their mental health. Adam Peaty, Simone Biles, Ben Stokes and Naomi Osaka are a few examples of elite athletes who have withdrawn from events or taken breaks from sport citing mental health – be it burnout, depression or anxiety. When athletes are withdrawing from competitions because the cost of their pursuit outweighs any potential outcome, we have to question the conditions, cultures and values in the environments being created in pursuit of high performance.

Indeed, the cultures within high-performance sport have been under scrutiny in recent years. In her landmark report for the UK government, Baroness Tanni Grey-Thompson stated, 'Winning medals is, of course, really important, but should not be at the expense of the Duty of Care towards athletes, coaches and others involved in the system' (2017, 4). While a number of undesirable cultures have been unveiled in elite sport, it is worth noting that few environments consciously choose to be damaging to their people. Rather, the development of unethical practices can gradually be normalized under certain environmental conditions (e.g. Feddersen, 2021; Feddersen and Phelan, 2021). A 'winning matters most' mentality can contribute to an environment that does not adequately consider the human cost of pursuing success. To mitigate against this, we believe that leaders and anyone working in elite sport environments should be openly considering and evaluating the costs being paid for success.

Some things matter more than the win

There are a wide range of factors that athletes and staff reference when describing what value was generated from their success. Many of these factors extend beyond the fact that they won a trophy or a medal. Instead, significant value is often placed on how they won and what their win means. Meaningful outcomes relate to both them and others and can be short and long term.

Examples of what matters beyond the win include

- the *broader social impact of the result* (e.g. how much good does the winning generate in the world for all those involved in the short and long term?),
- *the content of the narrative* (e.g. to what extent does the story arc capture something inherently good about human potential?),
- *the evidence of personal and collective growth* and
- *the relationships that are part of the experience and journey towards winning.*

Olympic hockey champion Alex Danson-Bennett MBE summed the latter up powerfully when she retired, saying: 'It's not the winning, it's how you win, the people you win with, the group of people you are connected to… I think that human connection is the ultimate marker of success' (*The Telegraph*, 2020).

Taken together, these stories point us towards an understanding that coming first and winning is not necessarily what brings an athlete the most value. When athletes experience winning and it falls short of expectations, when it costs more to win than winning could ever return, or when the things that people truly value about winning extend beyond the medal or trophy, then we might want to shift our definitions of success. Our contention is that not all wins are equal in value; therefore, the simple act of winning cannot be the thing that matters most in elite sport.

How might we explore the value of winning?

If not all wins are equal in value then we must consider what factors contribute to the value of a win. We think about the value of winning as the *outcomes* from the achievement (i.e. what did anybody get out of it?) and the *process of achievement* (i.e. how was the winning achieved?) The outcomes that result from winning can be extrinsic, such as the external rewards gained, or intrinsic, such as the personal experience and applied meaning. Additionally, when we are determining value, we should also be cognizant of the costs – both resource and human – associated with the win.

A helpful way to think about the value of the win may be:

Competition Outcomes + Process of Achievement + Broader Social Impact – Costs = Value

We propose in this chapter that the winning itself is only part of the equation. There is value that comes from the moment of winning, of course; however, a preoccupation with this may lead us to underappreciate the value (or lack of value) held within the journey taken leading up to the result or in the longevity of positive outcomes stimulated by the win. Underpinning the value of the win is the *How* – the way in which winning was achieved – and the *Why* – the purpose that drove the process and the meaning that it has. Our view is that the true value of winning can only be determined with consideration of all of these factors.

Characteristics of meaningful wins

From our collective experiences as athletes, coaches, researchers and psychologists, we passionately believe that there are many different ways to win, and there are many different types of win. Our agenda is to champion the pursuit of winning in ways that are deeply fulfilling, growthful and of long-term value. In this section, we share some approaches (see table 1.1) to winning that we believe can support the creation of more meaningful wins.

These approaches to winning come from asking ourselves: Which type of win is worth pursuing? Which might offer more to celebrate? Which might have longer-lasting value for those involved, whether spectators, athletes or coaches? And what are the factors, beyond the win, that we could pay more attention to in our collective quest to explore the true potential of sport to bring out the best in human beings? (see Table 2.1)

Winning deep

Grange (2020) explains the difference between 'winning deep' and 'winning shallow'. Winning shallow comes from winning to avoid not being good enough, winning to beat the other person or to be seen as worthy. It's winning born of comparison, scarcity and self-doubt. This approach gives rise to insecure overachievers. Winning deep is where you actually feel the richness of your journey. You are attached to the joy and the struggle, to the mess, and it is generally done for reasons outside of yourself. The value of this was highlighted in a study by Houltberg et al. (2018) who examined athletes with different narrative profiles. Athletes with performance-based narrative identities were characterized by high perfectionism, contingent self-worth and fear of failure. Alternatively, those with purpose-based narrative identities were characterized by an intrinsic drive, broader self-worth and a positive sense of self after sport. Athletes who

Table 2.1. Approaches that help us redefine what winning means.

Winning Deep	To be 'all in' on your experience, living it fully. To be driven by a desire to explore what you are capable of rather than a need to be good enough. To coach wins that are fulfilling, growthful and have longevity.
Purpose-Driven	To have personally meaningful motivations beyond the result, often linked to being or doing good for others and for society.
Thriving Experiences	To pursue performance in a way that enables experiences of success, growth and well-being. Requires a range of personal and environmental factors.
Excellence	To be driven towards personal, collective and procedural excellence in all aspects of the performance pursuit. To be as passionate and rigorous about how things are done, as you are about the outcome. Typically exhibiting a mastery mindset.
Meaningful	To be purposeful in one's search for meaning in activity. To create opportunities to explore and experience meaning over the course of the performance pursuit.

reported a purpose-based narrative identity reported higher psychological well-being and life satisfaction and lower depression, anxiety and shame compared to their counterparts with a performance-based identity narrative. Athletes who reported a mixed-narrative identity reported better psychological outcomes than the performance-based group, but not as good as the purpose-based group.

Focusing on winning deep also enables us to see the value in all journeys taken towards performance, even if they ultimately don't all lead to coming first. Tom Mitchell, former GB Rugby 7s Captain, shared a few thoughts on falling short of his goal at the Tokyo Olympics:

As someone who has been fortunate to have come home with a medal and without one, any youngsters should know that hard work and following your passion are worthwhile in their own right. Don't get me wrong, achieving your goal feels great, and not achieving what you set out to get is painful for a while. But both outcomes contain emotions that only last for a while. The deep sense of fulfilment that comes from pursuing a passion and dedicating yourself to it lasts much longer.

Tom's comments remind us of what can be gained from losing and the opportunity to appreciate the value that comes with it that is all too often overlooked in a world where winning matters most. Ashe psychologist Susan Cain expressed:

We live in a culture that only wants to talk about what's going well. Anything that's not going well is positioned as a detour from the main road. The truth is that pain is not a detour from the main road. Pain is part of the road we walk as human beings.

(Cain, 2021)

Purpose-driven

It is common for practitioners to work with athletes on what their particular goals are, be they for a game, a season or a career (Bird, Swann and Jackman, 2023). Much of this type of work centres on the question '*what is it you are wanting to achieve?*' and helps the athlete or team to tease out the proposed value of such a goal or outcome. Frameworks such as those proposed by Goal Setting Theory (Locke and Latham, 2019) and Achievement Goal Theory (Elliott and McGregor, 2001) are helpful in this regard. But all this talk about goals and value focuses only on *what* can be gained. It fails to get into the more important (in our opinion) question: *why*? Why are these goals and things of perceived value important? What do they mean, and how do they connect to your purpose as a person and athlete?

When England women's football manager Sarina Wiegman left the scene of England's 2022 European Championships victory, she declared: 'We changed society'. The extra-time win against Germany was to be seen as the beginning, not the end. Three days later, all 23 Lionesses signed an open letter urging the UK prime minister to give every girl in the nation the chance to follow in their footsteps (BBC, 2022).

Their shared purpose was for every young girl in the UK to have the opportunity to play football at school. On 8 March 2023, the UK government made a historic pledge for girls to have equal access to all school sports, including football. The Lionesses shone a national spotlight on the importance of improving equality in sporting opportunity for the next generation, showing that their ambitions went beyond lifting a Silver trophy in the Wembley sunshine the previous summer.

In the FIFA Women's World Cup in 2023, it was clear to see this sense of purpose across all the teams, whether from Nigeria, Australia or Morocco. All these female athletes were focussed on both performing at their best – while acutely aware of their social responsibility as role models to show all the girls watching at home that they should expect to participate in sport equally – and believing that they can pursue their dreams, whether in sport or any other aspect of their life. It led to incredible scenes of connection across winning and losing teams immediately after matches, as these women shared a powerful purpose that went beyond the scoreline.

Thriving experiences

A meaningful win may be characterized by an athlete not just thriving in the arena but thriving holistically as they master their craft. Thriving is the positive developmental experience of success and well-being (Brown et al., 2017). Initial studies into the area of thriving in elite sport have indicated that athlete experiences of thriving are linked to having their basic psychological needs met (Brown and Arnold, 2019; Brown et al., 2021). Examining performance pursuits through this lens enables us to see beyond the objective outcome of performance and explore the lived experience of the participants involved in it.

Thriving is not an inevitable experience. Some high-performance journeys are characterized by feelings of overwhelm and (perceived) threat within the environment or situation, causing them to be preoccupied with safety and security. Jonny Wilkinson said, 'I spent my career surviving the pressure I put on myself. When you get to the end you look back and you say "what did I do with my career?" I survived it' (*The Guardian*, 2019). We question the value of winning if the experience of those that won can be characterized in this way.

It is possible and even frequent for athletes to have experiences in elite sport where they never fully reach their potential. Thriving is not just about well-being, it is also about growth. To be clear, our message in this section is not just about avoiding unnecessary distress or eradicating abuse (which of course we should). A focus on facilitating thriving experiences means that we proactively work to avoid people stagnating or meandering through an experience that leaves them wondering at the end of their career, 'what might I have been truly capable of?'

Excellence

Our experience across different performance domains has been that the most challenging but also the most inspiring and meaningful environments are those that are as vigorous in chasing excellence in how they do things and how they treat people, as they are about the outcome. This mentality is about a constant search for improvements in the processes of performance. The win-at-all-costs mentality is prepared to ignore sub-optimal processes or outcomes (e.g. athlete well-being, staff retention) as long as the outcome on the field/track/court is satisfactory. To our minds, a win-at-all-costs mentality is far from a commitment to excellence as it deprives participants of so much of the richness that winning can represent. If you win but do so with dysfunction in the staff team, an unwillingness for coaches and athletes to resolve conflict, a culture of fear and low psychological safety and a 'sticky plaster' approach to managing performance limiters, have you truly achieved excellence? What might your win represent in such circumstances? Is it as valuable and meaningful as it could have been?

Focusing on excellence promotes the quality of individual, team and organizational processes. It is about being the best you can be, in the circumstances you inhabit, on all levels while working towards a performance outcome. This performance philosophy has connections to concepts of mastery, flow and personal best which can be lost when the focus is solely on 'what it takes to win'. Indeed much of the performance psychology literature, be it individual, team or organization-focussed, is intended to support people to realize their performance potential rather than explicitly enable them to win. As an example, a recent scoping review conducted by Salcinovic and colleagues (2022) identified four key variables that were associated with team function and performance across a variety of industries: (i) leadership styles, (ii) supportive team behaviour, (iii) communication and (iv) performance feedback. A meaningful pursuit of winning would look to proactively work on excelling in many relevant performance processes, alongside a focus on trying to win.

Meaningful

According to Frankl (1959), it is our central driving force to find meaning in life. Given the deep commitment to hard work necessary for athletes to achieve their sporting dreams, the role of meaning has particular relevance to them. Athletes are faced with a number of potential events that may cause them to search for, or experience, the presence of meaning in their careers and lives. Examples include injury, selection and deselection, transition, loss of form, a significant win or loss, career termination and retirement. Despite the relevance of meaning to the lives of those in elite sport, this area receives relatively little attention in academic or applied spheres (Luzzari and Chow, 2020; Nesti, 2004). It is our experience that supporting athletes – and indeed coaches, staff and leaders – to find meaning in their work can enhance the value of the journey taken.

The presence of meaning in one's life has been described as an important indicator of well-being (Stager et al., 2013) and has been shown to facilitate adaptive coping (Stager et al., 2006). We believe that sport provides an incredible context in which people can find meaning. We support the calls from applied researchers such as Ronkainen and Nesti (2015) for a greater emphasis on *understanding existential meaning and purpose in applied sport psychology. Practitioners who have explored the existential issues of meaning and purpose with elite athletes have demonstrated deep and nuanced connections with identity, storytelling, well-being, and commitment* (e.g. Aggerholm, 2015; Nesti and Ronkainen, 2020; Obliger-Peters et al., 2023). Participants in elite sport are also seen to be susceptible to a lack of meaning owing to the potential for basic psychological need frustration, narrow identities based on sport and a preoccupation with winning and striving for perfectionism, all of which pose risks to mental health and well-being (Beckmann, 2023).

This insight should encourage us to explore the role that meaning can play when working with people in elite sport. With particular reference to the myth in question, we think that there is value in exploring the meaning of winning with those who seek it. The stories shared earlier on in the chapter, particularly those of Michael Phelps, Amy Tinkler and Jonny Wilkinson, should serve as reminders that winning is not inherently good, and part of our solution to this reality is to nurture the meaning that makes it fulfilling.

A practical model to achieve meaningful winning

In this section, Cath and Laurence offer a model (see Figure 2.1) that blends their two influential approaches to help people explore more valuable and meaningful experiences of sport – Long Win Thinking (LWT; Bishop, 2020) and The True Athlete Philosophy (TAP; Halsted, 2021). They have brought together the central and mutually compatible elements of their respective approaches to offer a helpful prompt for those seeking to redefine and redesign their approach to 'winning' in elite sport.

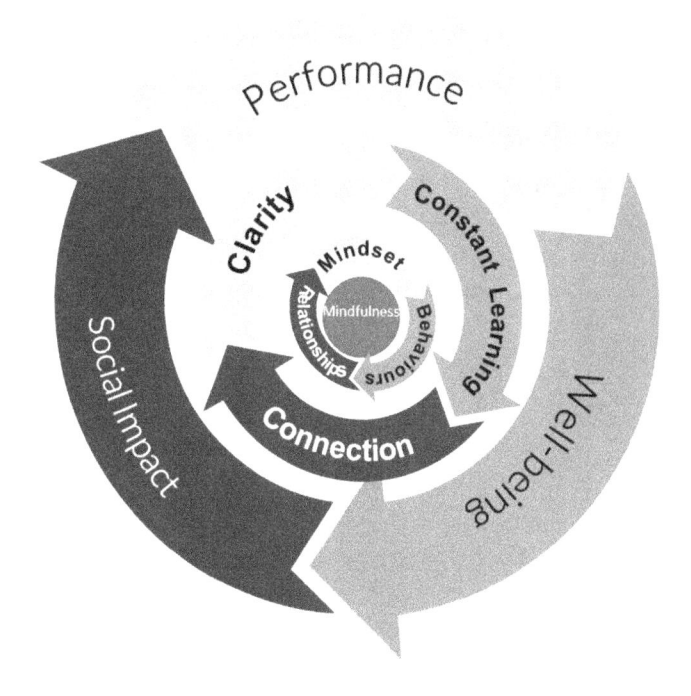

Figure 2.1. A proposed model integrating Long Wing Thinking (LWT) and the True Athlete Philosophy (TAP).

Model summary

The circular nature of each level symbolizes the evolution, ongoing journey and constant development that are inherent in this thinking and practice.

In the outer circle sit the principles of Performance, Well-being and Social Impact that comprise The TAP's holistic mission to create a more compassionate society through sport, in stark contrast to the damaging win-at-all-costs approach that we've seen has typically characterized sport in modern times. LWT provides us with the three Cs – Clarity, Constant learning and Connection – themes which broaden how we think, act and interact and are realized through a focus on developing our mindsets, behaviours and relationships in the next tier.

Finally, at the core of the model sits Mindfulness – the foundation, starting point and support for all the elements of the model.

Ring one: The purpose of sport – performance, well-being social impact

The TAP recognizes that performance is the driver of so much of what makes sport uniquely impactful, on both an individual and collective level, but that it should not sit alone on the pedestal of sport's purpose. Mental, emotional and physical well-being matter just as much, from grassroots up to, and including, the elite level. When talking about the purpose of sport, it's also important to go beyond the individual and recognize the unique position that sport holds for creating positive outcomes for society.

Sport could be an unequivocally positive force for physical and mental health, creating moments of flow and exhilaration and instilling a joy of life-long learning. It could also benefit communities and wider society. It could bridge social divides and bring people from every walk of life together under a universal language. It could provide inspirational role models for everyone.

Unfortunately, the reality looks depressingly different. As we've touched on, sport at all levels is rife with unwanted and destructive side effects, including stress, anxiety, depression, burnout, bullying, abuse, discrimination, and corruption. Sport has not come close to delivering on its potential for making the world a better place: neither for many of those involved nor for society.

We must find a way to bring sport closer to the vision of what it could be for society and its participants: the joy of movement, human connection and deep engagement in mental and physical endeavour, the incredible experiences that are accessible to all, the magical, historic moments that inspire those that witness them and connect generations. Sport can transcend time and culture to bring us closer together and go further as a species. What is needed is an approach that journeys deeper than the ego-driven, superficial realm of short-term wins and losses, medals, and the superiority of nations. A fundamentally different approach that puts athletes, coaches, teams and all those who support them back in touch with the core benefits and true purpose of sport – the pursuit of excellence, personal growth, teamwork and respect for all, including opponents and officials. This would light the way for athletes to excel at their sport while becoming exemplary citizens, family members and friends who have trained mind and body to better contribute to their community and ultimately to society as a whole.

Having set the scene for what the broader purpose of sport could be, the elements of the inner rings begin to show us how we can bring this approach to life and ground it in daily practice.

Ring two: Our guiding compass – clarity, constant learning and connection

Much like a compass that points north and helps us find our way in the physical world, the three Cs (3Cs) help us find direction in life without being prescriptive. When we open ourselves up to clarifying the 'why' in what we do, embrace learning and prioritize connecting more deeply with others, it brings fun, growth and meaning to us and what we do, whether it's a weekly fun training session or the Olympic final.

Clarity

This element involves developing clarity about what matters beyond the short term, developing a wider perspective on what success could look like over the longer term, clarifying the 'why' and defining the experience we want to have along the way. It's about more than short-term metrics and outcomes and encourages us to keep asking clarifying questions about what we do

- What's the lasting value from what we're doing in sport? What will we have gained when the training session or race is finished?
- Why does our involvement in sport matter? What impact will it have on ourselves and others involved?
- How do we want to go about the pursuit of excellence in sport? How do we want to show up when training and competing?

Constant learning

Asking clarifying questions leads naturally into a constant learning approach that defines success through personal and collective growth rather than external results (at the same time giving us the best chance of maximizing those results). This deepens the focus on the 'how' – the way we do things – and defines success in terms of a human currency: our development and growth – exploring what we're capable of individually and collectively, finding out what's possible, not constraining ourselves by defining everything in the non-human, inanimate currency of trophies and medals. It balances out the overwhelming focus on racking up achievements in life and ensures we keep growing and developing both when we succeed and when we fail, embedding a mastery mindset at the heart of what it means to play sport.

Connection

With a stronger human-focussed lens underpinning the 3Cs, the last focuses on the 'who' in our lives – our colleagues, partners, friends and others in our networks, as well as those we have yet to connect with. How are we actively looking to develop our connections with others, rather than compare ourselves against others or work 'against' others, allowing us to move away from a competitive zero-sum-game approach to relationships? This helps us develop a human-centred lens to our sporting lives, seeing training and competing in terms of relationships developed and deepened, not simply medals and trophies won. It reminds us that when we invest in our relationships as a priority in everything we do, we thrive. And that when we finish sport, whether it's at the end of competition or at the end of our sporting career, it's the relationships that we're left with which offer us lasting human value from our engagement with sport.

Ring three: Our road map – mindset, behaviours, relationships (MBR)

The MBR roadmap encourages us to recognize the importance of how we think, behave and interact in the pursuit of performance, well-being and social impact. All three aspects benefit from attention, intention and training and yet are often overlooked, undervalued and left unexplored as key elements in enhancing the quality of our performance and experience in sport.

We all bring a mindset, a way of behaving and relating to others to everything we do by shining a lens on these areas, we can start to think about how we might develop our mindset, behaviours and relationships to lead us towards greater performance, well-being and social impact.

The core: Mindfulness

Mindfulness is the golden thread that runs through this model. Mindfulness is, simply, an awareness of what is happening in the present moment – thoughts, feelings, sensations – in a way that is both unattached and non-judgemental.

This recognition that our thoughts and feelings need not define us and that we can treat ourselves with more compassion when we have thoughts or feelings that cause us suffering can provide the basis for incredible stability, equanimity and presence, in the face of whatever life throws at us. The opposite of mindfulness is being lost in thought, on auto-pilot or caught up in the storm of our emotions. In those states, there is no opportunity to be aware of the mindset we are bringing to bear, or of our behaviour in any given moment, as we are simply not present with them – we are instead lost in the past or future, buried in worry or rumination. If we are on auto-pilot, then we cannot meaningfully attend to the relationships that buoy us, and if we let emotions cloud our judgement, then we risk saying or doing things that we later regret. If we are not showing up mindfully, it's almost impossible to attend to the elements that we have seen bring greater value to our sporting endeavours: the outer ring of performance, well-being and social impact. Mindfulness is the essential ingredient to being more focussed, to connecting with others deeply and to responding to ourselves and the world around us with compassion. There is no other state, no other practice that holds the keys to what we hold dear in sport as explored in this chapter as mindfulness does.

To be clear, this model isn't saying that we shouldn't pursue medals; quite the contrary, it's saying that the way we pursue our best performance should entail elements that will bring lasting value and meaning as discussed in this chapter and within this model, none of which are dependent solely on outcomes.

Concluding remarks

Our aim in this chapter has been to challenge the pervasive myth in elite sport that winning matters most. We have come to understand through our extensive experience that the act of winning has little lasting value, but there is enormous potential value through how we define success and how we develop our approach to performance. Each win has its own value that we must be interested in enhancing if we are to enable sport to fulfil its potential for doing good in the world –for its participants, its spectators and wider society.

For winning to matter, it should connect positively to the journey to that point and the long-term impact of its positive outcomes. We believe that those in sport should be asking themselves not whether they want to win or not, but rather how and why they want to win. And when we embrace those that win, we must do so with a greater passion and curiosity for their 'how' and 'why', and a greater understanding of 'who' they are beyond being athletes. Doing so not only allows us to celebrate what is truly of value in winning but also enables us to recognize the value in the pursuits of those who fall just short of the win on the field of play but have still experienced deep meaning, joy and growth along the way.

In summary, we believe that:

- Sport has so much more to offer than only determining who comes first or last.
- A sole occupation on winning as the only thing that matters can lead to destructive behaviours and negative experiences and unfulfilled potential for individuals and sport more broadly.
- Not all wins are valuable and not all losses are worthless.
- It is the lasting value of winning and what meaning it represents that really matters – not just the act of winning itself.
- When we understand that the aims we are pursuing have value and meaning, we open ourselves up to truly exploring what we're capable of, together.

References

Agassi, A. (2009). *Open: An Autobiography*. London: Harper Collins.
Aggerholm, K. (2015). *Talent Development, Existential Philosophy and Sport: On Becoming an Elite Athlete*. Abingdon: Routledge.
Baldock, L., Cropley, B., Mellalieu, S. D. and Neil, R. (2022). A Longitudinal Examination of Stress and Mental Ill-/Well-Being in Elite Football Coaches. *The Sport Psychologist*, **36**(3), 171–182. https://doi.org/10.1123/tsp.2021-0184.
BBC. (2012). Olympics Rowing: Britain's Men's Coxless Four Win Gold. https://www.bbc.co.uk/sport/olympics/18911517.
BBC. (2022). Lionesses: England's Euro 2022 Winners Urge Tory Leadership Duo to Help Schoolgirls Play Football. https://www.bbc.co.uk/sport/football/62412348.
Beckmann, J. (2023). Meaning and Meaninglessness in Elite Sport. In I. Nixdorf et al. (Eds.), *Routledge Handbook of Mental Health in Elite Sport*. London: Routledge.

Bird, M. D., Swann, C. and Jackman, P. C. (2023). The What, Why, and How of Goal Setting: A Review of the Goal-Setting Process in Applied Sport Psychology Practice. *Journal of Applied Sport Psychology*, **35**(1). https://doi.org/10.1080/10413200.2023.2185699.

Bishop, C. (2020). *The Long Win: A Search for a Better Way to Succeed*. Great Britain: Practical Inspiration Publishing.

Brown, D. J. and Arnold, R. (2019). Sports Performers' Perspectives on Facilitating Thriving in Professional Rugby Contexts. *Psychology of Sport and Exercise*, **40**, 71–81. https://doi.org/10.1016/j.psychsport.2018.09.008.

Brown, D. J., Arnold, R., Fletcher, D. and Standage, M. (2017). Human Thriving: A Conceptual Debate and Literature Review. *European Psychologist*, **22**(3), 167–179. https://doi.org/10.1027/1016-9040/a000294.

Brown, D., Arnold, R., Standage, M. and Fletcher, D. (2021). A Longitudinal Examination of Thriving in Sport Performers. *Psychology of Sport and Exercise*, **55**. https://doi.org/10.1016/j.psychsport.2021.101934.

Cain, S. (2021). *Bittersweet: How Sorrow and Longing Make Us Whole*. Random House.

Elliot, A. J. and McGregor, H. A. (2001). A 2 X 2 Achievement Goal Framework. *Journal of Personality and Social Psychology*, **80**, 501–519.

Fedderson, N. B. (2021). The Emergence and Perpetuation of a Destructive Culture in a British Olympic Sport. In F. Cavallerio (Ed.), *Creative Nonfiction in Sport and Exercise Research*. New York: Routledge.

Fedderson, N. B. and Phelan, S. (2021). The Gradual Normalization of Behaviors Which Might Challenge Ethical and Professional Standards in Two British Elite Sports Organizations. *Journal of Sport Management*. http://dx.doi.org/10.1123/jsm.2021-0077.

Frankl, V. E. (1959). *Man's Search for Meaning*. Hodder & Stoughton. Boston, MA: Beacon Press.

Gallo, V., Motley, K., Kemp, S. P. T., et al. (2020). Concussion and Long-Term Cognitive Impairment among Professional or Elite Sport-Persons: A Systematic Review. *Journal of Neurolology, Neurosurgery and Psychiatry*, **91**, 455–468.

Grange, P. (2020). *Fear Less: How to Win at Life Without Losing Yourself*. London: Vermillian.

Grey-Thompson, T. (2017). Duty of Care in Sport. Independent Report to Government. https://assets.publishing.service.gov.uk/government/uploads/system/uploads/attachment_data/file/610130/Duty_of_Care_Review_-_April_2017__2.pdf.

Halsted, L. (2021). *Becoming a True Athlete: A Practical Philosophy for Flourishing Through Sport*. Sequoia Books.

Houltberg, B. J., Wang, K. T., Qi, W. and Nelson, C. S. (2018). Self-Narrative Profiles of Elite Athletes and Comparisons on Psychological Well-Being. *Research Quarterly for Exercise and Sport*, **89**(3), 1–7. https://doi.org/10.1080/02701367.2018.1481919.

Locke, E. A. and Latham, G. P. (2019). The Development of Goal Setting Theory: A Half Century Retrospective. *Motivation Science*, **5**(2), 93–105. https://doi.org/10.1037/mot0000127.

Luzzeri, M. and Chow, G. M. (2020). Presence and Search for Meaning in Sport: Initial Construct Validation. *Psychology of Sport and Exercise*, **51**. https://doi.org/10.1016/j.psychsport.2020.101783.

Mountjoy, M., Sundgot-Borgen, J., Burke, L., et al. (2014). The IOC Consensus Statement: Beyond the Female Athlete Triad—Relative Energy Deficiency in Sport (RED-S). *British Journal of Sports Medicine*, **48**, 491–497.

Nesti, M. S. (2004). *Existential Psychology in Sport: Theory and Application*. London: Routledge.

Nesti, M. S. and Ronkainen, N. J. (2020). Existential Approaches. In D. Tod and M. Eubank (Eds.), *Applied Sport, Exercise, and Performance Psychology: Approaches to Helping Clients*. London: Routledge.

Oblinger-Peters, V., Henriksen, K. and Ronkainen, N. (2023). Is it all About Medals? Meaning and Purpose in Elite Sport through the Eyes of Olympic Athletes. *Current Issues in Sport Science (CISS)*, **8**(76). https://doi.org/10.36950/2023.2ciss076.

Prior, E., Papathomas, A. and Rhind, D. (2022). A Systematic Scoping Review of Athlete Mental Health within Competitive Sport: Interventions, Recommendations, and Policy. *International Review of Sport and Exercise Psychology*, 1–23. https://doi.org/10.1080/1750984X.2022.2095659.

Ronkainen, N. J. and Nesti, M. S. (2015). An Existential Approach to Sport Psychology: Theory and Applied Practice. *International Journal of Sport and Exercise Psychology*, **15**(1). https://doi.org/10.1080/1612197X.2015.1055288.

Salcinovic, B., Drew, M., Dijkstra, P., et al. (2022). Factors Influencing Team Performance: What Can Support Teams in High-Performance Sport Learn from Other Industries? A Systematic Scoping Review. *Sports Med – Open*, **8**(2). https://doi.org/10.1186/s40798-021-00406-7.

Steger, M. F., Frazier, P., Oishi, S. and Kaler, M. (2006). The Meaning in Life Questionnaire. Assessing the Presence and Search for Meaning in Life. *Journal of Counseling Psychology*, **53**, 80–93. https://doi.org/10.1037/0022-0167.53.1.80.

Steger, M. F., Shin, J. Y., Shim, Y. and Fitch-Martin, A. (2013). Is Meaning in Life a Flagship Indicator of Well-Being? In A. Waterman (Ed.), *The Best Within Us: Positive Psychology Perspectives on Eudaimonia* (pp. 159–182). APA Press.

The Guardian. (2019). Jonny Wilkinson: 'It Took a Few Years for the Pressure to Really Build. And Then it Exploded. https://www.theguardian.com/sport/2019/sep/08/jonny-wilkinson-mental-iilness-rugby-union.

The Sunday Times. (2020). Olympic Medal Wasn't Worth What I Went Through, Says Amy Tinkler. https://www.thetimes.co.uk/article/olympic-medal-wasnt-worth-what-i-went-through-says-amy-tinkler-vw25k0xfg.

The Telegraph. (2020). Alex Danson has 'Zero Regrets' after Bringing Glittering Career to an End Following Her Cruel Head Injury. https://www.telegraph.co.uk/hockey/2020/02/20/alex-danson-has-zero-regrets-bringing-glittering-career-end/.

3 The Myth of the Zombie

Why Automaticity Is Insufficient for (Aspiring) Elite Athletes

Henrik Herrebrøden

Introduction

One of the more pleasurable effects of practice is the apparent ability to be in control despite spending little effort. When starting to learn a skill, it requires most of our attention. But after a while, perhaps years of practice, we can ride our bikes or play fluid tennis strokes while talking to a friend. This progression is summed up by the classic skill acquisition model by Fitts and Posner (1967). In their view, practice may take the motor performer from the early *cognitive phase* to the final destination, the *autonomous phase*, where the role of cognition is drastically diminished. Fitts and Posner's main tenet, that practice may take the performer from early stages characterized by cognition and analysis to later stages where the action runs rather effortlessly and largely outside conscious awareness, has remained influential in sport settings and theoretical frameworks (e.g. Carson & Collins, 2011; Gray, 2015).

Since skilled athletes have been through extensive amounts of practice, it is perhaps no wonder that they are often thought to run their actions on autopilot. It seems plausible that they can, and perhaps should, perform without thinking or attending. In its more extreme form, this view of elite athletes portrays them as zombies, moving around with little (conscious) awareness of their own actions, resembling sleepwalkers (Breivik, 2013). Indeed, attending to one's actions is frequently warned against and believed to disrupt skilled motor execution (e.g. Beilock, 2011; Gray, 2020). The drive towards automaticity also has implications for practice, exemplified by legendary basketball coach John Wooden (as cited in Gray, 2015, p. 74): 'The importance of repetition until automaticity cannot be overstated.'

Recent years have seen a pushback against the idea that automaticity is the key to becoming the best in the game. Based on recent evidence, this could be regarded as a myth, and the typical elite sporting action may instead be characterized by intensive attention and cognition.

Automaticity: Its definition and measurement

The call for automatic human actions is nothing new. In his book *Habit*, William James (1890) described automaticity as a relative absence of volition, effort and consciousness, something to be desired in everyday settings: 'The more of the details of our daily life we can hand over to the effortless custody of automatism, the more our higher powers of mind will be set free for their own proper work' (p. 54).

If an action is automatized, it may be carried out with no or few attentional resources directed towards task-related cues or execution (Gray, 2015, 2020). Actions that require mental effort, on the other hand, require more, if not most, of one's attentional capacity (Kahneman, 1973). Based on this understanding of automaticity, namely as inversely related to how much mental effort (i.e. intensive attention) one devotes to a given task, it can be measured in several different ways. First, one could ask the athlete to *self-report* by indicating the effort or cognition that goes into task execution. Second, since mental effort is usually accompanied by changes in one's arousal (Kahneman, 1973), one could measure athletes' heart rates, pupil sizes, cortical activity or any other physiological indicator of effort. A third option is to manipulate athletes' attention and see how it affects performance, for example, by engaging the athlete in dual tasking by drawing their attention to an extraneous cognitive task and seeing how this affects performance on a concurrent sports task. Assumedly, the athlete on autopilot should report relatively little task-related cognition and effort, demonstrate relatively modest task-related arousal and be able to attend to cues unrelated to task execution without hurting their sports performance. In the following, past studies measuring self-report, physiology and performance under various attentional constraints will be used to provide evidence for and against such automaticity in sports.

Support for automaticity in sports

After sporting events, athletes are usually interviewed or asked about their performance. In those situations, many skilled athletes demonstrate poor ability to recall details relating to skill execution. In fact, some appear to not remember the execution at all! For instance, Walter Chrintz scored the decisive goal in the highly important semi-final match of the European handball championships in 2022. When interviewed after the final whistle, he claimed he had experienced a 'blackout'; he could not remember the goal or running back to play defence after scoring (Overvik & Kristiansen, 2022). This is a case of what Beilock and Carr (2001) would call 'expertise-induced amnesia', an impoverished episodic memory of performance in experts. This was also demonstrated in a study where expert (intercollegiate) golfers and novices (with no golfing experience) were invited to execute golf putts towards targets that were 1.5 m away on an indoor carpet green (Beilock & Carr, Exp. 1). When asked about the steps involved in a typical golf putt, the experts demonstrated more general knowledge about the technical execution, relative to novices. When asked to recall their recent execution, on the other hand, experts provided less extensive descriptions than their novice counterparts. Beilock and Carr's proposed mechanism was based on automaticity: despite experts' extensive knowledge, they do not rely on online attention to the technical process during execution, and hence they fail to remember parts of the process when asked about it. This proposed mechanism has remained influential, although it has been questioned more recently (see, for example, Høffding & Montero, 2020).

Turning to psychophysiological research, studies have suggested that superior performers rely on relatively modest activation in their brain cortices when executing sport skills (Cheng et al., 2015, 2023; Filho et al., 2021). Such *neural efficiency* (Filho et al., 2021) was demonstrated in two studies by Cheng and colleagues using electroencephalography (EEG) to measure cortical activity. In a darts study, Cheng et al. (2015) recruited expert dart players with approximately 14 years of mean dart-throwing experience, as well as a group of novices with limited dart experience. During the two seconds before releasing the dart, experts demonstrated less activity in their sensorimotor cortex, an area involved in processing motor task information. In a more recent study by Cheng et al. (2023), the same brain area was investigated via EEG in skilled shooters (i.e. marksmen) with approximately three-and-a-half years of pistol shooting experience on average. Participants were divided into two groups based on their shooting performance. The results suggested that from three seconds before to one second after the trigger was pulled, the sensorimotor cortex activation was lower in the above-median performers than in the below-median performers. Overall, these EEG studies by Cheng and colleagues provide psychophysiological demonstrations of the common idea that 'skillful performers execute movement with lower conscious processing during execution as reflected by less cognitive involvement' (Cheng et al., 2015, p. 212).

Finally, since the late 1990s, numerous reports have suggested that sports performance is enhanced when athletes attend to external stimuli that are related to the outcome of their movements, such as their equipment or a target, as opposed to internal stimuli related to movement execution or the body itself. A darts player trying to hit the bullseye, for instance, would be well-advised to focus on the bullseye rather than their arm movement (Marchant et al., 2009). If you try to jump as far as possible, studies suggest that you should be focussing on a visual target ahead instead of focussing on 'extending your knees as rapidly as possible' (Ducharme et al., 2016, p. 278). Studies have even found that skilled athletes can tolerate distraction by attending to extraneous stimuli that are irrelevant to the sports task, without impairing sports performance (Gabbett & Abernethy, 2012; Gray, 2004). Gray (2004, Exp. 1), for example, found that college baseballers (competing in Division 1A) demonstrated similar performance and movement patterns in a single-task batting condition and a dual-task condition. In the latter, participants swung at balls while engaging in a tone recognition task where they responded by saying 'low' or 'high' depending on tone frequency. For novice batters, on the other hand, the dual task led to worse performance than the single-task condition. Another study found that skilled golfers' putting performance *improved* when simultaneously attending to an extraneous task, as compared to a single-task putting condition (Land & Tenenbaum, 2012). A common explanation for such findings has been that automaticity facilitates superior performance and that focussing on execution components can disrupt the ideal automatic processing (Land & Tenenbaum, 2012; for reviews, see Gray, 2015, 2020).

Support for mental effort in sports

Arsal et al. (2016) conducted a self-report golf putting study that was similar to the one by Beilock and Carr (2001) in several respects. That is, they recruited skilled and lesser-skilled golfers (with mean handicaps of 4.42 and 23.19, respectively) to putt on an indoor golf green and report on the steps involved in making golf putts. However, Arsal and colleagues' study had two distinct features, relative to the study by Beilock and Carr. First, they increased task complexity by adding more variability in the putting conditions, for example, by letting participants execute putts that were relatively short (101 cm; 3.3 feet) and relatively long (203 cm; 6.7 feet). Second, participants were asked to *think aloud*, that is, verbalize their current thinking while performing, as opposed to providing episodic recollections of a previous putt. The results indicated more task-related thoughts in skilled than lesser-skilled golfers. Experts demonstrated a greater increase in task-relevant thinking when going from short putts to longer putts, and they particularly demonstrated more thoughts related to strategy. This study presents an intriguing aspect of skilled performance: experts may rely on mental effort, but they may use it differently from novices. For example, experts can shift their attention from mechanical execution elements to higher-order elements such as strategy or tactics (see Christensen et al., 2015).

Reports of physiological measurements have also suggested greater cognitive activity in skilled athletes than in lesser-skilled athletes (e.g. Cooke et al., 2014; Mann et al., 2011). For instance, Cooke et al. (2014) asked expert golfers (with handicaps < 5) and novices (with no formal handicap) to make 2.4-m golf putts. EEG was used to measure cortical activity from four seconds before to one second after the putting movement was initiated. The results indicated more cognitive effort in novices than experts two to three seconds before initiating putting movement. However, from there until the one-second mark past movement initiation, experts appeared to increase their effort to a greater level than novices. This was indicated by, for example, a greater reduction in cortical high-alpha power, assumed to be inversely related to cortical activity and focussed attention. Such findings suggest that skilled sports performance involves mental effort that varies across time.

Finally, studies have manipulated attentional focus to demonstrate that, instead of merely disrupting automaticity and causing performance decline, focussing on task execution, and even one's body can be helpful during motor performance (for a review, see Herrebrøden, 2023). Neumann et al. (2020) conducted an attentional focus study by inviting participants to perform with internal and external foci with a counterbalanced design. Yet, in this study, internal focus led to better performance. That is, novice participants used a rowing ergometer and demonstrated greater distance and power output when focussing on cues related to their body or technique (e.g. legs or breathing) as opposed to focussing externally on cues related to the ergometer (e.g. seat movement or sound). The fact that results in this study differed from those obtained in most past studies with a similar design could be due to the fact that the internal focus cues appeared highly relevant and appropriate, given the rowing task. Past studies, on the other hand, have often used internal cues with questionable relevance for the task at hand (Herrebrøden, 2023).

Multi-methodological approach to investigating mental effort in elite athletes

I recently led a study that combined different measures to test the idea that elite athletes can perform on autopilot without much mental effort (Herrebrøden et al., 2023a, 2023b). The participants were elite rowers from the Norwegian national rowing team as well as a group of non-elites representing Norwegian rowing clubs. Their task was to use a dynamic rowing ergometer, mimicking on-water rowing, under varying conditions. This involved single-task trials where the athletes rowed with certain speed levels, and dual-task trials where the athletes rowed with certain speeds while solving math problems at the same time. The results gave no support to the idea that elite athletes can run their actions automatically. First, we found no difference in self-reported mental effort between the groups. Second, both the elites and non-elites demonstrated kinematic changes and performance decline when going from single-task to dual-task rowing. Third, elites' pupil sizes indicated that they spent more mental effort across the various trials than the non-elites.

Some methodological aspects and strengths of our study may partly explain these results and why they contradict several past findings. For one, our task demands were arguably greater than those in several past studies. Specifically, we used a physically demanding and continuous motor task, engaging athletes in complex movements involving coordination between upper and lower body limbs, and our extraneous math problems were likely more challenging than some of the cognitive tasks used in past dual-task conditions (e.g. Gabbett & Abernethy, 2012; Gray, 2004). Further, we used a highly distinguished elite sample, where most athletes were qualified for the Olympic Games and several had experienced success in international events. This kind of sample might be more inclined to use mental effort than, say, an expert sample competing at the college level or having a few years of experience (see the next section).

Why would athletes need mental effort?

Mental effort is, well, effortful. Spending cognitive resources can, in fact, often be a somewhat aversive experience in human beings, something we do not necessarily enjoy (Vogel et al., 2020). It seems much more pleasant and economical to run actions automatically. So why would we want, or even need, to use mental effort to succeed in competitive sports? One reason could lie in the competitive element. In sports competitions, it is not sufficient to just complete a task. We want to win and keep improving. When engaging in everyday habits such as tying our shoelaces, on the other hand, we are happy as long as we complete the task within a reasonable time frame. But suppose you entered a competition with a peer and decided to see who can tie their shoelaces faster one month from now. Chances are you would become much more focussed and spend more effort when practicing (and competing) with your shoelaces (see Bermúdez, 2017). Such motivation and intent to excel could be part of the reason why we observed relatively substantial amounts of mental effort in athletes preparing for the Olympic Games (Herrebrøden et al., 2023a). For skilled and ambitious athletes, automaticity could lead to what Anders Ericsson called 'arrested development', a plateau in one's development due to a lack of further improvement (e.g. Ericsson, 2008). Opting for automaticity could involve sacrificing progression by ignoring task-relevant cues that can propel one's performance standard beyond the 'good' or 'acceptable'.

Further, real-world sports performance occurs under complex and variable conditions. Automatic processing, on the other hand, is a common result of fairly constant practice conditions (Anderson, 1992). Highly familiar and easy performance settings may allow for somewhat automatic execution of certain motor components (see the next section). Typical research settings seem inclined to provide such conditions with less complexity than the conditions that are found in a real sporting environment. For example, research participants may putt from the same distance on an indoor carpet (Beilock & Carr, 2001), which stands in contrast to the variable putting conditions in a real golf round. When challenged, one should expect to see athletes relying on mental effort to provide appropriate motor responses (Christensen et al., 2016). Examples of challenges could include changes in contextual factors (e.g. changing wind conditions or opponents' tactics), technical demands (e.g. increased speed or difficulty) or internal factors (e.g. increased fatigue or bodily tension). Successful athletes should be able to deal with such challenges. Hence, *flexibility* seems more desirable than automaticity (Pacherie & Mylopoulos, 2021).

Implications for coaches and athletes

An extensive practice manual is beyond the scope of this chapter. However, it seems warranted to provide some advice for practitioners and address the question:

What place, if any, is there for 'repetition until automaticity' as emphasized by John Wooden? A plausible answer would be that automaticity in sports should be reserved for cases that mimic everyday chores as closely as possible. First, the action to be automatized should be relatively simple, presenting modest demands from a technical, tactical, mental and physical point of view. Second, the action should be familiar, to be performed with fairly constant task conditions and a similar motion pattern each time (Anderson, 1992; Christensen et al., 2016). Overall, few motor actions appear to meet these requirements in elite sports. Even movement patterns during walking (Oh & LaPointe, 2017) or elite rowers' movement patterns on a rowing ergometer (Herrebrøden et al., 2023b) can be affected when attention is drawn away from the motor task at hand.

Conceivably, however, certain components of routine actions in sports could be automatized to some degree. Hand or foot motion involved in routine passing or ball handling in soccer or basketball, respectively, could be practiced repeatedly until they require little deliberate attention. The aim of such practice could be the ability to shift attention towards task-relevant cues other than foot or hand motion. For example, the experienced soccer or basketball player can now employ a higher-order focus, for example, by focussing *holistically* on the general feeling of the movement (Becker et al., 2019) or shifting attention towards strategic elements such as finding gaps in the opponents' defence.

It seems that practice should promote better use of mental effort, not a lack of mental effort. Based on this view, practice frameworks such as *implicit motor learning* (e.g. Masters & Maxwell, 2004), where a lack of attention to execution is a prime target, appear questionable. Rather, coaches may want to help athletes explore optimal ways of attending to the task at hand. One starting point would be to identify the task goal, namely, what one tries to accomplish in a given sporting situation. Next, one could ask: Where may the athlete find task-relevant information, based on that goal (Herrebrøden, 2023)? That is, what cues or stimuli may the athlete focus on to facilitate task success? Since performance contexts are complex and ever-changing, any sporting task presents an abundance of potential focus cues. The coach and athlete may become creative and explore novel foci. For example, while vision is a key and dominant sense in most sports, athletes may explore auditory cues or rhythm cues by trying to recreate the sound of successful execution (see MacPherson et al., 2009). Any practice session will offer an opportunity to test out different foci, and practice may become a learning process where the coach and athlete deliberately attend to various task-relevant cues and reflect on their experiences (i.e. what seems fruitful and not). This would be in line with *deliberate practice*, where effort and reflection are key ingredients and improved performance is the all-important and overarching goal (Ericsson, 2008).

Over the last 50 years, the educational psychology literature has presented evidence that recommends a shift from low-effort repetition to more variable and effortful (i.e. deep) information processing (e.g. Craik & Lockhart, 1972; McDaniel & Masson, 1985). It seems that sports practice could take a similar route by encouraging athletes, at all levels, to apply their attentional resources to a variety of cues and stimuli in accordance with their goals and performance context, instead of merely repeating actions until they become automatic.

Conclusion

While it might be pleasant and suited for everyday chores, automaticity seems insufficient to explain real-world sporting success. Evidence from recent self-reports, psychophysiological measurements and dual-task studies suggest that complex motor actions require mental effort, even when the performer has extensive experience with the task at hand. Elite athletes, far from acting zombie-like (Breivik, 2013), may rely on cognition to a greater extent than what has been appreciated and acknowledged in the past. Indeed, their fluid actions may *seem* effortless to the outside viewer, and elites may have a hard time explaining how they carry out their amazing feats (Høffding & Montero, 2020). However, it appears that they do not stop applying attentional effort with practice. Rather, skilled performers may apply mental effort differently from novices.

References

Anderson, J. R. (1992). Automaticity and the ACT theory. *The American Journal of Psychology, 105*(2), 165–180. https://doi.org/10.2307/1423026

Arsal, G., Eccles, D. W., & Ericsson, K. A. (2016). Cognitive mediation of putting: Use of a think-aloud measure and implications for studies of golf-putting in the laboratory. *Psychology of Sport and Exercise, 27,* 18–27. https://doi.org/10.1016/j.psychsport.2016.07.008

Becker, K. A., Georges, A. F., & Aiken, C. A. (2019). Considering a holistic focus of attention as an alternative to an external focus. *Journal of Motor Learning and Development, 7*(2), 194–203. https://doi.org/10.1123/jmld.2017-0065

Beilock, S. (2011). *Choke: What the secrets of the brain reveal about getting it right when you have to.* Free Press.

Beilock, S. L., & Carr, T. H. (2001). On the fragility of skilled performance: What governs choking under pressure? *Journal of Experimental Psychology: General, 130*(4), 701. https://doi.org/10.1037/0096-3445.130.4.701

Bermúdez, J. P. (2017). Do we reflect while performing skillful actions? Automaticity, control, and the perils of distraction. *Philosophical Psychology, 30*(7), 896–924.

Breivik, G. (2013). Zombie-like or superconscious? A phenomenological and conceptual analysis of consciousness in elite sport. *Journal of the Philosophy of Sport, 40*(1), 85–106. https://doi.org/10.1080/00948705.2012.725890

Carson, H. J., & Collins, D. (2011). Refining and regaining skills in fixation/diversification stage performers: The Five-A Model. *International Review of Sport and Exercise Psychology, 4*(2), 146–167. https://doi.org/10.1080/1750984X.2011.613682

Cheng, M.-Y., Hung, C.-L., Huang, C.-J., Chang, Y.-K., Lo, L.-C., Shen, C., & Hung, T.-M. (2015). Expert-novice differences in SMR activity during dart throwing. *Biological Psychology, 110*, 212–218. https://doi.org/10.1016/j.biopsycho.2015.08.003

Cheng, M.-Y., Wang, K.-P., Doppelmayr, M., Steinberg, F., Hung, T.-M., Lu, C., Tan, Y. Y., & Hatfield, B. (2023). QEEG markers of superior shooting performance in skilled marksmen: An investigation of cortical activity on psychomotor efficiency hypothesis. *Psychology of Sport and Exercise, 65*, 102320. https://doi.org/10.1016/j.psychsport.2022.102320

Christensen, W., Sutton, J., & McIlwain, D. (2015). Putting pressure on theories of choking: Towards an expanded perspective on breakdown in skilled performance. *Phenomenology and the Cognitive Sciences, 14*(2), 253–293. https://doi.org/10.1007/s11097-014-9395-6

Christensen, W., Sutton, J., & McIlwain, D. J. F. (2016). Cognition in skilled action: Meshed control and the varieties of skill experience. *Mind & Language, 31*(1), 37–66. https://doi.org/10.1111/mila.12094

Cooke, A., Kavussanu, M., Gallicchio, G., Willoughby, A., McIntyre, D., & Ring, C. (2014). Preparation for action: Psychophysiological activity preceding a motor skill as a function of expertise, performance outcome, and psychological pressure. *Psychophysiology, 51*(4), 374–384. https://doi.org/10.1111/psyp.12182

Craik, F. I. M., & Lockhart, R. S. (1972). Levels of processing: A framework for memory research. *Journal of Verbal Learning and Behavior, 11*(6), 671–684. https://doi.org/10.1016/S0022-5371(72)80001-X

Ducharme, S. W., Wu, W. F., Lim, K., Porter, J. M., & Geraldo, F. (2016). Standing long jump performance with an external focus of attention is improved as a result of a more effective projection angle. *The Journal of Strength & Conditioning Research, 30*(1), 276–281. https://doi.org/10.1519/JSC.0000000000001050

Ericsson, K. A. (2008). Deliberate practice and acquisition of expert performance: A general overview. *Academic Emergency Medicine, 15*(11), 988–994. https://doi.org/10.1111/j.1553-2712.2008.00227.x

Filho, E., Dobersek, U., & Husselman, T.-A. (2021). The role of neural efficiency, transient hypofrontality and neural proficiency in optimal performance in self-paced sports: A meta-analytic review. *Experimental Brain Research, 239*(5), 1381–1393. https://doi.org/10.1007/s00221-021-06078-9

Fitts, P. M., & Posner, M. I. (1967). *Human performance.* Brooks/Cole Publishing Company.

Gabbett, T. J., & Abernethy, B. (2012). Dual-task assessment of a sporting skill: Influence of task complexity and relationship with competitive performances. *Journal of Sports Sciences, 30*(16), 1735–1745. https://doi.org/10.1080/02640414.2012.713979

Gray, R. (2004). Attending to the execution of a complex sensorimotor skill: Expertise differences, choking, and slumps. *Journal of Experimental Psychology: Applied, 10*(1), 42–54. https://doi.org/10.1037/1076-898X.10.1.42

Gray, R. (2015). Movement automaticity in sport. In J. Baker & D. Farrow (Eds.), *Routledge handbook of sport expertise* (pp. 74–83). Routledge.

Gray, R. (2020). Attentional theories of choking under pressure revisited. In G. Tenenbaum & R. C. Eklund (Eds.), *Handbook of sport psychology* (pp. 595–610). John Wiley & Sons, Inc.

Herrebrøden, H. (2023). Motor performers need task-relevant information: Proposing an alternative mechanism for the attentional focus effect. *Journal of Motor Behavior, 55*(1), 125–134. https://doi.org/10.1080/00222895.2022.2122920

Herrebrøden, H., Espeseth, T., & Bishop, L. (2023a). Mental effort in elite and nonelite rowers. *Journal of Sport and Exercise Psychology, 45*(4), 208–223. https://doi.org/10.1123/jsep.2022-0164

Herrebrøden, H., Jensenius, A. R., Espeseth, T., Bishop, L., & Vuoskoski, J. K. (2023b). Cognitive load causes kinematic changes in both elite and non-elite rowers. *Human Movement Science, 90*, 103113. https://doi.org/10.1016/j.humov.2023.103113

Høffding, S., & Montero, B. G. (2020). Not being there: An analysis of expertise-induced amnesia. *Mind & Language, 35*(5), 621–640. https://doi.org/10.1111/mila.12260

James, W. (1890). *Habit*. Henry Holt.

Kahneman, D. (1973). *Attention and effort*. Prentice-Hall.

Land, W., & Tenenbaum, G. (2012). An outcome- and process-oriented examination of a golf-specific secondary task strategy to prevent choking under pressure. *Journal of Applied Sport Psychology, 24*(3), 303–322. https://doi.org/10.1080/10413200.2011.642458

MacPherson, A. C., Collins, D., & Obhi, S. S. (2009). The importance of temporal structure and rhythm for the optimum performance of motor skills: A new focus for practitioners of sport psychology. *Journal of Applied Sport Psychology, 21*(S1), S48–S61. https://doi.org/10.1080/10413200802595930

Mann, D. T., Coombes, S. A., Mousseau, M. B., & Janelle, C. M. (2011). Quiet eye and the Bereitschaftspotential: Visuomotor mechanisms of expert motor performance. *Cognitive Processing, 12*(3), 223–234. https://doi.org/10.1007/s10339-011-0398-8

Marchant, D. C., Clough, P. J., Crawshaw, M., & Levy, A. (2009). Novice motor skill performance and task experience is influenced by attentional focusing instructions and instruction preferences. *International Journal of Sport and Exercise Psychology, 7*(4), 488–502. https://doi.org/10.1080/1612197X.2009.9671921

Masters, R. S., & Maxwell, J. P. (2004). Implicit motor learning, reinvestment and movement disruption: What you don't know won't hurt you. In A. M. Williams & N. J. Hodges (Eds.), *Skill acquisition in sport* (pp. 231–252). Routledge.

McDaniel, M. A., & Masson, M. E. (1985). Altering memory representations through retrieval. *Journal of Experimental Psychology: Learning, Memory, and Cognition, 11*(2), 371. https://doi.org/10.1037/0278-7393.11.2.371

Neumann, D. L., Walsh, N., Moffitt, R. L., & Hannan, T. E. (2020). Specific internal and external attentional focus instructions have differential effects on rowing performance. *Psychology of Sport and Exercise, 50*, 101722. https://doi.org/10.1016/j.psychsport.2020.101722

Oh, C., & LaPointe, L. L. (2017). Changes in cognitive load and effects on parameters of gait. *Cogent Psychology, 4*(1), 1372872. https://doi.org/10.1080/23311908.2017.1372872

Overvik, J., & Kristiansen, T. (2022). Svensk matchvinner i tårer: – Jeg fikk blackout. *Aftenposten*. https://www.aftenposten.no/sport/i/oWPaPj/svensk-matchvinner-i-taarer-jeg-fikk-blackout

Pacherie, E., & Mylopoulos, M. (2021). Beyond automaticity: The psychological complexity of skill. *Topoi, 40*(3), 649–662. https://doi.org/10.1007/s11245-020-09715-0

Vogel, T. A., Savelson, Z. M., Otto, A. R., & Roy, M. (2020). Forced choices reveal a trade-off between cognitive effort and physical pain. *eLife, 9*, e59410. https://doi.org/10.7554/eLife.59410

4 Busting Myths

Navigating Pregnancy as an Elite Athlete

Melanie J Hayman, Margie H Davenport, Nicola Bullock and Amy E. Whitehead

Throughout the 19th and early 20th centuries, women were encouraged to avoid participating in exercises in order to 'rest' and 'relax' during pregnancy despite women engaging in physically demanding labour for centuries (Davenport & Hayman, 2022). Medical and public sentiment rapidly changed course when the American College of Obstetricians and Gynecologists (ACOG) released the first guidelines for exercise during pregnancy in 1985. Although this was a progressive change, they included significant restrictions on exercise duration and intensity, recommending a limit of 15 minutes per session at a maximal heart rate of 140 beats/min. which equates to 'moderate' intensity exercise for most women of childbearing age (American College of Obstetricians and Gynecologists (ACOG), 1985). Over the subsequent five decades, a substantial body of empirical evidence consistently reveals that exercise intensities of up to at least 80% of maximal effort in healthy individuals do not lead to any additional adverse outcomes for both the mother and the foetus. As such, most exercises during pregnancy guidelines now recommend women accumulate at least 150 min of moderate-intensity activity each week (Hayman et al., 2023) to achieve clinically meaningful reductions in pregnancy complications (Mottola et al., 2019). Although exercise during pregnancy guidelines have continued to evolve, they are not 'fit for purpose' for recreational and elite athletes who typically engage in high intensity, duration and/or volumes of training well beyond current recommendations.

In 2016, the International Olympic Committee (IOC) formed an expert working group to develop a series of reviews specific to recreational and elite athletes (Bø, Artal, Barakat, Brown, Davies, et al., 2016; Bø, Artal, Barakat, Brown, Davies, Dooley, Evenson, Haakstad, Kayser, Kinnunen, Larsén, et al., 2017; Bø et al., 2018; Bø, Artal, Barakat, Brown, Davies, Dooley, Evenson, Haakstad, Kayser, Kinnunen, Mottola, et al., 2017; Bø, Artal, Barakat, Brown,

Dooley, et al., 2016). Their aims were to: (1) summarize common conditions, illnesses and complaints that may interfere with strenuous exercise and competition during pregnancy and after childbirth; (2) provide recommendations for exercise training during pregnancy and after childbirth, for high-level regular exercisers and elite athletes; and (3) identify major gaps in the literature that limit the confidence with which recommendations can be made. Unfortunately, due to limited empirical evidence at the time, the IOC were unable to establish any concrete recommendations regarding the safety of high intensity, duration and/or volumes of training beyond guidelines recommendations; nor were they able to provide any practical guidance regarding training or performance optimization for recreational and elite athletes. Since the publication of these reviews, there has been renewed interest and uptake in research specifically related to pregnant and postpartum athletes. Based on emerging research, novel systematic reviews and meta-analyses have examined pregnancy, labour and delivery outcomes, as well as postpartum health outcomes, between elite athletes and active/sedentary controls (Kimber et al., 2021; Wowdzia et al., 2021). These reviews found similar health outcomes between the groups, laying the foundation for research that challenges traditional beliefs pertaining to the safety risks associated with high intensity (Anderson et al., 2021; Beetham et al., 2019; Kardel, 2005; Wowdzia et al., 2022) and types of exercise including heavy strength training (Prevett et al., 2023). As the number and visibility of athlete mothers who continue to engage in high-performance sport grows, so does societal acceptance of these athletes. Yet, numerous myths persist regarding the safety and potential benefits of continued sport participation for athletic mothers.

There is no evidence to support the myth that 'women with a healthy pregnancy should take it easy', especially amongst athletes who are already highly active before conception. In contrast, a dose-response relationship between higher intensities, durations and volumes of physical activity during pregnancy with greater reductions in the odds of developing gestational diabetes, gestational hypertension and preeclampsia has been identified (Davenport et al., 2018). In fact, inactivity is an established risk factor for the development of adverse outcomes and complications. Even if absolute contraindications to exercise during pregnancy develop, light-intensity exercise (i.e. activities of daily living) is associated with health benefits (Mottola et al., 2019). Irrespective of whether the athlete chooses to maintain or reduce their exercise behaviours during pregnancy, the priority should always be the health and well-being of the athlete and the child.

During pregnancy, many athletes will experience some degree of detraining during pregnancy. This will be highly variable between athletes as the development of complications, medical advice and desire to continue training will be key influences. Limiting the effects of detraining can be critical for elite athletes who aim to return to the high-performance environment within a short time frame, typically pre-determined by competition dates. For some athletes, a degree of deconditioning, as a result of detraining, is unavoidable, due to the nature of the sport (e.g. cardiovascular demands of rugby can be replicated, but the contact/collision demands cannot, as a rugby player must cease all contact activities, upon pregnancy confirmation) (Mujika & Padilla, 2000, 2001). However, smart and well-planned programming, under the guidance and supervision of appropriately qualified healthcare professionals who can monitor and tailor the training to meet the athlete's specific needs, is imperative (Hayman et al., 2023.

Athletes commonly participate in rigorous aerobic training to develop and sustain their cardiovascular fitness and endurance, concurrently incorporating strength training to enhance muscular power and endurance. Yet, two of the most common approaches to athletic training – high-intensity exercise and heavy weight training – are typically discouraged during pregnancy.

High-intensity exercise

A recent systematic review of 15 studies focussed on vigorous-intensity exercise in the third trimester (up to 85% maximal heart rate [HR_{max}]) found a small but significant increase in gestational age and reduced risk of prematurity (Beetham et al., 2019). However, only three studies to date have investigated the effect of high-intensity exercise surpassing 90% HR_{max} in pregnant women with a key focus on assessing the safety of vigorous-intensity exercise on foetal wellbeing (Salvesen et al., 2012; Szymanski & Satin, 2012; Wowdzia et al., 2023). Foetal bradycardia assessed via ultrasound is considered an abnormal response to maternal exercise that may be caused by abnormalities in maternal/foetal circulation (e.g. decreased blood flow to the foetus and/or increased resistance to blood flow by the placenta). Two studies examining the impact of a graded (2–5-minute stage) exercise test to maximal effort lasting 20–25-minutes identified transient foetal bradycardia (<110 beats per minute) in some participants that resolved within minutes (Salvesen et al., 2012; Szymanski & Satin, 2012). Based on this data, the IOC and other organizations suggested an upper limit of 90% HR_{max} during pregnancy.

In the interim, two additional studies of interval exercise with intensities up to 90% HR_{max} have been conducted. Anderson and colleagues (2021) examined the impact of three rounds of six exercises performed at 80–90% HR_{max} for the 20s interspersed with 60s of recovery, while Ong et al. (2016) tested six, 15-second self-paced bouts of high-intensity exercise repeated every three minutes. Neither study identified adverse maternal or foetal outcomes with brief bouts of high-intensity exercise. High-intensity interval training (HIIT) has been a top 10 fitness trend for more than a decade, with many women opting to continue this form of training even in the absence of safety guidelines (Nagpal et al., 2021). To address this question, Wowdzia and colleagues (2022) recruited 15 pregnant women in the second and third trimester of pregnancy to engage in a session of HIIT *(10 × 1-minute intervals ≥ 90% HR_{max})* interspersed with one minute of active recovery and moderate-intensity continuous training *(30 minutes at 64–76% HR_{max})*. Participants achieved an average of 96% HR_{max}, and maternal and foetal well-being including foetal heart rate and umbilical blood flow metrics were assessed; no adverse effects were identified. They also illustrated similar glucose responses to both HIIT and more traditional moderate-intensity continuous exercise, and the potential for an increase in the duration of maternal sleep following exercise (Wowdzia et al., 2022). These data demonstrate an alternative for athletes to engage in high-intensity exercise to maintain fitness, without adversely affecting the foetus. However, additional work is needed to establish the safety of other forms of high-intensity exercise, including heavy weightlifting.

Heavy lifting

Heavy weightlifting during pregnancy has been a topic of intense concern and debate amongst healthcare professionals, researchers and pregnant women. Heavy weightlifting during pregnancy has traditionally been discouraged due to concern for the health of the foetus and potential stress on the pelvic floor due to the associated (and significant) increases in blood pressure that occurs when lifting heavy loads with and without the Valsalva manoeuver (Prevett et al., 2023). Concern for maternal and foetal well-being is supported by meta-analysed data from observational studies that revealed occupational lifting objects ≥ 11 kg was associated with an increased odds ratio of miscarriage (odds ratio, 1.31; 95% confidence interval, 1.08–1.58; I2 = 79%) and preeclampsia (odds ratio, 1.35; 95% confidence interval, 1.07–1.71; I2 = 0%). Lifting objects for a combined weight of ≥ 100kg per day was associated with increased odds of preterm delivery (odds ratio, 1.31; 95% confidence interval, 1.11–1.56; I2 = 0%) and having a low birthweight neonate (odds ratio, 2.08; 95% confidence interval, 1.06–4.11; I2 = 73%) in an occupational setting (Cai et al., 2019). Yet, occupational and recreational heavy lifting cannot be equated (Cai & Davenport, 2022). Heavy lifting in an occupational setting is often repetitive with poor form and limited time for recovery, warranting the development of occupational lifting limits, such as those developed by the National Institute for Occupational Safety and Health in 2015 (Waters et al., 2014). These recommendations are based on frequency and duration of lifting, the object distance from the body, as well as gestational age. In the first half of pregnancy (<20 weeks gestation), the maximum recommended lift weight is 16 kg/36 lbs, while the maximum recommended lift weight in the second half of pregnancy reduces to 12 kg/26 lbs. Conversely, heavy lifting in a recreational setting focusses on proper technique and appropriate recovery time between lifts. There is no evidence to date that suggests lifting in a recreational setting during pregnancy is associated with increased pregnancy complications or adverse events. As such, it is not appropriate to apply occupational lifting limits to lifting in a recreational setting, despite many women being advised to do so.

Current prenatal physical activity guidelines around the world recommend moderate-intensity strength training, but heavy weightlifting is traditionally not advised due to a lack of research (Hayman et al., 2023). To date, only two studies have investigated the use of a Valsalva manoeuvre during prenatal resistance but no adverse maternal or foetal responses have been identified, albeit at relatively low training loads (up to a maximum of 23 kg/50 lbs with incline bench press (Gould et al., 2021) and 40% of 10 RM in a seated leg press (Meah et al., 2021)). Only one cross-sectional study of 679 athletes has examined the impact of chronic heavy weightlifting (>80% 1 RM) before and during pregnancy on pregnancy outcomes (Prevett et al., 2023). Athletes in the Prevett et al. (2023) study commonly engaged in activities discouraged by many prenatal physical activity guidelines (Olympic lifting, Valsalva and supine exercise). Overall rates of maternal and foetal complications were low, and those who maintained pre-pregnancy training levels until delivery had a 51% reduction in the odds of having pregnancy and delivery complications than those who reduced their training level prior to delivery (OR: 0.49, 95% CI, 0.29–0.81).

The IOC guidelines recommend focussing on technique and safety during strength training for pregnant athletes (Bø, Artal, Barakat, Brown, Davies, et al., 2016). Proper technique is essential to reduce injury risk and ensure the changing body is accommodated. Those who perform bar work and Olympic lifts may wish to consider switching to dumbbells or kettlebells to avoid the growing belly and maintain proper technique. However, individualization to support the athlete's unique needs and pregnancy experiences is essential. This individualization is of critical importance, as pregnancy is a uniquely individual experience; no two pregnancies are the same. Sport-specific considerations for individualization should also be applied. Three-time Olympic Kayaker and World Champion Alyce Wood (nee Burnett) explains how working closely with her sport science team and setting individualized, adaptable and manageable training goals were vital to her training during pregnancy:

> Whilst at times it was very challenging, training through pregnancy gave me a lot of purpose in my day-to-day life as I had small and manageable goals to work towards every day. I set these goals with my immediate support team (Coach, sport scientist and physiotherapist) early in my pregnancy, with the idea that we didn't want to make them too specific or outcome related as there are so many unknowns throughout a pregnancy. Rather, they were overarching goals that meant I could pivot training modalities or remove exercises from my program whenever I felt I needed, without having to change training philosophies completely. This helped me remain incredibly positive and driven right throughout my pregnancy.

Depending on the nature of the sport, various modifications will be necessary to accommodate pregnant athletes. For instance, sprint kayaking is a highly technical sport requiring paddling with a high degree of rotation under load. As the conceptus (embryo) grows, eventually the athlete's rotation will become restricted which subsequently has biomechanical implications around technique. Additionally, sprint kayakers also require a high level of balance and coordination. However, pregnancy-induced physical and physiological changes (e.g. change in centre of gravity, increase in breast and stomach size, reduced abdominal strength) as pregnancy progresses will impact balance and coordination. As such, the athlete should cease kayaking sessions when the pregnancy starts to negatively impact their technique to avoid the potential introduction of bad technical habits and/or increase the risk of injury due to a potential decline in balance and coordination. Rather than focussing on on-water kayaking sessions, pregnancy might present an opportunity for the athlete to undertake strength training with the goal to prevent injury and optimize strength in areas that could not be addressed otherwise due to requirements to periodize different traits around the racing and the competition blocks. For instance, strength training blocks that typically only last 6–12 weeks could potentially be extended (e.g. up to six months) and the volume increased (e.g. repetitions per exercise could increase from the traditional 3 to 6 repetitions to 10 repetitions) to build the athletes' strength capacity.

Elite athletes with a healthy pregnancy need not 'compromise' their training routine or shy away from opportunities to improve their overall performance. However, achieving athletic goals must consider the health and well-being of both the mother and foetus. The training program should be reviewed weekly/bi-weekly and adjusted based on the athlete's feedback and training monitoring data. In all cases, regular and open dialogue between the athlete, coaching staff and healthcare providers is essential to ensure that appropriate modifications are being made while maintaining an athlete-centred decision-making process (Davenport et al., 2023).

Importantly, due to the unpredictable nature of birth, some athletes will require a longer postpartum recovery period, which will ultimately delay their return to activity, thus also likely delaying their return to sport. It is imperative this period is not 'rushed' and that the athlete be provided with the necessary support structures to allow adequate time to engage in the necessary rehabilitation and recovery before returning to sport (Tighe et al., 2023). While there is currently limited evidence to guide women, especially elite athletes, through this return to sport postpartum phase, those involved with the elite athletes' care may benefit from the utilization of emerging frameworks, rather than the 'arbitrary 6-week check-up' (Tighe et al., 2023).

An athlete's perspective

This chapter highlighted some of the training complexities and nuances of the elite athlete-mother's journey. As the number of athlete mothers continues to grow, so does the need for high-quality research to inform 'fit for purpose' guidelines to appropriately support them. Preliminary research, addressed in this chapter, suggests that elite athletes may continue to engage in exercises (e.g. high-intensity exercise and heavy weight training) that were once believed to be unsafe during pregnancy; however, there is still much work to be done before we can confidently and unequivocally prescribe elite athletes with exercise guidance during pregnancy. What we do know for sure is that athletes need an individualized program, unique to both their sport and pregnancy-specific considerations and a highly skilled and knowledgeable multi-disciplinary team to monitor their physical, physiological and psychological health and well-being. Finally, athletes need a supportive environment, one where decisions are based on evidence and best practices, and not beliefs of the past that do nothing but propagate uncertainty and unsubstantiated myths. In the words of Alyce Wood:

> Servicing a high-performance athlete in their daily training environment is incredibly technical and requires a lot of high-level support. However, when it comes to servicing a pregnant athlete, there is a gap in knowledge and lack of policies/strategies within many sports. That's why I recommend that athletes who are planning on starting a family to be really open and honest about their intent as early as practicable, as it gives sports ample time to be able to plan and build a best-practice environment.
>
> I think it's also incredibly important for sports to expose athletes to female health information sessions early in their career. Knowledge is power, and having a solid understanding of this topic is incredibly useful for all female athletes, but more so for athletes entering motherhood as our bodies are simultaneously sustaining a life while performing at a high level.

MYTHS OF SPORT PERFORMANCE

ARE YOU AN ATHLETE WHO IS CURRENTLY PREGNANT?

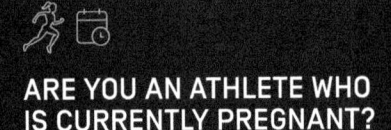

AIS

MEDICAL CHECK-UPS

Prioritise an appointment with your Sports Doctor or Health Care Professional (e.g., General Practitioner, Midwife, Obstetrician) to discuss the following:

> Your pregnancy plan
> How to best manage current health conditions
> Safety of current medications and supplements, including compliance with WADA
> Supplements to consider such as folate, iodine, iron and vitamin D
> Pelvic floor health and potential referral to a Women's Health Physiotherapist

You should also make an appointment with your Sports Doctor or Health Care Professional if:

> You have a medical concern or have concerns about performing exercise
> You are having difficulty eating or drinking because of continued nausea and/or vomiting
> You experience any pelvic floor symptoms such as incontinence (leaking urine, wind or faeces), prolapse (dragging, bulging or heaviness sensation in the vagina), persistent bladder urgency/pressure or pelvic pain.
> You are experiencing continued musculoskeletal pain (e.g., lower back or pelvic girdle pain)
> You are experiencing reduced foetal movements or have concerns regarding your pregnancy or baby

EXERCISE

Exercising while pregnant in accordance with the Australian evidence-based physical activity guidelines for pregnant women is SAFE, has HEALTH BENEFITS for the mother and her child and REDUCES THE RISK of some pregnancy-related complications (e.g., gestational diabetes, preeclampsia).

There is **LIMITED** evidence to guide exercise prescription for pregnant elite athletes. There is **NO KNOWN SAFE UPPER LIMIT** to exercise intensity or duration. If **EXCEEDING** the recommended amount of exercise (high intensity >90% of womans maximum heart rate, duration >60 min and/or high volume >300 min), seek advice from an appropriately qualified Health Care Professional.

DO NOT ignore any of the following signs and symptoms that may put your pregnancy at risk. These include chest pain, persistent excessive shortness of breath that does not resolve with rest, regular painful uterine contractions, persistent loss of fluid and/or bleeding from the vagina, severe headache or persistent dizziness / feeling faint that does not resolve with rest.

A small number of women may develop medical conditions (contraindications) where exercise may not be recommended. These conditions can be pre-existing or develop at any point during your pregnancy. Depending on the contraindication, you may be recommended to continue, modify or cease engaging in moderate to vigorous activity. If your health changes, it is important you screen for contraindications again.

ABSOLUTE CONTRAINDICTATIONS TO EXERCISE (reasons not to continue): This includes but is not limited to an incompetent cervix, ruptured membranes, preterm labour, persistent second or third trimester bleeding, placenta previa; pre-eclampsia, evidence of intrauterine growth restriction, multiple gestation (triplets or higher number), poorly controlled type 1 diabetes, hypertension or thyroid disease and other serious cardiovascular, respiratory or systemic disorders as specified by Health Care Professional. **RECOMMENDATION:** Continue activities of daily living, but do not take part in moderate or vigorous exercise and take guidance from your Medical Practitioner.

Busting Myths

ARE YOU AN ATHLETE WHO IS CURRENTLY PREGNANT?

RELATIVE CONTRAINDICATIONS TO EXERCISE (reasons to consider modification): This includes but is not limited to mild/moderate cardiovascular or chronic respiratory disease, pregnancy induced hypertension / gestational hypertension, poorly controlled seizure disorder, type 1 diabetes, symptomatic anaemia, malnutrition, significantly underweight or eating disorder, twin pregnancy after the 28th week, history of spontaneous miscarriage, preterm labour or foetal growth restriction or other significant medical conditions. **RECOMMENDATION:** Discuss advantages and disadvantages of exercise with your Health Care Professional and continue exercise with appropriate modification.

DO: Accumulate 150-300 minutes of moderate-vigorous exercise per week consisting of aerobic, resistance and pelvic floor exercises.

DO: Modify training as required to accommodate physiological changes as pregnancy progresses including pregnancy weight gain, the growing baby bump, increased joint laxity and change in balance.

DO: Ensure adequate hydration, especially when exercising in hot and/or humid conditions.

> Core body temperature should remain between 36°C-39°C so avoid exercise, training and recovery in excessively cold, hot and/or humid conditions (including ice baths, cryotherapy, spas, saunas and heat chambers) especially during the first trimester.
> Exercise in supine position (lying on your back) if causing light headedness or dizziness.
> Those considering altitude training above 2000m (including chambers and tents) should seek supervision from a Health Care Professional with knowledge in this area.
> Avoid training and competition that might involve a risk of contact, collision or falls.

NUTRITION & WEIGHT GAIN

Work with a Sports Dietitian to help monitor and meet the nutritional needs of being an athlete and being pregnant.

> **Extra nutrients:** The basic principles of healthy eating remain the same during pregnancy, though the recommended dietary intake is higher for some nutrients during pregnancy. You should have at least 500 micrograms of folate and 150 micrograms of iodine per day.
> **Supplements:** Checking your supplements (pregnancy or sport related) is your responsibility and you should ensure that these supplements do not contain prohibited substances.
> **Iron deficiency:** Is a common issue for female athletes and pregnant women. Your Health Care Professional can check iron levels, whilst your Sports Dietitian can provide advice on strategies to meet iron needs, as well as other important nutrients such as calcium.
> **Nausea and/or vomiting:** Can occur at any point during the day. Drink plenty of fluids, eat small portion meals/snacks often throughout the day, get rest and avoid foods and smells that trigger nausea. Try to avoid training on an empty stomach.
> **Avoid:** Foods that may contain listeria bacteria, salmonella or high levels of mercury. Also avoid smoking, alcohol and the use of illicit drugs. Caffeine (a stimulant present in coffee, tea, energy drinks, some soft drinks and sports products) should be limited to 200mg day - approximately two cups of coffee per day.
> **Weight Gain:** Healthy weight gain over the course of a pregnancy is important. The Institute of Medicine (IOM) guidelines recommend 11.5-16.0kg over the entire course of the pregnancy for women who are a healthy pre-conception weight. Do not engage in unhealthy practices that attempt to minimise weight gain via restriction in food quantity and range. Concerns around changes in weight/physique are best addressed with a Dietitian.

MYTHS OF SPORT PERFORMANCE

ARE YOU AN ATHLETE WHO IS CURRENTLY PREGNANT?

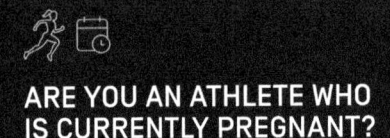

SLEEP

While there are no specific studies examining the sleep behaviours of elite athletes during pregnancy, we know that pregnant women, including elite athletes, usually obtain well below the recommendation of 7-9 hours of **GOOD QUALITY SLEEP** per night, and that sleep worsens as pregnancy progresses. To improve sleep:

- **Create a good sleep routine:** Wind down 30 minutes before bedtime and turn off all electronic devices and bright lights.
- **Avoid:** Caffeine, sleeping tablets, spicy and/or heavy meals close to bedtime and irregular sleep routines.
- **Avoid:** Sleeping on your back (particularly after 28 weeks gestation) and consider pregnancy pillow for additional support.
- **Napping:** Is ideal for pregnant athletes as it may help to supplement inadequate sleep. Consider napping between 20-90 minutes per day and aim to take your nap between the hours of 1-4:00pm.
- **Allow 30 minutes upon wakening:** To reduce sleep inertia (feeling sluggishness immediately on waking) before training / competing for better performance outcomes.

BRA SUPPORT

A well-designed and fitted sports bra is essential during pregnancy to support growing and often tender breasts. You will often require more support and a larger bra size so choose a sports bra that provides 'higher support' or wear two bras simultaneously with these features:

- **Band:** High-quality elastic fabric that does not curl up and can stretch yet retain its shape and includes several adjustment options (hook, clip, zip) to allow for ongoing change.
- **Cups:** Completely cover your breasts (near your armpits and at the top of each breast) and comfortably compress each breast. Non-underwire sports bras with elastic material in the cups adapt more easily to changing breast shape and size. Any underwire MUST sit on your breastbone (at the front) and ribs (near your armpits) and NOT on your breast tissue. Cups should be able to accommodate pads to manage any leakage that can occur in the latter stages of your pregnancy.
- **Straps:** Adjustable, wide and padded. If wearing two bras simultaneously, make sure each bra has a different strap orientation (e.g., vertical straps and bra and racerback) for comfort and weight distribution.
- **Material:** Smooth, soft to touch and moisture-wicking (cool to wear), non-abrasive and no seams particularly on the inside of the cups.

PELVIC FLOOR

- The combined load of pregnancy and heavy lifting and/or high-impact exercise may overload the pelvic floor for some women and can lead to the development of pelvic floor symptoms either during pregnancy or after childbirth.
- Pelvic floor exercises are recommended before, during and after pregnancy as they can help to preserve your pelvic floor health. Speak with your Sports Physiotherapist early, to find a Women's Health Physiotherapist that understands your sport demands as well as pregnancy plans.

Busting Myths

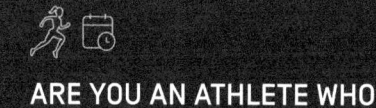

ARE YOU AN ATHLETE WHO IS CURRENTLY PREGNANT?

OTHER CONSIDERATIONS

TRAVEL: During pregnancy, restrictions apply for most modes of commercial travel. Most domestic airlines will not permit pregnant women to travel for more than four hours after 36 weeks gestation, international flights restrict travel from 32 weeks. Always check with your Health Care Professional prior to planning travel to ensure it is safe for you to do so. When travelling, move often by flexing and extending knees and ankles and stop to stretch your legs every two hours, consider wearing knee-high fitted compression stockings and stay well hydrated to also reduce the risk of blood clots. It is also important to ensure that travel insurance covers both you and your unborn baby.

MENTAL HEALTH: Engaging in exercise during pregnancy also has a positive effect on mental health. However, pregnancy can also uncover or worsen pre-existing mental health issues. If you have any concerns you should discuss this with your sports doctor or health professional, or the AIS Mental Health Referral Network.

Please note, this factsheet does not replace individualised medical advice.

Contributors

Dr Melanie Hayman (CQUniversity), Dr Margie Davenport (University of Alberta, Canada), Dr Rachel Harris (AIS FPHI), Dr Clare Minahan (Griffith University), Dr Louise Burke (Australian Catholic University), Dr Jodie Dakic (Monash University), Dr Deirdre McGhee (University of Wollongong), Dr Julie Steele (University of Wollongong), Dr Michele Lastella (CQUniversity)

References

1. Brown WJ, Hayman MJ, Haakstad L. et al. (2020) Evidence-based physical activity guidelines for pregnant women: Report for the Australian Government Department of Health. Australian Government Department of Health: Canberra. Available from: **https://www.health.gov.au/resources/publications/evidence-based-physical-activity-guidelines-for-pregnant-women**

2. Mottola M, Davenport M, Ruchat S. et al. (2018) 2019 Canadian guideline for physical activity throughout pregnancy. BJSM. Available from: **https://bjsm.bmj.com/content/52/21/1339**

3. Department of Health, Australian Government. (2020) Australian Clinical Practice Guidelines: Pregnancy Care. Available from: **https://www.health.gov.au/resources/pregnancy-care-guidelines**

4. Department of Health, Australian Government. (2013) Australian dietary guidelines: healthy eating during pregnancy. Available from: **https://www.eatforhealth.gov.au/guidelines**

5. The Royal Australian and New Zealand College of Obstetricians and Gynaecologists. (2021) Planning for Pregnancy. Available from: **https://ranzcog.edu.au/womens-health/patient-information-resources/planning-for-pregnancy**

6. Royal Australian College of General Practitioners (2018) Guidelines for preventative activities in general practice, 9th edition. Available from: **https://www.racgp.org.au/getattachment/1ad1a26f-9c8b-4e3c-b45b-3237272b3a04/Guidelines-for-preventive-activities-in-general-practice.aspx**

7. Australian Government. Eat for health - Healthy eating during your pregnancy (2015). Available from: **https://www.eatforhealth.gov.au/sites/default/files/files/the_guidelines/n55h_healthy_eating_during_pregnancy.pdf**

8. The Royal Australian and New Zealand College of Obstetricians and Gynaecologists. (2021) Why your weight matters during pregnancy. Available from: **https://ranzcog.edu.au/wp-content/uploads/2022/06/Why-your-weight-matters-during-pregnancy-pamphlet.pdf**

9. Lastella M et al. (2021) To Nap or not to nap? A systematic review evaluating napping behavior in athletes and the impact on various measures of athletic performance. Nature and Science of Sleep. Available from: **https://www.ncbi.nlm.nih.gov/pmc/articles/PMC8238550/**

10. Ravanelli N et al. (2019) Heat stress and fetal risk. Environmental limits for exercise and passive heat stress during pregnancy: a systematic review with best evidence synthesis. BJSM. Available from: **https://bjsm.bmj.com/content/53/13/799**

References

American College of Obstetricians and Gynecologists (ACOG). (1985). *During pregnancy and the postnatal period*. Wolters Kluwer Health, Inc.

Anderson, J., Pudwell, J., McAuslan, C., Barr, L., Kehoe, J., & Davies, G. A. (2021). Acute fetal response to high-intensity interval training in the second and third trimesters of pregnancy. *Applied Physiology, Nutrition, and Metabolism, 46*(12), 1552–1558. https://doi.org/10.1139/apnm-2020-1086

Beetham, K., Giles, C., Noetel, M., Clifton, V., Jones, J., & Naughton, G. (2019). The effects of vigorous intensity exercise in the third trimester of pregnancy: A systematic review and meta-analysis. *BMC Pregnancy Childbirth, 19*(281), 1-. https://doi.org/10.1186/s12884-019-2441-1

Bø, K., Artal, R., Barakat, R., Brown, W., Davies, G. A. L., Dooley, M., Evenson, K. R., Haakstad, L. A. H., Henriksson-Larsen, K., Kayser, B., Kinnunen, T. I., Mottola, M. F., Nygaard, I., Poppel, M. V., Stuge, B., & Khan, K. M. (2016). Exercise and pregnancy in recreational and elite athletes: 2016 evidence summary from the IOC expert group meeting, Lausanne. Part 1—exercise in women planning pregnancy and those who are pregnant. *British Journal of Sports Medicine, 50*, 571–589. https://doi.org/10.1136/bjsports-2016-096218

Bø, K., Artal, R., Barakat, R., Brown, W., Davies, G. A. L., Dooley, M., Evenson, K. R., Haakstad, L. A. H., Kayser, B., Kinnunen, T. I., Larsén, K., Mottola, M. F., Nygaard, I., Poppel, M. V., Stuge, B., & Khan, K. M. (2017). Exercise and pregnancy in recreational and elite athletes: 2016/17 evidence summary from the IOC expert group meeting, Lausanne. Part 4— Recommendations for future research. *British Journal of Sports Medicine*, 1–3. https://doi.org/10.1136/bjsports-2017-098387

Bø, K., Artal, R., Barakat, R., Brown, W., Davies, G. A. L., Dooley, M., Evenson, K. R., Haakstad, L. A. H., Kayser, B., Kinnunen, T. I., Larsén, K., Mottola, M. F., Nygaard, I., Poppel, M. V., Stuge, B., & Khan, K. M. (2018). Exercise and pregnancy in recreational and elite athletes: 2016/2017 evidence summary from the IOC expert group meeting, Lausanne. Part 5. Recommendations for health professionals and active women. *British Journal of Sports Medicine, 52*, 1080–1085. https://doi.org/10.1136/bjsports-2018-099351

Bø, K., Artal, R., Barakat, R., Brown, W., Davies, G. A. L., Dooley, M., Evenson, K. R., Haakstad, L. A. H., Kayser, B., Kinnunen, T. I., Mottola, M. F., Nygaard, I., Poppel, M. V., Stuge, B., & Khan, K. M. (2017). Exercise and pregnancy in recreational and elite athletes: 2016/17 evidence summary from the IOC Expert Group Meeting, Lausanne. Part 3—exercise in the postpartum period. *British Journal of Sports Medicine, 51*, 1516–1525. https://doi.org/10.1136/bjsports-2017-097964

Bø, K., Artal, R., Barakat, R., Brown, W., Dooley, M., Evenson, K. R., Haakstad, L. A. H., Henriksson-Larsen, K., Kayser, B., Kinnunen, T. I., Mottola, M. F., Nygaard, I., Poppel, M. V., Stuge, B., & Davies, G. A. L. (2016). Exercise and pregnancy in recreational and elite athletes: 2016 evidence summary from the IOC expert group meeting, Lausanne. Part 2—the effect of exercise on the fetus, labour and birth. *British Journal of Sports Medicine, 50*, 1297–1305. https://doi.org/doi:10.1136/bjsports-2016-096810

Cai, C., & Davenport, M. H. (2022). Prenatal physical activity paradox: occupational versus leisure-time physical activity. *British Journal of Sports Medicine, 56*(7), 365–366. https://doi.org/10.1136/bjsports-2021-104945

Cai, C., Vandermeer, B., HKhurana, R., Nerenberg, K., Featherstone, R., Sebastianski, M., & Davenport, M. (2019). The impact of occupational shift work and working hours during pregnancy on health outcomes: A systematic review and meta-analysis. *American Journal of Obstetrics and Gynecology*. https://doi.org/10.1016/j.ajog.2019.06.051

Davenport, M., Ruchat, S., Poitras, V., Garcia, A., Gray, C., Barrowman, N., Skow, R., Meah, V., Riske, L., Sobierajski, F., James, M., Kathol, A., Nuspl, M., Marchand, A., Nagpal, T., Slater, L., Weeks, A., Adamo, K., Davies, G., Barakat, R., & Mottola, M. (2018). Prenatal exercise for the prevention of gestational diabetes mellitus and hypertensive disorders of pregnancy: A systematic review and meta-analysis. *British Journal of Sports Medicine, 52*, 1367–1375. https://doi.org/10.1136/bjsports-2018-099355

Davenport, M. H., & Hayman, M. (2022). Physical activity during pregnancy: Essential steps for maternal and fetal health. *Obstetric Medicine, 15*(3), 149–150. https://doi.org/10.1177/1753495X221122540

Davenport, M. H., Khurana, R., Thornton, J. S., & McHigh, T. L. F. (2023). 'It's going to affect our lives, our sport and our career': Time to raise the bar for pregnant and postpartum athletes. *British Journal of Sports Medicine, 57(14)*, 893–894. https://doi.org/10.1136/bjsports-2023-107256

Gould, S., Cawyer, C., Dell'Italia, L., Harper, L., McGwin, G., & Bamman, M. (2021). Resistance training does not decrease placental blood flow during Valsalva Maneuver: A novel use of 3D Doppler power flow ultrasonography. *Sports Health, 13*(5), 476–481. https://doi.org/10.1177/19417381211000717

Hayman, M., Davenport, R., Harris, R., Minahan, C., Burke, L., McGhee, D., Steele, J., & Lastelle, M. (2002). Are you an athlete who is currently pregnant fact sheet. Accessed via: https://www.ais.gov.au/__data/assets/pdf_file/0005/1085099/36945_Pregnancy-Fact-Sheet_D3.pdf

Hayman, M., Brown, W. J., Brinson, A., Budzynski-Seymour, E., Bruce, T., & Evenson, K. R. (2023). Public health guidelines for physical activity during pregnancy from around the world: A scoping review. *British Journal of Sports Medicine*, bjsports-2022-105777. https://doi.org/10.1136/bjsports-2022-105777

Kardel, K. R. (2005). Effects of intense training during and after pregnancy in top-level athletes. *Scandinavian Journal of Medicine & Science in Sports, 15*(2), 79–86. https://doi.org/10.1111/j.1600-0838.2004.00426.x

Kimber, M. L., Meyer, S., McHugh, T. L., Thornton, J., Khurana, R., Sivak, A., & Davenport, M. H. (2021). Health outcomes following pregnancy in elite athletes: A systematic review and meta-analysis. *Medicine & Science in Sports & Exercise*. https://doi.org/10.1249/MSS.0000000000002617

Meah, V. L., Strynadka, M. C., Steinback, C. D., & Davenport, M. H. (2021). Cardiac responses to prenatal resistance exercise with and without the Valsalva Maneuver. *Medicine & Science in Sports & Exercise, 53*(6), 1260–1269. https://doi.org/10.1249/mss.0000000000002577

Mottola, M., Davenport, M., Ruchat, S., Davies, G., Poitras, V., Gray, C., Garcia, A., Barrowman, N., Adamo, K., Duggan, M., Barakat, R., Chilibeck, P., Fleming, K., Forte, M., Korolnek, J., Nagpal, T., Slater, L., Stirling, D., & Zehr, L. (2019). 2019 Canadian guideline for physical activity throughout pregnancy. *British Journal of Sports Medicine, 52*(21), 1339–1346. https://doi.org/10.1136/bjsports-2018-100056

Mujika, I., & Padilla, S. (2000). Detraining: Loss of training-induced physiological and performance adaptations. Part II. *Sports Medicine, 30*(3), 145–154. https://doi.org/10.2165/00007256-200030030-00001

Mujika, I., & Padilla, S. (2001). Muscular characteristics of detraining in humans. *Medicine and Science in Sports and Exercise, 33*(8), 1297–1303.

Nagpal, T. S., Everest, C., Goudreau, A. D., Manicks, M., & Adamo, K. B. (2021). To HIIT or not to HIIT? The question pregnant women may be searching for online: A descriptive observational study. *Perspectives in Public Health*, 1757913920985898–1757913920985898. https://doi.org/10.1177/1757913920985898

Ong, M. J., Wallman, K. E., Fournier, P. A., Newnham, J. P., & Guelfi, K. J. (2016). Enhancing energy expenditure and enjoyment of exercise during pregnancy through the addition of brief higher intensity intervals to traditional continuous moderate intensity cycling. *BMC Pregnancy and Childbirth*, *16*(1), 161. https://doi.org/10.1186/s12884-016-0947-3

Prevett, C., Kimber, M., Forner, L., deVivo, M., & Davenport, M. (2023). Impact of heavy resistance training on pregnancy and postpartum health outcomes. *International Urogynecology Journal*, *34*, 405–411. https://doi.org/10.1007/s00192-022-05393-1

Salvesen, K. Å., Hem, E., & Sundgot-Borgen, J. (2012). Fetal wellbeing may be compromised during strenuous exercise among pregnant elite athletes. *British Journal of Sports Medicine*, *46*(4), 279–283. https://doi.org/10.1136/bjsm.2010.080259

Szymanski, L., & Satin, A. (2012). Strenuous exercise during pregnancy: Is there a limit? *American Journal of Obstetrics and Gynecology*, *207*, 179. https://doi.org/10.1016/j.ajog.2012.07.021

Tighe, B. J., Williams, S. L., Porter, C., & Hayman, M. (2023). Barriers and enablers influencing female athlete return-to-sport postpartum: A scoping review. *British Journal of Sports Medicine*. https://doi.org/10.1136/bjsports-2023-107189

Waters, T. R., MacDonald, L. A., Hudock, S. D., & Goddard, D. E. (2014). Provisional recommended weight limits for manual lifting during pregnancy. *Human Factors*, *56*(1), 203–214. https://doi.org/10.1177/0018720813502223

Wowdzia, J. B., Hazell, T. J., Berg, E. R. V., Labrecque, L., Brassard, P., & Davenport, M. H. (2023). Maternal and fetal cardiovascular responses to acute high-intensity interval and moderate-intensity continuous training exercise during pregnancy: A randomized crossover trial. *Sports Medicine*, *53*(9), 1819–1833. https://doi.org/10.1007/s40279-023-01858-5

Wowdzia, J. B., Hazell, T. J., & Davenport, M. H. (2022). Glycemic response to acute high-intensity interval versus moderate-intensity continuous exercise during pregnancy. *Physiological Reports*, *10*(18), e15454. https://doi.org/10.14814/phy2.15454

Wowdzia, J. B., McHugh, T. L., Thornton, J., Sivak, A., Mottola, M. F., & Davenport, M. H. (2021). Elite athletes and pregnancy outcomes: A systematic review and meta-analysis. *Medicine & Science in Sports & Exercise*, *53*(3), 534–542. https://doi.org/10.1249/mss.0000000000002510

5 'All Feedback Is Beneficial':

A Deconstruction of Feedback

Ross Corbett, Mark Partington, Lisa Ryan and Ed Cope

Introduction

This chapter focusses on the coach behaviour of feedback which is a popular coaching intervention implemented in some form by coaches in all sports and domains. According to Butler and Winne (1995), 'feedback is information with which a learner can confirm, add to, overwrite, tune, or restructure information in memory'. However, not all feedback in a sports setting is equal and is provided in many ways (Williams & Hodges, 2005). One is through intrinsic feedback, where learners use their senses and evaluate their own performances (Williams & Hodges, 2005). Another is through augmented feedback, where external sources (e.g. a coach) provide information about performance (Anderson, Rymal, & Ste-Marie, 2014). While augmented feedback has been researched in a variety of different modes including verbal, visual, auditory, haptic and multimodal (Sigrist et al., 2013; Frikha et al., 2019), practically, augmented verbal feedback (AVF) is the most readily available mode of feedback in sporting environments. For this reason, AVF is the focus of this chapter. The purposes of this chapter are to (1) highlight the myth regarding feedback, (2) review the literature on feedback, (3) evaluate why feedback is delivered in certain ways and then finally (4) offer some thoughts and recommendations on feedback.

The proposed myth and review of the feedback literature

The overarching myth for this chapter is that all feedback is beneficial and improves learning and performance when given in any format. Later in this chapter, we discuss this myth in relation to what, when, to whom and how much AVF practitioners provide. This myth has been constructed from reading the literature and research undertaken in sports coaching environments, while also encountering this myth when working in the sport industry. As authors, we suggest that more consideration on the type of feedback that is provided and the influences that impact implementation is needed. By highlighting this myth, we hope to help practitioners to consider the different types of feedback that exist. Also, by suggesting some of the influences that impact implementation, readers will then be able to resonate with how they provide feedback in a sporting context to best support their own athletes.

The effectiveness of feedback has been mostly understood from either its impact on motor learning or a broader pedagogical strategy that supports learning (Petancevski et al., 2022; Wisniewski, Zierer & Hattie, 2020). Research has highlighted the position of the coach as a key provider of feedback to athletes (Markland & Martinek, 1988; Ford et al., 2010; Millar, Oldham & Donovan, 2011). Coaches have highlighted their perceived importance of AVF (Raya Castellano et al., 2020) and suggested they see feedback as a tool to improve performance, build athlete confidence, help athletes to monitor progress and as a tool to improve their own performance (Mason, Farrow & Hattie, 2020a). AVF has consistently been shown to have positive effects on the performance and learning of gross motor and sport-specific skills (Wulf, 2013; Ericsson, 2020; Petancevski et al., 2022). This is due to the ability of feedback to speed up the learning process so that a higher skill level is achieved sooner (Wulf, 2013).

Meta-analyses from education environments have highlighted how effective AVF focussed on providing reinforcement, high levels of information and detail on what is deemed to be correct rather than incorrect performance (Hattie & Timperley, 2007; Wisniewski, Zierer & Hattie, 2020). AVF has been observed to be beneficial to learning and performance in skill acquisition when promoting an external focus of attention (Halperin et al., 2016a), is autonomy-supportive (Hooyman, Wulf, & Lewthwaite, 2014) and is based on positive performance (Wulf & Lewthwaite, 2016). However, not all feedback is beneficial for learning (Petancevski et al., 2022). From an educational standpoint, meta-analyses (Hattie & Timperley, 2007; Wisniewski, Zierer & Hattie, 2020) have highlighted how feedback linked to punishment, reward and/or praise had minimal, if any, effect on learning. AVF has been shown to hinder learning in skill acquisition when the learner develops a dependency on the feedback provided and when feedback is provided too frequently (Magill, 1994). Feedback can also hinder performance when it promotes an internal focus of attention (Halperin et al., 2016a), is controlling in nature (Hooyman, Wulf, & Lewthwaite, 2014) and is based on negative performance, in turn affecting the performer's motivational state, perceptions of competence and self-efficacy (Wulf & Lewthwaite, 2016).

Types of feedback

When discussing how feedback is provided in sports performance, we can take several different approaches. For the purpose of this chapter, we will discuss the use of feedback through the framework of what (types of feedback are/can be used), when (in relation to timing relative to performance), who (the feedback is given to) and how much (feedback is given acutely or chronically). We do this with the aim of dispelling the myth that all feedback is beneficial and one size fits all when using feedback to improve learning and performance. If people understand the different ways in which feedback can be provided, hopefully it will support them in making more evidence-informed choices when supporting their athletes.

What? The potential myth: All types of feedback are beneficial

Information

When observing the type of information given from feedback, we can view this as either knowledge of results (KR) or knowledge of performance (KP) (Petancevski et al., 2022). KR can be described as the information-related outcome of an action (e.g. whether a penalty kick has been scored or not), whereas KP is related to specific movement characteristics (e.g. the follow-through of the kicking leg on the penalty kick) (Kernodle & Carlton, 1992; Williams & Hodges, 2005). While in some circumstances KR may be beneficial to learning and performance (see Andersen et al., 2019), research at present suggests that KP may be of greater benefit due to the added level of information garnered from such feedback (Wisniewski et al., 2020). When giving KP feedback, this can then also be distinguished as either descriptive (e.g. you had excellent range on your follow-through on that kick) or prescriptive (e.g. you need to follow-through further on your kick next time) in nature (Mason, Farrow & Hattie, 2020b). Research from nonlinear pedagogies suggests that feedback should function as facilitative rather than being overly prescriptive in nature (Chow et al., 2016), creating opportunities for performers to process previous actions which guide solutions to improve further performance (Otte et al., 2020). It may be suggested therefore that descriptive KP feedback may be most optimal to facilitate learning as it allows for an element of decision-making and autonomy from the performer. This emphasizes the shared responsibility between coach and performer in processing feedback, which can be a common oversight in our discussion regarding feedback.

Autonomy

We can also view the information we give athletes through the level of autonomy the athlete has in utilizing the feedback. For example, was the feedback autonomy-supportive, neutral or controlling (Halperin et al., 2016b)? Autonomy-supportive feedback allows the athlete to think as their own individual performer, while controlling feedback forces the athlete to think, feel or act in a certain way prescribed by the coach (Carpentier & Mageau, 2013). Autonomy-supportive feedback is empathetic and can include providing choices of potential solutions, providing a rationale, asking for an opinion, acknowledging feelings or making a suggestion (Mouratidis, Lens, & Vansteenkiste, 2010). In many instances, the autonomy-supportive feedback can be evident in the use of questions (e.g. what do you think will allow that pass to reach the winger quicker?), while controlling feedback simply gives the coach's opinion on what the athlete should do to improve performance in the next attempt (e.g. your foot needs to come through the ball more on the pass). Halperin et al. (2016b) and Mason, Farrow and Hattie (2020b) describe some common instances of autonomy-supportive, neutral and controlling AVF observed in boxing and Australian Football League (AFL), respectively.

Autonomy-supportive AVF has been seen to enhance learning and performance when compared with controlling feedback (Teixeira et al., 2012). Similarly, Hooyman, Wulf and Lewthwaite (2014) found autonomy-supportive language during a cricket bowling task led to superior performance improvements when compared to controlling feedback. Autonomy-supportive language also resulted in perceptions of greater choice and higher self-efficacy among undergraduate student athletes. Mason, Farrow and Hattie (2020b) observed that controlling AVF was used significantly more during losing quarters AFL competition, while Halperin et al. (2016b) found boxing coaches used controlling AVF 10% more often in losing rather than winning bouts.

Valence

The valence attached to feedback messages is another important consideration in how we use feedback to impact sporting performance. We can view the valence of any feedback message as positive, negative or neutral (Halperin et al., 2016b). Valence has an influence on individual's expectancies (Stoate, Wulf & Lewthwaite, 2012), which are an important factor in performance environments. Positive AVF enhances athletes' performance expectancies and prepares the performer for successful movement (Stoate, Wulf & Lewthwaite, 2012; Wulf & Lewthwaite, 2016).

Research suggests that learning is facilitated if feedback is provided after good rather than poor trials (Chiviacowsky & Wulf, 2007), with AVF emphasizing successful rather than unsuccessful performances enhancing motor learning. During boxing competition, Halperin et al. (2016b) observed coaches to provide more positive (36% vs. 18%) feedback in winning rather than losing bouts. Mason, Farrow and Hattie (2020b) observed similar results during AFL competition with significantly more positive (17.66% vs 7.86%) feedback provided during winning rather than losing quarters. While positive feedback has a superior impact on learning and performance, an important differentiation exists in terms of the level of information associated with a positive feedback message. Praise alone has been shown to have minimal if any impact on learning and performance (Hattie & Timperley, 2007; Wisniewski, Zierer & Hattie, 2020), therefore it is important to recognize that it is the level of information attached to a positive feedback message which appears to impact performance.

Level (Hattie and Timperley Model)

Another important consideration in the use of AVF is the level at which feedback is provided. This was first discussed by Hattie and Timperley (2007), who claimed that there are four major levels and that the level at which feedback is directed influences its effectiveness. The four levels include self, task, process and self-regulation. This model has been discussed primarily in education settings, with the notable exception of Mason, Farrow and Hattie (2020b). While there are of course areas of overlap with information and autonomy as already discussed, there are some important elements we can take from this model. Carrying on our examples related to a kick/pass, we will discuss this continuum with this skill in mind. AVF at the self-level includes personal statements about the learner (Mason, Farrow & Hattie, 2020b) (e.g. well done, John). AVF targeted at the task level refers to how well tasks are understood or performed referring to any action and whether the action is performed correctly or incorrectly (e.g. good pass there, John). AVF at the process level involves the main processes needed to perform a task and aids the athletes' understanding of what is necessary to perform the task well (e.g. good speed on the pass, John). The final level, self-regulation, encourages self-monitoring, directin, and regulating actions, supporting confidence to engage further on a task (e.g. how can we make that pass more damaging to our attack, John?), quite similarly to autonomy-supportive AVF.

It is argued that looking at AVF across these levels helps to elucidate the function of the feedback provided during performance and whether the feedback we use helps the athlete to self-regulate and correct future performances (Mason, Farrow & Hattie, 2020b). This chapter observed slight increases in higher-level feedback (process and self-regulation) during winning quarters. It is argued that feedback at the self and task levels is too often unrelated to performance to provide information that can guide improvements in future performance (see Hattie & Timperley, 2007).

Attentional focus

How feedback directs an athlete's attentional focus has been shown to play an important role in the learning and performance of sport skills (Wulf, 2013). Feedback related to attentional focus can promote an internal, neutral or external focus (Halperin et al., 2016b). External focus of attention refers to instructing an individual to focus on the effects of the movement in relation to the environment (e.g. let's get speed on the pass, to her feet). In contrast, internal focus of attention refers to instructing an individual to focus on a specific body part or muscle group during a movement (e.g. make sure your foot comes through the ball).

Research indicates that sporting performance is enhanced via the use of feedback that promotes an external as opposed to an internal focus of attention (Wulf, 2013). For example, jumping (Wu, Porter, & Brown, 2012), agility (Porter et al., 2010), punching (Halperin et al., 2016a) and golf putting (Wulf, Lauterbach & Toole, 1999) performances have all been shown to be enhanced by feedback promoting an external focus of attention.

When? The potential myth: Feedback should be provided at all times

The timing of when AVF is given is also an important consideration, which has been acknowledged by team sport coaches (Mason, Farrow & Hattie, 2020a). Timing can be considered in different ways, which of course depends on the sporting context (e.g. during a live football game or during golf putting practice). Commonly, research has looked at a dichotomy between concurrent (during the performance of a task, which could represent during a set of four putts in golf or during a live football game) and post/terminal (information provided after a performance attempt which could represent at full time or half time of a football game or after a set of four putts in golf). Partridge and Franks (1996) also looked at a 'stopped' categorization (e.g. a brief message of AVF when a coach has stopped a group activity or stopped an individual participating in the activity). Depending on the sporting context, post/terminal feedback can also come immediately post activity or delayed (e.g. at the following training session) (Andersen et al., 2019).

It must be acknowledged that knowledge of the effects of timing of AVF on learning or performance in sporting contexts is quite minimal (Petancevski et al., 2022). While Salmoni, Schmidt and Walter (1984) suggested that providing concurrent feedback can be detrimental to performance due to a dependency on the feedback that can be developed, Wulf and Shea (2002) have shown this may not be applicable to more complex tasks. Regarding post/terminal AVF, it is suggested that delaying feedback provision allows for memory consolidation and the development of error detection and correction abilities (Magill & Anderson, 2017). In sporting contexts, we must acknowledge that it is also unknown whether AVF should be provided immediately or delayed (Petancevski et al., 2022).

Who? The potential myth: Feedback should always be provided to individuals

To whom feedback is directed may also be an important consideration when providing AVF to athletes. While research on the impact of AVF on learning or performance has been conducted via providing AVF to individuals, we know that, particularly in team sports, AVF is commonly provided to a full team or to a group of athletes from within a team (Raya Castellano et al., 2020). This lack of research as to the variety in the recipient of AVF appears to be a distinct oversight. For example, Mason, Farrow and Hattie (2020b) observed 30% of in-game feedback to be directed at groups and 70% to individuals.

While research comparing the effectiveness of AVF to groups vs. individuals is unknown, in terms of an individual's learning or performance improvement, it is fair to suggest that individual AVF may be of value. This is due to the importance of high information detail in the learning and performance process, as already discussed. It is also important to consider the impact the feedback to one individual may have on other individuals within earshot, or the group if delivered in a group setting. For example, if I play as a defender and I hear another defender receive positive feedback on the speed of their pass to a teammate, it may stand to reason that I also take that feedback on board and try to use this information in future performances. On the other hand, AVF to groups may be of particular importance when aiming to improve team/group performance due to the ability of this AVF to stimulate dialogue within the group and develop solutions to improve the performance of the group (Mason, Farrow & Hattie, 2020a). Research has identified the importance of dialogic feedback to engage learners (Mortimer & Scott, 2003; Cope et al., 2016) and develop a reflective attitude by listening to their ideas (Oslin & Mitchell, 2006). Wright and Forrest (2007) suggest that learners' ability to articulate components of their performance demonstrates their ability to successfully play their sport.

How Much? The potential myth: Frequency of feedback should always be low, to not overload the learner

Coaches often highlight the 'struggle to find the right balance between providing enough feedback to ensure the most salient points were covered, but also keeping feedback quantity within a range that was manageable for athletes to use' (Mason, Farrow & Hattie, 2020a). This struggle highlights the importance of the recipient as well as the provider, something which can be commonly overlooked. Mason et al. (2020c) observed AFL athletes' retention of AVF messages from individual review meetings one week later. This study found that coaches averaged 30 AVF messages per meeting of which players recalled 50% of summarized feedback messages, but just 6% of all feedback a week later. This study also highlighted that longer video feedback meetings led to lower athlete recall. Tribolet et al. (2021) found that the relationship between the number of feedback interventions and average feedback duration was dependent on the previous match result in an AFL context. Lower feedback intervention frequencies after a loss were associated with lower feedback durations, while higher feedback intervention frequencies after a win were associated with greater feedback duration (Tribolet et al., 2021).

It is accepted that providing AVF too frequently, particularly concurrently, can generate a dependency, which can be detrimental to performance when learners are required to perform the skill without feedback (Salmoni, Schmidt & Walter, 1984). Research has shown that providing AVF less frequently and spaced out across practice can have a positive effect on performance retention (Andersen et al., 2019). While providing detail on the desirable frequency and amount of AVF to provide to athletes is not possible based on current literature, some guidelines may be possible. When providing AVF to individuals, where task complexity is high and learner skill is low, a higher feedback frequency may be recommended, with the opposite for simpler tasks and skilled learners (Guadagnoli & Lee, 2004).

Influences on the implementation of feedback

One of the influences on the implementation of feedback in sport performance settings is the social impact. Sports performance practitioners are immersed in the culture and traditions of the organization they are working in and have been shown to reproduce practice and behaviours (Partington & Cushion, 2013). One of the reasons for a 'one size fits all' approach to the implementation of feedback could be due to this reproduction of 'what has always been done'. This means that instead of the feedback being evidence-informed and based on the individual who is to receive it, it is based on feedback that has been seen and heard before. The problem with the reproduction of feedback is that it does not always align to the specific situation in which it is needed.

A practitioner in a sport performance setting is not simply an isolated cognitive being, but instead a socially embedded individual within that context (e.g. Cushion & Jones, 2014; Jones & Ronglan, 2018. Indeed, Cushion et al.'s (2006) critical review of the coaching process highlighted that practice is firmly embedded within specific social and cultural sporting contexts. The specific context, then, where an individual (e.g. a coach) is providing feedback will ultimately shape how, when and what is delivered. Collectively the growing body of sociological research in sport argues that coaching methods, including feedback, need to change and adapt to the situations that occur because of the social context. The impact of the sporting setting on the type of feedback therefore needs to be appreciated and considered. The downplaying or lack of consideration of the culture, tradition and historical influence of the context on the implementation of feedback is problematic. The social impact needs to be considered when thinking about the type of feedback to be used as well as focus on who the specific athlete is and the specific situation that is being evaluated.

Another issue to consider, on what could influence a practitioner's implementation of feedback, is the possible gap between the articulation of an approach and continuing to do it in a traditional way due to a lack of understanding (e.g. Grecic & Collins, 2013; Christian et al., 2017). This was apparent in Partington and Cushion (2013) and Stodter and Cushion (2014) studies where the authors used systematic observation to identify what coaches did in practice, including the types of feedback and interviews to understand why. Both studies identified a gap between the articulated reason for feedback and actual implementation. Therefore, coaches have been identified as having poor self-awareness of the feedback they provide to athletes (Partington & Cushion, 2013). Clearly, practitioners need self-awareness of the feedback they are providing and clarity on what informs and guides their knowledge and understanding to provide the optimal sporting setting for their athletes.

The coach learning literature consistently and repeatedly demonstrates that coaches' main source for developing knowledge is experience (Nelson & Cushion, 2006; Cushion et al., 2010). Nelson and Cushion (2006) reviewed the literature exploring how sports coaches acquire the knowledge that underpins their professional practice. Coaches' learning experiences range from being involved as a participant in a coaching session to actual coaching. The knowledge and understanding gained in these types of informal settings have been conceptualized as coaches' 'practice theories' (Cassidy, 2010); that is, experience and a body of informal knowledge and developed assumptions about coaching where often these assumptions are viewed as taken-for granted or normal (Cassidy, 2010; Lyle & Cushion, 2017). This means that practice is uncritically reproduced (Cushion & Jones, 2014; Townsend, Smith & Cushion, 2015) and the unconscious nature of practice reproduction is influenced by socio-political issues (Light & Evans, 2013; Cushion & Jones, 2014; Hassanin & Light, 2014; Hassanin, Light & MacFarlane, 2018). Some examples of the influence of social structure on practice include the status of ex-professionals in coaching practice (Cushion & Jones, 2014), the underlying culture on a coach education course (Townsend & Cushion, 2015) and the powerful influence of the traditional culture of club rugby shaped by the resilient amateur ideal in New Zealand (Hassanin, Light & MacFarlane, 2018). A more realistic position is to conceptualize individual coaches as agents-in-relation, meaning that 'actors who operate within networks of interdependence and who embody differential distributions of power and authority' (Jones & Ronglan, 2017).

Feedback: Moving forward

Coaches spend much of their time planning practice design, while of course this is a vitally important part of the coaching process. We propose that planning the use of AVF may also be a key consideration. For instance, if we plan a certain activity to work on a tactical issue in our game, can we also consider the types of AVF we think will be important to our coaching of that activity? The coach may plan to feed back to or engage in dialogue with certain individuals, after a certain number of attempts and in a controlling or autonomy-supportive manner. There may be individuals with whom the coach plans to reinforce positive behaviours from a previous practice, while for others the coach may want to plan their language to be quite autonomy-supportive to encourage the self-regulation capacity of the athlete. This planning process may also aid coaches in understanding how they use feedback, something that research suggests coaches find difficult (Partington & Cushion, 2013). This enhanced level of understanding may, in turn, help practitioners working in sport to develop a rationale for their usage of feedback and the feedback types they use. This ability to rationalize behaviour is also an element of the coaching process which coaches appear to find difficult (Partington & Cushion, 2012).

In some cases, feedback can be viewed as an endpoint in the delivery of information. The authors encourage practitioners to consider what can follow on from well-used feedback. Feedback can be a vital starting point for dialogue between practitioner and athlete. This dialogue can be an important step in promoting reflection on the athlete's part (Mouratidis, Lens, & Vansteenkiste, 2010; Cope et al., 2016). This process can be vital in developing problem-solving athletes who have a deeper understanding of the skills and tactics needed to excel in their sport (Otte et al., 2020). It can be important to allow time for this reflection, but also to follow up with the performer to check for understanding and learning the athlete's needs and wants (O Connor et al., 2022).

It is vital that practitioners place consideration on the receiver of feedback. Just as a coach's biography affects how they learn (Stodter & Cushion, 2017), an athlete's biography and previous experiences (e.g. family and previous coaches) may affect how they learn and wish to receive feedback. Coaches interviewed as part of Mason et al. (2020a) research cited the need to differentiate feedback for players, which involved tailoring the amount or the valence of the feedback used. More experienced or highly skilled athletes may also not need as high a frequency of feedback as more novice athletes (Guadagnoli & Lee, 2004).

Practitioners providing feedback need to develop awareness of the characteristics and qualities of feedback in relation to the context, individual's needs and the specific situation. This knowledge and understanding could help those providing feedback to counter the effects of the social, including the organization's tradition and culture, and the person's past experiences to then make more informed decisions before implementation. An opportunity for people to develop an evidence-informed understanding of feedback and the influence of social factors can better support the development and performance of their athletes (Partington & Walton, 2020).

As well as acquiring knowledge, practitioners need to be educated about the possible influences of culture and tradition, but this is not currently provided in coach education courses (Stodter & Cushion, 2014; Cushion & Partington, 2016). Ideally, providing practitioners with the understanding of the possible impact of culture and tradition early in their education could make them more aware of the possible influences when entering a sporting organization. Knowledge and understanding can then support reflections, leading to awareness, and provide a degree of freedom so those providing feedback can make a more informed decision about the implementation. Sport education (e.g. coaching courses) should encourage quality feedback, which is more about the process, athlete and environment than just providing simple step-by-step guides (Denison et al., 2015).

Recommendations for feedback

1) Plan feedback processes or types you wish to use during upcoming coaching.
2) Take time to understand and rationalize (to yourself or to other practitioners) why you think these processes or feedback types are important in your coaching.
3) Don't see the use of feedback as an end point.
   a) Well-used feedback should prompt reflection from the performer that the practitioner may want to check in on later.
   b) Use feedback to encourage dialogue between the coach and the performer. Allow time for this dialogue as part of the process.
4) Consider the person receiving the feedback; is the feedback provided encourages understanding, autonomy, confidence and self-efficacy?
5) Think about how the sporting environment where you are using feedback could or is impacting your implementation. Make sure the feedback you are providing is most beneficial to the learner receiving it and the specific situation being carried out.

References

Anderson, D. I., Magill, R. A., Mayo, A. M., & Steel, K. A. (2019). Enhancing motor skill acquisition with augmented feedback. In *Skill acquisition in sport: Research, theory and practice* (3rd ed.). New York, NY: Routledge.

Anderson, D. I., Rymal, A. M., & Ste-Marie, D. M. (2014). Modeling and feedback. In Athanasios, P. & Dieter, H. (Eds.), *The Routledge handbook of sport and exercise psychology* (pp. 272–288). New York, NY: Routledge.

Butler, D. L., & Winne, P. H. (1995). Feedback and self-regulated learning: A theoretical synthesis. *Review of Educational Research*, *65*(3), 245–281.

Carpentier, J., & Mageau, G. A. (2013). When change-oriented feedback enhances motivation, well-being and performance: A look at autonomy-supportive feedback in sport. *Psychology of Sport and Exercise*, *14*(3), 423–435.

Cassidy, T. (2010). Understanding athlete learning and coaching practice: Utilising 'practice theories' and 'theories of practice'. In John, L. and Chris C. *Sports coaching: Professionalisation and practice* (pp. 177–192).

Chiviacowsky, S., & Wulf, G. (2007). Feedback after good trials enhances learning. *Research Quarterly for Exercise and Sport*, *78*(2), 40–47.

Chow, J. I., Davids, K., Button, C., & Renshaw, I. (2016). *Nonlinear pedagogy in skill acquisition: An introduction*. New York, NY: Routledge.

Christian, E., Berry, M., & Kearney, P. (2017). The identity, epistemology and developmental experiences of high-level adventure sports coaches. *Journal of Adventure Education and Outdoor Learning*, *17*(4), 353–366.

Cope, E., Partington, M., Cushion, C. J., & Harvey, S. (2016). An investigation of professional top-level youth football coaches' questioning practice. *Qualitative Research in Sport, Exercise and Health*, *8*(4), 380–393.

Cushion, C. J., & Jones, R. L. (2014). A Bourdieusian analysis of cultural reproduction: Socialisation and the 'hidden curriculum' in professional football. *Sport, Education and Society*, *19*(3), 276–298.

Cushion, C., & Partington, M. (2016). A critical analysis of the conceptualisation of 'coaching philosophy'. *Sport, Education and Society*, *21*(6), 851–867.

Cushion, C. J., Armour, K. M., & Jones, R. L. (2006). Locating the coaching process in practice: Models 'for' and 'of' coaching. *Physical Education and Sport Pedagogy*, *11*(1), 83–99.

Cushion, C., Nelson, L., Armour, K., John Lyle, Jones, R., Sandford, S., & O'Callaghan, C. (2010). "*Coach learning and development: A review of literature* (pp. 166–180)." Sports Coach UK.

Denison, J., Pringle, R., Cassidy, T., & Hessian, P. (2015). Informing coaches' practices: Toward an application of Foucault's ethics. *International Sport Coaching Journal*, *2*(1), 72–76.

Ericsson, K. A. (2020). Towards a science of the acquisition of expert performance in sports: Clarifying the differences between deliberate practice and other types of practice. *Journal of Sports Sciences*, *38*(2), 159–176.

Ford, P. R., Yates, I., & Williams, A. M. (2010). An analysis of practice activities and instructional behaviours used by youth soccer coaches during practice: Exploring the link between science and application. *Journal of Sports Sciences*, *28*(5), 483–495.

Frikha, M., Chaari, N., Elghoul, Y., Mohamed-Ali, H. H., & Zinkovsky, A. V. (2019). Effects of combined versus singular verbal or haptic feedback on acquisition, retention, difficulty, and competence perceptions in motor learning. *Perceptual and Motor Skills*, *126*(4), 713–732.

Grecic, D., & Collins, D. (2013). The epistemological chain: Practical applications in sports. *Quest*, *65*(2), 151–168.

Guadagnoli, M. A., & Lee, T. D. (2004). Challenge point: A framework for conceptualizing the effects of various practice conditions in motor learning. *Journal of Motor Behavior*, *36*(2), 212–224.

Halperin, I., Chapman, D. W., Martin, D. T., & Abbiss, C. (2016a). The effects of attentional focus instructions on punching velocity and impact forces among trained combat athletes. *Journal of Sports Sciences*, *35*(5), 500–507.

Halperin, I., Chapman, D. W., Martin, D. T., Abbiss, C., & Wulf, G. (2016b). Coaching cues in amateur boxing: An analysis of ringside feedback provided between rounds of competition. *Psychology of Sport and Exercise, 25*, 44–50.

Hassanin, R., & Light, R. (2014). The influence of cultural context on rugby coaches' beliefs about coaching. *Sports Coaching Review, 3*(2), 132–144.

Hassanin, R., Light, R. L., & MacFarlane, A. (2018). Developing 'good buggers': Global implications of the influence of culture on New Zealand club rugby coaches' beliefs and practice. *Sport in Society, 21*(8), 1223–1235.

Hattie, J., & Timperley, H. (2007). The power of feedback. *Review of Educational Research, 77*(1), 81–112.

Hooyman, A., Wulf, G., & Lewthwaite, R. (2014). Impacts of autonomy-supportive versus controlling instructional language on motor learning. *Human Movement Science, 36*, 190–198.

Jones, R. L., & Ronglan, L. T. (2018). What do coaches orchestrate? Unravelling the 'quiddity' of practice. *Sport, Education and Society, 23*(9), 905–915.

Kernodle, M. W., & Carlton, L. G. (1992). Information feedback and the learning of multiple-degree-of-freedom activities. *Journal of Motor Behavior, 24*(2), 187–195.

Light, R. L., & Evans, J. R. (2013). Dispositions of elite-level Australian rugby coaches towards game sense: Characteristics of their coaching habitus. *Sport, Education and Society, 18*(3), 407–423.

Lyle, J., & Cushion, C. J. (2017). *Sport coaching concepts: A framework for coaches' practice*. London: Routledge.

Magill, R. A. (1994). The influence of augmented feedback on skill learning depends on characteristics of the skill and the learner. *Quest, 46*(3), 314–327.

Magill, R. A., & Anderson, D. (2017). *Motor learning and control: Concepts and applications* (11th ed.). Berkshire: McGraw-Hill Education.

Markland, R., & Martinek, T. J. (1988). Descriptive analysis of coach augmented feedback given to high school varsity female volleyball players. *Journal of Teaching in Physical Education, 7*(4), 289–301.

Mason, R. J., Farrow, D., & Hattie, J. A. (2020a). Sports coaches' knowledge and beliefs about the provision, reception, and evaluation of verbal feedback. *Frontiers in Psychology, 11*, 552–571.

Mason, R. J., Farrow, D., & Hattie, J. A. C. (2020b). An analysis of in-game feedback provided by coaches in an Australian Football League competition. *Physical Education and Sport Pedagogy, 25*(5), 464–477.

Mason, R. J., Farrow, D., & Hattie, J. A. C. (2020c). An exploratory investigation into the reception of verbal and video feedback provided to players in an Australian Football League club. *International Journal of Sports Science & Coaching, 16*(1), 181–191.

Millar, S.-K., Oldham, A. R., & Donovan, M. (2011). Coaches' self-awareness of timing, nature and intent of verbal instructions to athletes. *International Journal of Sports Science & Coaching, 6*(4), 503–513.

Mortimer, E., & Scott, P. (2003). *Meaning making in secondary science classrooms*. Berkshire: McGraw-Hill Education.

Mouratidis, A., Lens, W., & Vansteenkiste, M. (2010). How you provide corrective feedback makes a difference: The motivating role of communicating in an autonomy-supporting way. *Journal of Sport and Exercise Psychology, 32*(5), 619–637.

Nelson, L. J., Cushion, C. J., & Potrac, P. (2006). Formal, nonformal and informal coach learning: A holistic conceptualisation. *International Journal of Sports Science & Coaching, 1*(3), 247–259.

O'Connor, D., Larkin, P., Robertson, S., & Goodyear, P. (2022). The art of the question: The structure of questions posed by youth soccer coaches during training. *Physical Education and Sport Pedagogy*, *27*(3), 304–319.

Oslin, J., & Mitchell, S. (2006). Game-centred approaches to teaching physical education. In D. Kirk, D. Macdonald & M. O'Sullivan (Eds.), *Handbook of physical education*. London: Sage.

Otte, F. W., Davids, K., Millar, S. K., & Klatt, S. (2020). When and how to provide feedback and instructions to athletes? How sport psychology and pedagogy insights can improve coaching interventions to enhance self-regulation in training. *Frontiers in Psychology*, *11*, 1444.

Partington, M., & Cushion, C. (2013). An investigation of the practice activities and coaching behaviors of professional top-level youth soccer coaches. *Scandinavian Journal of Medicine and Science in Sports*, *23*(3), 374–382.

Partington, M., & Cushion, C. J. (2012). Performance during performance: Using Goffman to understand the behaviours of elite youth football coaches during games. *Sports Coaching Review*, *1*(2), 93–105.

Partington, M., & Walton, J. (2020). A guide to analysing coaching behaviours. In Ed Cope & Mark Partington (Eds.), *Sports coaching: A theoretical and practical guide* (pp. 18–29).

Partridge, D., & Franks, I. M. (1996). Analyzing and modifying coaching behaviors by means of computer aided observation. *Physical Educator*, *53*(1), 8.

Petancevski, E. L., Inns, J., Fransen, J., & Impellizzeri, F. M. (2022). The effect of augmented feedback on the performance and learning of gross motor and sport-specific skills: A systematic review. *Psychology of Sport and Exercise*, *63*, 102277.

Porter, J. M., Nolan, R. P., Ostrowski, E. J., & Wulf, G. (2010). Directing attention externally enhances agility performance: A qualitative and quantitative analysis of the efficacy of using verbal instructions to focus attention. *Frontiers in Psychology*, *1*, 216.

Raya-Castellano, P. E., Reeves, M. J., Littlewood, M., & McRobert, A. P. (2020). An exploratory investigation of junior-elite football coaches´ behaviours during video-based feedback sessions. *International Journal of Performance Analysis in Sport*, *20*(4), 729–746.

Salmoni, A. W., Schmidt, R. A., & Walter, C. B. (1984). Knowledge of results and motor learning: A review and 791 critical reappraisals. *Psychological Bulletin*, *95*(3), 355–386.

Sigrist, R., Rauter, G., Riener, R., & Wolf, P. (2013). Augmented visual, auditory, haptic, and multimodal feedback in motor learning: A review. *Psychonomic Bulletin & Review*, *20*(1), 21–53.

Stoate, I., Wulf, G., & Lewthwaite, R. (2012). Enhanced expectancies improve movement efficiency in runners. *Journal of Sports Sciences*, *30*(8), 815–823.

Stodter, A., & Cushion, C. J. (2014). Coaches' learning and education: A case study of cultures in conflict. *Sports Coaching Review*, *3*(1), 63–79.

Stodter, A., & Cushion, C. J. (2017). What works in coach learning, how, and for whom? A grounded process of soccer coaches' professional learning. *Qualitative Research in Sport, Exercise and Health*, *9*(3), 321–338.

Teixeira, P. J., Carraça, E. V., Markland, D., Silva, M. N., & Ryan, R. M. (2012). Exercise, physical activity, and self-determination theory: A systematic review. *International Journal of Behavioral Nutrition and Physical Activity*, *9*(1), 1–30.

Townsend, R. C., Smith, B., & Cushion, C. J. (2015). Disability sports coaching: Towards a critical understanding. *Sports Coaching Review*, *4*(2), 80–98.

Tribolet, R., Sheehan, W. B., Novak, A. R., Watsford, M. L., & Fransen, J. (2021a). A descriptive and exploratory study of factors contributing to augmented feedback duration in professional Australian football practice. *International Journal of Sports Science & Coaching, 17*(3), 609–618.

Williams, A. M., & Hodges, N. J. (2005). Practice, instruction and skill acquisition in soccer: Challenging tradition. *Journal of Sports Sciences, 23*(6), 637–650.

Wisniewski, B., Zierer, K., & Hattie, J. (2020). The power of feedback revisited: A meta-analysis of educational feedback research. *Frontiers in Psychology, 10*, 3087.

Wright, J., & Forrest, G. (2007). A social semiotic analysis of knowledge construction and games centred approaches to teaching. *Physical Education and Sport Pedagogy, 12*(3), 273–287.

Wu, W. F., Porter, J. M., & Brown, L. E. (2012). Effect of attentional focus strategies on peak force and performance in the standing long jump. *The Journal of Strength & Conditioning Research, 26*(5), 1226–1231.

Wulf, G. (2013). Attentional focus and motor learning: A review of 15 years. *International Review of Sport and Exercise Psychology, 6*(1), 77–104.

Wulf, G., & Lewthwaite, R. (2016). Optimizing performance through intrinsic motivation and attention for learning: The OPTIMAL theory of motor learning. *Psychonomic Bulletin and Review, 23*(5), 1382–1414.

Wulf, G., & Shea, C. (2002). Principles derived from the study of simple skills do not generalise to complex skill learning. *Psychonomic Bulletin & Review, 9*(2), 185–211.

Wulf, G., Lauterbach, B., & Toole, T. (1999). The learning advantages of an external focus of attention in golf. *Research Quarterly for Exercise and Sport, 70*(2), 120–126.

6 The Myth of 'Periodization'

James Steele, James Fisher, Jeremy Loenneke and Samuel Buckner

Introduction

> … *Science must begin with myths, and with the criticism of myths; neither with the collection of observations, nor with the invention of experiments, but with the critical discussion of myths, and of magical techniques and practices.*
>
> (Popper, 1968)

Few realize that, as Karl Popper noted, myths are often the starting point of our science – the bold conjecturing of explanations for the phenomena we observe in the world. Indeed, myths begin in origin with ontology in that they are about what is purportedly real and often serve the function of explanation of observations and inferred phenomena (Mills, 2020a). As such, while not one and the same, myths and scientific theories are more closely related than most typically appreciate (Cresswell, 2020; Mills, 2020b). Though Popper felt that induction – the inference from particulars to generalization – could not succeed as a scientific epistemology, he realized that the myths which often arose from this and what is called abduction as explanation:[1]

> … may be developed, and become testable; that historically speaking all--or very nearly all--scientific theories originate from myths, and that a myth may contain important anticipations of scientific theories.

That is, they can become such that the formal logical consequences of them can be deductively inferred, and thus the conditions for their testing and possible falsification are clear, that is, *Modus tollens* can be applied. Indeed, the more precise the deductive consequences of a theory are, the 'riskier' the conjecture is said to be and the stronger the subsequent test (Meehl, 1990).

The world of sport, exercise and health is rife with so-called 'myths' (Tiller, 2020; Whitehead & Coe, 2021). In this chapter, we will discuss what we believe is a highly prominent myth within the sport and exercise sciences: periodization. Our aim is to first introduce periodization and discuss its definition and historical development. We will then consider the common argument that strength and hypertrophic adaptations are optimized through the application of periodization and provide alternative interpretations that we think likely reflect more parsimonious explanations than appeals to periodization 'theory'. Lastly, we will consider its structure as a myth vs as a scientific theory.

What is 'periodization' theory[2]?

The more consistent components of modern periodization theory – the planned variation in a training process with the aim of achieving specific goals – are recognizable long before attempts at formalization of the concept (Stone et al., 2021). However, modern conceptualizations of periodization theory emerged in the 1960s and developed over the latter part of the 20th century with authors in many countries publishing seminal texts: Russia (e.g. (Matveyev, 1982), (Ozolin, 1971) and (Verkhoshansky & Verkhoshansky, 2011)), Germany (Harre, 1964), Hungary (Nadori, 1962), Ukraine (Platonov, 2009), America (Stone et al., 1981) and Romania (Bompa, 1965). It appears to have emerged in its early modern form from observation and inductive inferences of how successful athletes trained, particularly in Eastern bloc countries (Krüger, 2016; Stone et al., 2021), and observation of successful athletes continues to be cited as a primary source of evidence (Hornsby et al., 2020; Stone et al., 2021). Accompanying the inductive inferences from successful athletes was abductive inference and the borrowing of a host of auxiliary theories as possible explanatory mechanisms stemming from those conjectured in other areas of physiology. The primary theory adopted was Hans Selye's General Adaptation Syndrome (Selye, 1936, 1938, 1956)[3] from which concepts such as 'adaptation energy' had seeming plausibility for explaining the process of adaptation to exercise stimulus. Notably, this continues to be cited as an instructive framework for understanding this mechanistically (Cunanan et al., 2018). Often emphasized too have been the primacy of the coach and their ability to plan and predict based on their inductive inferences from their trial and error experience of varying the training plan (Verkhoshansky & Verkhoshansky, 2011) which is also learnt on to this day (Hornsby et al., 2020).

The terminology used within the literature surrounding periodization can be a source of confusion when trying to discern exactly what 'periodization theory' is and how one might go about testing it. In particular, there seems to be a case of what has been called in the social sciences the *Jingle-Jangle Fallacy*.[4] Discrepancies between definitions of periodization and experimental investigations testing the concept seem to have created confusion between what is 'periodization' and what is 'programming' in particular (Hammert et al., 2021).

We will see that each of these points lends itself to the conclusion that, at present, periodization perhaps constitutes more myth than scientific theory. But before that, we will briefly review the common claims within the periodization literature that it presents a means of optimizing training[5] to enhance both strength and hypertrophic adaptations.

Periodization for strength adaptation

It has been suggested that periodized resistance training programs result in superior strength adaptations when compared to non-periodized resistance training programs (Stone et al., 1981; Willoughby, 1993). When examining the experimental evidence testing this claim, it appears that some studies demonstrate training interventions comparing a group that employs variation in the set and repetition scheme across time to experience greater strength increases when compared to a training group that has no variation in their set and repetition scheme across the same period of time. For example, Stone et al. (Stone et al., 1981) conducted a six-week study that compared strength adaptations between a training group that had variation in the set and repetition scheme ('periodized' condition) and a training group that had no variation in the set and repetition over the course of the training program. Following the six-week training period, the authors observed greater 1 repetitions maximum (RM) strength increases in the periodized group compared to the non-periodized training condition. The set and repetition scheme from this study are provided in Table 6.1. Although many would suggest that this study is actually examining different 'programming' strategies rather than the concept of periodization (Hammert et al., 2021) (see discussion below), this study is often cited as evidence that a periodized training program results in superior strength gains compared to a non-periodized training program. In the context of this study, what is thought to make the periodized program better is the variation in the exercise stimulus, particularly, the increase in training load, along with the decrease in training volume over time. However, it has also been pointed out that the periodization group lifted heavier than

Table 6.1. Training set and repetition scheme from Stone et al. (Stone et al., 1981).

	Weeks 1–3	Week 4	Week 5	Week 6
Periodized Condition	5 sets of 10 RM	5 sets of 5 RM	3 sets of 3 RM	3 sets of 2 RM
Non-Periodized Condition	3 sets of 6 RM	3 sets of 6 RM	3 sets of 6 RM	3 sets of 6 RM

RM = repetitions maximum

Table 6.2. Training program from O'Bryant et al. (O'Bryant et al., 1988).

	Weeks 1–4	Weeks 5–8	Weeks 9–11
Periodized	5 sets of 10	3 sets of 5 (1 set of 10)*	3 sets of 2 (1 set of 10)**
Non-Periodized	3 sets of 6	3 sets of 6	3 sets of 6
	Monday and Friday: • Parallel Squat • Bench Press • Hyperextensions • Sit-ups	**Wednesday:** • Clean Pulls (floor) • Clean Pulls (mid-thigh) • Shoulder Shrugs • Behind Neck Press • Sit-ups	

Sets in parenthesis represent follow-up sets performed with 70%* or 75%** of the original training loads.

the non-periodized training group prior to 1 RM strength testing (Mattocks et al., 2016). Thus, superior strength changes may simply be due to the fact that the periodized group lifted heavier weights in the weeks leading up to strength testing compared to the non-periodized training condition. As such, studies following this design do not seem to constitute strong tests of periodization theory generally speaking, unless it is the narrow claim that planning training to more closely reflect the outcome tested as proximity to the testing day decreases/enhances said outcome. But this can be explained more parsimoniously by the 'principle of specificity'.

Similar trends in strength adaptation can be observed across other studies that make up the periodization literature. For example, O'Bryant et al. (O'Bryant et al., 1988) examined strength adaptations following a 11-week periodized or a non-periodized training program. The set and repetition schemes across the study are provided in Table 6.2. Over the 11 weeks, the non-periodized training group performed three sets of six repetitions the entire time (O'Bryant et al., 1988). However, the periodized group gradually increased the training load across time, performing three sets of two repetitions for the final three weeks. Following the 11-week period, both training conditions increased 1 RM parallel squat strength; however, the periodized group demonstrated greater increases in strength when compared to the non-periodized training condition. Like the investigation of Stone et al. (Stone et al., 1981), the periodization group lifted heavier weight than the non-periodized group, particularly in the later weeks of the training program around the time of post-testing. Thus, it is possible that 'periodization' had nothing to do with the superior strength gains and that the specificity of training load provides a more parsimonious explanation for the superior changes in 1 RM strength.

The two studies reviewed in this section are intended to provide examples of how periodization research has typically been conducted. Regarding both investigations, proponents of periodization will suggest that strength adaptations were superior in the periodization groups due to the proper stress management (less fatigue accumulation) and variation within the program design. However, it seems reasonable to suggest that the periodized groups in these studies demonstrated greater strength increases because they were given exposure to lifting heavier weights (trained closer in load to 1 RM) in comparison to the non-periodized training conditions which only ever performed three sets of six repetitions. If the non-periodized condition was given periodic exposure to lifting heavy weights in these training studies, it seems reasonable to assume that strength adaptations would be similar between conditions. With this in mind, it is also important to note that in the context of periodization, variation in the exercise stimulus is meant to serve the purpose of proper stress management (Buckner et al., 2017). Yet, in the investigations reviewed, it seems likely that there was no risk of overtraining and thus no need to introduce variation in the set and repetition scheme across time. These studies would be more interesting if the non-periodized groups would perform low volume high load training (two to three sets of two to three RM) for the entire study duration and see if the periodized groups still see greater strength adaptations over time.[6]

Periodization for muscle growth

Muscle growth can occur through hypertrophy (increased fibre size) and/or hyperplasia (increased fibre number). Traditionally, it is thought that hypertrophy is the dominant factor associated with muscle growth in humans, but this has been mostly inferred from small-scale cross-sectional studies (MacDougall et al., 1984). Position stands for resistance training across multiple organizations recommend periodized programs in order to optimize the muscle growth response to resistance training (American College of Sports Medicine, 2009; Fragala et al., 2019). That is, having a plan in place to manipulate volume and intensity across time in an effort to optimize muscle growth. If periodization is as important as has been suggested, then evidence for this effect should be plentiful. Prior to discussing what the experimental work suggests, it might be worthwhile to briefly review how muscle is mechanistically thought to grow. When considering mechanisms, it will be important to keep the following question in mind: How could periodization, considering the manner in which it is theorized to work, impact these systems to a greater extent than traditional progressive resistance training?

Exercise-induced muscle hypertrophy is thought to be a local response (Bell et al., 2023; Dankel et al., 2020). In other words, training the right bicep can induce growth in the right bicep that is trained but not in the opposite untrained left bicep. The contraction takes a mechanical stimulus and converts it into a chemical one (Marcotte et al., 2015). This is referred to as mechanotransduction. One of the key pathways associated with exercise-induced growth is the mechanistic target of rapamycin (mTORC1). Although mTORC1 is important (Bodine et al., 2001), it would be an oversimplification to imply that it is the only important pathway for muscle growth. Following a single bout of resistance exercise, the muscle is sensitized to anabolic stimuli for up to 72 hours (Miller et al., 2005). This anabolic window potentially shortens with repeated training (Damas et al., 2015), but it is still thought to last a considerable amount of time (~24 hours) (Burd et al., 2011). When food is consumed in this post-exercise window, the protein synthetic response is augmented above levels in the absence of that resistance training bout, and protein breakdown is suppressed (Joanisse et al., 2020). When synthesis exceeds breakdown, growth will occur. Given that synthesis occurs at the ribosome, the ability to grow might be related in part to an increase in the number of ribosomes (Bamman et al., 2018). The majority of the ribosome is thought to be composed of ribosomal RNA (rRNA). Since rRNA is a final gene product, the only way to increase rRNA is to increase gene transcription (Adams & Bamman, 2012). Gene transcription occurs in the myonuclei, which can also increase in response to resistance exercise (Petrella et al., 2006). This is a simplified summary of how muscle growth can occur following bouts of resistance exercise. For periodization to result in superior growth to that of traditional progressive resistance training, it would need to be able to enhance at least one part of the aforementioned processes. Although mechanistic work is of importance for the development of theory regarding adaptation, the ultimate test of superiority is the measurement of muscle size in response to theoretically optimal training interventions (i.e. periodization) compared to other approaches.

Muscle growth is determined by measuring the muscle size before and after a training program. This is estimated through changes in lean body mass, fat-free mass or by specifically imaging the muscle of interest. There are studies that find that periodized programs are more effective than traditional progressive resistance training, but the majority of the studies do not support this (Buckner et al., 2020). One thing to consider is that moving from phase to phase in a periodization program may inadvertently lead to greater progression in load because some of the comparator groups in the early studies were allowed to progress load at their own pace. The inability of periodization to consistently result in superior muscle growth is in line with how muscle is mechanistically thought to occur. The recruitment and activation of muscle fibres for a sufficient (not well-defined) duration of time appear to be one of the important factors in signalling a muscle to grow (Dankel et al., 2017). How that muscle is overloaded appears to be influenced very little by complex and precise manipulation of extrinsic variables (load, repetitions, rest, etc.) in the manner of periodized training and can largely be selected by preference. Of course, some would argue that periodization has never been properly studied and that the conclusions drawn in this book chapter are premature (Cunanan et al., 2018). We do not necessarily disagree with this point. If that is true though, then that is even more of a reason to be sceptical of the claims made about periodization. Still, some might argue that changing anything in a program is periodization. If that is true, then virtually everything could be considered periodization. That would make any comparison between periodized and non-periodized programs nonsensical.

Periodization for strength and hypertrophic adaptations

To summarize: (1) the periodization literature does not consistently result in superior changes in strength or muscle size, (2) muscle strength adaptation is more parsimoniously explained by the principle of specificity and (3) the lack of superiority for muscle growth can be predicted based on how muscle growth is theorized to mechanistically occur. This is not to say that periodization programs cannot be used to produce changes in strength and muscle size. They certainly can be effective (just not superior), and one might make the argument that implementing different phases within a training cycle may be important for maintaining long-term motivation with resistance training. But that is also only an idea and to date remains untested.

But is periodization a myth or a theory?

As we have seen from this brief review, there is reason to doubt the veracity of periodization as a theory to explain the strength and hypertrophic adaptations to training. But the question raised at the beginning of this chapter remains; is periodization a theory, albeit one likely falsified, or did it never really emerge from its origins as a myth in the first place? This last section will consider this broader question and examine each part of its structure and origin to determine its status as one or the other.

Under-specification, deductive infertility and weak tests

As noted, from a Popperian perspective, the under-specification of periodization limiting its testability is alone sufficient to consider it more myth than scientific theory. Over the course of its development periodization theory has, though often accompanied in some form by various graphical 'models', typically been defined as a *verbal theory*.[7] Indeed, while the various iterations of periodization have been proposed as explanatory theories of the adaptive process in response to the management of training variables in certain developmental orders, explanation presumes accurate deduction (Hempel & Oppenheim, 1948). A primary issue of verbal theories is their deductive infertility; it is unclear what should indeed follow from the theory were it a true explanation of the phenomena to be explained. It is not specifically clear what exactly we should, or should not, observe if periodization theory were an accurate explanation of the adaptive response to training, partly because it is not clear exactly 'what' periodization theory is. Reviews note the lack of clarity conceptually in periodization (Afonso et al., 2017; Kiely, 2012) as well as the varying definitions of periodization that crop up in the literature noting that, while some loose themes emerge (e.g. that periodization is proposed to serve as a 'macro-' management of the training process), there is inconsistency amongst author's definitions[8] and as a result it is not even clear what would constitute an appropriate test of the theory (Kataoka et al., 2021).[9] At best we might deduce that training following broadly the tenets of periodization should produce larger adaptations than those which do not or allows for continued adaptation to occur as opposed to plateaus, or that possibly training to target adaptations of particular kinds in a specific order ultimately optimizes outcomes (Buckner et al., 2020).

As we have seen, in so far as it has been tested, it is not clear that periodization, as it is typically studied, produces superior outcomes, at least for strength and hypertrophy. Further, it is not clear that there is any evidence that it is possible to overcome the typical plateauing of adaptation that occurs over time (Counts et al., 2017; Fisher et al., 2018; Steele et al., 2022), or that particular ordering of training for specific adaptations enhances outcomes (Buckner et al., 2020). But, as it has typically been studied, periodization in so far as we can discern some clarity regarding what it *is* has not been strongly tested in that form.

For example, periodization as it is presented typically appears to be a long-term coaching framework where periods of time are created to manage the stress of training alongside the other stressors in an athlete's life. These periods of time are intended to manage stress, avoid overtraining and acute fatigue and peak performance at a time relevant to competition (Kataoka et al., 2021). Indeed, we are not arguing that these are not sensible things to consider in planning training. However, studies have attempted to examine this concept over a relatively short period of time where there is no risk of overtraining and no competing stressors (see the previous studies given as examples). In such short studies, it appears that none of the imposed training variation serves the purpose of stress management. Thus, it is important to ask the question, 'what is the purpose of the variation?'. Within a typical periodized program, it would be common to train hypertrophy (higher volume) when less time is being dedicated to sport. As other stressors increase (including sport-specific training and competition), it would be common to decrease training volume in order to balance the competing stressors in an athlete's life. This would take place over the course of an entire training season. It appears that Stone et al. (Stone et al., 1981), for example, attempted to condense this process down to six-weeks' time. However, over six-weeks' time, it seems that there is little risk of overtraining from performing the same set and repetition scheme and no apparent reason to change the set and rep scheme (unless the training goal has changed). This is problematic, as studies such as these have perpetuated the idea that weekly (Bartolomei et al., 2015) or daily (Zourdos et al., 2016) changes in programming variables make a program 'periodized', whereas no variation in programming variables makes it 'non-periodized'. However, periodization is more so the idea that there is an extended period focussing on hypertrophy, strength or other attributes within a larger overall program with training tailored towards these in order to manage stress. If a six- to eight-week hypertrophy block existed within the larger plan, this would represent a period of time created with a specific intention that has considered other stressors in an athlete's life at that time. The programming within this eight-week block should be designed in a manner that would best maximize muscle growth. This goal can likely be accomplished with or without variation. With this in mind, it is important to note that nearly every experimental intervention that tests the efficacy of periodization employs a 6–12-week study design where one group has variation in the set and rep scheme and the other group has no variation in the set and repetition scheme (Kataoka et al., 2021). Thus, it is possible (and perhaps likely) that none of these studies actually test periodization as it is broadly conceived anyway.

The mythology of Eastern bloc Olympic success due to periodization

One argument in opposition to the criticism that periodization theory is underspecified is that it does in fact entail a deductive consequence; we should observe that athletes who follow its principles and practices should perform better and be more successful. Indeed, as noted, this continues to be a source of evidence which is pointed to corroborate periodization (Hornsby et al., 2020; Stone et al., 2021). However, this does not seem to be an appropriate test of the theory. Such logic is flawed and is a case of begging the question of circular reasoning.[10] The initial formalization of periodization theory stemmed from the inductive inferences made by way of generalizing from observations of successful athletes, particularly in Eastern bloc countries during the 1950s–1960s (Krüger, 2016; Stone et al., 2021). At this time, sport – and particularly Olympic success – was heavily politicized particularly between the Soviet Union and the United States echoing Cold War tension and the competition between state-planned communism and individualistic capitalism (Keys, 2012; Krüger, 2016; Stone et al., 2021). The success of the USSR during this time seemingly spawned a mythos in the West and resulted in the application of periodization and other 'Soviet Secrets'. This likely spawned the cottage industry of research and practice we see today (Nuckols, 2017; Stone et al., 2021). A common point of contention for this explanation was that heavy state-supported use of performance-enhancing drugs in fact better explained Soviet success; however, the use of such substances was likely widespread in many countries during these years (Stone et al., 2021). But, at the same time, there were wider efforts to formalize sport and talent identification in the USSR (Parks, 2009); during the Cold War years, its population outstripped that of the United States (US Census Bureau, 1991).

Statistically speaking, the probability of the Eastern bloc countries identifying successful athletes (larger population to sample from and focussed well-resourced efforts to identify talent) would have been far greater. Indeed, population size and selection pressures have influenced anthropometric trends in athletes (Norton & Olds, 2001) and, as such, are strong predictors of Olympic success (Rewilak, 2021). Thus, alternative explanatory theories exist for the success of athletes during these years. But the mythology of periodization was taken up in the West, and now is the accepted 'gold standard' such that it is widely applied to modern athletes. This presents a problem for the contemporary arguments that the observations that modern successful athletes employ these practices provide evidence to corroborate the theory; almost all athletes are employing such principles whether successful or not. It is entirely possible that a sociological explanation better fits this observation. Due to the alluring mythos of periodization and the widespread uptake of such practices, it has been employed with athletes; that is, athletes are not necessarily successful because they have engaged in periodization, but they engage in periodization because they are athletes. Kenneth Gergen (Gergen, 1976) wrote of the impact that social science theories had upon themselves by way of a feedback loop from the public and practitioners who became aware of them. A similar point can be made here whereby the 'successes' of periodization have meant it is so widely used that the predictions of the theory no longer bear out in observation. As is hopefully clear anyway, such evidence cannot constitute a test of periodization theory as it is unable to differentiate between competing explanations.

Mis-borrowing of auxiliary theory

It is not uncommon for newly emerging disciplines without a long history of theory construction and testing to abductively 'borrow' theory from other disciplines as a kind of analogy albeit one with the intention to provide an explanation (Fellows & Liu, 2020; Murray & Evers, 1989). This process involves the transportation of theory from its original context in order to explain phenomena in another, or it could be said to be an expansion of the boundary conditions within which the theory is thought to apply. In the case of periodization, Selye's General Adaptation Syndrome (Selye, 1936, 1938, 1956) was the primary (though not only) theory borrowed in order to explain athlete success from the planning and organization of the training process in specific ways (Cunanan et al., 2018). Indeed, a key assumption of periodization theory was that biological adaptation to training followed a predictable pattern (Kiely, 2012). The reason for its borrowing was seemingly due to an interest in not only explicating the *how* but the *why* of periodization – a desire to provide a plausible biological flourish for that assumption (Verkhoshansky & Verkhoshansky, 2011). However, a key element of good theory borrowing is consideration of the original context in which the theory was formed and that testable theories are indeed constrained by this in terms of their testable consequences. The original context of the General Adaptation Syndrome (and indeed other theories of biological adaptation employed) was clearly not training processes and indeed a review of Selye's original work suggests the ideas may have been misapplied (Buckner et al., 2017; Kiely, 2012, 2018; Kiely et al., 2019; Vasenina et al., 2020). Further, it is not clear what the application of such auxiliary theories to the training process achieves in terms of yielding deductive consequences due to their own vagueness alongside periodization; indeed, they seem to offer little more than truisms (Kiely et al., 2019). Their application however seems likely to have furthered the mythology around periodization similarly to other fields where the inclusion of 'sciencey' sounding biological information is seductively alluring in convincing people of a given explanation (Weisberg et al., 2008, 2015). The use of these theories by proponents of periodization seems more in line with pragmatic views of theory (i.e. that a theory is useful to believe to be true) as opposed to correspondence views (i.e. that a theory is true in so far as it describes the world with a high degree of verisimilitude).

The limitations of appeals to coaches' experience

Like the allure of auxiliary biological theories, appeals to coaching experience can be instinctively persuasive to many in sport particularly the experiences of those who have seemingly had a lot of success. There is the assumption that the practices employed by those coaches with their athletes *must* be at least in some part responsible for their success. But this is far from clear. While it is clear that what athletes do impact their performance, their genetics also play an important role (Davids & Baker, 2007) and the selection pressures on this likely play a much larger role (Norton & Olds, 2001). In fact, at the elite level deliberate practice accounts for only 1% of overall variance in performance (Macnamara et al., 2016). Given this, and the fact that in countless other fields time and time again expert prediction based on induction from prior success has been found wanting (Meehl, 1954; Tetlock, 2005), it seems overconfident to weigh professional experience so highly. This is not to say that sometimes simple heuristics used by experts can't be useful (Katsikopoulos et al., 2008), but similarly to retrospective analyses of successful athletes, the input of experts' experience is better placed to inductively generalize phenomena and to abductively build theories for more severe deductive testing. Instead, in the case of periodization there seems to have been an application of the genetic fallacy (i.e. judging something as good or bad based on the source) to shore up further the mythology surrounding it.

The structure of the myth

Mills (Mills, 2020a) notes that a myth must have (1) source, (2) force, (3) form, (4) object and (5) goal. *Source* relates to a myth's attempts to answer the question of fundamental ontology. *Force* is the essence of the myth and the organizing principles behind the narrative. *Form* is the organizational style, the story, the development of characters and plot within meta-narratives. The *object* of myth refers to its contents, the phenomena and concepts it contains. Lastly, the *goal* is the purpose of the myth.

With regard to periodization, it is hopefully clear that the source lies in ontology – an attempt to explain observable phenomena. Its force is the various vague and under-specified models employed to explain training adaptation. Its forms are the stories surrounding its origins and the various characters involved in its development over the years. The goal of periodization is hard to say without presupposing the intentions of the characters involved, but it has certainly penetrated the field widely in its application.

Does this all constitute labelling periodization as myth? In the introduction, we noted Popper's distinction between myth and theory and note that it is sufficient merely that periodization is unclear in its testability to label it the former as opposed to the latter. Indeed, Mills (Mills, 2020b) echoes the distinction:

> Theory is far more scrutinized for its validity, generalizability, and applied consequences, while the premises of myth are often historically and culturally presupposed.

From our perspective and analysis, it does not feel unfair to label periodization as a myth. At the very least, it has strong elements of mythos about it, particularly in terms of its origin and development. This is not necessarily a bad thing. Strong scientific theories begin as myths. But in the case of periodization, there was never the required strengthening and specification such that it became a strong theory. As we have seen, the vagueness and under-specification of it have made it difficult to test rigorously, and we continue to see debates in the literature regarding its conceptualization and definition to this day. If periodization is to take a step forward into the beginnings of a scientific theory, then consensus specification and definition such that it yields clear deductively testable consequences should be the next point in its journey from mythical origins.

Notes

1. Indeed, Francis Bacon even wove myth and allegory into his work in the development of his inductive reasoning in the *Novum Organum* (MacIntyre, 1994). Abduction is also considered to be the process of inferring possible explanations for observations and phenomena (Douven, 2021).
2. Periodization is often referred to as a 'theory'. As such to begin, we should probably provide a definition of 'periodization theory' for the reader; yet, we have to confess we are somewhat at a loss for how to do this. In fact, the difficulty of providing a definition highlights a key theme within the literature on periodization that, at least from a falsificationist epistemological stance regarding the nature of scientific theories (*ala* Karl Popper, Imre Lakatos, Paul Meehl), we feel prevents it from being considered at present a strong scientific theory. We will first give a brief historical and descriptive overview.
3. Others such as Ivan Pavlov's work on Classical Conditioning (Pavlov, 1927), Nikolai Yakolev's work on glycogen supercompensation (Yakolev, 1949), Nicolai Bernstein's Theory of the Self-Regulated Motor System (Bernshteĭn, 1967) and Peter Anokhin's Theory of the Functional System (Anokhin, 1974) were also co-opted by various authors.
4. Edward Thorndike (Thorndike, 1904) introduced the *Jingle* fallacy as being when two things are falsely assumed to be the same because the terms used for them are the same. Contrastingly the *Jangle* fallacy is falsely assuming that two things are different because the terms used for them are different.
5. Optimal is not easily defined in this context so it will be used here as programs that produce superior adaptations.
6. Some pilot work has explored this type of approach in powerlifters (Androulakis-Korakakis et al., 2018) and does not appear to support the need for traditional 'periodized' training approaches to optimize strength adaptation, or indeed manage stress.
7. By 'verbal theory' we mean to say a theory expressed in structure through the use of words and thus limited by the imprecision of natural language compared to computational or mathematical expressions of theory (Smaldino, 2017).
8. There is even inconsistency in the terminology used, varying between 'periodization' and 'programming' (Kataoka et al., 2021). Some proponents of 'periodization' have argued that criticisms have been based largely upon studies that have examined 'programming' (Cunanan et al., 2018; Hornsby et al., 2020; Suchomel et al., 2018); yet even examination of this distinction highlights confusion (Hammert et al., 2021). Further, this terminological confusion appears as far back as the early debates of Matveyev and Verkhoshanksy and indeed even appears to reflect the opposite of what today's periodization proponents argue these terms denote; see appendix 4 in Verkhoshansky and Verkhoshansky (Verkhoshansky & Verkhoshansky, 2011).
9. Indeed, similarly to in fields such as psychology, it could be said that periodization in this sense is *not even wrong* as its critical under specification means that empirical attempts at falsification or corroboration are doomed to fail (Scheel, 2022).

10 The logic is as follows: successful athletes engaged in certain practices, the inference being that these practices explained their success leading to development of periodization theory, thus athletes following practices stemming from periodization theory should be successful, and lo and behold successful athletes today follow such practices. It often goes unmentioned that many unsuccessful athletes also tend to follow such practices in modern sport, and indeed that now almost anything that includes some variation gets labelled as 'periodization' anyway.

References

Adams, G. R., & Bamman, M. M. (2012). Characterization and regulation of mechanical loading-induced compensatory muscle hypertrophy. *Comprehensive Physiology*, *2*(4), 2829–2870. https://doi.org/10.1002/cphy.c110066

Afonso, J., Nikolaidis, P. T., Sousa, P., & Mesquita, I. (2017). Is empirical research on periodization trustworthy? A comprehensive review of conceptual and methodological issues. *Journal of Sports Science & Medicine*, *16*(1), 27–34.

American College of Sports Medicine. (2009). Progression models in resistance training for healthy adults. *Medicine & Science in Sports & Exercise*, *41*(3), 687. https://doi.org/10.1249/MSS.0b013e3181915670

Androulakis-Korakakis, P., Fisher, J. P., Kolokotronis, P., Gentil, P., & Steele, J. (2018). Reduced volume 'daily max' training compared to higher volume periodized training in powerlifters preparing for competition-a pilot study. *Sports (Basel, Switzerland)*, *6*(3), 86. https://doi.org/10.3390/sports6030086

Anokhin, P. K. (1974). *Biology and neurophysiology of the conditioned reflex and its role in adaptive behavior: International series of monographs in cerebrovisceral and behavioral physiology and conditioned reflexes, volume 3*. Pergamon Press.

Bamman, M. M., Roberts, B. M., & Adams, G. R. (2018). Molecular regulation of exercise-induced muscle fiber hypertrophy. *Cold Spring Harbor Perspectives in Medicine*, *8*(6), a029751. https://doi.org/10.1101/cshperspect.a029751

Bartolomei, S., Stout, J. R., Fukuda, D. H., Hoffman, J. R., & Merni, F. (2015). Block vs. weekly undulating periodized resistance training programs in women. *The Journal of Strength & Conditioning Research*, *29*(10), 2679. https://doi.org/10.1519/JSC.0000000000000948

Bell, Z. W., Wong, V., Spitz, R. W., Yamada, Y., Song, J. S., Kataoka, R., Chatakondi, R. N., Abe, T., & Loenneke, J. P. (2023). Unilateral high-load resistance training influences strength changes in the contralateral arm undergoing low-load training. *Journal of Science and Medicine in Sport*. https://doi.org/10.1016/j.jsams.2023.06.011

Bernshteĭn, N. A. (1967). *The co-ordination and regulation of movements*. Pergamon Press.

Bodine, S. C., Stitt, T. N., Gonzalez, M., Kline, W. O., Stover, G. L., Bauerlein, R., Zlotchenko, E., Scrimgeour, A., Lawrence, J. C., Glass, D. J., & Yancopoulos, G. D. (2001). Akt/mTOR pathway is a crucial regulator of skeletal muscle hypertrophy and can prevent muscle atrophy in vivo. *Nature Cell Biology*, *3*(11), 1014–1019. https://doi.org/10.1038/ncb1101-1014

Bompa, T. (1965). Periodization of strength. *Sports Review*, *1*, 26–31.

Buckner, S. L., Jessee, M. B., Mouser, J. G., Dankel, S. J., Mattocks, K. T., Bell, Z. W., Abe, T., & Loenneke, J. P. (2020). The basics of training for muscle size and strength: A brief review on the theory. *Medicine and Science in Sports and Exercise*, *52*(3), 645–653. https://doi.org/10.1249/MSS.0000000000002171

Buckner, S. L., Mouser, J. G., Dankel, S. J., Jessee, M. B., Mattocks, K. T., & Loenneke, J. P. (2017). The General Adaptation Syndrome: Potential misapplications to resistance exercise. *Journal of Science and Medicine in Sport*, *20*(11), 1015–1017. https://doi.org/10.1016/j.jsams.2017.02.012

Burd, N. A., West, D. W. D., Moore, D. R., Atherton, P. J., Staples, A. W., Prior, T., Tang, J. E., Rennie, M. J., Baker, S. K., & Phillips, S. M. (2011). Enhanced amino acid sensitivity of myofibrillar protein synthesis persists for up to 24 h after resistance exercise in young men1–3. *The Journal of Nutrition*, *141*(4), 568–573. https://doi.org/10.3945/jn.110.135038

Counts, B. R., Buckner, S. L., Mouser, J. G., Dankel, S. J., Jessee, M. B., Mattocks, K. T., & Loenneke, J. P. (2017). Muscle growth: To infinity and beyond? *Muscle & Nerve*, *56*(6), 1022–1030. https://doi.org/10.1002/mus.25696

Cresswell, J. (2020). Theories as modern myths: Giving up the pursuit of good theory to focus on good theorizing. *Journal for the Theory of Social Behaviour*, *50*(4), 429–434. https://doi.org/10.1111/jtsb.12261

Cunanan, A. J., DeWeese, B. H., Wagle, J. P., Carroll, K. M., Sausaman, R., Hornsby, W. G., Haff, G. G., Triplett, N. T., Pierce, K. C., & Stone, M. H. (2018). The general adaptation syndrome: A foundation for the concept of periodization. *Sports Medicine*, *48*(4), 787–797. https://doi.org/10.1007/s40279-017-0855-3

Damas, F., Phillips, S., Vechin, F. C., & Ugrinowitsch, C. (2015). A review of resistance training-induced changes in skeletal muscle protein synthesis and their contribution to hypertrophy. *Sports Medicine (Auckland, N.Z.)*, *45*(6), 801–807. https://doi.org/10.1007/s40279-015-0320-0

Dankel, S. J., Bell, Z. W., Spitz, R. W., Wong, V., Viana, R. B., Chatakondi, R. N., Buckner, S. L., Jessee, M. B., Mattocks, K. T., Mouser, J. G., Abe, T., & Loenneke, J. P. (2020). Assessing differential responders and mean changes in muscle size, strength, and the crossover effect to 2 distinct resistance training protocols. *Applied Physiology, Nutrition, and Metabolism = Physiologie Appliquee, Nutrition Et Metabolisme*, *45*(5), 463–470. https://doi.org/10.1139/apnm-2019-0470

Dankel, S. J., Mattocks, K. T., Jessee, M. B., Buckner, S. L., Mouser, J. G., & Loenneke, J. P. (2017). Do metabolites that are produced during resistance exercise enhance muscle hypertrophy? *European Journal of Applied Physiology*, *117*(11), 2125–2135. https://doi.org/10.1007/s00421-017-3690-1

Davids, K., & Baker, J. (2007). Genes, environment and sport performance: Why the nature-nurture dualism is no longer relevant. *Sports Medicine (Auckland, N.Z.)*, *37*(11). https://doi.org/10.2165/00007256-200737110-00004

Douven, I. (2021). Abduction. In E. N. Zalta (Ed.), *The Stanford Encyclopedia of Philosophy* (Summer 2021). Metaphysics Research Lab, Stanford University. https://plato.stanford.edu/archives/sum2021/entries/abduction/

Fellows, R., & Liu, A. M. M. (2020). Borrowing theories: Contextual and empirical considerations. *Construction Management and Economics*, *38*(7), 581–588. https://doi.org/10.1080/01446193.2020.1727541

Fisher, J. P., Steele, J., Smith, D., & Gentil, P. (2018). Periodization for optimizing strength and hypertrophy; the forgotten variables. *Journal of Trainology*, *7*(1), 10–15. https://doi.org/10.17338/trainology.7.1_10

Fragala, M. S., Cadore, E. L., Dorgo, S., Izquierdo, M., Kraemer, W. J., Peterson, M. D., & Ryan, E. D. (2019). *Resistance training for older adults: Position statement from the national strength and conditioning association.*

Gergen, K. J. (1976). Social psychology as history. In L. H. Strickland, F. E. Aboud, & K. J. Gergen (Eds.), *Social psychology in transition* (pp. 15–32). Springer US. https://doi.org/10.1007/978-1-4615-8765-1_2

Hammert, W. B., Kataoka, R., Vasenina, E., Ibrahim, A. H., & Buckner, S. L. (2021). Is "periodization programming" periodization or programming? *Journal of Trainology*, *10*(2), 20–24. https://doi.org/10.17338/trainology.10.2_20

Harre, D. (1964). *Einführung in die allgemeine Trainings—Und Wettkampflehre: Anleitung fürdas Fernstudium [Introduction to general training and competition theory: Instructions for distance learning]*. DHfK.

Hempel, C. G., & Oppenheim, P. (1948). Studies in the logic of explanation. *Philosophy of Science*, *15*(2), 135–175. https://doi.org/10.1086/286983

Hornsby, W. G., Fry, A. C., Haff, G. G., & Stone, M. H. (2020). Addressing the confusion within periodization research. *Journal of Functional Morphology and Kinesiology*, *5*(3), Article 3. https://doi.org/10.3390/jfmk5030068

Joanisse, S., Lim, C., McKendry, J., Mcleod, J. C., Stokes, T., & Phillips, S. M. (2020). Recent advances in understanding resistance exercise training-induced skeletal muscle hypertrophy in humans. *F1000Research*, *9*, F1000 Faculty Rev-141. https://doi.org/10.12688/f1000research.21588.1

Kataoka, R., Vasenina, E., Loenneke, J., & Buckner, S. L. (2021). Periodization: Variation in the definition and discrepancies in study design. *Sports Medicine*, *51*(4), 625–651. https://doi.org/10.1007/s40279-020-01414-5

Katsikopoulos, K., Pachur, T., Machery, E., & Wallin, A. (2008). *From Meehl to fast and frugal heuristics (and back): New insights into how to bridge the clinical—actuarial divide*. https://journals.sagepub.com/doi/10.1177/0959354308091824

Keys, B. (2012). The early cold war olympics, 1952–1960: Political, economic and human rights dimensions. In H. J. Lenskyj & S. Wagg (Eds.), *The Palgrave handbook of Olympic studies* (pp. 72–87). Palgrave Macmillan UK. https://doi.org/10.1057/9780230367463_6

Kiely, J. (2012). Periodization paradigms in the 21st century: Evidence-led or tradition-driven? *International Journal of Sports Physiology and Performance*, *7*(3), 242–250. https://doi.org/10.1123/ijspp.7.3.242

Kiely, J. (2018). Periodization theory: Confronting an inconvenient truth. *Sports Medicine (Auckland, N.Z.)*, *48*(4). https://doi.org/10.1007/s40279-017-0823-y

Kiely, J., Pickering, C., & Halperin, I. (2019). Comment on 'biological background of block periodized endurance training: A review'. *Sports Medicine (Auckland, N.Z.)*, *49*(9), 1475–1477. https://doi.org/10.1007/s40279-019-01114-9

Krüger, A. (2016). From Russia with Love? Sixty years of proliferation of L.P. Matveyev's concept of Periodisation? *Staps*, *114*(4), 51–59.

MacDougall, J. D., Sale, D. G., Alway, S. E., & Sutton, J. R. (1984). Muscle fiber number in biceps brachii in bodybuilders and control subjects. *Journal of Applied Physiology*, *57*(5), 1399–1403. https://doi.org/10.1152/jappl.1984.57.5.1399

MacIntyre, W. P. (1994). Francis Bacon's use of ancient myths in Novum Organum. *Alicante Journal of English Studies / Revista Alicantina de Estudios Ingleses*, *7*, Article 7. https://doi.org/10.14198/raei.1994.7.10

Macnamara, B., Moreau, D., & Hambrick, D. (2016). The relationship between deliberate practice and performance in sports: A meta-analysis. *Perspectives on Psychological Science: A Journal of the Association for Psychological Science*, *11*(3). https://doi.org/10.1177/1745691616635591

Marcotte, G. R., West, D. W. D., & Baar, K. (2015). The molecular basis for load-induced skeletal muscle hypertrophy. *Calcified Tissue International, 96*(3), 196–210. https://doi.org/10.1007/s00223-014-9925-9

Mattocks, K. T., Dankel, S. J., Buckner, S. L., Jessee, M. B., Counts, B. R., Mouser, J. G., Laurentino, G. C., & Loenneke, J. P. (2016). Periodization: What is it good for? *Journal of Trainology, 5*(1), 6–12. https://doi.org/10.17338/trainology.5.1_6

Matveyev, L. (1982). *Fundamentals of sports training*. Victor Kamkin.

Meehl, P. E. (1954). *Clinical versus statistical prediction: A theoretical analysis and a review of the evidence* (pp. x, 149). University of Minnesota Press. https://doi.org/10.1037/11281-000

Meehl, P. E. (1990). Appraising and amending theories: The strategy of Lakatosian defense and two principles that warrant it. *Psychological Inquiry, 1*(2), 108–141.

Miller, B. F., Olesen, J. L., Hansen, M., Døssing, S., Crameri, R. M., Welling, R. J., Langberg, H., Flyvbjerg, A., Kjaer, M., Babraj, J. A., Smith, K., & Rennie, M. J. (2005). Coordinated collagen and muscle protein synthesis in human patella tendon and quadriceps muscle after exercise. *The Journal of Physiology, 567*(Pt 3), 1021–1033. https://doi.org/10.1113/jphysiol.2005.093690

Mills, J. (2020a). Toward a theory of myth. *Journal for the Theory of Social Behaviour, 50*(4), 410–424. https://doi.org/10.1111/jtsb.12249

Mills, J. (2020b). Why theory is not myth. *Journal for the Theory of Social Behaviour, 50*(4), 435–438. https://doi.org/10.1111/jtsb.12262

Murray, J. B., & Evers, D. J. (1989). Theory borrowing and reflectivity in interdisciplinary fields. *ACR North American Advances, NA-16*. https://www.acrwebsite.org/volumes/6929/volumes/v16/NA-16/full

Nadori, L. (1962). *Training and competition*. Sport.

Norton, K., & Olds, T. (2001). Morphological evolution of athletes over the 20th century: Causes and consequences. *Sports Medicine (Auckland, N.Z.), 31*(11), 763–783. https://doi.org/10.2165/00007256-200131110-00001

Nuckols, G. (2017, August 22). Periodization: History and theory • stronger by science. *Stronger by Science*. https://www.strongerbyscience.com/periodization-history-theory/

O'Bryant, H. S., Byrd, R., & Stone, M. H. (1988). Cycle ergometer performance and maximum leg and hip strength adaptations to two different methods of weight-training. *The Journal of Strength & Conditioning Research, 2*(2), 27.

Ozolin, N. (1971). *Sovremennaia Systema Sportivnoi Trenirovky [Athlete's training system for competition]*. Fizkultura i Sport.

Parks, J. (2009). *Red sport, red tape: The Olympic games, the soviet sports bureaucracy, and the cold war, 1952—1980*. University of North Carolina at Chapel Hill.

Pavlov, I. P. (1927). *Conditioned reflexes: An investigation of the physiological activity of the cerebral cortex* (pp. xv, 430). Oxford University Press.

Petrella, J. K., Kim, J., Cross, J. M., Kosek, D. J., & Bamman, M. M. (2006). Efficacy of myonuclear addition may explain differential myofiber growth among resistance-trained young and older men and women. *American Journal of Physiology. Endocrinology and Metabolism, 291*(5), E937–946. https://doi.org/10.1152/ajpendo.00190.2006

Platonov, B. H. (2009). Theory of annual training background, status, discussions, ways to modernize. *Theory and Practice of Physical Culture, 9*, 18–34.

Popper, K. R. (1968). *Conjectures and refutations: The growth of scientific knowledge*. Harper & Row.

Rewilak, J. (2021). The (non) determinants of Olympic success. *Journal of Sports Economics, 22*(5), 546–570. https://doi.org/10.1177/1527002521992833

Scheel, A. M. (2022). Why most psychological research findings are not even wrong. *Infant and Child Development*, *31*(1), e2295. https://doi.org/10.1002/icd.2295

Selye, H. (1936). A syndrome produced by diverse nocuous agents. *Nature*, *138*(3479), Article 3479. https://doi.org/10.1038/138032a0

Selye, H. (1938). Experimental evidence supporting the conception of 'adaptation energy'. *American Journal of Physiology*, *123*(3), 758–765.

Selye, H. (1956). *The stress of life* (pp. xvi, 324). McGraw-Hill.

Smaldino, P. E. (2017). Models are stupid, and we need more of them. In Robin, R. & Vallacher, et al., (Eds.), *Computational social psychology*. Routledge.

Steele, J., Fisher, J. P., Giessing, J., Androulakis-Korakakis, P., Wolf, M., Kroeske, B., & Reuters, R. (2022). Long-term time-course of strength adaptation to minimal dose resistance training through retrospective longitudinal growth modeling. *Research Quarterly for Exercise and Sport*, 1–18. https://doi.org/10.1080/02701367.2022.2070592

Stone, M. H., Hornsby, W. G., Haff, G. G., Fry, A. C., Suarez, D. G., Liu, J., Gonzalez-Rave, J. M., & Pierce, K. C. (2021). Periodization and block periodization in sports: Emphasis on strength-power training—A provocative and challenging narrative. *The Journal of Strength & Conditioning Research*, *35*(8), 2351. https://doi.org/10.1519/JSC.0000000000004050

Stone, M. H., O'Bryant, H., & Garhammer, J. (1981). A hypothetical model for strength training. *The Journal of Sports Medicine and Physical Fitness*, *21*(4), 342–351.

Suchomel, T. J., Nimphius, S., Bellon, C. R., & Stone, M. H. (2018). The importance of muscular strength: Training considerations. *Sports Medicine*, *48*(4), 765–785. https://doi.org/10.1007/s40279-018-0862-z

Tetlock, P. E. (2005). *Expert political judgement: How good is it? How can we know?* (pp. xvi, 321). Princeton University Press.

Thorndike, E. L. (1904). *An introduction to the theory of mental and social measurements* (p. 277). The Science Press.

Tiller, N. (2020). *The skeptic's guide to sports science: Confronting myths of the health and fitness industry*. Routledge & CRC Press. https://www.routledge.com/The-Skeptics-Guide-to-Sports-Science-Confronting-Myths-of-the-Health-and/Tiller/p/book/9781138333130

US Census Bureau. (1991). *Cold War: U.S. and USSR populations 1970–1990*. Statista. https://www.statista.com/statistics/1072400/population-us-ussr-cold-war/

Vasenina, E., Kataoka, R., & Buckner, S. L. (2020). Adaptation energy: Experimental evidence and applications in exercise science. *Journal of Trainology*, *9*(2), 66–70. https://doi.org/10.17338/trainology.9.2_66

Verkhoshansky, Y., & Verkhoshansky, N. (2011). *Special strength training: Manual for coaches*. Verkhoshansky.

Weisberg, D. S., Keil, F. C., Goodstein, J., Rawson, E., & Gray, J. R. (2008). The seductive allure of neuroscience explanations. *Journal of Cognitive Neuroscience*, *20*(3), 470–477. https://doi.org/10.1162/jocn.2008.20040

Weisberg, D. S., Taylor, J. C. V., & Hopkins, E. J. (2015). Deconstructing the seductive allure of neuroscience explanations. *Judgment and Decision Making*, *10*(5), 429–441. https://doi.org/10.1017/S193029750000557X

Whitehead, A., & Coe, J. (2021). *Myths of sport coaching*. Sequoia Books. https://www.sequoia-books.com/catalog/whiteheadcoe/

Willoughby, D. S. (1993). The effects of mesocycle-length weight training programs involving periodization and partially equated volumes on upper and lower body strength. *The Journal of Strength & Conditioning Research*, *7*(1), 2.

Yakolev, N. (1949). Biochemical foundations of muscle training. *Uspekhi Sovr Biol, 27*, 257–271.

Zourdos, M. C., Jo, E., Khamoui, A. V., Lee, S.-R., Park, B.-S., Ormsbee, M. J., Panton, L. B., Contreras, R. J., & Kim, J.-S. (2016). Modified daily undulating periodization model produces greater performance than a traditional configuration in powerlifters. *The Journal of Strength & Conditioning Research, 30*(3), 784. https://doi.org/10.1519/JSC.0000000000001165

7 The Myth That Being a Good Mother and an Elite Athlete Are Not Compatible

Kelly Massey and Amy E. Whitehead

Introduction

Despite the emergence of high-profile athlete mothers – such as Fanny Blankers-Koen, a Dutch track and field athlete known as the Flying Housewife in the 1940s – historically motherhood has been linked to sport-career termination. However, more and more female elite athletes (e.g. Serena Williams, Allyson Felix, Dame Sarah Storey and Helen Glover) are demonstrating how they can simultaneously manage both motherhood and a successful career as an athlete. So why does the belief that motherhood signifies the end of a sporting career continue, and why are we only recently starting to challenge this myth?

Historically, women's involvement in sport within the Western world was constrained by gender norms and medical myths (Gregg & Taylor, 2019). Nineteenth-century medical opinions of women were one of frailty and that women are unsuitable for participation in sport. In the previous book *Myths of Sport Coaching*, Bowes (2021) explains how doctors warned against serious strenuous activity for women because of their perceived fragility due to menstruation, which resulted in women being restricted in the types of activities they could participate in. For instance, women were even told that cycling would cause a physiological condition called 'bicycle face' where the strain of cycling would cause paleness, permanently drawn lips and dark circles under the eyes (Bailey et al., 2013). This practice is believed to represent a manifestation of gender discrimination that was used to discourage women from engaging in 'non ladylike' behaviours such as cycling (Bailey et al., 2013).

Stereotypical socio-cultural norms, coupled with gender stereotypes, historically confined women to being seen to have a 'place' in society and a role to be mothers and wives. These gender stereotypes have led to the idea that being an athlete and a mother is incompatible resulting in many athletes terminating their career to start a family (Nash, 2011). From a socio-cultural 'normative' perspective, the strain between a mother giving their child what they need and managing the demands of competitive sport has been evident in research, along with pressures to uphold traditional a 'good mother' identity (Talbot & Maclennan, 2016), consisting of childcare, ensuring their child's needs are met first, and compromising training and sporting goals (Darroch & Hillsburg, 2017).

As a result of the historical perpetuation of both the socio-cultural gender norms and outdated beliefs that female athletes are unable to sustain the rigours of sport, athletes continue to experience negative stereotypes/perceptions when they become athlete mothers. However, in this chapter, we discuss how this discourse is starting to change and present contemporary literature that explores how elite athlete mothers have successfully renegotiated their identity as both mothers and athletes to maintain a successful career.

Good mother vs good athlete

So, what does it take to be a 'good mother' and what does it take to be an elite athlete? Historical expectations highlight that a 'good mother' identity is related to 'intensive mothering' practices which are child-centred, self-sacrificing, emotionally absorbing and all-consuming for the mother (Hays, 1996; Spowart & McGannon, 2022). An athlete identity refers to the extent to which an individual aligns themself to an athlete which tends to be high within the elite athlete population (Rasquinha & Cardinal, 2017). This identity is often associated with characteristics such as addictive exercise behaviours, sacrifice in the pursuit of sporting excellence (Ryan, 2018) and an exclusive identity that limits the development of other roles (Rasquinha & Cardinal, 2017). Considering the requirements for being a good mother and a good athlete, it would seem illogical that someone could simultaneously adopt both identities, thus supporting the myth that it is impossible to be 'good' at both. Yet, as society evolves and cultural stereotypes change, elite athlete mothers challenge and renegotiate this 'good mother' concept.

Training and competing as an elite athlete and being a mother have been highlighted to be mutually beneficial for one another. This is connected to an ethic of care where mothers through their sporting engagements act as role models to their children. This is displayed through behaviours that demonstrate a high work ethic, commitment, a healthy lifestyle and good time management (Darroch & Hillsburg, 2017). Sport is also considered a necessity to support positive mental well-being and the ability to cope with the challenges of motherhood. Martinez-Pascual et al. (2014) showed how Spanish elite athlete mothers consider sport as a part of who they are and challenge those who consider them to be a 'bad mother' for continuing their involvement in sport postpartum, highlighting the need to look after themselves to be able to look after their child. Thus, challenging hegemonic discourse and renegotiating what it means to be a 'good mother' to include taking time for oneself to exercise. As sport has been shown to enhance well-being as a mother, so too has becoming a mother on well-being as an elite athlete. Darroch and Hillsburg (2017) found elite athlete mothers develop a relaxed approach to their sport and find themselves in an empowered position, as confidence and comfortableness increased along with a sense of completeness – an approach that has been associated with enhancements in performance, which may also be influenced by the increased commitment and focus to each identity (Massey & Whitehead, 2022). Thus, rather than the historic notion that believes the presence of the mother or athlete identity diminishes the capabilities of the other (Talbot & Maclennan), they in fact enhance each other.

There is an understandable shift in priorities upon becoming a mother, yet the need to uphold sporting commitments such as training, recovery and sponsorship demands (Darroch & Hillsburg, 2017) and balancing the needs of the child and athlete is not without challenge. However, what if fulfilling the requirements of the athlete coincided with addressing the needs of the child? For many, being an elite athlete is a source of financial income. Therefore, actions such as taking time away from their child to address sporting commitments that may be considered selfish to outsiders are considered necessary by athlete mothers to be successful in elite sport (Massey & Whitehead, 2022). Although these actions often result in guilt (Martinez-Pascual et al., 2014), they allow athlete mothers to justify family sacrifices and financially provide for their family (Massey & Whitehead, 2022). Therefore, rather than the traditional 'good mother' identity requiring athletes to retire, the definition of this identity has been renegotiated to include space for the athlete, and in some instances the necessity of time for self. Overcoming the myth of the impossibility of simultaneously being a 'good mother' and 'good athlete' is not achieved without challenge. Individualized strategies such as identity renegotiation, childcare and financial security are required.

The elite athlete mother identity

Three-time Olympic Kayaker and World Champion Alyce Wood (nee Burnett) explains how she felt about embarking on motherhood:

> My biggest worry was juggling a child with my demanding schedule, but I've learnt that if I'm upfront and honest with my situation, there is always a work around. If motherhood has taught me anything, it's that there's more than one pathway to success.

Throughout pregnancy and postpartum, several identities come into play (e.g. physical identity, social identity, personal identity, athletic identity), which shift and encounter periods of renegotiation. For example, Appleby and Fisher (2009) examined the athletic experiences of elite distance runners who returned to competition after having children. Prior to motherhood, these athletes defined themselves and their identity through their running performance and accomplishments. However, motherhood led to a multidimensional identity which led to an increase in both life quality and performance. Additionally, McGannon et al. (2019) examined the nuanced psychosocial aspects of one elite athlete's (Jo Pavey) athletic journey into motherhood. This study illustrated how Pavey was able to construct an elite athlete mother identity grounded in family relationships to facilitate training and competition goals. The narrative presented within Pavey's story (McGannon et al., 2019) provided resistance to a narrow performance narrative (Carless & Douglas, 2012, 2013), which rendered pregnancy, motherhood and elite athletics incompatible (Cosh & Crabb, 2012; Douglas & Carless, 2009).

Massey and Whitehead (2022) followed the longitudinal postpartum journey (2–16 months postpartum) of two elite athletes to explore how becoming a mother impacted their perceived personal and physical identity. They found that the first few months post-birth created feelings of uncertainty about physical identity, athlete identity and the goals associated with elite sport. Gaining the mother identity brought about a loss of the athlete identity on a cognitive and physical level. However, over time, identities were renegotiated in terms of priorities, goals and space to accommodate both the mother and athlete roles. Massey and Whitehead (2022) found athlete mothers compartmentalize these identities, which was deemed healthy practice as it allowed them to feel 'fresh' in each role. Yet, the dual identity of being an athlete mother and the positivity of having their child present and a part of their sporting environment was considered 'quite special'. Although athletes had their own unique journeys and challenges, they were able to successfully manage their roles as both athlete and mother.

What is evident within both the literature and the media is the ability of elite athlete mothers to be successful in the negotiation of both motherhood and elite athlete status. How this negotiation occurs is nuanced and individual to the athlete. However, there appears to be key determinants that are evident within the literature that can be seen to support this athlete mother identity. So, what are these determinants that allow elite athlete mothers to exist?

Alyce Wood (nee Burnett) explains how her team were vital in her success:

> When I first made the decision to continue sport whilst becoming a Mum, I had a list of worries that felt endless, but the further I got through my journey and the more I learnt about myself and what's possible, the more comfortable I became. Physiologically, there were a lot of unknowns through both the pregnancy and post-partum periods, but the trust I built in my team gave me a lot of confidence that we were on the right path.

Social support has been identified as a key influence in the successful transition to elite athlete mother. This comes in the form of a supportive family, teammates and athlete support personal such as coaches as they may provide emotional support and ease logistical challenges. Spouses are often considered essential for providing both emotional and financial support, and facilitating training opportunities (Darroch & Hillsburg, 2017). This support in turn enhances the drive to succeed, motivated by the dedication of their spouse. Tekavc, Wylleman and Erpic (2020) show that parents offer support in terms of understanding, a trusted source of childcare and even adjusting their own lifestyle to accommodate their daughters' sporting pursuits. When this support is not available, athlete mothers take longer to return to sport. Other elite athlete mothers are considered vital to the support network due to their shared experience. They are considered the most trusted and valued source to fill gaps in knowledge of how to train safely before medical professionals and coaches (Darroch et al., 2016). There has been evidence of increased support for elite athlete mothers including from those working within high-performance sport (e.g. coaches). However, this environment may not always be accepting, particularly for those who compete on the international stage but fall outside of the remit for support from high-performance organizations (Massey et al., under review).

Massey and Whitehead (2022) found that there is little flexibility to sacrifice requirements to be successful in the mother and athlete identity. However, lifestyle sacrifices such as reduced socializing (e.g. cinema trips) are considered acceptable. Additional lifestyle adjustments, such as developing a structure and increasing organization, along with a reduced emphasis on sport dictating routine aid the transition to an elite athlete mother – although these adjustments often require social support.

Within elite sport, discriminative conditions such as the omission of pregnancy-related contract conditions (Culvin & Bowes, 2021), financial penalty (Scott et al., 2022) and the oversight of pregnancy within selection criteria (McGannon et al., 2023) highlight the remanence of the myth of motherhood in high-performance sport. Specifically, the absence of maternity policy in two-thirds of Canadian sports organizations (Davenport et al., 2022) and cultures of silence within the UK around discussing pregnancy are the underlying assumptions that pregnancy signifies the terminations of athletes' sporting career (Culvin & Bowes, 2021; Pullen et al., 2023). Yet, gradual improvements have been made which have supported the successful transition to athlete mother. As previously mentioned, it is now a possibility for pregnant and postpartum athletes to still earn an income. Examples of these are through the continuation of funding during pregnancy and into the postpartum period within North American and some European sporting organization (Davenport et al., 2022) and employment status and protection within professional contracts (Culvin & Bowes, 2021). Furthermore, the myth that motherhood does not belong in the elite sport environment is thwarted by the developing cultural acceptance of motherhood in the high-performance sport environment (Pullen, Miller & Plateau, 2021).

Recommendations

Below are recommendations that can be put into place by elite athletes who become or wish to become mothers during their time in elite sport. These can be used as guidance for athlete support personal and elite sport organizations to support female elite athletes their decision and journey.

- Identify what it means to you (i.e. the athlete) to be a 'good mother' in relation to your personal values and your individual needs in relation to your physical and mental well-being.
- Prepare for the expected loss of physical and mental athlete identity. Develop the understanding that this is a necessary temporary phase during the journey to becoming a mother. Yet, over time and with support the athlete identity can return.
- Create a supportive network of family, friends, athlete support personal and other elite athlete mothers.
- Develop research and athlete-informed individualized support strategies for childcare, training logistics, emotional support and financial security.[1]

Note

1 We would like to thank Alyce Wood (nee Burnett) for providing quotes for this chapter. Hearing from real-world elite athletes who are negotiating motherhood and being an elite athlete is vital for informing policy and support for future elite athlete mothers.

References

Appleby, K. M., & Fisher, L. A. (2009). "Running in and out of motherhood": Elite distance runners' experiences of returning to competition after pregnancy. *Women in Sport & Physical Activity Journal, 18(1)*, 3–17.

Bailey, J., Steeves, V., Burkell, J., & Regan, P. (2013). Negotiating with gender stereotypes on social networking sites: From "bicycle face" to Facebook. *Journal of Communication Inquiry, 37*(2), 91–112. https://doi.org/10.1177/0196859912473777

Bowes, A. (2021). The stepping stone? Challenging the myth that women's sport is less significant than men's sport. In A. Whitehead & J. Coe (Eds.), *Myths of Sport Coaching*. Sequoia.

Carless, D., & Douglas, K. (2012). Stories of success: Cultural narratives and personal stories of elite and professional athletes. *Reflective Practice, 13,* 387–398. http://doi.org/10.1080/14623943.2012.657793

Carless, D., & Douglas, K. (2013). Living, resisting, and playing the part of athlete: Narrative tensions in elite sport. *Psychology of Sport and Exercise, 14,* 701–708. http://doi.org/10.1016/j.psychsport.2013.05.003

Cosh, S., & Crabb, S. (2012). Motherhood within elite sport discourse: The case of Keli Lane. *Psychology of Women Section Review, 14,* 41–49.

Culvin, A., & Bowes, A. (2021). The incompatibility of motherhood and professional women's football in England. *Frontiers in Sports and Active Living, 3,* 730151–730151. https://doi.org/10.3389/fspor.2021.730151

Darroch, F., Giles, A., & McGettigan-Dumas, R. (2016). Elite female distance runners and advice during pregnancy: Sources, content, and trust. *Women in Sport & Physical Activity Journal, 24*(2), 170–177. https://doi.org/10.1123/wspaj.2015-0040

Darroch, F., & Hillsburg, H. (2017). Keeping pace: Mother versus athlete identity among elite long distance runners. *Women's Studies International Forum, 62,* 61–68. https://doi.org/10.1016/j.wsif.2017.03.005

Davenport, M. H., Ray, L., Nesdoly, A., Thornton, J. S., Khurana, R., & McHugh, T. F. (2022). Pushing for change: A qualitative study of experiences of elite athletes during pregnancy. *British Journal of Sports Medicine, 56,* 452–457. http://dx.doi.org/10.1136/bjsports-2021-104755

Douglas, K., & Carless, D (2009). Abandoning the performance narrative: Two women's stories of transition from professional sport. *Journal of Applied Sport Psychology, 21*(2), 213—231. https://doi.org/10.1080/10413200902795109

Gregg, E. A., & Taylor, E. (2019). History and evolution of women's sport. In Nancy L. & Andrea N. G. (Eds.), *Routledge handbook of the business of women's sport* (pp. 11–22).

Hays, S. (1996). *The cultural contradictions of motherhood*. New Haven and London: Yale University Press.

Massey, K., Cronin, C., & Whitehead, A. (2024). 'Baby Ban' and 'we are not the same': Creative non-fiction dialogue exploring pregnancy and motherhood for a funded Paralympic and unfunded Olympic athlete. *Qualitative Research in Sport, Exercise and Health*, 1–16.

Massey, K., & Whitehead, A. (2022). Pregnancy and motherhood in elite sport: The longitudinal experiences of two elite athletes. *Psychology of Sport and Exercise, 60*. https://doi.org/10.1016/j.psychsport.2022.102139.

McGannon, K. R., Kulkarni, S., Hladun, W., Bundon, A., & Pegoraro, A. (2023). Exposing a motherhood penalty in sport: a feminist narrative inquiry of media stories of Canadian athlete mothers' journeys to the 2020 Tokyo Games. *Communication & Sport*. https://doi.org/10.1177/21674795231187916

McGannon, K. R., Tatarnic, E., & McMahon, J. (2019). The long and winding road: An autobiographic study of an elite athlete mother's journey to winning gold. *Journal of Applied Sport Psychology. 31(4),* 385–404. https://doi.org/10.1080/10413200.2018.1512535

Martinez Pascual, B., Alvarez Harris, S., Fernández De Las Peñas, C., & Palacios-Ceña, D. (2014). Maternity in Spanish elite sportswomen: A qualitative study. *Women & Health, 54*(3), 262–279. https://doi.org/10.1080/03630242.2014.883660

Nash, M. (2011). "You don't train for a marathon sitting on the couch": Performances of pregnancy 'fitness' and 'good' motherhood in Melbourne, Australia. *Women's Studies International Forum, 34*(11), 50–65. https://doi.org/10.1016/j.wsif.2010.10.004

Pullen, E., Miller, B., & Plateau, C. (2021). Experiences of pregnancy in elite female athletes on the world class programmes – Research report, 1—17. www.uksport.ov.uk: Loughborough University.

Pullen, E., Miller, B., Wiltshire, G., & Plateau, C. (2023). A feminist materialist inspired analysis of the meaning and management of pregnancy and reproductive health in Olympic and Paralympic female athletes. *Qualitative Research in Sport, Exercise and Health, 15*(3), 332–344. https://doi.org/10.1080/2159676X.2022.2146162

Rasquinha, A. M., & Cardinal, B. J. (2017). Association of athletic identity by competitive sport level and cultural popularity. *Journal of Sport Behavior, 40*(2), 191–204.

Ryan, C. (2018). Navigating the athlete role: identity construction within New Zealand's elite sport environment. *Qualitative Research in Sport, Exercise and Health, 10*(3), 306–317. http://dio.org/10.1080/2159676X.2017.1399923

Scott, T., Smith, S., Darroch, F., & Giles, A. (2022). Selling vs. supporting motherhood: How corporate sponsors frame the parenting experiences of elite and Olymic athletes. *Communication and Sport,* 1–22. http://doi.org/10.1177/21674795221103415

Spowart, L., & McGannon, K. R. (Eds.). (2022). *Motherhood and sport: Collective stories of identity and difference.* Taylor & Francis.

Talbot, L., & Maclennan, K. (2016). Physiology of pregnancy. *Anaesthesia & Intensive Care Medicine, 17*(7), 341–345. https://doi.org/10.1016/j.mpaic.2019.05.001

Tekavc, J., Wylleman, P., & Cecic Erpic, S. (2020). Becoming a mother-athlete: Female athletes' transition to motherhood in Slovenia. *Sport in Society*. https://doi.org/10.1080/17430437.2020.1720200

8 Stretching the Truth

A Critical Examination of Stretching for Athletes

Tim Pigott

The myth

'Stretching is a waste of time – it doesn't prevent injuries or improve performance, it can even make you weaker, athletes should just focus on strength training.'

The reality

While it is tempting to boil down complex topics into bit-sized nuggets of information, the truth is far from simple. Yes, there are some studies that failed to find any links between stretching and injury risk reduction, or even reduced explosive power, but that isn't the whole story, and their methodology needs further critical appraisal.

Why the myth persists

Headlines and social media 'influencers' love a good controversy. The more polarizing the better. But when it comes to topics such as stretching, the devil is in the details – or, in this case, the muscle fibres, tissue mechanics and the individuals' physiology, history and sporting demands.

Stretching has become a polarizing topic over the past decade, with many headlines in mainstream media and social media 'influencers' along the lines of 'stretching does not prevent injury' or well-meaning coaches have stated that stretching is bad and has a negative impact on strength or performance. However, this is an oversimplification of the evidence base, and a much more nuanced approach is required.

> **Origin of the myth**
>
> Over the years, there has been a number of conflicting articles both within research and the media, for example:
>
> *'Stretching before exercise does not reduce the risk of local muscle injury: a critical review of the clinical and basic science literature.' (Shrier, 1999)*
>
> *'To stretch or not to stretch: the role of stretching in injury prevention and performance.' (McHugh & Cosgrave, 2010)*
>
> *'Stretching to prevent or reduce muscle soreness after exercise.' (Herbert et al., 2011)*
>
> *'The impact of stretching on sports injury risk: a systematic review of the literature.' (Thacker et al., 2004)*
>
> This then leads to mainstream media commenting on these findings:
>
> BBC (2019) 'why stretching might not make you a better runner?'
> Hutchinson, A. 2020 – outside online
> McMahan, I. (2014) – stretching is overrated
>
> Also, many social media influencers misinterpret the data and push the binary position that 'you should stop stretching'.

The myth and complexity

Every individual possesses a unique biomechanical profile, influenced by genetic, environmental, injury history and lifestyle factors. One such area of variability lies in natural joint mobility, with a spectrum ranging from hypermobility where joints easily move beyond the normal range to hypomobility characterized by restricted joint movement. Yet, when exploring the role of stretching for injury reduction or sports performance, this variability is often overlooked.

Stretching prior to athletic activities has long been standard practice for both competitive and recreational athletes, advocated to prevent injury, alleviate muscle soreness and even enhance performance (Rubini et al., 2007; Trehearn & Buresh, 2009). Indeed, flexibility is crucial in activities like jumping, sprinting and agility (García-Pinillos et al., 2015), with disciplines like gymnastics, martial arts and ballet demanding high levels of flexibility (Hart et al., 2018; Spanias et al., 2019). Furthermore, restricted motion in certain muscle groups is associated with various injuries (Maselli et al., 2020; Hamilton & Velasquez, 2011; Wahlstedt & Rasmussen-Barr, 2015 Witvrouw et al., 2003; Kaufman et al., 1999; Backman & Danielson, 2011; Malliaras et al., 2006).

However, the efficacy of stretching in improving performance or reducing injury risk has faced scrutiny in several reviews (Yeung & Yeung, 2001; Shrier, 2001; Herbert & Gabriel, 2002; Thacker et al., 2004; Gremion, 2005; Herbert et al., 2011; Behm, 2015). This has led to a dichotomy where mainstream advice often contradicts the practices observed in elite athletes' warm-up routines.

So, why does this apparent discrepancy exist? Hemingway's words of caution against oversimplification resonate deeply in this context: 'Be careful, he said to himself, it is all very well for you to write simply and the simpler the better. But do not start to think so damned simply. Know how complicated it is and then state it simply.' The science of stretching, like many areas of sports science, is complex. It encompasses tissue mechanics, individual physiology, nutrition, psychological state and much more. A critical examination reveals that many of these studies suffer from methodological limitations, such as failing to account for the type of stretching employed, the timing relative to exercise or the specific athletic discipline under investigation.

Therefore, while the available literature on stretching may at times appear contradictory or even dismissive of its benefits, it's crucial to recognize the inherent complexity. The goal of this chapter is not to dismiss or champion stretching universally but to critique the literature and contextualize it. Adopting a Dostoevsky approach, examination of various factors that influence the efficacy of stretching ranging from tissue mechanics and sporting demands to individual physiology, nutrition, psychological state and more, thus viewing the science and the individual as a cohesive whole. Ultimately, it enables you to understand how and when to apply research findings to specific individuals and situations.

Historical context of stretching

The practice of stretching dates back millennia and has roots in diverse cultures worldwide. Ancient civilizations, including the Egyptians, Greeks and Chinese, have documented the use of stretching for both therapeutic and preparatory purposes.

The athletes in the original Olympic Games, held as far back as 776 BC, were depicted in vases and sculptures as practicing stretching exercises to prepare for their competitions. In the East, stretching has been an integral component of traditional practices like yoga and martial arts which place a significant emphasis on flexibility and stretching. The origins of yoga can be traced back to ancient India, around 5000 years ago (Feuerstein, 1996). The postures, or 'asanas', in yoga involve a combination of stretches, holds and breathing techniques aimed at aligning and balancing the body, mind and spirit. Postural yoga is an adaptable, low-impact intervention that increases strength, stabilization (Hayden et al., 2005), flexibility and balance (Roland et al., 2011; Ross & Thomas, 2010). Studies examining yoga for musculoskeletal conditions have noted pain relief and functional benefits, and, in the context of ageing, have found benefits for balance and mental health improvements in the elderly (Denham-Jones et al., 2022).

Fast-forwarding to the 20th century, the scientific community began to study the physiological effects of stretching more systematically. The 1950s and 1960s saw a surge in research focussed on flexibility and its role in athletic performance and injury prevention (Gleim & McHugh, 1997). Flexibility is often measured as joint range of motion but can also be measured in terms of muscle fascicle length. The methods we use to measure flexibility are often determined by the passive mechanical properties of the joint shape, ligaments, muscles, tendons and nerves and thus the individual's tolerance to stretch and ability to relax the muscles being stretched. The contribution to each of these components will vary across different joints, individuals and clinical conditions.

As sports medicine evolved, so did the understanding of stretching's biomechanics and its implications for athletes and the general population alike. Prolonged sitting, for example, has been associated with limited hip extension (Boukabache et al., 2021). Thus, in recent decades, with the growth of sedentary lifestyles and an increased understanding of holistic well-being, stretching has become a staple for not just athletes but also for those seeking to alleviate the physical strains of modern life.

In conclusion, stretching is not a modern phenomenon, it is a practice deeply rooted in human history, evolving over time and transcending cultures. Its sustained relevance speaks to its fundamental role in human health, performance and well-being. While some studies have questioned its importance, the absence of evidence (for performance or injury prevention) is not evidence of absence. As Hemingway said 'do not start to think so damned simply'.

The underlying issue: defining 'stretching'

The first challenge we have in this debate is what do we mean by 'stretching'. At its core, 'stretching' refers to techniques used to enhance muscle flexibility. However, this broad term encapsulates several distinct methodologies, each with its own mechanisms and outcomes. There are three main types of stretching used to increase flexibility. Static stretching, whereby the muscle is slowly elongated to tolerance and the position held with the muscle in this greatest tolerated length (ACSM, 2000). Proprioceptive Neuromuscular Facilitation (PNF) techniques utilize contract-relax or hold-relax involving either an isometric contraction of the muscle to be stretched prior to a static stretch being administered or a contraction of the antagonistic muscle prior to a passive stretch. The theory proposed is that a PNF stretch can alter the muscle spindle (Ia and II afferents) and the Golgi tendon organ (Ib afferents) output to the central nervous system (De Deyne, 2001), thus influencing the activity of the a-motorneurons. Although the original hypothesis was that PNF stretching would decrease Electromyography activity of the muscles, studies have shown it is actually increased (Shrier, 1999). The third type of stretching, the ballistic method, uses bouncing or jerking movements, which can theoretically exceed the extensibility limits of the muscle in an uncontrolled manner and thus cause injury. For this reason, it is not widely supported in the literature (Anderson & Burke, 1991: Bandy & Irions, 1994; ACSM, 2000).

Along with the classic stretching methods described above, there is growing evidence to support the use of eccentric muscle training, lengthening the muscle under tension, to alter the optimum length of tension development, resulting in longer muscle lengths (Brughelli & Cronin, 2007; Diong et al., 2022). Static stretching induces only transient alterations in tissue length, attributable either to changes in neural stretch tolerance or to 'creep,' a temporary elongation of tissue fibres with stress lower than that of microscopic failure. See stress–strain graph shown in Figure 8.1.

When a tissue is subjected to a passive stretch, it will deform according to its material properties in a time-dependent manner known as creep (De Deyne, 2001). When the force is no longer applied, the tissue will return to its original length, also in a time-dependent manner. For a stretch force to reach the muscle, it is transmitted via the perimysium and endomysium (connective tissues), and the stiffness of muscle tissue is affected by the relationship between the contractile (actin–myosin interactions) and non-contractile cytoskeletal components (titin–dystrophin). However, it has also been shown that changes in the range of

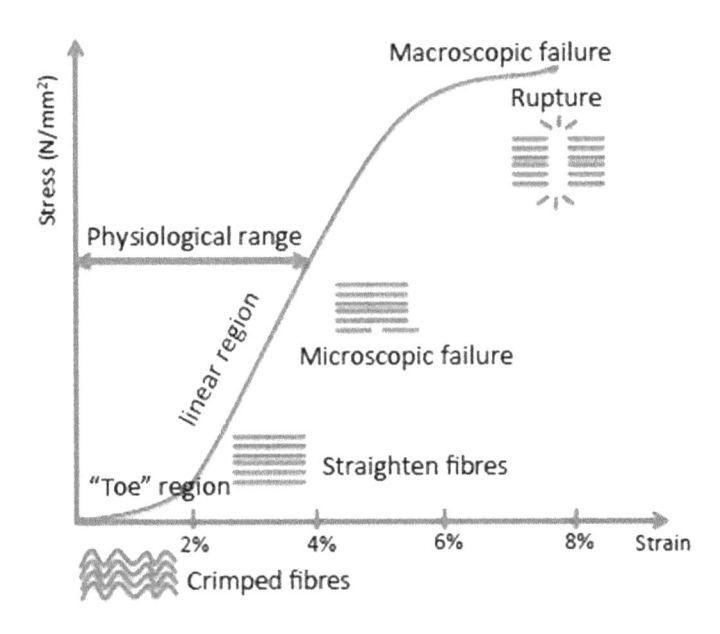

Figure 8.1. An introduction to biomechanics and mechanobiology – Scientific Figure on ResearchGate. Available from: https://www.researchgate.net/figure/Typical-stress-straincurve-for-tendons-and-ligaments_fig4_328496314 [accessed 26 Nov. 2023].

motion achieved through stretching programs are a consequence of an increase in stretch tolerance, being able to tolerate the sensation of the stretch, rather than a change in the mechanical or viscoelastic properties of the muscle (Støve et al., 2019; Magnusson et al., 1996).

Eccentric muscle strength training has been shown to lead to a longer-lasting change in muscle length due to the generation of sarcomeres in series, more protein strands within each muscle and thus creating structurally longer tissues (Brughelli & Cronin, 2007). Another possible method for myofibrilogenesis (new muscle fibres) is through the release of growth factors, such as insulin-like-growth factor 1 (IGF-1), platelet-derived growth factor and fibroblastic growth factor that stimulate either myoblast proliferation or muscle maturation (De Deyne, 2001).

While stretching is often associated with simple muscle elongation, the science behind it is multifaceted. Different methods operate via unique mechanisms, influencing how our muscles respond and adapt. By understanding these nuances, practitioners can tailor their approach to better serve their individual needs. Frequently, the criticisms levied against stretching are specifically targeting static stretching techniques. Yet, all forms of mobility work may have their place and the language we use to describe stretching matters. The following section will thus address each of these critiques in turn.

Critiquing the protocols used

There have been significant variations between the studies regarding the stretching protocols employed by the researchers which make it challenging to compare their findings. Many of the primary research papers commonly referenced are over 20 years old and often do not reflect training practices athletes generally employ. The shortest stretch being 10-second stretch by Bello et al. (2011) in their control group versus the PNF stretch in their intervention group, 20 seconds by Pope et al. (2000), Amako et al. (2003) and 30 seconds by Jamveldt (2009). Bandy et al. (1997) found that, for the hamstrings, a minimum stretch duration of 30 seconds was required to increase range of motion (ROM), whereas Thomas et al. (1998) found that at least 60 seconds 5 days a week was required to have an effect. Therefore, the studies referenced that show no beneficial effect of stretching and that have protocols using short-duration stretching should be questioned as to their real-world application. Studies that included longer-duration stretching protocols include 40 seconds by Pope et al. (1998) and 45 seconds by Cross and Worrell (1999). Arnason et al. (2008) used 60 seconds pre-exercise and 135 seconds as a separate flexibility session, with the longest stretch duration employed by Hartig and Henderson (1999) with 150 seconds ×3 per day.

In older adults, over the age of 65 years, the longer-duration hold of 60 seconds was shown to be superior to 15- and 30-second stretches in terms of rate of gains of ROM and sustained increase in ROM (Feland et al., 2001).

Much of the contradictory opinions on the time duration of stretching can be explained by considering the viscoelasticity of the tissues. Pure elastic substances will lengthen for a given force and return immediately to their original length upon release of that force. However; muscles, tendons and other connective tissues have viscoelastic properties, with the viscous elements having flow and movement dependent on time. If a tissue is placed under stretch and held at a constant length, then the tension at that length will decrease over time. This decrease in tension is known as the stress relaxation. The immediate short-term changes seen after 60 seconds of stretching are therefore attributed to the passive viscoelastic changes, which reduce muscle stiffness and decrease actin–myosin bridging due to reflex inhibition. Therefore, tissues with altered viscoelastic properties may require longer stretches, or more repetitions, compared to healthy tissues (Malliaropoulos et al., 2004).

Rehabilitation after hamstring injuries includes restoring ROM, with Comfort et al. (2009) recommending a static stretching protocol of 4 × 30–45 seconds, repeated three to five times per week. In the acute phase, after 48 hours, this can be increased to 4 × 30 seconds, three to four times per day, which can reduce the time to restore normal ROM compared with stretching only once per day (5.7 vs 7.3 days).

In summary, the science of stretching is multifaceted; it is a complex interplay of biomechanical, physiological and temporal factors. The duration, type and context of stretching all contribute to its efficacy and safety. While acute stretching may offer immediate benefits, chronic stretching protocols appear to provide more sustainable changes in muscle–tendon unit properties. Understanding these nuances is crucial for athletes, clinicians and researchers alike, as it informs more individualized and effective stretching regimens.

Short-term (acute) stretching

Merits
Immediate Flexibility: Acute stretching can quickly increase your ROM, making it ideal for pre-activity warm-ups.

Reduced Muscle Stiffness: Short bouts of stretching can alleviate muscle tightness, enhancing comfort and ease of movement.

Quick Activation: It's like a quick espresso shot for your muscles, prepping them for the activity ahead.

Drawbacks
Temporary Effects: The benefits are often short-lived, dissipating within a few minutes to hours.

Risk of Overstretch: The immediate flexibility gains can sometimes lead to overshooting your natural range, increasing the risk of injury.

Long-term (chronic) stretching

Merits
Sustained Flexibility: Think of this as your base mileage; it builds up over time, leading to lasting improvements in flexibility.

Muscle Adaptation: Chronic stretching can lead to muscle–tendon adaptations, making your body more resilient to strains and injuries.

Improved Athletic Performance: Over time, a more flexible muscle–tendon unit can enhance your power output and efficiency in sports.

Drawbacks

Time Consuming: Just like those long weekend rides, it requires a consistent time commitment.

Risk of Imbalance: Overemphasis on flexibility can sometimes lead to muscle imbalances, affecting your biomechanics and performance.

Stretching makes you weaker!

In the early 2000s, a surge of research emerged highlighting the potential deleterious effects of static stretching on strength and power performance (Behm et al., 2001; Cornwell et al., 2002; Power et al., 2004; Shrier, 2004; Young et al., 2006). However, these studies often had the stretch protocol immediately prior to a maximal contraction. Thus, while an immediate loss of strength or power might be observed, perhaps due to a temporary change in neural signalling or musculotendinous stiffness reduction, this does not replicate the real-world scenario of how stretching is incorporated into a training practice.

In comparison, a systematic review by Thomas et al. (2023) found that chronic stretching exercises (those done for a minimum of four weeks) could significantly improve muscular strength, albeit a small magnitude. Eccentric loading also involves greater muscle forces compared to concentric or isometric, so in addition to the generation of sarcomeres in series, the stretch of the titin filaments also causes a release of calcium ions (Ca^+) which in turn determines additional binding during cross-bridge creation enabling the muscle to resist stretches of greater magnitudes (Thomas et al., 2023).

This has led to more recent recommendations (Blazevich et al., 2018; Reid et al., 2018) to suggest that provided stretching is incorporated into a full warm-up routine then there are no subsequent strength or power impairments, aligning more closely with real-world practices.

We need an individual approach

A significant limitation in the existing literature on stretching and flexibility training in athletes is the lack of an individualized approach. Human mobility exists on a continuum, ranging from individuals with natural stiffness to those with inherent flexibility. At one end of this spectrum is hypermobility syndrome, also known as congenital laxity of ligaments and joints. Although joint hypermobility is relatively common in the general population, reports of related musculoskeletal complaints are infrequent (Grahame & Bird, 2001). Hypermobility can be idiopathic or part of a syndrome, such as Ehlers-Danlos or Marfan's (Castori, 2012). Its relevance to primary research into the effects of stretching is related to the classification of the populations' natural flexibility, whereby the introduction of a stretching protocol may have detrimental effects. The relationship between ligamentous laxity and injury risk is complex, with studies indicating both increased and decreased risks (Krivickas & Feinberg, 1996). While increased flexibility might seem advantageous, especially in certain sports, it can lead to joint instability, frequent dislocations and a higher risk of soft tissue injuries (Remvig et al., 2007). The prevalence of hypermobility syndrome in children and adults has been reported in between 2% and 65%, although the variance in reporting is largely due to different scoring and assessment methods (Reuter & Fichthorn, 2019). In patients with hypermobility syndrome, it has been suggested that there is alteration of proprioceptive acuity (Hall et al., 1995). Reduced sensory feedback may lead to biomechanically unsound limb positions being adopted, which could result in injury. It appears reasonable; therefore, to advise individuals with hypermobility to use stretching exercises cautiously, distinguishing between stretching muscles and stretching joints, as the former may be beneficial, but the latter may be harmful (Russek, 1999). Emphasis should therefore be on strengthening exercises to stabilize the hypermobile joints, rather than increasing flexibility.

Conversely, individuals with hypomobility often benefit from regular stretching to improve joint ROM and decrease the risk of musculoskeletal complaints. In the context of injury prevention, several studies have established a correlation between restricted ROM and elevated injury risk (Pope et al., 1998; Tak et al., 2017; Storm et al., 2018; Pozzi et al., 2020). However, it's essential to identify the cause of the hypomobility, as certain conditions, such as ankylosing spondylitis, may require specialized interventions (Braun & Sieper, 2007).

Thus, understanding the individual's natural mobility state is pivotal to any training program. It will inform the risk-benefit ratio of different stretching protocols and ensure the goals of flexibility training align with the individual's health and performance needs. As such, the coach or medical practitioner must perform a thorough assessment of joint mobility, stability and screen for underlying conditions prior to prescribing any stretching exercises.

Physiological shifts over time

Most of the research on stretching has either been on athletes or university age participants, and thus there is little research examining older populations. There are physiologic changes which occur with ageing that include muscle atrophy, loss of strength and elasticity and increased joint stiffness with increased amounts of fibrous connective tissues (Feland et al., 2001). These physiological changes subsequently alter tissue biomechanics and responsiveness to various training stimuli, such as stretching and flexibility exercises. A survey conducted by Herbert et al. (2020) revealed that contractures, chronic shortening of tissues impacting on joint ROM, were reported in 6.7% of individuals aged 55 and over, escalating to 13.4% in those aged 85 and above. This was greater in men, 7.1% rising to 15.2% vs women 6.3% rising to 12.3% in the 85 year+ (Herbert et al., 2020).

The ageing process involves a range of cellular and molecular changes which contribute to muscle atrophy, decreased tissue elasticity and increased joint stiffness. At the heart of it is an imbalance between protein synthesis and breakdown, exacerbated by declining anabolic hormones and the inhibitory effects of myostatin (White & LeBrasseur, 2016). The loss of muscle and tendon elasticity is linked to increased collagen cross-linking and the accumulation of Advanced Glycation end-products, which stiffen the tissues (Verzijl et al., 2000). Additionally, joint stiffness is related to changes in the joint capsule, synovoial fluid alterations, cartilage degeneration, all under the backdrop of chronic low-grade inflammation (Lotz & Loeser, 2012). Increased inflammation can accelerate joint degeneration due to elevated levels of inflammatory cytokines including IL-6 and TNF-α (Franceschi et al., 2007). Appreciating these intricate cellular pathways provides insight into the age-related musculoskeletal changes and thus the application of any research to specific populations.

While changes in flexibility have been noted in shorter-duration stretch protocols in younger individuals, the study by Feland et al. (2001) found that in people aged 65 years or older a 60-second stretch produced greater rate of gains, and the gains persisted for longer. Their results may differ due to the age-related physiological changes which occur.

A study by Andrade et al. (2015 demonstrated that ankle joint ROM is influenced by both the head and hip position, thus the ROM at the ankle is influenced by the peripheral nerves and fascia, not solely the muscles and tendons in the lower leg. In older individuals, increased collagen cross-linking and reduced collagen fibril diameter have been observed. While some studies report no change in tendon stiffness (Couppé et al., 2009), age-related alterations may lead to increased muscular stiffness, compensating for decreased tendon stiffness (Baudry et al., 2012). Therefore, the influence of neurodynamics (the ability for the nerves to slide and stretch) as well as the fascia on joint ROM might be changed by ageing due to the alterations in tissue mechanical properties. This is supported by the study by Hirata, Yamadera and Akagi (2020) who found that in older individuals the influence of nerve stiffness is greater than the influence of muscle stiffness, compared to younger individuals.

Handrakis et al. (2010) found that stretching enhanced dynamic balance in middle-aged adults (40–60 years), contrasting with Gurjão et al. (2009), who reported an immediate short-term reduction in strength post-stretching in older women (64.6 years +/- 7.1 years).

In summary, the influence of ageing on stretching and flexibility is a complex interplay of physiological, biomechanical and neurological factors. While the existing literature predominantly focusses on younger athletic populations, emerging studies on older individuals reveal nuanced outcomes. Age-related changes in muscle–tendon units, collagen properties and neurodynamics necessitate a more individualized approach to stretching, particularly in older populations. The evidence suggests that older individuals may respond differently to stretching protocols, both in terms of benefits and potential risks. Therefore, it is imperative for future research to address this gap in the literature, providing more comprehensive guidelines that consider the age-related variables influencing stretching and flexibility.

Stretching for injured muscles

Injury management and prevention is a multifaceted challenge, with stretching playing a pivotal role in both the rehabilitation and re-injury risk reduction process. Understanding the biomechanical differences between injured and healed tissues is critical for effective rehabilitation and injury prevention. While the acute management of various injuries is beyond the scope of this chapter, an important message is the challenge doesn't end once the tissue has ostensibly healed. Chronic management, aimed at reducing the risk of re-injury, remains paramount. The study by De Vos et al. (2014) underscores that clinical findings at the point of return to play can predict hamstring re-injury, indicating the importance of a thorough assessment before an athlete's return to full activity. Complementing this with targeted stretching exercises can help address any residual deficits, ensuring that the athlete is not just fit to play but also less susceptible to future injuries.

Thus, understanding the biomechanical integrity of healed tissues compared to their uninjured counterparts is key, especially in understanding the predisposition of healed tissues to re-injury. Jarvinen et al. (2005) provide a comprehensive overview of muscle injuries and their treatment. The study emphasizes that the healing process involves inflammation, regeneration and remodelling phases, which can lead to scar tissue formation and potential changes in the mechanical properties of the muscle. Magnusson et al. (2001) studied the load-displacement properties of the triceps surae aponeurosis and found that previously injured tissues displayed different elastic properties compared to healthy tissues. Muscle and tendon injuries, whether acute or chronic, bring about significant alterations in the tissue's viscoelastic properties. Viscoelasticity dictates how tissues deform and recover in response to external forces, a crucial aspect when considering stretching protocols.

Muscle and tendon injuries bring about significant alterations in tissue's viscoelastic properties. Such changes, whether in muscle connective tissues (Purslow, 2002) or in tendon structures (Andarawis-Puri et al., 2015), influence the tissue's response to stretching. The intertwined nature of muscle and tendon behaviour, especially at musculotendinous junctions, further complicates this biomechanical interplay.

This becomes particularly relevant as changes in connective tissue composition and alignment might modify the tissue's response to stretching. Specifically, the rate at which a stretch is applied can produce different responses in the muscle. Best et al. (1995) highlighted that the viscoelastic properties of muscle tissue can be strain-rate dependent. This suggests that post-injury muscles might benefit from a more controlled stretching rate, emphasizing the potential advantage of longer, gradual (static) stretches over rapid ones.

Muscle and tendon injuries bring about significant alterations in tissue's viscoelastic properties. Such changes, whether in muscle connective tissues (Purslow, 2002) or in tendon structures (Andarawis-Puri et al., 2015), influence the tissue's response to stretching. The intertwined nature of muscle and tendon behaviour, especially at musculotendinous junctions, further complicates this biomechanical interplay.

Furthermore, while the focus has often been on muscles, the intertwined nature of muscle and tendon behaviour cannot be overlooked. Overuse or strain can lead to alterations in tendons' viscoelastic properties, which, in turn, can impact muscle function (Maganaris et al., 2004). Such biomechanical interplay becomes even more critical at the musculotendinous junctions, where muscles and tendons meet. There may also be the need to incorporate dynamic stretches to improve the functional flexibility of the muscle–tendon unit, especially in the context of the altered biomechanical interplay post-injury.

Understanding these biomechanical changes is essential not just for immediate post-injury care but also for long-term management. Noonan and Garrett (1999) emphasized that acknowledging the altered mechanical behaviour of injured muscles, including changes in their viscoelastic properties, is pivotal for tailoring effective rehabilitation strategies. Only by doing so can we hope to prevent re-injury and ensure optimal recovery. Therefore, it's vital to appreciate the complex tapestry of biomechanical alterations that occur. By understanding these changes and their implications, we can be better equipped to educate the athlete and tailor their stretching protocols that are both safe and effective for injured individuals.

Do we need short-term changes or long-term changes?

Stretching can have two types of effects: short-term and long-term effects. Short-term or acute effects (seconds to minutes) could include events such as a change in tendon length (i.e. a change in its stress–strain properties), a change in the series elastic component (SEC) or parallel elastic component (PEC) elements or a change in the distribution of sarcomere lengths within the muscle fibres. Immediate increases in ROM following stretching are partly due to changes in the viscoelastic behaviour of muscles. When a tissue is subjected to a passive stretch, it will deform according to its material properties in a time-dependent manner known as creep (De Deyne, 2001). When the force is no longer applied, the tissue will return to its original length, also in a time-dependent manner. For a stretch force to reach the muscle, it is transmitted via the perimysium and endomysium (connective tissues), and the stiffness of muscle tissue is affected by the relationship between the contractile (actin–myosin interactions) and non-contractile cytoskeletal components (titin–dystrophin).

Long-term effects (days to weeks) could include any of the above plus a change in the composition (i.e. isoforms) of either the tendon or SEC/PEC of the muscle, which could change the viscoelastic properties of the muscle–tendon unit. In order to create a permanently longer muscle fibre, we need to add more of its smallest contractile units called sarcomeres. This process of adding sarcomeres is known as myofibril genesis. This has been shown to happen with static passive stretching in a study by De Deyne (2001); however, the stretches in this study were applied for several days or incrementally increased over a two-week period, which does not mirror pre- or post-exercise practices (but is relevant to specific health conditions such as stretching contractures). Thus, to establish long-term effects we need to be considering the eccentric loading protocols, as stretching under load is arguably still 'stretching'.

A literature review by Witvrouw et al. (2004) proposed a possible explanation for why there is disagreement on the issue of whether stretching prevents injury. They recommend that the type of sports activity in which an individual is participating needs to be considered. Sports that involve a lot of bouncing and jumping activities, like basketball or football, rely heavily on rapid stretching and contracting of muscles, known as stretch-shortening cycles. For these activities, the muscle and tendon need to be flexible and responsive. If the muscle–tendon unit is not compliant enough, the demands in energy absorption and release may rapidly exceed its capacity. This may lead to an increased risk of injury to this structure.

Conclusion

Stretching has often been dismissed as a futile exercise and criticized for the lack of evidence of its direct role in preventing injuries, alleviating muscle soreness or boosting performance. However, this narrow viewpoint overlooks the nuanced roles stretching can play in different contexts and fails to mirror how it is implemented in real-world training. Coaches and therapists should avoid painting with a broad brush; instead, they should appreciate the intricate web of factors that shape an athlete's risk of injury and performance metrics. For medical practitioners, consider employing diagnostic tools like the Beighton Score to assess hypermobility. Coaches could use movement screenings to tailor stretching protocols to athletes' specific needs. While the existing body of research provides some insights, there is a need for more longitudinal studies that track the effects of different stretching protocols over time and in different population groups. It's crucial to note that while stretching can be beneficial, it is not a one-size-fits-all solution. Factors such as age, sport-specific demands and pre-existing conditions can significantly influence its effectiveness.

The advice to athletes, coaches and therapists is therefore to assess each individual and determine whether a stretching program would be beneficial for them or not. In a field rife with myths and oversimplifications, a nuanced, evidence-based approach to stretching can make all the difference.

Reference list

ACSM. (2000). *American College of Sports Medicine's Guidelines for Exercise Testing and Prescription*. Sixth Ed. Lippincott Williams and Wilkins.

Amako, M., Oda, T., Masuoka, K., Yokoi, J., & Campisi, P. (2003). Effect of static stretching on prevention of injuries for military recruits. *Military Medicine*, 168(6), 442–446.

Andarawis-Puri, N., Flatow, E. L., & Soslowsky, L. J. (2015). Tendon basic science: Development, repair, regeneration, and healing. *Journal of Orthopaedic Research*, 33(6), 780–784.

Anderson, B., & Burke, E. R. (1991). Scientific, medical, and practical aspects of stretching. *Clinics in Sports Medicine*, 10, 63–86.

Andrade, R. J., Lacourpaille, L., Freitas, S. R., McNair, P. J., & Nordez, A. (2015). Effects of hip and head position on ankle range of motion, ankle passive torque, and passive gastrocnemius tension. *Scandinavian Journal of Medicine and Science in Sports*, 26(1), 41–47.

Arnason, A., Andersen, T. E., Holme, I., Engebretsen, L., & Bahr, R. (2008). Prevention of hamstring strains in elite soccer: An intervention study. *Scandinavian Journal of Medicine and Science in Sports*, 18, 40–48.

Backman, L. J., & Danielson, P. (2011). Low range of ankle dorsiflexion predisposes for patellar tendinopathy in junior elite basketball players: A 1-year prospective study. *The American Journal of Sports Medicine*, 39(12), 2626–2633.

Bandy, W. D., & Irion, J. M. (1994 Sep). The effect of time on static stretch on the flexibility of the hamstring muscles. *Phys Ther.*, 74(9), 845–50; discussion 850-2. doi: 10.1093/ptj/74.9.845. PMID: 8066111.

Bandy, W., Irion, J., & Briggler, M. (1997). The effect of time and frequency of static stretching on flexibility of the hamstring muscles. *Physical Therapy*, 77, 1090–1096.

Baudry, S., Lecoeuvre, G., & Duchateau, J. (2012). Age-related changes in the behaviour of the muscle-tendon unit of the gastrocnemius medialis during upright stance. *Journal of Applied Physiology*, 112(2), 296–304.

Bello, M., et al. (2011). Rythmic stabilization versus conventional passive stretching to prevent injuries in indoor soccer athletes: A controlled clinical trial. *Journal of Bodywork and Movement Therapies*, 15, 380–383.

Behm, D. G., Blazevich, A. J., Kay, A. D., & McHugh, M. (2015). Acute effects of muscle stretching on physical performance, range of motion, and injury incidence in healthy active individuals: A systematic review. *Applied Physiology, Nutrition, and Metabolism*, 41(1), 1–11.

Behm, D. G., Button, D. C., & Butt, J. C. (2001). Factors affecting force loss with prolonged stretching. *Canadian Journal of Applied Physiology*, 26, 262–272.

Best, T. M., McElhaney, J. H., Garrett Jr, W. E., & Myers, B. S. (1995). Axial strain measurements in skeletal muscle at various strain rates. *Journal of Biomechanical Engineering*, 117(3), 262–265.

Blazevich, A. J., Gill, N. D., Kvorning, T., Kay, A. D., Goh, A. G., Hilton, B., et al. (2018). No effect of muscle stretching within a full, dynamic warm-up on athletic performance. *Medicine & Science in Sports & Exercise*, 50, 1258–1266.

Boukabache, A., Preece, S., & Brookes, N. (2021). Prolonged sitting and physical inactivity are associated with limited hip extension: A cross-sectional study. *Musculoskeletal Science and Practice*, 51, 102282.

Braun, J., & Sieper, J. (2007). Ankylosing spondylitis. *The Lancet*, 369(9570), 1379–1390.

Brughelli, M., & Cronin, J. (2007). Altering the length-tension relationship with eccentric exercise. Implications for performance and injury. *Sports Medicine*, 37(9), 807–826.

Castori, M. (2012). Ehlers-Danlos syndrome, hypermobility type: An underdiagnosed hereditary connective tissue disorder with mucocutaneous, articular, and systemic manifestations. *ISRN Dermatology*, 2012.

Cornwell, A., Nelson, A. G., & Sidaway, B. (2002). Acute effects of stretching on the neuromechanical properties of the triceps surae muscle complex. *European Journal of Applied Physiology*, 86, 428–434.

Couppé, C., Hansen, P., Kongsgaard, M., Kovanen, V., Suetta, C., Aagaard, P., Kjær, M., & Magnusson, S. P. (2009). Mechanical properties and collagen cross-linking of the patellar tendon in old and young men. *Journal of Applied Physiology*, 107(3), 880–886.

Comfort, P., Green, C., & Matthews, M. (2009). Training Considerations after Hamstring Injury in Athletes. *Strength & Conditioning Journal*, 31, 68–74. 10.1519/SSC.0b013e318195d225.

Cross, K. M., Worrell, T. W. (1999 Jan). Effects of a static stretching program on the incidence of lower extremity musculotendinous strains. J Athl Train,. 34(1), 11–4. PMID: 16558540; PMCID: PMC1322867.

De Deyne, P. G. (2001). Application of passive stretch and its implications for muscle fibers. *Physical Therapy*, 81(2), 819–827.

De Vos, R. J., Reurink, G., Goudswaard, G. J., et al. (2014). Clinical findings just after return to play predict hamstring re-injury, but baseline MRI findings do not. *British Journal of Sports Medicine*, 48, 1377–1384.

Denham-Jones, L., Gaskell, L., Spence, N., & Pigott, T. (2022). A systematic review of the effectiveness of yoga on pain, physical function, and quality of life in older adults with chronic musculoskeletal conditions. *Musculoskeletal Care*, 20(1), 47–73.

Diong, J., Carden, P., O'Sullivan, K., & Sherrington, C. (2022). Eccentric exercise improves joint flexibility in adults: A systematic review update and meta-analysis. *Musculoskeletal Science and Practice*, 60, 102556.

Feland, J. B., Myrer, J. W., Schulthies, S. S., Fellingham, G. W., & Measom, G. W. (2001). The effect of duration of stretching of the hamstring muscle group for increasing range of motion in people aged 65years or older. *Physical Therapy*, 81(5), 1110–1117.

Feuerstein, G. (1996). The classical yoga: The essential texts for the study and practice of yoga. Rochester, VT: Inner Traditions.

Franceschi, C., Bonafè, M., Valensin, S., et al. (2007). Inflamm-aging: An evolutionary perspective on immunosenescence. *Annals of the New York Academy of Sciences*, 908(1), 244–254.

García-Pinillos, F., Ruiz-Ariza, A., Moreno del Castillo P., & Latorre-Román, P. Á. (2015). Impact of limited hamstring flexibility on vertical jump, kicking speed, sprint, and agility in young football players. *Journal of Sports Sciences*, 33(12), 1293–1297.

Gleim, G. W., & McHugh, M. P. (1997). Flexibility and its effects on sports injury and performance. *Sports Medicine*, 24(5), 289–299.

Gray, R. (2019). https://www.bbc.com/future/article/20190327-why-stretching-might-not-make-you-a-better-runner

Grahame, R., & Bird, H. (2001 May). British consultant rheumatologists' perceptions about the hypermobility syndrome: a national survey. Rheumatology (Oxford), 40(5), 559–62. doi: 10.1093/rheumatology/40.5.559. PMID: 11371666.

Gremion, G. (2005). The effect of stretching on sports performance and the risk of sports injury: A review of the literature. *Sportmedizin und Sporttraumatologie*, 53(1), 6–10.

Gurjao, A. L., Goncalves, R., de Moura, R. F., & Gobbi, S. (2009). Acute effect of static stretching on rate of force development and maximal voluntary contraction in older women. *Journal of Strength & Conditioning Research*, 23, 2149–2154.

Handrakis, J. P., Southard, V. N., Abreu, J. M., Aloisa, M., Doyen, M. R., Echevarria, L. M., Hwang, H., Samuels, C., Venegas, S. A., & Douris, P. C. (2010). Static stretching does not impair performance in active middle-aged adults. *Journal of Strength & Conditioning Research*, 24, 825–830.

Hall, M. G., et al. (1995). The effect of hypermobility syndrome on knee joint proprioception. *Rheumatology*, 34, 121–125.

Hamilton, M., & Velasquez, J. (2011). Ankle flexibility and jump landing mechanics: Implications for ACL injury risk. *International Journal of Athletic Threapy and Training*, 16(6), 14–16.

Hayden, J., van Tulder, M. W., Malmivaara, A., & Koes, B. W. (2005). Exercise therapy for treatment of non-specific low back pain. *Cochrane Database of Systematic Reviews*, (3). . Art. No.: CD000335. DOI: 10.1002/14651858.CD000335.pub2. Accessed 26 April 2024.

Hart, E., Meehan, W., Bae, D., d'Hemecourt, P., & Stracciolini, A. (2018). The young injured gymnast: A literature review and discussion. *Current Sports Medicine Reports*, 17(11), 366–375.

Hartig, D. E., & Henderson, J. M. (1999). Increasing hamstring flexibility decreases lower extremity overuse injuries in military basic trainees. *American Journal of Sports Medicine*, 27(2), 173–176.

Herbert, R. D., & Gabriel, M. (2002). Effects of stretching before and after exercising on muscle soreness and risk of injury: systematic review. *British Medical Journal*, 325, 1–5.

Herbert, R., de Noronha, M., & Kamper, S. (2011). Stretching to prevent or reduce muscle soreness after exercise (Review). *The Cochrane Collaboration*, 7, 1–50.

Herbert, R. D., Taylor, J. L., Lord, S. R., & Gandevia, S. C. (2020). Prevalence of motor impairment in residents of New South Wales, Australia aged 55years and over: Cross-sectional survey of the 45 and up cohort. *BMC Public Health*, 20, 1353.

Hirata, K., Yamadera, R., & Akagi, R. (2020). Associations between range of motion and tissue stiffness in young and old people. *Medicine and Science in Sports and Exercise*, 52(10), 2179–2188.

Hutchinson, A. (2020). The case against stretching. Outside Online. https://www.outsideonline.com/health/training-performance/case-against-stretching-flexibility-research/

Jamtvedt, G., Herbert, R., Flottorp, S., Odgaard-Jensen, J., Håvelsrud, K., Barratt, A., Mathieu, E., Burls, A., & Oxman, A. (2009). A pragmatic randomised trial of stretching before and after physical activity to prevent injury and soreness. *British journal of sports medicine*, 44, 1002–9. 10.1136/bjsm.2009.062232.

Jarvinen, T. A., Jarvinen, T. L., Kaariainen, M., Kalimo, H., & Jarvinen, M. (2005). Muscle injuries: biology and treatment. *The American Journal of Sports Medicine*, 33(5), 745–764.

Kaufman, K. R., Brodine, S. K., Shaffer, R. A., Johnson, C. W., & Cullison, T. R. (1999). The effect of foot structure and range of motion on musculoskeletal overuse injuries. *The American Journal of Sports Medicine*, 27(5), 585–593.

Krivickas, L. S., & Feinberg, J. H. (1996). Lower extremity injuries in college athletes: Relation between ligamentous laxity and lower extremity muscle tightness. *Archives of Physical Medical Rehabilitation*, 77, 1139–1143.

Lotz, M., & Loeser, R. F. (2012). Effects of aging on articular cartilage homeostasis. *Bone*, 51(2), 241–248.

Maganaris, C. N., Narici, M. V., & Almekinders, L. C. (2004). Biomechanics and pathophysiology of overuse tendon injuries: Ideas on insertional tendinopathy. *Sports Medicine*, 34(14), 1005–1017.

Magnusson, S. P., Simonsen, E. B., Aagaard, P., Sørensen, H., Kjaer, M. (1996). A mechanism for altered flexibility in human skeletal muscle. *The Journal of Physiology*, 497(1), 291–298.

Magnusson, S. P., Aagaard, P., Rosager, S., Dyhre-Poulsen, P., & Kjaer, M. (2001). Load–displacement properties of the human triceps surae aponeurosis in vivo. *Journal of Physiology*, 531(1), 277–288.

Malliaras, P., Cook, J., & Kent, P. (2006). Reduced ankle dorsiflexion range may increase the risk of patella tendon injury among volleyball players. *Journal of Science and Medicine in Sport*, 9(4), 304–309.

Malliaropoulos, N., Papalexandris, S., Papalada, A., & Papacostas, E. (2004). The role of stretching in rehabilitation of hamstring injuries: 80 athletes follow up. *Medicine & science in Sports & Exercise*, 36(5), 756–759.

Maselli, F., Storari, L., Barbari, V., et al. (2020). Prevalence and incidence of low back pain among runners: A systematic review. *BMC Musculoskeletal Disorders*, 21, 343.

McHugh, M. P., & Cosgrave, C. H. (2010). To stretch or not to stretch: The role of stretching in injury prevention and performance. *Scandinavian Journal of Medicine & Science in Sports*, 20(2), 169–181.

McMahan, I. (2014). Stretching is overrated. *The Atlantic*. https://www.theatlantic.com/health/archive/2014/08/stretching-before-exercise-is-overrated/376089/

Noonan, T. J., & Garrett Jr, W. E. (1999). Muscle strain injury: Diagnosis and treatment. *The Journal of the American Academy of Orthopaedic Surgeons*, 7(4), 262–269.

Pope R., Herbert, R., & Kirwan, J. (1998). Effects of ankle dorsiflexion range and pre-exercise calf muscle stretching on injury risk in Army Recruits. *Australian Journal of Physiotherapy*, 44, 165–177.

Pope, R. P., Herbert, R. D., Kirwan, J. D., & Graham, B. J.(2000). A randomized trial of preexercise stretching for prevention of lower-limb injury. *Medicine and Science in Sports and Exercise*, 32(2), 271-7. https://doi.org/10.1097/00005768-200002000-00004

Power, K., Behm, D., Cahill, F., Carroll, M., & Young, W. (2004). An acute bout of static stretching: Effects on force and jumping performance. *Medicine & Science in Sports & Exercise*, 36, 1389–1396.

Pozzi, F., Plummer, H. A., Shanley, E., et al. (2020). Preseason shoulder range of motion screening and in-season risk of shoulder and elbow injuries in overhead athletes: Systematic review and meta-analysis. *British Journal of Sports Medicine*, 54, 1019–1027.

Purslow, P. P. (2002). The structure and functional significance of variations in the connective tissue within muscle. *Comparative Biochemistry and Physiology Part A: Molecular & Integrative Physiology*, 133(4), 947–966.

Reid, J. C., Greene, R., Young, J. D., Hodgson, D. D., Blazevich, A. J., & Behm, D. G. (2018). The effects of different durations of static stretching within a comprehensive warm-up on voluntary and evoked contractile properties. *European Journal of Applied Physiology*, 118, 1427–1445.

Remvig, L., Jensen, D. V., & Ward, R. C. (2007). Epidemiology of general joint hypermobility and basis for the proposed criteria for benign joint hypermobility syndrome: Review of the literature. *Journal of Rheumatology*, 34(4), 804–809.

Reuter, P. R., & Fichthorn, K. R. (2019). Prevalence of generalized joint hypermobility, musculoskeletal injuries, and chronic musculoskeletal pain among American university students. Peer Journal, Sep 11, 7.

Roland, K. P., Jakobi, J. M., & Jones, G. R. (2011). Does yoga engender fitness in older adults? A critical review. *Journal of Aging and Physical Activity*, 19(1), 62–79.

Ross, A., & Thomas, S. (2010). The health benefits of yoga and exercise: A review of comparison studies. *Journal of Alternative & Complementary Medicine*, 16(1), 3–12.

Rubini, E. C., Costa, A. L., & Gomes, P. S. (2007). The effects of stretching on strength performance. *Sports Medicine*, 37(3), 213–224.

Runners World. (2022). https://www.runnersworld.com/training/a41535703/why-you-should-stop-ballistic-stretching/

Russek, L. N. (1999). Hypermobility syndrome. *Physical Therapy*, 79(6): 591–599.

Shrier, I. (1999). Stretching before exercise does not reduce the risk of local muscle injury: A critical review of the clinical and basic science literature. *Clinical Journal of Sports Medicine*, 9, 221–227.

Shrier, I. (2001). Should people stretch before exercise? *West Journal Medicine*, 174(4), 282–283.

Shrier, I. (2004). Does stretching improve performance?: A systematic and critical review of the literature. *Clinical Journal of Sport Medicine*, 14(5), 267–273.

Spanias, C., Nikolaidis, P. T., Rosemann, T., & Knechtle, B. (2019). Anthropometric and physiological profile of mixed martial art athletes: A brief review. *Sports*, 7(6), 146.

Storm, J. M., Wolman, R., Bakker, E. W. P., & Wyon, M. A. (2018). The relationship between range of motion and injuries in adolescent dancers and sportspersons: A systematic review. *Frontiers in Psychology*, 9, 287.

Støve, M., Hirata, R., & Palsson, T. (2019). Muscle stretching – The potential role of endogenous pain inhibitory modulation on stretch tolerance. *Scandinavian Journal of Pain*, 19(2), 415–422.

Tak, I., Engelaar, L., Gouttebarge, V., et al. (2017). Is lower hip range of motion a risk factor for groin pain in athletes? A systematic review with clinical applications. *British Journal of Sports Medicine*, 51, 1611–1621.

Thacker, S. B., et al. (2004). The impact of stretching on sports injury risk: A systematic review of the literature. *Medicine Science Sports Exercise*, 36(3), 371–378.

Thomas, E., Bianco, A., Paoli, A., & Palma, A. (1998). The relation between stretching typology and stretching duration: the effects on range of motion. *International Journal of Sports Medicine*, 39(4), 243–254.

Thomas, E., et al. (2023). Does stretching training influence muscular strength? A systematic review with meta-analysis and meta-regression. *Journal of Strength and Conditioning Research*, 37(5), 1145–1156.

Trehearn, T., & Buresh, R. (2009). Sit-and-reach flexibility and running economy of men and women collegiate distance runners. *Journal of Strength and Conditioning Research*, 23(1), 158–162.

Verzijl, N., DeGroot, J., Thorpe, S. R., et al. (2000). Effect of collagen turnover on the accumulation of advanced glycation end products. *Journal of Biological Chemistry*, 275(50), 39027–39031.

Wahlstedt, C., & Rasmussen-Barr, E. (2015). Anterior cruciate ligament injury and ankle dorsiflexion. *Knee Surgery, Sports Traumatology Arthroscopy*, 23, 3202–3207.

White, T. A., & LeBrasseur, N. K. (2016). Myostatin and sarcopenia: Opportunities and challenges - A mini-review. *Gerontology*, 62(3), 289–293.

Witvrouw, E., Danneels, L., Asselman, P., D'Have, T., & Cambier, D. (2003). Muscle flexibility as a risk factor for developing muscle injuries in male professional soccer players: A prospective study. *The American Journal of Sports Medicine*, 31(1), 41–46.

Witvrouw, E., et al. (2004). Stretching and injury prevention: An obscure relationship. *Sports Medicine*, 34, 443–449.

Yeung, E. W., & Yeung, S. S. (2001). A systematic review of interventions to prevent lower limb soft tissue running injuries. *British Journal of Sports Medicine*, 35, 383–389.

Young, W., Elias, G., & Power, J. (2006). Effects of static stretching volume and intensity on plantar flexor explosive force production and range of motion. The Journal of Sports Medicine and Physical Fitness, 46, 403–411.

9 Distinguishing the Truths from the Myths

The Dual-Axis Framework

Philip E. Kearney, Frank Nugent and Andrew Harrison

Introduction

> … at the heart of science is an essential balance between two seemingly contradictory attitudes – an openness to new ideas, no matter how bizarre or counterintuitive, and the most ruthlessly sceptical scrutiny of all ideas, old and new. This is how deep truths are winnowed from deep nonsense. The collective enterprise of creative thinking and sceptical thinking, working together, keeps the field on track. Those two seemingly contradictory attitudes are, though, in some tension.
>
> – Carl Sagan (1996, p. 304)

Consider the following brief case study. In the second half of their competitive season, an elite athlete suffered two broken bones in their upper arms. Having completed their initial assessment, the athlete, coach and support team believed there was a small but realistic chance of recovering in time for the upcoming World Championships. Even if the ambitious rehabilitation timeline did not make sufficient progress ahead of the championships, pursuing it was thought to provide a more positive and focussed end to the athlete's season. The challenge facing the athlete, coach and support team was to determine the most appropriate 'package of care' to optimize recovery. Standard medical support (e.g. use of a cast, initial rest, progressive strengthening exercises, etc.) would provide the core of the programme. The team also drew upon their personal experiences, current practices of their peers and potential innovations as they considered what other interventions might reasonably be employed to accelerate recovery. Amongst the additional interventions considered were novel methods which do not have sufficient evidence to support or refute their effectiveness (e.g. hyperbaric oxygen therapy – Bennett et al., 2012; Gambhir et al., 2020), traditional remedies which appear to have sound empirical support but which also have had concerns raised about them (e.g. comfrey root extract ointment – Gianetti et al., 2010; Food & Drug Administration, 2001) and methods which are classified as complementary and alternative medicines (e.g. homeopathy and acupuncture –Singh & Ernst, 2008; Tiller, 2020).

It is not within the scope of this chapter to evaluate all of the interventions used within the scope of the case study; this would require multiple chapters. Instead, our purpose in presenting the case is to illustrate the general challenge facing the coach or applied scientist. Whether in the context of enhancing performance or facilitating rehabilitation, a coach and/or sport scientist is required to make a series of judgement calls regarding which interventions to pursue and which to reject. Making these judgement calls is complicated by the wide range of interventions they might choose from, the limited resources available (e.g. time, energy, finances), the inadequate investigations into some interventions, the pseudoscience presented in support of others and the inevitable trade-off between trying to be innovative while ensuring that they are evidence-based. As suggested by the opening quotation from Carl Sagan, the scientist must be a sceptic, not a cynic. However, that scepticism applies both ways: assuming an intervention will work because of its antiquity is flawed, but so is assuming that an intervention will *not* work because of its antiquity (Tiller, 2020). This chapter will explore the challenge facing the coach and applied practitioner when evaluating a prospective intervention. As outlined in Whitehead and Coe (2021) and again in this volume, deciding which intervention to use is made more difficult because sport is replete with examples of myths (e.g. learning styles; Stodter, 2021) and misconceptions (e.g. deliberate practice; Coughlan, 2021). While books explicitly exploring these myths are useful, the evolving nature of scientific knowledge exacerbates the challenge facing coaches and applied practitioners; a standard treatment in the 20th century may be relegated to a placebo effect within the 21st century as new evidence is uncovered (Kamper & Williams, 2013). Thus, in addition to books such as this one which provide an update on the current state of knowledge, practitioners also require a process to aid their decision-making. The centrepiece of this chapter is such a process: the Dual-Axis Framework (see Figure 9.1) that can guide practitioners when evaluating their practices both individually and in cooperation with their peers. Finally, we outline a range of factors that need to be considered to assist coaches and applied practitioners to make appropriate decisions about where interventions should

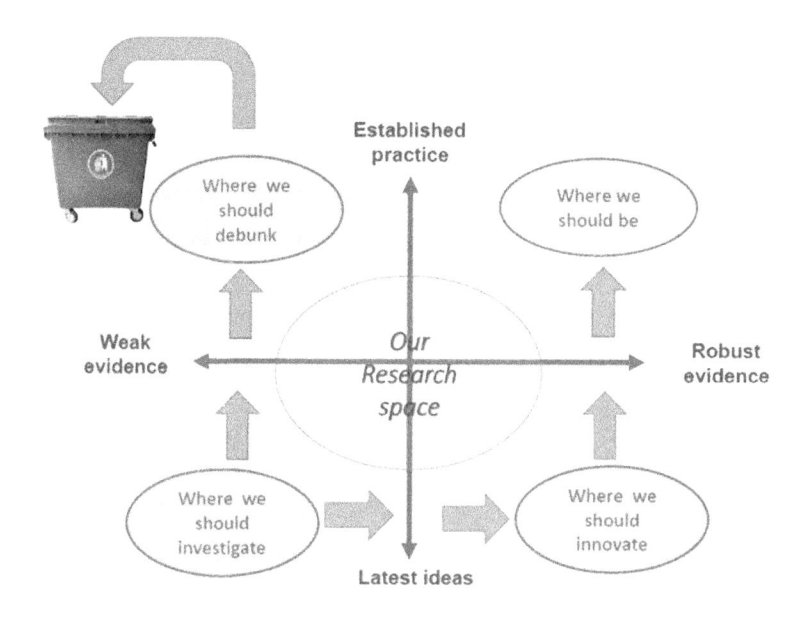

Figure 9.1. The Dual-Axis Framework.

be placed in the framework. The framework is also intended to guide students as they learn to critically evaluate the literature.

The Dual-Axis Framework

We begin with the understanding that all credible science is underpinned by evidence from research and, therefore, at the centre of the framework is *our research space*. The vertical axis (continuum) presents *the latest ideas* at one end and *established practice* at the other end. The horizontal axis (continuum) describes the strength of evidence supporting a practice or treatment. The two axes form an orthogonal grid with four quadrants. In the lower left quadrant, we see the *latest ideas* (i.e. novel practices) that have minimal or weak supporting evidence. Since these ideas or practices are new, they remain worthy of investigation to determine whether evidence can be found to support their continued use. If research uncovers evidence supporting a novel practice, then the practice progresses towards the lower right quadrant and will become an innovative practice. These new ideas with robust supporting evidence are *where we should innovate*. Over time, with the support of research replication, innovative practices could become established and progress to the upper right quadrant and become evidence-based practice – this is, *where we should be*. Unfortunately, this ideal is not always achieved, and sometimes ideas or practices become established despite the supporting evidence being weak. These established practices that lack robust evidence are the myths that occupy the upper left quadrant, and these are the practices *where we should debunk* (e.g. see Whitehead & Coe, 2021). Where a practice has become established in the absence of supportive evidence, it may hover on the boundary between *where we should be* and *where we should debunk*, until such time that sufficient evidence is found to support or debunk its use. Therefore, any research that fails to produce robust evidence in support of any idea or practice provides an important role in science, since it challenges or debunks the establishment of myths and pseudoscience.

The Dual-Axis Framework can be used as a tool to evaluate and classify the level of scientific underpinning for new ideas and established practices by guiding personal reflections and research, or conversations with peers. A key aspect in determining where a particular intervention belongs is the critical evaluation of the strength of the scientific evidence supporting any practice or idea. The vertical continuum only describes the extent to which a practice is established; it is the interaction with the horizontal axis that determines the extent to which the use of the practice is justified.

What does it mean for an intervention to 'work'?

'It worked for me': Why you cannot trust your personal experience to determine the cause of an effect.

Consider the following account from a physiotherapist working in professional sport (cited by Coveney et al., 2020, p. 4):

> I've often said why does it need to be peer reviewed literature, and actually be proven in a research study to say it's working. I know it's working. My players are feeling better […] there's techniques out there like Bowen Technique, there's Reiki, all these kinds of techniques that are out there, that people are doing through alternative medicine that are having good results with their clients. And there is no reason why they can't be used in a football setting. (I4, Physiotherapist)

It is not unusual for athletes, coaches or practitioners to base their evaluation of the effectiveness of an intervention on their personal experience: do I feel like the intervention worked? While we do not dispute that an individual might feel like an intervention has worked, there are multiple ways in which personal experience may be deceived as to the *cause* of an improvement (Singh & Ernst,

2008). We will consider these sources of deception using the physiotherapist's example of Reiki[1] to facilitate recovery after a competition, but we encourage you to consider whether each of these reasons might also apply to the interventions discussed in our opening case study (i.e. comfrey root extract, hyperbaric oxygen therapy, homeopathy and acupuncture). The first source is *post hoc ergo proctor hoc* (after this, therefore because of this) – the fact that one event (I feel better) follows another (a session of Reiki) does not necessarily mean that one event caused the other. There are many other factors that might have influenced the athlete's recovery, including the quality of their night's sleep, their activity post competition, the circumstances of their travel home from the competition and so forth, which are not being considered. Unless these additional variables are also considered, the true cause of a benefit may be missed.

Singh and Ernst (2008, p. 231) describe three further ways in which the cause of an effect may be misunderstood. Expectations of benefit (i.e. thinking a treatment will work) may also lead to confusion as to the effectiveness of an intervention due to a *placebo effect*: a benefit arising from a physically inert treatment due to a psychobiological effect (Bérdi et al., 2015). *Confirmation bias* may also play a role, whereby on occasions where an athlete feels like recovery has been enhanced, the benefit is attributed to the session of Reiki, but on occasions where an athlete does not feel like recovery has been enhanced, despite a session of Reiki, some other reason for the lack of recovery is identified. We might also consider *regression to the mean*: normal day-to-day variation in muscle soreness can occasionally result in some days that are a little worse than others, but such extremes are generally followed by a return to more typical levels without treatment (i.e. a regression to the mean). An athlete might seek out Reiki treatment when feeling particularly sore and attribute their feeling better the next day to the effects of the treatment, whereas the improvement was simply due to natural variation.

Personal experience may initially seem like an appropriate source of evidence for judging the efficacy of interventions. However, once an understanding is gained of the multiple factors which can influence the outcome of an individual case and one's perceptions, it becomes clear that the only way of understanding the true value of an intervention comes from aggregating effects across individuals (Singh & Ernst, 2008). Thus, we turn to the scientific method: 'a system in which the likelihood of being wrong is reduced by methods used by individual scientists and by the scepticism and interactions of the community of scientists working together' (Lee, 2000, p. 14). Fundamentally, the fallibility of personal experience is so pronounced that only through appropriately controlled and blinded trials can the true effect of an intervention be known (Goldacre, 2009; Singh & Ernst, 2008).

Weight of quality evidence

> *If it disagrees with experiment, it is wrong. In that simple statement is the key to science. It does not make any difference how beautiful your guess is, it does not make any difference how smart you are, who made the guess, or what his name is – if it disagrees with experiment, it is wrong.*
>
> —Richard Feynman

Today, we need to add two clarifications to Feynman's 'key to science'. The first is that even a well-designed, well-conducted experiment may, due to chance variation, produce an aberrant result. Thus, championed by Archie Cochrane, the standard for evidence has shifted away from the individual study to the systematic review of high-quality studies (Spence, 2020). The word systematic refers to the use of clearly defined methods of searching and evaluating research papers to produce a comprehensive and reproducible collation and synthesis of the available evidence relating to a particular question (Bennie et al., 2017) – where does the weight of evidence point?

The second clarification of Feynman's statement relates to the importance of a well-designed and conducted experiment. Not all experiments are equally informative. There are multiple sources of bias which may call into question an experiment's findings (Midgley et al., 2007), sources of bias which a snake oil salesperson may all too readily ignore while focussing on the finding produced. For example, are the participants involved in the study representative of the group that you are interested in (e.g. recreational vs high-performance athletes)? Was the study of sufficient duration to replicate a typical training cycle? In what phase of the season was the study conducted (e.g. were athletes coming back from pre-season and likely to respond better to an intervention)? Were placebo effects considered when designing the control condition? Apart from the experimental manipulation, were each group of participants treated equally? Were sensitive, reliable and valid measures used? Were appropriate statistical analysis procedures followed? Understanding the characteristics of high-quality scientific experiments is vital – and no easy matter (Borg et al., 2020; Lohse et al., 2016; Willingham, 2012). Tools have been developed to assist researchers to evaluate the quality of individual studies, such as the Risk of Bias 2 (Sterne et al., 2019) or the Critical Appraisal Skills Program checklists (https://casp-uk.net/

casp-tools-checklists/). The range of questions considered within these checklists emphasizes the care required when conducting and interpreting scientific research to ensure that the answers obtained are trustworthy.

An intervention may not work for everybody

Establishing that a training intervention is generally effective (i.e. that it sits in the upper right quadrant: Where we should be) does not mean that it will be effective for all individuals (Pickering & Kiely, 2019). The complexity of human beings in terms of their genetic make-up, maturational status, training history and lifestyle mean that training prescriptions or interventions which work best for all people all of the time are unlikely to exist (Mann et al., 2014; Pickering & Kiely, 2019; Radnor et al., 2017). A clear example of this individualized response to training was provided by Gaskill et al. (1999). Fourteen cross-country skiers participated in an annual training programme comprising primarily high-volume and low-intensity activity. Seven of the participants showed a marked improvement in $\dot{V}O_2$ max over the course of the season (average response from baseline +5.4%), while the remainder did not respond to the programme (average response –1.5%). The seven participants who had shown improvement remained on a high-volume low-intensity programme the following year (control group), whereas those who did not respond were assigned to a programme with an increased proportion of high-intensity training (treatment group). In the second year, the control group again responded positively to their training prescription (+6.1%), but this time so did the treatment group (+5.5%). Although evidence is limited from performance sport contexts, studies on exercising populations consistently support Gaskill et al.'s finding that individuals who are low responders to one training intervention are likely to have a positive response to an alternative intervention (Bonafiglia et al., 2016; Hautala et al., 2006). Thus, it is important to consider interventions within the upper right quadrant as those which *may* work rather than interventions which will always work for every individual.

While we cannot conclusively identify interventions that will work for all athletes all of the time, we can identify interventions which do not work, beyond a potential placebo effect. Skrabanek (1986) emphasized the need for a *Demarcation of the Absurd*: we must have a point at which we suspend belief in plausibility. Skrabanek gives the example of the physicist dismissing the inventor of a perpetual motion machine based on the laws of thermodynamics. Likewise, a homeopathic remedy such as that used by the athlete in our opening case study may be relegated to, at best, a placebo effect because the dilution is to such an extent that not one single molecule of the original substance remains within the ingested tonic or pill (Gorski & Novella, 2014; Singh & Ernst, 2008). The plausibility of an explanatory mechanism for an effect is important when determining what potential interventions to implement. In relation to sports performance, the relative age effect is a well-established phenomenon observed in many sports, whereby children born closer to the cut-off date for inclusion in one age grade or another are more likely to be selected for representative teams than their peers born later in the year (Kelly et al., 2021; Smith et al., 2018). Why does being born early in the year confer an advantage? We are more likely to derive effective practical solutions by following established theories about the specific roles that parents, coaches and athletes may play in producing relative age effects (Hancock et al., 2013; Wattie et al., 2015) than by considering that Capricorns, Aquarians and Pisces have benefited from some peculiar quirk of the arrangement of the stars at the moment of their birth (Frawley, 2007). While openness is critical for a scientist, so is a demarcation of the absurd, otherwise time and energy are wasted (Gorski & Novella, 2014).

Deterministic evidence based on laws of science or mathematics

There are aspects of knowledge in sports sciences where we can establish evidence through proof. The burden of proof may be a considerable challenge in experimental science, but in mathematics the notion of proof is fundamental and frequently demanded. Deterministic models in biomechanics are based on the laws of physics and mathematics, and they carry perhaps the most robust form of evidence to support their predictions (i.e. mathematical and scientific proof). Deterministic models were proposed by Hay (1993), and they demonstrate an analysis of the biomechanical factors that determine performance in various activities. The deterministic models are presented in the form of a flow chart and follow specific rules which require that the outcome variable is at the top of the chart and the factors below determine the factors above using clearly defined mathematical expressions. Figure 9.2 provides an example of a deterministic model for running (Hay, 1993). The main objective of running is to reduce the time taken to cover a set distance, so time is at the top of the flow chart and the factors of distance and average speed determine the time via the equation: *time = distance ÷ average speed*. Average speed in running is determined by *stride length × stride frequency*, and stride frequency is determined by stride time where *stride frequency = 1 ÷ stride time*. In an equivalent way, each factor in the model is determined mathematically by the factors below.

```
                          Time
                           │
                      Distance (m)
                           │
                     Average Speed
                    ┌──────┴──────┐
              Stride Length    Stride Frequency
          ┌────────┼────────┐         │
      Take-off  Flight   Landing   Stride Time
      Distance  Distance Distance      │
      ┌───┬────┴──┬─────┐         ┌────┴────┐
   Speed at Angle of Height of  Air      Time on  Time in
   Take-off Take-off Take-off Resistance  Ground    Air
```

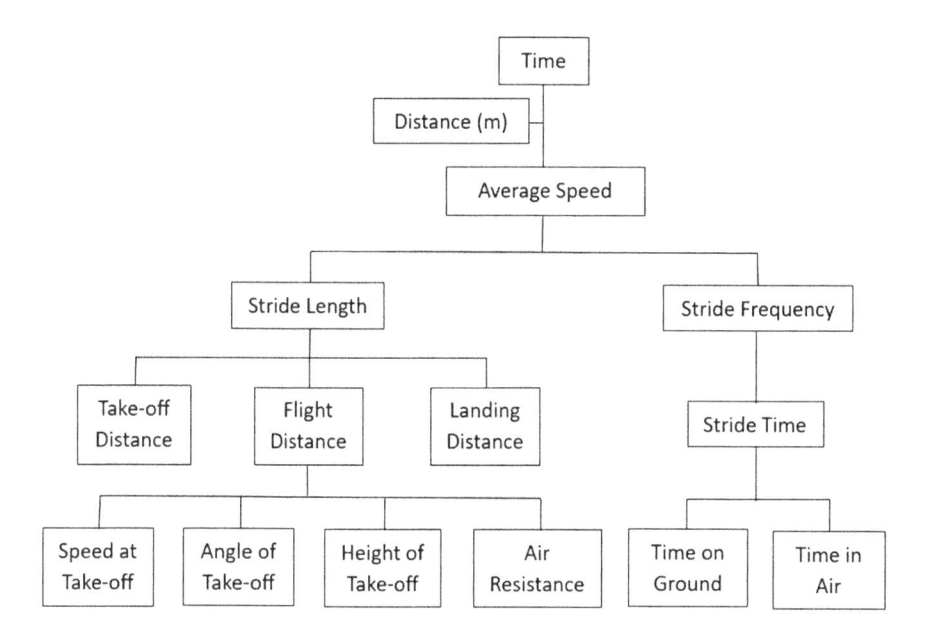

Figure 9.2. A deterministic model for running (Hay, 1993).

Similar examples exist in other areas of sports sciences (e.g. the Hick-Hyman Law in motor control [Hick, 1952; Hyman, 1953]). Unfortunately, in the sports sciences this source of evidence is often overlooked. For example, how often do we see the sport scientist gathering data of vertical jumping and through correlation and regression analysis they may conclude that flight height (or take-off velocity) is strongly correlated with performance (i.e. jump height)? Unfortunately, such analyses are at best pointless and at worst may be misleading since we already know from Galileo's equations of uniformly accelerated motion (projectiles) that take-off velocity (VTO) determines flight height (H) (H = VTO^2 ÷2g, where H is the vertical flight height of the centre of mass during the jump, VTO is the vertical velocity at take-off and g is the acceleration due to gravity). On balance, deterministic models should take precedence over correlation-based models derived solely from experimental data.

Is there a role for professional judgement derived from practical experience?

> *'the likelihood of success increases when training implementation is founded upon an interaction between best practice and science'* (Haugen, 2020, p. 297).

Due to the unknown and unmeasured variables inherent in any intervention, it is very difficult to determine the cause of a benefit for a single individual (Goldacre, 2009; Singh & Ernst, 2008). Thus, coaches and applied practitioners take evidence that is derived from studies of groups of athletes and apply it to the individual they are working with. The primary value of these group-based studies is that they account for the myriad unmeasured variables through the process of randomization (Kunz & Oxman, 1998), allowing for the true cause of an effect to be identified. However, the individual athlete at the centre of the decision in question may not fit within the precise inclusion and exclusion criteria of the participants in the research study; experiments 'tell us what interventions are effective, but not necessarily which athletes should receive them, under which environmental and system constraints and at which phase of their training and competition cycle' (Ross et al., 2018, p. 202). Consequently, the coach or applied practitioner must also apply their professional judgement when determining the course to follow; that is, they must extrapolate from the existing evidence, based upon their theoretical understanding of the scenario and their knowledge of the individual in question (Spence, 2020). This 'knowledge of the individual' includes the values and preferences of the athlete, which also play a role in determining buy-in and adherence to an intervention (Ross et al., 2018; Sackett et al., 1996). The *integration* of relevant scientific evidence, the athlete's values and preferences and the practitioner's professional judgement is termed evidence-based practice (Amonette et al., 2010; English et al., 2012; Sackett et al., 1996; see Figure 9.3).

The concept of evidence-based practice is often misinterpreted (Ioannidis, 2017), and a careful reading of the original position paper by Sackett et al. (1996) is highly recommended. The first misconception is that within evidence-

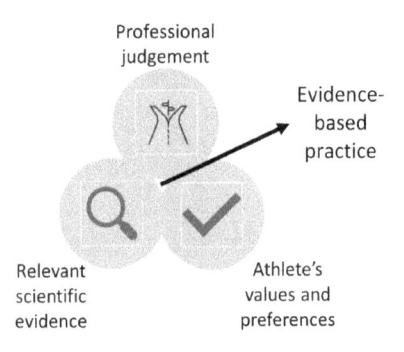

Figure 9.3. Contributions to evidence-based practice (based upon Sackett et al., 1996).

based practice, scientific evidence outweighs professional judgement. This is not the case. When a practitioner applies scientific findings without sufficient consideration of the specific individual context, results are likely to be suboptimal, especially when that literature is unrepresentative of the context (e.g. based upon sub-elite rather than elite athletes). Furthermore, that evidence is viewed as 'current best evidence' (English et al., 2012) – evidence which may (and typically does) evolve over time (Ritchie, 2020). Hence, it is important that the summary of research evidence is regularly re-evaluated (Amonette et al., 2010).[2]

The value of professional judgement is not limited to contextualizing research; the practice of the World's best coaches is often more advanced than the scientific literature (Haugen, 2021). As such, professional judgement also incorporates results-proven practice: lessons from the training practices of coaches with a track record of consistent success (Haugen et al., 2022). Recent scientific publications have provided comprehensive training information on the World's best runners such as the double Olympic Gold medallist Eliud Kipchoge and previous World Marathon Record holder Paula Radcliffe (Haugen et al., 2022; Haugen et al., 2021). Similar publications have occurred in Judo (Franchini & Takito, 2014), triathlon (Mujika, 2014) and swimming (Hellard et al., 2019), to name but a few. Critically, the value afforded to professional judgement does not extend to permitting biologically implausible or 'magic' (Gorski & Novella, 2014) interventions into practice. Similarly, when a practitioner relies upon their professional judgement, without routinely calibrating that judgement against current literature, they risk rapidly becoming out of date in their practice, and again results for the athlete are likely to be suboptimal. Evidence-based practice emphasizes the *balanced* integration of both professional judgement and a careful evaluation of the scientific literature, in light of the specific individual and context, to arrive at an optimal decision.

Other factors guiding decision-making

Alternative reasons for alternative treatments

Examples of the use of alternative and unproven treatments by high-performance athletes (e.g. Michael Phelps' use of cupping at the 2016 Olympic Games; Tiller, 2020) may be used to rationalize their use by their peers or lower-level athletes. How valid is this argument? Interventions such as acupuncture are often presented as an alternative choice to mainstream medical treatments; however, particularly in the context of elite sport, athletes and practitioners more commonly choose to *supplement* one course of treatment with another rather than rejecting conventional medicine in favour of an alternative treatment (Coveney et al., 2020). Within the case study that we introduced at the start, the athlete and coach reported how the consultant overseeing their rehabilitation 'was well in for the hyperbaric chamber … was definitely all on board from an acupuncturist point of view … he wasn't at all surprised when we mentioned it and he said, yeah, you go for it'. In contrast, with another consultant '… we mentioned the chamber and the laser therapy. And he said "No; won't make a difference". And I was like "OK". Yeah; we haven't gone back to him.' While the decision to discontinue working with the second consultant was primarily due to his pessimistic prognosis on a time to recovery, his attitude to the coach and athlete's proposals for supplementary complementary and alternative medicine also contributed to the decision.

Why do practitioners utilize unproven, or even debunked, interventions? Drawing upon interviews conducted with 27 leading sports medicine physicians working in professional football and cycling in the United Kingdom, Coveney et al. (2020) concluded that, rather than due to a genuine belief in their efficacy, alternative treatments could be supported as a means of managing the expectations of players and managers that everything possible was being done, to buy time for healing to occur and stop the pursuit of a potentially more harmful practice: 'If I have a player and I am offering him a treatment for something, in some respects, what it does is it stops him going and getting a treatment from somewhere else because he hasn't been offered it by me. And I would rather control the degree of mismanagement (I23, Medical Doctor)' (Coveney et al., 2020, p. 6). Coveney et al. also reported occasional concerning examples where practitioners recognized that one's reputation might be enhanced if one could be seen to be using innovative treatments at the cutting edge of rehabilitation, irrespective of their efficacy. The more common rationale reported by practitioners interviewed by Coveney et al. was to incorporate additional, harmless treatments which may have a placebo effect, as a means to maintain control over the therapeutic decision-making and build an effective relationship with the client. Thus, the use of an intervention in high-performance sport is not sufficient justification for its broader use.

Are we all scientific experts now?

More than ever before, the availability of original manuscripts within repositories makes the research underpinning interventions accessible to all.

However, while repositories give the public access to primary source material, they do not provide the historical, methodological and theoretical context (collectively termed interactional expertise; Collins, 2014) through which to interpret that work. Minor omissions or errors in procedure can nullify a reported finding, and the peer review process is not faultless. Within motor learning, it is well-established that some interventions which provide an immediate boost to performance during practice may show little to no long-term benefit, while other interventions which produce less of an immediate benefit show a marked long-term benefit (Magill & Anderson, 2017; Schmidt et al., 2019). Consequently, knowledgeable readers of motor learning research know that some measure of the long-term effects of an intervention is essential for an accurate evaluation (Kantak & Winstein, 2012; Soderstrom & Bjork, 2015). This measure of long-term practice effects may take the form of a retention test (participants are re-tested in the same conditions after a period of no practice) or a transfer test (participants are tested in a new context). Critically, without the interactional expertise to understand what to look for, a reader unfamiliar with core principles of motor learning may misinterpret reported findings. Thus, while 'Do your own research' may be a sensible rule of thumb, real-world examples on topics such as Coronavirus suggest that many people are doing very poor-quality research. Engaging with research is akin to examining a position on a chess board – without knowledge of the rules of chess, an accurate interpretation of the situation is not possible. In the information age, interactional expertise is essential to filter out the noise so that the true signal can be identified.

While the previous paragraph relates to athletes and coaches, applied practitioners may face another challenge which disrupts their capacity to make effective decisions: time. Coaches and athletes may be keen for rapid responses to their queries, limiting time for a thorough review of research. Likewise, coaches may be keen to adopt new technology or training methods, so as not to 'miss out'. Consequently, the applied practitioners will often rely more on a 'dashboard analytic approach', fusing knowledge and intuition to make a judgement (Coutts, 2016). In such a fast-paced environment, the available research may not be interrogated to the same extent as would a research scientist. Thus, we endorse Coutts' (2016) call for building partnerships between the contemplative research scientist and the reactive applied practitioner to provide 'a conscience that can inform the judgments and decisions in athlete preparation' to provide athletes and coaches with the optimal benefits of the scientific method.

A Practical Task

We recommend the following practical task to help you make the most of the Dual-Axis Framework:

1. Make a complete list of the interventions that you currently use (Table 9.1).
2. Assign each intervention to one quadrant of the Dual-Axis Framework; write a brief explanation (rationale) of why you placed each intervention in its assigned quadrant. You may be confident about the assignment of some interventions, and less certain about others; that is normal. Beside each intervention, place a number from 0 to 100 to reflect your confidence in its position.
3. Discuss your organization with another coach or applied scientist, ideally one who has completed a similar exercise with their practices. On what practices do you agree and disagree?
4. Your discussion may indicate a need for further exploration on your part, through engaging with research or conversations with other coaches and scientists. Update your Dual-Axis Framework.

Table 9.1. In which quadrant would you place each of the interventions you might use?

Intervention	Quadrant	Rationale	Confidence (0–100)

Conclusion

When attempting to improve performance or to accelerate rehabilitation, coaches and applied practitioners must make recommendations on which interventions to pursue or reject. The quotation which opened this chapter reminds us that effective decision-making requires an openness to new ideas balanced against a sceptical scrutiny. The Dual-Axis Framework provides a tool for coaches and applied practitioners to structure their evaluation of the evidence base underpinning their practice, to engage in productive peer discussions and to decide where to invest, innovate, investigate and debunk. The framework will also help students to critically evaluate the literature which is an essential skill that underpins future scientific investigations. When conducting these discussions and determining where an intervention should fall on the Dual-Axis Framework, remember that personal experience is a poor indicator of the cause of an effect. Instead, coaches and applied practitioners must consider the weight of evidence from high-quality experiments on the effectiveness of an intervention. The availability of research papers is not sufficient to make all readers scientific experts; knowledge of the domain is essential to facilitate correct understanding. Deterministic evidence is based on the laws of science and mathematics and should be considered amongst the most robust forms of evidence available. It is unlikely that there will be universally effective interventions, but there may be universally ineffective interventions. While both scientific research and results-proven practice can provide valuable guidance in many cases, the final decision for a specific individual in a particular context should be derived from evidence-based practice; that is, the fusion of the latest scientific research and professional judgement in light of athlete values and perceptions. Practitioners may consider alternative treatments to manage therapeutic decision-making and build a relationship with a client, rather than for any perceptions of efficacy. Partnerships, between researchers and applied practitioners, or between scientists and coaches, may provide the most fruitful means to enhance the information-base underpinning coaches' decisions and the quality of athletes' experiences.

> **Recommended reading**
>
> 1. Tiller, N. B. (2020). *The skeptic's guide to sports science: Confronting myths of the health and fitness industry*. Routledge.

2. Ritchie, S. (2020). *Science fictions: Exposing fraud, bias, negligence and hype in science*. Random House.
3. Sagan, C. (1996). *The demon-haunted world: Science as a candle in the dark*. Ballantine books.

Notes

1 Reiki refers to a form of alternative medicine in which a practitioner channels healing energy into a patient (Zadro & Stapleton, 2022).
2 For a practical guide on how to efficiently find and integrate research evidence, see English et al. (2012).

References

Amonette, W. E., English, K. L., & Ottenbacher, K. J. (2010). Nullius in verba: A call for the incorporation of evidence-based practice into the discipline of exercise science. *Sports Medicine, 40*, 449–457.

Bennett, M. H., Stanford, R. E., & Turner, R. (2012). Hyperbaric oxygen therapy for promoting fracture healing and treating fracture non-union. *Cochrane Database of Systematic Reviews*, (11), Article CD004712.

Bennie, A., Apoifis, N., Caron, J., Falcão, W., Marlin, D., Bengoechea, E. G., ... George, E. (2017). A guide to conducting systematic reviews of coaching science research. *International Sport Coaching Journal, 4*(2), 191–205.

Bérdi, M., Köteles, F., Hevesi, K., Bárdos, G., & Szabo, A. (2015). Elite athletes' attitudes towards the use of placebo-induced performance enhancement in sports. *European Journal of Sport Science, 15*(4), 315–321.

Bonafiglia, J. T., Rotundo, M. P., Whittall, J. P., Scribbans, T. D., Graham, R. B., & Gurd, B. J. (2016). Inter-individual variability in the adaptive responses to endurance and sprint interval training: A randomized crossover study. *PloS One, 11*(12), e0167790.

Borg, D. N., Lohse, K. R., & Sainani, K. L. (2020). Ten common statistical errors from all phases of research, and their fixes. *PM&R, 12*(6), 610–614.

Collins, H. (2014). *Are we all scientific experts now?*. John Wiley & Sons.

Coughlan, E. (2021). Myths about deliberate practice. In A. Whitehead & J. Coe (Eds.), *Myths of sports coaching* (pp. 1–13). Sequoia Books.

Coutts, A. J. (2016). Working fast and working slow: The benefits of embedding research in high-performance sport. *International Journal of Sports Physiology and Performance, 11*(1), 1–2.

Coveney, C., Faulkner, A., Gabe, J., & McNamee, M. (2020). Beyond the orthodox/CAM dichotomy: Exploring therapeutic decision making, reasoning and practice in the therapeutic landscapes of elite sports medicine. *Social Science & Medicine, 251*, 112905.

Edwards, S. E., da Costa Rocha, I., Williamson, E. M., & Heinrich, M. (2015). *Phytopharmacy: An evidence-based guide to herbal medicinal products*. Wiley Blackwell.

English, K. L., Amonette, W. E., Graham, M., & Spiering, B. A. (2012). What is "evidence-based" strength and conditioning?. *Strength & Conditioning Journal, 34*(3), 19–24.

Ernst, E. (2011). Fatalities after CAM: An overview. *British Journal of General Practice, 61*(587), 404–405.

Food and Drug Administration. (2001). FDA advises dietary supplement manufacturers to remove comfrey products from the market. USFDA. *Center for Food Safety and Applied Nutrition.* https://wayback.archive-it.org/7993/20170722024314/https:/www.fda.gov/Food/RecallsOutbreaksEmergencies/SafetyAlertsAdvisories/ucm111219.htm

Franchini, E., & Takito, M. Y. (2014). Olympic preparation in Brazilian judo athletes: Description and perceived relevance of training practices. *The Journal of Strength & Conditioning Research, 28*(6), 1606–1612.

Frawley, J. (2007). *Sports astrology.* Apprentice Books.

Gambhir, S., Kulshrestha, V., Sood, M., & Sahu, S. (2020). Does hyperbaric oxygen therapy have a role in acute fracture healing-A Randomised Controlled Trial. *Journal of Marine Medical Society, 22*(2), 175–181.

Gaskill, S. E., Serfass, R. C., Bacharach, D. W., & Kelly, J. M. (1999). Responses to training in cross-country skiers. *Medicine & Science in Sports & Exercise, 31*, 1211–1217.

Giannetti, B. M., Staiger, C., Bulitta, M., & Predel, H. G. (2010). Efficacy and safety of comfrey root extract ointment in the treatment of acute upper or lower back pain: Results of a double-blind, randomised, placebo controlled, multicentre trial. *British Journal of Sports Medicine, 44*(9), 637–641.

Goldacre, B. (2009). *Bad science.* Fourth Estate.

Gorski, D. H., & Novella, S. P. (2014). Clinical trials of integrative medicine: Testing whether magic works?. *Trends in Molecular Medicine, 20*(9), 473–476.

Hancock, D. J., Adler, A. L., & Côté, J. (2013). A proposed theoretical model to explain relative age effects in sport. *European Journal of Sport Science, 13*(6), 630–637.

Haugen, T. (2020). Key success factors for merging sport science and best practice. *International Journal of Sports Physiology and Performance, 15*(3), 297–297.

Haugen, T. (2021). Best-practice coaches: An untapped resource in sport-science research. *International Journal of Sports Physiology and Performance, 16*(9), 1215–1216.

Haugen, T., Sandbakk, Ø., Enoksen, E., Seiler, S., & Tønnessen, E. (2021). Crossing the golden training divide: The science and practice of training world-class 800-and 1500-m runners. *Sports Medicine, 51*(9), 1835–1854.

Haugen, T., Sandbakk, Ø., Seiler, S., & Tønnessen, E. (2022). The training characteristics of world-class distance runners: An integration of scientific literature and results-proven practice. *Sports Medicine-Open, 8*(1), 1–18.

Hautala, A. J., Kiviniemi, A. M., Mäkikallio, T. H., Kinnunen, H., Nissilä, S., Huikuri, H. V., & Tulppo, M. P. (2006). Individual differences in the responses to endurance and resistance training. *European Journal of Applied Physiology, 96*, 535–542.

Hay, J. G. (1993). *The biomechanics of sports techniques* (4th ed.). Englewood Cliffs, NJ: Prentice-Hall.

Hellard, P., Avalos-Fernandes, M., Lefort, G., Pla, R., Mujika, I., Toussaint, J. F., & Pyne, D. B. (2019). Elite swimmers' training patterns in the 25 weeks prior to their season's best performances: Insights into periodization from a 20-years cohort. *Frontiers in Physiology, 10*, 363.

Hick, W. E. (1952). On the rate of gain of information. *Quarterly Journal of Experimental Psychology, 4*(1), 11–26.

Hyman, R. (1953). Stimulus information as a determinant of reaction time. *Journal of Experimental Psychology, 45*(3), 188–196.

Ioannidis, J. P. (2017). Hijacked evidence-based medicine: Stay the course and throw the pirates overboard. *Journal of Clinical Epidemiology, 84*, 11–13.

Kamper, S. J., Williams, C. M. (2013 Jan). The placebo effect: powerful, powerless or redundant? Br J Sports Med, 47(1), 6–9. doi: 10.1136/bjsports-2012-091472. Epub 2012 Aug 14. PMID: 22893511.

Kantak, S. S., & Winstein, C. J. (2012). Learning–performance distinction and memory processes for motor skills: A focused review and perspective. *Behavioural Brain Research, 228*(1), 219–231.

Kelly, A. L., Côté, J., Jeffreys, M., & Turnnidge, J. (Eds.). (2021). *Birth advantages and relative age effects in sport: Exploring organizational structures and creating appropriate settings.* Routledge.

Kunz, R., & Oxman, A. D. (1998). The unpredictability paradox: Review of empirical comparisons of randomised and non-randomised clinical trials. *British Medical Journal, 317*(7167), 1185–1190.

Lee, J. A. (2000). *The scientific endeavor: A primer on scientific principles and practice.* Pearson.

Lohse, K., Buchanan, T., & Miller, M. (2016). Underpowered and overworked: Problems with data analysis in motor learning studies. *Journal of Motor Learning and Development, 4*(1), 37–58.

Magill, R., & Anderson, D. I. (2017). *Motor learning and control.* McGraw-Hill Publishing.

Mann, T. N., Lamberts, R. P., & Lambert, M. I. (2014). High responders and low responders: Factors associated with individual variation in response to standardized training. *Sports Medicine, 44*, 1113–1124.

Midgley, A. W., McNaughton, L. R., & Jones, A. M. (2007). Training to enhance the physiological determinants of long-distance running performance: Can valid recommendations be given to runners and coaches based on current scientific knowledge?. *Sports Medicine, 37*, 857–880.

Mujika, I. (2014). Olympic preparation of a world-class female triathlete. *International Journal of Sports Physiology and Performance, 9*(4), 727–731.

Pickering, C., & Kiely, J. (2019). Do non-responders to exercise exist—and if so, what should we do about them?. *Sports Medicine, 49*, 1–7.

Radnor, J. M., Lloyd, R. S., & Oliver, J. L. (2017). Individual response to different forms of resistance training in school-aged boys. *Journal of Strength and Conditioning Research, 31*(3), 787–797.

Ritchie, S. (2020). *Science fictions: Exposing fraud, bias, negligence and hype in science.* Random House.

Ross, E., Gupta, L., & Sanders, L. (2018). When research leads to learning, but not action in high performance sport. *Progress in Brain Research, 240*, 201–217.

Sackett, D. L., Rosenberg, W. M., Gray, J.A., Haynes, R. B., & Richardson, W. S. (1996 Jan). Evidence based medicine: what it is and what it isn't. *BMJ*, 13;312(7023):71-2. doi: 10.1136/bmj.312.7023.71. PMID: 8555924; PMCID: PMC2349778.

Sagan, C. (2000). *The demon-haunted world: Science as a candle in the dark.* Random House.

Schmidt, R. A., Lee, T. D., Winstein, C., Wulf, G., & Zelaznik, H. N. (2019). *Motor control and learning: A behavioral emphasis.* Human Kinetics.

Singh, S., & Ernst, E. (2008). *Trick or treatment? Alternative medicine on trial.* Bantam Press.

Skrabanek, P. (1986). Demarcation of the absurd. *The Lancet, 327*(8487), 960–961.

Smith, K. L., Weir, P. L., Till, K, Romann M, & Cobley S. (2018 Jun). Relative Age Effects Across and Within Female Sport Contexts: A Systematic Review and Meta-Analysis. Sports

Med., 48(6):1451–1478. doi: 10.1007/s40279-018-0890-8. Erratum in: Sports Med. 2018 Apr 17;: PMID: 29536262.

Soderstrom, N. C., & Bjork, R. A. (2015). Learning versus performance: An integrative review. *Perspectives on Psychological Science*, *10*(2), 176–199.

Spence, J. D. (2020). The need for clinical judgement in the application of evidence-based medicine. *BMJ Evidence-Based Medicine*, *25*(5), 172–177.

Sterne, J. A. C, Savović, J., Page, M. J., Elbers, R. G., Blencowe, N. S., Boutron, I., Cates, C. J., Cheng, H. Y., Corbett, M. S., Eldridge, S. M., Emberson, J. R., Hernán, M. A., Hopewell, S., Hróbjartsson, A., Junqueira, D. R., Jüni, P., Kirkham, J. J., Lasserson, T., Li, T., McAleenan, A., Reeves, B. C., Shepperd, S., Shrier, I., Stewart, L. A. Tilling, K., White, I.R., Whiting, P. F., & Higgins, J. P. T. (2019 Aug). RoB 2: a revised tool for assessing risk of bias in randomised trials. BMJ, 28;366:l4898. doi: 10.1136/bmj.l4898. PMID: 31462531.

Stodter, A. (2021). Myths about learning styles in sport coach education. In A. Whitehead & J. Coe (Eds.), *Myths of sports coaching* (pp. 66–77). Sequoia Books.

Tiller, N. (2020). *The skeptic's guide to sport science: Confronting myths of the health and fitness industry*. Routledge.

Wattie, N., Schorer, J., & Baker, J. (2015). The relative age effect in sport: A developmental systems model. *Sports Medicine*, *45*, 83–94.

Whitehead, A., & Coe, J. (2021). *Myths of sports coaching*. Sequoia Books.

Willingham, D. T. (2012). *When can you trust the experts?: How to tell good science from bad in education*. John Wiley & Sons.

Zadro, S., & Stapleton, P. (2022). Does Reiki benefit mental health symptoms above placebo?. *Frontiers in Psychology*, *13*, 3274.

10 Smoke and Mirrors

The Superficial Rise of Women's Sport

Alex Lascu

It would be easy to believe that we have done enough for women's sport by now. After all, many female athletes are getting paid for playing sport in 2023, which is the classical benchmark for professionalism. But when we move beyond the positive smoke that often features in media headlines and social media channels, we realize that there is still so much to do. This chapter aims to hold up a mirror to the recent rise of women's sport, because for every story of success and cause for celebration, every respite that sport (and therefore society) has come a long way, we are reminded that this is a false sense of security.

There is an abundance of resources available now that did not a mere five years ago, such as the *Professionalisation of Women's Sport* by Ali Bowes and Alex Culvin (2021), Bowes' (2022) chapter in *Myths of Sport Coaching* (Chapter 5: The Stepping Stone?) and, most recently, *Girls Don't Play Sport* by Chloe Dalton (2023). I will be leaning heavily on their narratives, especially their exploration of language and sentiment of women's sport, while also weaving in the themes I uncovered about professionalization of women's sport in my recent doctoral thesis (Lascu et al., 2021).

There is an imbalance in sport that we have been hiding behind smoke and mirrors, (un)intentionally halting the progress of women. Despite explicitly trying to unstick the notion that women's sport is an add-on, or stepping stone (Bowes, 2022), through clever advertising campaigns and equal prize money guarantees and paid contracts, there is plenty of work to be done. First, we'll set the ground rules around the language of 'professionalization' before wading through the smoke (all the good news stories that may not be so good) and holding up the mirror (the not-so-good things) to inspire a new wave of action for women in sport.

What do we mean by 'professionalization'?

Professionalism in women's sport is a topic that has garnered increasing attention in the past five years in particular, but the movement is not limited to this time frame. If anything, the fight for women's sport to stand equally with men's sport has been ongoing, featuring battles that men's sport never had to fight. In this chapter, I am defining professionalization in accordance with Bowes and Culvin (2021):

> *Professionalization:* The process of professionalization, underpinned by progressive gender ideologies, involves women's sports organization's demonstrating an increasing formalization of their administration and structure, through policy and practice, resulting in the formal contracting of women as athletes for financial remuneration.

> *Professional sportswoman:* A woman whose financial income from her involvement in sport as an athlete enables her to commit full time, without the need[1] to pursue a second occupation. Any sportswoman who earns enough from participating in sport to cover at least expenses, or is reimbursed in some way, but not enough to warrant a full-time commitment, will be considered semi-professional.

Equipped with these words, we can now continue our exploration of the sporting landscape, keeping in mind that professionalization is not a destination to be reached but rather part of an 'evolving, complex, uncertain and disorderly process' (Woods et al., 2020). The following sections will centre on Australia as a cultural context that is often exacerbated as the 'gold standard' of women's sport (Lascu et al., 2021) and a number of popular sporting events that female athletes seem to be thriving in – the smoke to our mirror.

The smoke

Women's sport has experienced a record-breaking year in 2023 across many facets of sport. The attendance record for a women's sporting event has been broken multiple times over the last three years, most recently at a college volleyball match in Nebraska (Kuta, 2023) where 92,003 people filled the stands. Just before stands were emptied and crowd noises were computer-generated due to a global pandemic, attendance at women's sporting fixtures was growing exponentially (see Figure 10.1). While sport has often garnered a strong

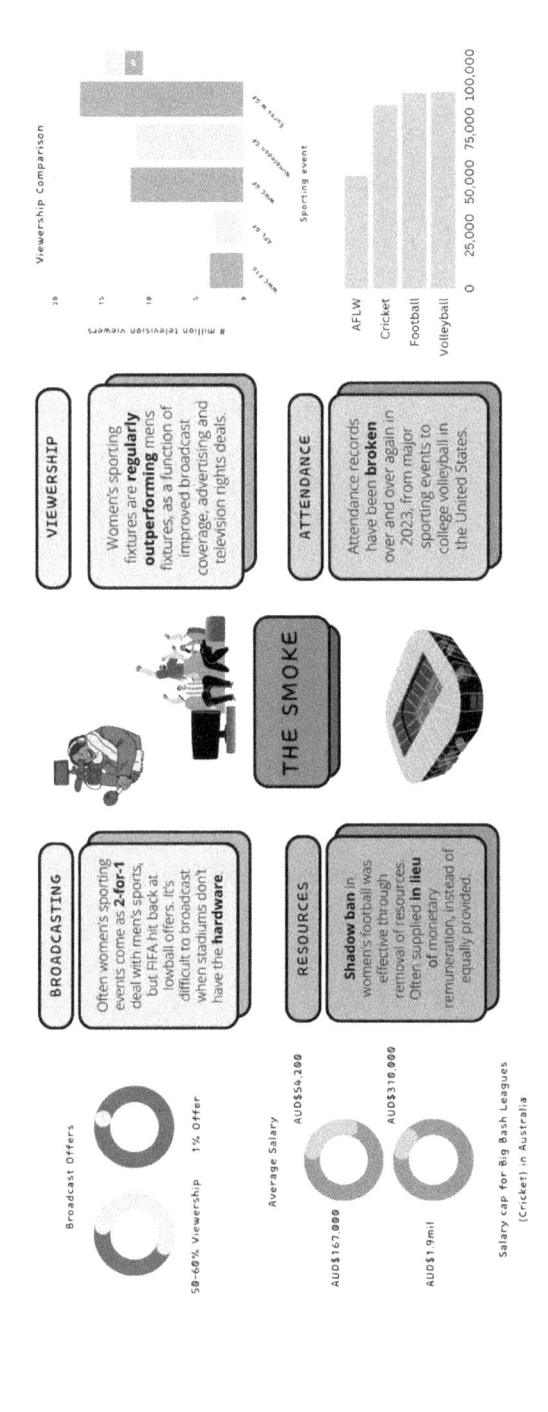

Figure 10.1. A summary of key statistics across The Smoke section: broadcasting, viewership, attendance and resources.

following for male athletes and teams, attention is more recently being turned towards women in sport with more viewers watching the FIFA 2023 Women's World Cup final in the UK than the men's Wimbledon final. During the Euros football competition, a peak viewership of 17.4 million was recorded, making it difficult to continue the rhetoric that people don't want to watch women's sport. Personally, my favourite example comes from the FIFA 2023 Women's World Cup in Australia, where fans left their seats at a live men's AFL match to watch their national team qualify for the semi-final with a penalty shootout on the tiny television screens around the stadium instead of the AFL match they paid to see.

Such popularity does not happen overnight. There is a systematic approach to filling a stadium for a women's sporting fixture, one detailed by Lucy Mills and Julia Belas Tindade (as cited in Dalton, 2023): (1) skill is not enough, players build their own brand and win over thousands of existing men's fans with their style of play; (2) advertise everywhere, make it almost impossible not to know that the game is on that weekend and boldly feature female athletes on posters and billboards; (3) make tickets reasonably priced and play at an iconic venue; and (4) societal attitudes are reflected in sport. These considerations highlight that the rise of women's sport is not accidental. If anything, this response has been delayed due to the saturation of men's sporting events on television, social media and stadiums worldwide.

Setting new standards and expectations for women's sport will take some time as broadcasters and fans alike adjust, but it is a worthwhile fight. Recently, threats of a broadcast blackout overshadowed the beginning of the FIFA 2023 Women's World Cup with broadcasters from Britain, Spain, Italy, Germany and France submitting unacceptably low offers for the television rights (Ingle, 2023). This has not been an issue in the past because the broadcast rights for the Women's World Cup were often offered as part of the package when awarding the men's World Cup rights, a two-for-one deal that broadcasters were not willing to part with yet. The World Cup boasts the highest viewership event for women's football, but broadcasting rights were 20 to 100 times lower for the Women's World Cup. FIFA's response to the broadcast offers was a welcome change given how little advocacy has been made for the value of the women's game previously.

Monetary remuneration is often considered the hallmark of professionalization in sport, and a number of sports are beginning to provide equal prize money for male and female athletes as a demonstration of their evolution. In the meantime, it fell to organizations to fill the gap: FIFA paid every player at the 2023 Women's World Cup a minimum sum to compensate for a lack of federations who could match the amount; and Cricket Australia topped up the prize money for the 2020 T20 Women's World Cup to ensure parity with the men's earnings (Savage, 2023). Such advancements in monetary remuneration need to go deeper into the sporting system if they are to have exponential impact. As a result, the average Women's Big Bash League player (professional T20 competition in Australia) now has double the earning capacity ($54,200 from $26,900).

Across viewership, attendance and monetary remuneration, there are a lot of good stories. But as the subheading suggests, these stories are largely smoke to hide the pervasive inequalities and systemic issues underneath. For every good story here, there is an equally troubling story. As the Independent Commission for Equity in Cricket (ICEC) report (2023) highlights, it's time to hold up a mirror to sport.

The mirror

'Unequal treatment and pay perpetuated by a culture of sexism' was the resounding finding from the ICEC (2023) report into England Cricket. The report was commissioned to review a number of ethical and cultural issues within the sport, and the findings revealed an undercurrent of misalignment and mistreatment of women's sport and the people within it. Not just an add-on to the game, the report found evidence that 'women continue to be treated as subordinate to men within, and at all levels of, cricket. This is evident both from the lived experience of professional and recreational women cricketers and from the structural barriers that women continue to face'. The pay breakdown adds to the damning results, with the average women's salary at just 20.6% of the men's, who received 13 times the amount of overall remuneration. The most recent Ashes competition was undoubtedly one of the biggest in terms of engagement and spectatorship, with side-by-side advertising seen at the grounds around England. Despite this, the women are yet to play a test match at the coveted Lord's Oval, which is colloquially considered the 'home of cricket'.

These findings are symptomatic of a global issue and should not be interpreted as a localized event. Across football, cycling, tennis, Australian rules football (AFL/W), basketball and cricket, the disparity between women's and men's sports in terms of remuneration, resources and media coverage appears almost insurmountable. The underrepresentation of women's sport is not unheard of, but the statistics are dismal with just 5.4% of all televized sports airtime featuring women across three decades as collated by Cooky and colleagues (2021).

After tracking and analysing over 30 years of data to report this underwhelming percentage, Cooky had this to say in a press release:

> Women's coverage is absent, largely, of the elements that we know make watching sport highlights compelling and interesting: exciting commentary, colourful, descriptive, animated delivery, and thoughtful, high-production value interviews and game footage. When you compare women's coverage to men's, the women's comes across as quite bland.

It is difficult to overcome this assessment when games are live-streamed from a camera in the corner of an empty stadium (if it's not glitching or dropping out; Meade, 2021). Even statistics surrounding decreases in television viewership and crowd attendance are skewed when you consider the systematic difficulties some sports face, such as fixtures across 37 venues, inconvenient timing, stadiums without hardware to broadcast effectively or sell more than 8,000 tickets and low-quality playing surfaces (Vinall, 2023a). There was a time when playing sports like Australian rules football and rugby league seemed unlikely given women's football/soccer was banned in 1921.

'*Complaints having been made as to football being played by women, Council felt impelled to express the strong opinion that the game of football is quite unsuitable for females and should not be encouraged*', the Football Association's famous ruling read.

Instead of outrightly banning football in Australia, a shadow ban was implemented for 50 years by refusing to provide resources, facilities and opportunities for women to play (Lewis, 2023). Even though the ban was technically lifted in 1971, the game still hasn't recovered in the 50 years since. This is why providing resources and facilities is often done in the absence of monetary remuneration (Lascu et al., 2021). Amateur status is easily reinforced when you have to fundraise your own way to the first invitational tournament which essentially piloted the Women's World Cup in 1988, and you borrow the kits from U15 boys team to have some sort of playing uniform (Lewis, 2023). In contrast, each team was given the same living conditions, resources and access to facilities that men have received for decades at the 2023 Women's World Cup. But that is not to say every team had a seamless lead-up to the tournament.

Spain did not take a full-strength side into the 2023 Women's World Cup after 15 players publicly refused to be selected in an incendiary letter to the Spanish football federation detailing condescending treatment of the players, poor training sessions and subpar facilities (Thomas, 2023). The World Cup celebrations for the ultimately successful Spanish team were overshadowed by the story of how much the team had overcome to achieve their first major trophy (Williams, 2023), which is a common rhetoric in women's sport. Similarly, Nigeria almost didn't make it to the World Cup because they were still battling their national federation over equal rights and equitable pay in the lead-up to the event, while Canada was fighting for recognition with no existing professional league to develop their players despite being Olympic champions (Elcombe, 2023). To have the same opportunities to prepare and perform as a woman in sport, there are arbitrary systemic barriers that do not need to exist but continue to remain.

Regarding monetary remuneration, Jodie Hawkins illustrated the issue perfectly while she was the general manager of a Big Bash League team (cricket) in Australia (Greenway, 2023): '*We've got some of the most marketable people in the country, in the world running around in our sports, and they're getting paid not even what the minimum contract of a men's BBL player or even grade cricketers. It just does my head in*'. That frustration is likely a shared global burden for advocates, especially in instances where the funding to support women's sport is sacrificed when a club or competition is under financial stress. Just recently, a professional netball team in Australia (funded by a wealthy AFL team) was discontinued due to a 'lack of financial viability' despite turning an AUD $7 million profit in 2022 (Carter, 2023). Similarly, an Indian football/soccer team 'paused' their women's team to pay a fine incurred by the men's team for protesting a controversial decision (D'Cunha, 2023). This sentiment that women's sporting teams are add-ons that can be removed when convenient is arguably more insidious than the disparity of pay. The stark differences in pay and allocation of funds are highlighted in the New Economy of Sport report (Wasserman's The Collective & Royal Bank of Canada, 2023) and reiterated in Figure 10.1.

It is difficult to hold up this mirror and influence change in sport when faced with a number of misconceptions that remain present in the public's mind. The next section targets two of the most 'sticky' phrases in relation to women's sport to highlight what we must overcome to move forward.

Common misconceptions

Women's sport is not profitable

For every $1 a corporate sponsor invests into the visibility of women's elite sport results in $7.29 in customer value for that organization, on average. This was the most compelling statistic to come out of a recent report by Change the Game (2023) in Australia, an initiative designed to 'encourage the sport and recreation sector to challenge gender stereotypes and help women and girls become leaders'. Furthermore, early corporate supporters of women's elite sport benefit from more than $650 million in customer value annually. The sponsorship of women's elite sporting properties also outperform the men's on brand awareness, brand consideration and customer conversion as well as improved brand attributes and increased employee satisfaction as a key point of difference between the sponsorship of men's and women's elite sports. As the 2023 FIFA WWC came to a close, they reported AUD $888 million (USD $570 million) in revenue – the most successful iteration of the competition. While the argument around revenue and/or profit may have been viable in the past, it is no longer relevant.

Part-time athletes, full-time expectations

This dichotomy is a common refrain in women's sport as investment doesn't yet afford the opportunity to pursue sport full time. And yet, the lack of performance is often confounded as a lack of skill or aptitude, not preparation. Bowes (2022) details the rich socio-cultural history that reinforces that sport is not a place for women, which is then operationalized by the systemic underfunding and underrepresentation that makes it increasingly difficult to go above and beyond these misguided perceptions of female athletes. Dalton (2023) details the exhaustion of balancing work, training and university, chasing the dream of representing your country in a sport that you've dedicated your life to, while also working a job that is flexible enough to exist outside of training hours. '[The] expectations on our performance and demanding hours required are completely incongruous with our status as part-time athletes', Dalton writes, with inadvertent consequences such as four anterior cruciate ligament ruptures in the first four rounds of the 2022 season, stagnant growth in skills because training time is limited, low competition scores as talent is stretched thinly across 16 clubs and only 10 matches per season. This makes vying for a full-time contract increasingly difficult, despite the full-time hours dedicated to performance preparation.

This mirror acts as a point of reflection to inspire progression in women's sport that goes beyond the superficial smoke.

Inspiring a solid foundation

It has become increasingly apparent that the disparities seen in women's sport have very little to do with the athletes themselves – or the product they produce as elite performers – and more to do with prevailing systemic barriers and societal perceptions. There is now a moral responsibility to redress the imbalance from historical inequities in sport (Archer & Prange, 2019) and the growing body of literature (Serpell et al., 2023; Martinez-Rosales et al., 2021) and media (Elting, 2023) addressing the underrepresentation of women is a positive first step. The findings from a Sport England (2022) report reiterate why dispelling this myth is important: 22% fewer girls than boys play team sport in England, which means about 860,000 children are missing out on team sport, and less than 1.2 million girls are playing football than boys.

If we look at the economic implications of these figures, involvement in sport to improve physical health can take a significant load off healthcare services, mental health providers and combat the rise of obesity levels. Together, they account for 6.2% GDP in the UK, which is approximately £34.72 million. When estimated across Europe, €16.1 billion could be saved by helping one person in every five reach the recommended levels of daily activity, which sport has the power to do. There is an opportunity to truly harness the power of women in sport, but investment needs to come at a higher cost than saving face.

The first step beyond structural and systemic changes to remuneration and resourcing is to evolve athlete partnerships. Women athletes exist at the heart of the intersection between social impact, brand building and fan engagement (Wasserman's The Collective & Royal Bank of Canada, 2023). They are conduits to fans with spending power, connect with fans beyond their on-field performances and drive double the engagement on social media with half the number of followers (ibid, p. 13–20).

To leverage this capacity for impact and connection, women athletes should be considered as commercial partners above and beyond remuneration to match their commitment to elite performance. To do so, the New Economy of Sport report (ibid.) suggests capturing the right data and letting it guide decision-making, crafting long-term deals for mutually beneficial equity and playing the long game by viewing women athletes as long-term investments. After all, 'As women athletes become more sought after, and endorsements more prevalent, the economic standards for women athletes will shift to reflect their true value' (ibid., p. 26).

Note

1   May want to pursue a second occupation, but it is not out of necessity.

References

Soccerscene. https://www.soccerscene.com.au/football-coaches-australia-upholds-the-need-for-fair-pay-and-suitable-employment-conditions-in-coach-survey-report/

Bowes, A. (2021). The stepping stone? Challenging the myth that women's sport is less significant than men's sport. In Whitehead, A., & Coe, J. Myths of Sport Coaching. Sequoia

Bowes, A., & Culvin, A. (Eds.). (2021). *The professionalisation of women's sport: Issues and debates* (First edition). Emerald Publishing Limited.

Carter, B. (2023a, May 25). *Just asked Netball Australia CEO Kelly Ryan whether netball feels a bit used*. Twitter. https://twitter.com/_BrittanyCarter/status/1661596156038873088

Carter, B. (2023b, May 25). *Netball competition will impact the rest of the league*. Twitter. https://twitter.com/_BrittanyCarter/status/1661598265492783106

Change our Game (2023). https://changeourgame.vic.gov.au/the-initiative/change-our-game-grants/change-our-game-aicd-foundations-of-directorship/women-in-sports-media-program

Cooky, C., Council, L. D., Mears, M. A., & Messner, M. A. (2021). *One and done: The long eclipse of women's televised sports, 1989–2019*. Retrieved August 27, 2023, from https://journals.sagepub.com/doi/full/10.1177/21674795211003524?_ga=2.41830817.2086131400.1688575652-1678371732.1688575652

Dalton, C. (2023). Girls Don't Play Sport: The game-changing, defiant rise of women's sport, and why it matters. Allen & Unwin

D'Cuhna, Z. (2023, June 6). *Play, Pause, Stop: Kerala Blasters nix women's team with spectacular own goal*. ESPN. https://www.espn.in/football/story/_/id/37806050/kerala-blasters-pause-womens-football-team-spectacular-own-goal

Elcombe, T. (2023, August 3). *The upside to Canada being knocked out of the FIFA Women's World Cup*. https://theconversation.com/the-upside-to-canada-being-knocked-out-of-the-fifa-womens-world-cup-210782

Elting, L. (2023, July 12). *Women's sports are profitable—When brands, media and broadcast buy in*. https://www.forbes.com/sites/lizelting/2023/07/12/going-for-gold-womens-sports-are-profitable-when-brands-media-and-broadcast-buy-in/amp/

Greenway, L. (2023). Women and girls' cricket: How we can grow the game together. *Sequoia Books*. https://www.sequoia-books.com/catalog/greenway/

Ingle, S. (2023, May 2). FIFA threatens Women's World Cup broadcast blackout in Europe. *The Guardian*. https://www.theguardian.com/football/2023/may/02/fifa-threatens-womens-world-cup-broadcast-blackout-in-europe-offers-rights-infantino

Kuta, S. (2023, September 1). *Nebraska Volleyball Sets New World Record for Attendance at a Women's Sporting Event*. Smithsonian Magazine. https://www.smithsonianmag.com/smart-news/with-92003-fans-nebraska-sets-new-world-record-for-attendance-at-womens-sporting-event-180982844/

Lascu, A., Spratford, W., Pyne, D. B., & Etxebarria, N. (2021). Talent development in women's cricket: Perceptions and practices of elite players and coaches. *International Journal of Sports Science & Coaching, 16*(4), 900–912.

Lewis, S. (2023, July 19). *Out of the shadows: How women's football flourished after 50 years of darkness*. ABC (Australian Broadcasting Corporation). https://www.abc.net.au/news/2023-07-20/out-of-the-shadows-womens-football-soccer-fifa-world-cup-2023/102321436

Martínez-Rosales, E., Hernández-Martínez, A., Sola-Rodríguez, S., Esteban-Cornejo, I., & Soriano-Maldonado, A. (2021). Representation of women in sport sciences research, publications, and editorial leadership positions: Are we moving forward? *Journal of Science and Medicine in Sport, 24*(11), 1093–1097. https://doi.org/10.1016/j.jsams.2021.04.010

Nic Savage. (2023, July 15). *'One piece of the puzzle': ICC announces equal prize money for men's and women's teams at World Cup events.* https://www.foxsports.com.au/cricket/one-piece-of-the-puzzle-icc-announces-equal-prize-money-for-mens-and-womens-teams-at-world-cup-events/news-story/1cba046c1a83153438a85d6bae0757de

Serpell, B. G., Harrison, D., Dower, R., & Cook, C. J. (2023). The under representation of women coaches in high-performance sport. *International Journal of Sports Science & Coaching, 18*(4), 1320–1332. https://doi.org/10.1177/17479541231160229

Sport England. (2022).https://www.sportengland.org/research-and-data/data/active-lives

The Associated Press. (2023, August 25). *Nike to sell replicas of England goalkeeper Mary Earps' Jersey after backlash in U.K.* NPR. https://www.npr.org/2023/08/25/1195854315/nike-to-sell-replicas-of-england-goalkeeper-mary-earps-jersey-after-backlash-in-

The Female Athlete Project. (2023, August 20). *The [female] athlete project on Instagram: "The players of the Australian Wallaroos (15s rugby) shared this statement today."* Instagram. https://www.instagram.com/p/CwJ7MQULt9_/

Thomas, L. (2023, July 23). *The World Cup and the frustrating, inspiring state of women's soccer.* The New Yorker. https://www.newyorker.com/sports/sporting-scene/the-world-cup-and-the-frustrating-inspiring-state-of-womens-soccer

Vinall, M. (2023, July 10). *'The broadcast was almost unwatchable': The insiders' view on why Australia switched off AFLW.* The Age. https://www.theage.com.au/sport/afl/the-broadcast-was-almost-unwatchable-the-insiders-view-on-why-australia-switched-off-aflw-20230706-p5dm7b.html

Vinall, M. (2023, June 26). *'Culture of silence': Survey shows angst among players.* The Age. https://www.theage.com.au/sport/afl/culture-of-silence-survey-shows-angst-among-players-20230626-p5djiv.html

Wasserman's The Collective & Royal Bank of Canada. (2023). *The new economy of sports.* Wasserman's The Collective. https://www.wearethecollective.com/new-economy-of-sports

Williams, Ra. (2023, August 22). *Women's World Cup 2023: The good, the bad and the stupid.* Women in Sport. https://womeninsport.org/news/womens-world-cup-2023-the-good-the-bad-and-the-stupid/

Williams, R. (2023, August 14). *Australia is too sexist to embrace female coaches across men's and women's sport, says Rennae Stubbs.* Daily Telegraph. https://www.dailytelegraph.com.au/sport/womens-sport/insight/australia-is-too-sexist-to-embrace-female-coaches-across-mens-and-womens-sport-says-rennae-stubbs/news-story/092263f53e5a65df01ad22d8cfd447e9

Women in Sport. (2023, July 16). *Girls' sporting lives stagnant despite the glory of the lionesses – Action is needed to close the gender gap.* https://womeninsport.org/news/girls-sporting-lives-stagnant-despite-the-glory-of-the-lionesses-action-is-needed-to-close-the-gender-gap/

Woods, C. T., Robertson, S., Rudd, J., Araújo, D., & Davids, K. (2020). 'Knowing as we go': A Hunter-Gatherer Behavioural Model to Guide Innovation in Sport Science. *Sports Medicine - Open, 6*(1), 52. https://doi.org/10.1186/s40798-020-00281-8

11 Physical Fatigue in Football

A Challenge to the Importance of Fatigue in Determining Performance in Football Match Play

Liam Anderson, Thomas Brownlee, Barry Drust and Matej Varjan

Introduction: The demands of football

Physically, football is a highly demanding sport where short bouts of intense activity are superimposed amongst longer periods of low-to-moderate intensity activity over 90 minutes (Stolen et al., 2005). Football match play's intermittent pattern exposes players to significant mechanical and metabolic stress, which in turn induces physiological changes both during and after match play. Within match play, players cover 10–13 km of total distance with ~80–90% being at speeds <19.8 km·hr^{-1}, ~10–20% at speeds >19.8 km·hr^{-1} (Bradley et al., 2009; Di Salvo et al., 2010). In addition to the locomotive demands, there are instances when players are required to transition from low-to-moderate intensities to higher-intensity activities and vice versa which results in ~1200 accelerations and decelerations during match play (Russell et al., 2016), which results in a change in activity every 4–6 seconds (Bangsbo, 1994; Mohr et al., 2003). To meet these demands, running performance must be sustained for a prolonged period of time (across the entire match) requiring a high level of force and energy production.

Fatigue in football

The available research would suggest that the demands of the game prevent players from performing at a consistent level across the time of a game. Fatigue can be broadly defined as an acute impairment of performance that includes both an increase in the perceived effort to exert a desired force or power and/or any reduction in the ability to exert maximal force or power (Gandevia, 2001).

Within football, fatigue can be described by changes in physical performance that are reflected in reductions in the external load. Table 11.1 provides an overview of reductions in external load at various time periods throughout a match. It has been suggested that players experience fatigue from the first half to second half, towards the end of the match as well as temporarily during the game (Bangsbo et al., 2006). These temporary reductions are associated with the parts of the game after the most demanding 5-minute period of match play and within the last 15-minute period of the game (Mohr et al., 2003). The performance on different physical assessments such as maximal strength, jumping ability and sprint performance have also shown reductions immediately after matches when compared with data collected before (Mohr et al., 2004; Krustrup et al., 2006). This would seem to indicate that the ability to generate optimal physical performances in such tests is reduced albeit temporarily. The rules of football allow players who start the game to be replaced by substitutes. As these players typically don't play the entire game, their activity may provide a useful insight into the existence of fatigue in games. For example, substitutes who are introduced into the latter stages of a match would be expected to perform more activity in the equivalent time period than those who have completed the full match from the start. Bradley et al. (2014) found that substitutes who come on within the second half had a higher physical performance level (15% more high-intensity running) than those who had played the full game (when expressed relative to time playing). That substitutes are playing within the same match yet performing to a greater level of physical performance supports the notion that players who are completing full matches experience fatigue during the second half.

The available evidence would therefore seem to suggest that fatigue is an issue that impacts the performance of players. The extent of this fatigue may, however, be partly related to the way that the available research conceptually operationalizes and assesses the concept of fatigue within the sport. This chapter will attempt to examine these approaches with a view to providing critical insights that may support a reconsideration of the importance of fatigue in determining the physical performance of players within football matches.

Challenging the existence of fatigue in football

Methodological approaches used to evaluate fatigue in football

Outlining the conceptual approaches to identifying fatigue in football is an important first step in reconsidering the extent to which the fatigue that is

Table 11.1. External loading data to display different methods of assessing fatigue within football match play.

Half-to-Half Comparison		Total Distance			High-Speed Running Distance (m)		
	Population	1st Half	2nd Half	Difference (%)	1st Half	2nd Half	Difference (%)
Barros et al. (2007)	Brazilian 1st Division	5173	4808	-7.1	1541	1308	-15.1
Bradley et al. (2009)	English Premier League	5422	5292	-2.4	1328	1295	-2.5
Carling and Dupont (2011)	French Ligue 1	5694	5432	-4.6	1404	1273	-9.3
Zubillaga et al. (2006)	La Liga	5121	5218	+0.9	1028	1148	+11.7
	English Premier League	5297	5252	+0.9	991	1069	+7.8
Mohr et al. (2003)	Serie A	5510	5350	-2.9			
	Danish Superliga	5200	5130	-1.3			

Discrete Period Comparison

	Population	Comparison Details	High-Speed Running Distance (m)		
			0–15 mins	75–90 mins	Difference (%)
Bradley et al. (2009)	English Premier League	0–15 minutes vs. 75–90 minutes	446	374	-16

Post Intese Period Comparison

	Population	Comparison Details	High-Speed Running Distance (m)				
			Peak 5 min	Average 5 min	Post Peak 5 min	Difference to peak (%)	Difference to average (%)
Mohr et al. (2003)	Serie A	Peak 5 min period vs the following 5 min period and 5 min average	219	121	106	-51.6	-12.4
	Danish Superliga		172	105	94	-45.3	-10.5
Bradley et al. (2009)	English Premier League		231	134	126	-45.5	-6

observed in games is a key performance determinant in the sport. Within any research study, the measured outcomes may be a function of the direct influence of one variable on another or merely a result of the experimental design and specific methodologies employed to measure the dependent variable. Analysing the physical performance of players during different specific time periods in match play is a common and practical approach to understanding when fatigue occurs (see Table 11.1). Typically, this is done by examining the differences from the first half to the second half of a match but can also be done by examining differences between specific discrete periods (i.e. initial 15 minutes of the first half and the last 15 minutes of the second half). In addition, short periods after the most intense periods can be examined and can be compared to the match average. The data for this analysis is collected using tracking cameras or global positioning system devices and then analysing the data to highlight when fluctuations in physical performance occur. Knowledge of when these changes occur can then allow practitioners to understand why they happen (i.e. the underlying physiology) and enable strategies (i.e. training) to build the physical capabilities of players so that physical performance is not then subsequently limited by fatigue. Other approaches to examine fatigue include pre-, during (i.e. half time) and post-match performance testing. For example, examinations of sprinting performance before the game, at half time and after the match found that repeated sprint performance was reduced at half time and markedly reduced after the game (Krustrup et al., 2006). These approaches are based on an assumption that reductions in test performance are associated with a number of changes in the physiological status of a player as a consequence of performing the activities required in the game.

Methodological approaches used to evaluate fatigue in football: Some challenges to the approaches used

This section will attempt to highlight some of the potential issues with the conceptual and methodological approaches outlined above for the calculation of fatigue in football. These ideas do not in themselves rule out the existence of players exhibiting fatigue in the game but merely challenge the extent to which fatigue can be assumed to exist. The typical approach of subtracting specific periods that occur late in the game from other periods of match play can be challenged. The typical period used as a comparator for later phases of the game is the first period of the match (e.g. 15 minutes). It is well recognized that this initial phase of play is not actually representative of the overall demands of the game. These phases are typically associated with very demanding high-intensity activities that are not seen when the teams start to settle in the general rhythm of the match. As such using this as the basis for comparison with other periods automatically biases findings towards the identification of less activity later in the match. There are also issues of applying arbitrary time bins to activities (e.g. five-minute periods) that do not accurately capture the stochastic nature of football match play. Physical performance changes are unlikely to fall within the predetermined time points often used and so such approaches may lack sensitivity to detect the highest or lowest physically demanding phases of play. Other statistical procedures such as rolling averages have been employed in an attempt to address this issue, though this type of analysis may not also capture the activity in a way that is really meaningful to performance. We also know that the activity profiles of players are highly variable. Few studies have examined repeat observations of the same player across a game to determine the variability that we might expect to see. Without this type of data, any variation we come across in games may merely be a function of the inherent variability in players' activities rather than an accurate representation of fatigue.

The research that has used pre- and post-game testing protocols can also pose methodological issues. The majority of these tests reflect an individual's willingness to produce a maximal effort as much as the physiological capability of the body's systems to function optimally. As a result, these reductions in performance that are seen post-game may simply be a function of the motivation of participants to give a maximal effort. Typically, the reductions observed are also small and may well be within the inherent variability that is often seen in such field-based tests. This may also be partly a function of small changes in the specific conditions that such field tests are often performed in such studies.

The nature of the sport and the importance of context as a moderating factor in the observation of fatigue profiles in football

When analysing the fluctuation in physical performance, the data seems to indicate that there are reductions as the game progresses and after intense periods. Analysing physical performance like this assumes that the opportunity for players to engage in physical activity maximally during the game is

Contextual Considerations

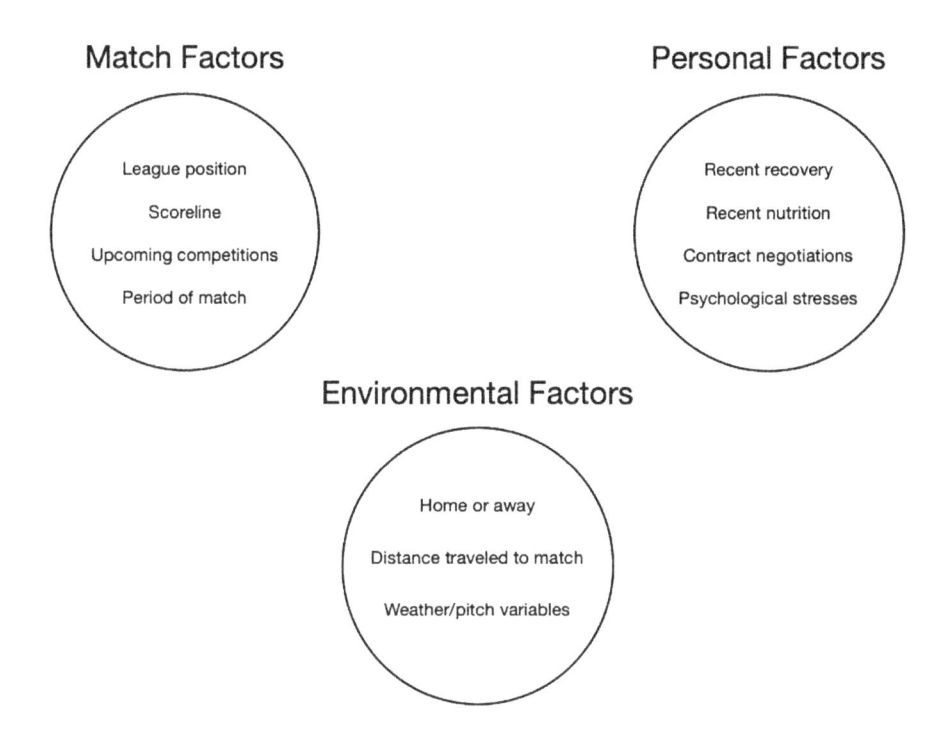

Match Factors
- League position
- Scoreline
- Upcoming competitions
- Period of match

Personal Factors
- Recent recovery
- Recent nutrition
- Contract negotiations
- Psychological stresses

Environmental Factors
- Home or away
- Distance traveled to match
- Weather/pitch variables

Figure 11.1. Schematic outlining groups of 'situational variables' that may contextually impact physical match output with examples.

constant. However, football is an intermittent sport where players perform at various intensities throughout the match play depending on the demands placed upon them in relation to the contextual aspects of the game that are happening at the specific time. Indeed, this means that there are occasions when players do not use their full capabilities as factors such as tactical strategy that result in inherent variation of physical performance both within-game and game-to-game (Drust et al., 2007; Gregson et al., 2010). Therefore, the reductions in physical performance that are observed may not be due to fatigue but are merely alterations as a function of the players performing to the demands placed upon them at the time. Given that contextual aspects will change frequently within matches, it may be difficult to directly attribute the reductions in physical performance to fatigue. Figure 11.1 outlines a range of contextual factors that exist in football that can impact the physical performance of players.

The context of the game: An outline of the importance of context in determining fatigue profiles in football

Having considered how we might look to monitor for the presence of fatigue, as well as the potential issues around these methods, we should also consider how the context of the game might impact these metrics. The reason that this is important is that just because we think we may be able to identify reductions in physical output, it does not necessarily mean that this fatigue is responsible. It is reasonable to think that there are likely a number of contextual factors that may also play a part in the levels of exertion required or applied by players during competition. For example, when looking at GPS outputs in isolation, our ability to draw conclusions is limited. We may see a consistent output of typical metrics, such as high-speed running, throughout a match that then increases in the final 10 minutes. In absolute isolation, we may take this to refute the existence of fatigue as a concept, as we may expect to see the opposite in the final stages of a match. However, considering context as simple as knowing that the team was winning 1-0 before the opposition scored an equalizer in the 80th minute might quickly explain this uptick in physical exertion. Score line is only one piece of context that perhaps is of interest. The remainder of this section will consider several others to help us better understand the potential presence of fatigue during match play.

Without applying a lens of context, we are limited to the conclusions we can draw from any isolated monitoring data we might have access to. This too is the case if we are interested in the potential presence of fatigue. Without context this provides us with no way of knowing whether drop-offs in any key variables are voluntary and are a result of reduced effort or are involuntary and a result of fatigue. We began to consider the importance of context by thinking about how the score of the game might influence the efforts of players during competition. Even within the score itself, we can delve deeper into how much of an impact context might have. We referred to going from leading 1-0 to drawing 1-1 in the final minutes of a match. Potentially, this would yield an increase in effort based on the hypothetical example above. Even here, further context might allow us to better understand what might happen. Going from 1-0 to 1-1 in the 80th minute may make the team work harder to rectify that. If, however, they are 10 points clear at the top of the league with an important European Cup game in 3 days, they may be less inclined to push towards a winning position. And, using the earlier extrapolation, we may see this, based solely on the score, as the team not being able to increase intensity. In reality, though, they simply may be favouring the next match over the current one when it comes to expending effort. They may even look to secure a draw and lower the tempo further. This might suggest fatigue whereas in reality this has simply been a decision based on context. This tells us that we cannot overlook context when looking to explain reductions in effort over time as fatigue is not a straightforward concept.

If we think solely about external load analysis, as it is often considered an important marker for physical effort, there is far more for us to think about than just the score line, as we have just established. These contextual considerations are sometimes known as 'situational variables' (Lago-Penas, 2012) and would include, though are not limited to, the position in the league of teams playing, as briefly mentioned, whether a team is playing at home or away, the distance travelled to the match, tactics, player availability and even weather conditions. When we consider whether teams are playing at home, it is anecdotally accepted that this is a favourable position in terms of match results based on familiarity and the benefits of a home crowd. From a tactical point of view when playing at home teams might adopt more aggressive tactics, which may lead to higher physical outputs from their players, compared to the more conservative approach for an away team. Again, for the away team, this may seem to suggest the presence of fatigue, while in reality it is a factor of the style of play. These tactics are unsurprising when we consider research showing that home players were more (Waters and Lovell, 2002). Beyond some of the more obvious contextual factors, some are perhaps less obvious with sudden weather changes, such as heavy rain, or playing on a sloped pitch, such as at St James' Park in Newcastle, UK, can alter playing conditions and affect player exertion levels. Here, players may seem to demonstrate fatigue while it is an unusual external factor acting upon them, in the case of the weather. In the case of the sloped pitch, players may be pacing themselves (voluntary easing of effort) as they know playing uphill may be more challenging. It seems therefore that it would be useful also to consider some of these situational variables when reporting physical match variables. The challenge comes when looking to understand how to specifically act upon these noted variables. Although initially, it may be something additional for practitioners to record to look for patterns over time, it is useful to keep in mind when considering the potential existence of fatigue in football. As we start to consider these additional variables, it makes it far more challenging to be certain.

It seems clear that researchers and sports scientists must consider a range of contextual factors. By incorporating game context, we can delve deeper into the dynamics of player performance. For example, the total distance covered by a player may indicate physical exertion, but the reasons behind that exertion

– whether it's due to defensive pressure, counter-attacking strategies or maintaining a lead – can only be fully comprehended by including the game context in the analysis. The presence of fatigue in football is not a straightforward concept. It is deeply entwined with the intricate context of the game. For example, Abbott et al. (2018) found that stress, mood and sleep were ≥ 12% worse after playing against higher-level opposition. This suggests that contextual factors are not only relevant during the match being played but also may have knock-on impacts on subsequent performance. Player match metrics may present as being reduced in subsequent games, but based on such data it could be that insufficient recovery has led to potential physical drop-offs rather than a presence of fatigue per se.

This importance of consideration for context is further compounded based on a study by Brito et al. (2016), who found that subsequent training sessions produced higher physical outputs following an away match than a home match. Polman et al. (2007) also found that eating habits were influenced following competition based on certain situational variables suggesting that even fuelling and recovery may be influenced by context. Taken together, these factors too will obviously have an impact on the potential for fatigue to occur or seem to occur. Match performance itself may not cause fatigue, but when compounded with poor recovery or nutrition, in these examples, it does seem to be evident if we only take things at face value. To comprehensively understand fatigue, external load analysis should extend beyond mere physical metrics to encompass the broader context of the match. By examining the various contextual factors, we can uncover the multifaceted influences on player fatigue, paving the way for more effective player management and improved performance outcomes.

As important as it is to consider contextual factors when looking to identify the existence of fatigue, it is important to think of the influence of ball-in-play (BIP) time as an umbrella over all of these. Having listed and explained how these situational factors might present us with data that suggests the presence of fatigue, we should consider these combined with BIP trends. Ball-out-of-play (BOP) times in football matches have been shown to be low in English Premier League (42.3%), Chinese Super League (45.2%) (Zhao and Liu, 2022) and in two FIFA World Cups in 2006 (41.8%) and 2014 (43.3%) (Augste and Corders, 2016). The average number of interruptions has also been seen to be between 108 and 116 (Augste and Corders, 2016; Siegle and Lames, 2012). Interestingly, from recently collected unpublished data when controlling for the effect of BIP, we found that the decrease in relative running performance across a match diminished or disappeared completely (see Figure 11.2). This suggests

Physical Fatigue in Football

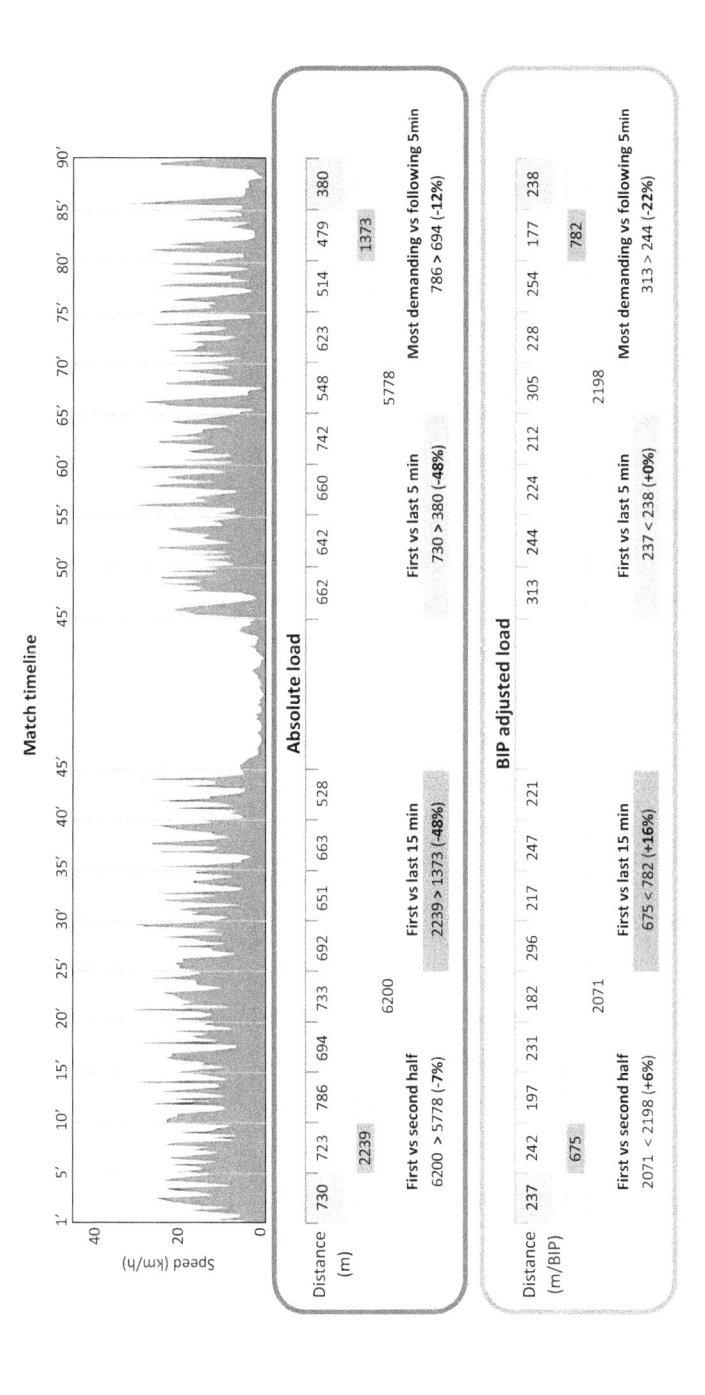

Figure 11.2. Image description: Real data of one player from the game. Presentation of external load in five-minute periods in absolute values (blue frame) – then relative data to Ball-in-play time (distane/BIP) (green frame). There was an injury in the last minutes of the game and long medical treatment + time wasting. It's nicely visible in the picture. In absolute values, in the last five minutes, significantly the lowest values of external load were recorded. Considering that there was almost no play (relative to BIP), the data is above average. It may be worth mentioning that this player also recorded his second-fastest run of the game in the last five minutes.

that fatigue may be largely context-dependent and not necessarily a given outcome of any match. This does not negate the need for the proper management of the physical attributes of players but rather points to the need to consider these within the coaching tactics and philosophies.

Individual pacing: The potential for an individual self-chosen activity to impact fatigue profiles

Football match play presents players with unpredictable and diverse requirements. This unpredictability provides the basis for players to employ conscious or subconscious pacing strategies so that they can maintain performance throughout an entire match. This is based on players deciding when and how to respond to the diverse situations that they are faced with in a game (Waldron and Highton, 2014). Although there are contextual factors that likely influence pacing during match play, it is unclear as to what extent these may affect the specific pacing strategies used. While the context of the game will no doubt affect all players' activity profiles, there is also clearly a potential role for these to be further influenced on an individual level. There is no information to date that attempts to link the broader contextual factors in the game to the patterns of activity that are produced across individual players so the extent of individual pacing strategies is hard to quantify. The potential for it to play a role though in the fatigue profiles that are often observed in games cannot however be ignored.

Conclusion

The purpose of this chapter is not to dispel the idea that there are reductions in the physical performance of footballers within games and that these reductions do not ultimately relate to the outcome of matches. There are clear examples where players will fatigue and obvious implications for these reductions in performance to clearly impact the performance of individual players, groups of players and then the team. The purpose of this chapter is instead to be purposefully provocative around the way that these important performance constructs are conceptually and methodologically operationalized in both research and practice. By challenging the dogma that exists, we are more likely to create better ways of both thinking about and practically addressing the issue of changes in activity profiles. Such new insights are the only way in which we are better able to inform practice and support both the performance and health aspirations of football organizations and players.

References

Abbott, W., Brownlee, T. E., Harper, L. D., Naughton, R. J. & Clifford, T. 2018. The independent effects of match location, match result and the quality of opposition on subjective wellbeing in under 23 soccer players: A case study. *Res Sports Med,* 26, 262–275.

Augste, C. & Corders, O. 2016. Game stoppages as a tactical means in soccer—A comparison of the FIFA World Cups (TM) 2006 and 2014. *Int J Perform Anal Sport,* 16, 1053–1064.

Bangsbo, J. 1994. The physiology of soccer--with special reference to intense intermittent exercise. *Acta Physiol Scand Suppl,* 619, 1–155.

Bangsbo, J., Mohr, M. & Krustrup, P. 2006. Physical and metabolic demands of training and match-play in the elite football player. *J Sports Sci,* 24, 665–674.

Bradley, P. S., Lago-Penas, C. & Rey, E. 2014. Evaluation of the match performances of substitution players in elite soccer. *Int J Sports Physiol Perform,* 9, 415–424.

Bradley, P. S., Sheldon, W., Wooster, B., Olsen, P., Boanas, P. & Krustrup, P. 2009. High-intensity running in English FA Premier League soccer matches. *J Sports Sci,* 27, 159–168.

Brito, J., Hertzog, M. & Nassis, G. P. 2016. Do match-related contextual variables influence training load in highly trained soccer players? *J Strength Cond Res,* 30, 393—399.

Di Salvo, V., Baron, R., Gonzalez-Haro, C., Gormasz, C., Pigozzi, F. & Bachl, N. 2010. Sprinting analysis of elite soccer players during European Champions League and UEFA Cup matches. *J Sports Sci,* 28, 1489–1494.

Drust, B., Atkinson, G. & Reilly, T. 2007. Future perspectives in the evaluation of the physiological demands of soccer. *Sports Med,* 37, 783–805.

Gandevia, S. C. 2001. Spinal and supraspinal factors in human muscle fatigue. *Physiol Rev,* 81, 1725–1789.

Gregson, W., Drust, B., Atkinson, G. & Salvo, V. D. 2010. Match-to-match variability of high-speed activities in premier league soccer. *Int J Sports Med,* 31, 237–242.

Krustrup, P., Mohr, M., Steensberg, A., Bencke, J., Kjaer, M. & Bangsbo, J. 2006. Muscle and blood metabolites during a soccer game: Implications for sprint performance. *Med Sci Sports Exerc,* 38, 1165–1174.

Lago-Penas, C. 2012. The role of situational variables in analysing physical performance in soccer. *J Hum Kinet,* 35, 89–95.

Mohr, M., Krustrup, P. & Bangsbo, J. 2003. Match performance of high-standard soccer players with special reference to development of fatigue. *J Sports Sci,* 21, 519–528.

Mohr, M., Krustrup, P., Nybo, L., Nielsen, J. J. & Bangsbo, J. 2004. Muscle temperature and sprint performance during soccer matches--beneficial effect of re-warm-up at half-time. *Scand J Med Sci Sports,* 14, 156–162.

Polman, R., Nicholls, A. R., Cohen, J. & Borkoles, E. 2007. The influence of game location and outcome on behaviour and mood states among professional rugby league players. *J Sports Sci,* 25, 1491–1500.

Russell, M., Sparkes, W., Northeast, J., Cook, C. J., Love, T. D., Bracken, R. M. & Kilduff, L. P. 2016. Changes in acceleration and deceleration capacity throughout professional soccer match-play. *J Strength Cond Res,* 30, 2839–2844.

Siegle, M. & Lames, M. 2012. Game interruptions in elite soccer. *J Sports Sci,* 30, 619–624.

Stolen, T., Chamari, K., Castagna, C. & Wisloff, U. 2005. Physiology of soccer: An update. *Sports Med,* 35, 501–536.

Waldron, M. & Highton, J. 2014. Fatigue and pacing in high-intensity intermittent team sport: An update. *Sports Med,* 44, 1645–1658.

Waters, A. & Lovell, G. 2002. An examination of the home advantage in a professional English soccer team from a psychological standpoint. *Football Studies,* 5, 46–59.

Zhao, Y. & Liu, T. 2022. Factors that influence actual playing time: Evidence from the chinese super league and English Premier League. *Front Psychol,* 13, 907336.

12 Seeking Clarity on Psychological Safety

Tackling Myths and Misconceptions in Competitive Sport

Michael Cooke, Kyle Paradis, Lee Ann Sharp, David Woods and Mustafa Sarkar

Introduction

'I hate it the most when you don't want the ball … I hate it. When we train every day for that. You have permission to make a mistake, you have permission to lose, you have permission for everything … when you have permission you accept, 'I want the ball!'". Those words echo from Manchester City head coach Pep Guardiola as he passionately addresses his players during a training session. It's clear he wants them to make themselves available to receive a pass and not be afraid to have the ball. The choice of words from the elite football coach is interesting. Permission to make mistakes? Permission to lose? In an era where success is crucial for all involved in the high-performance sport environment, the concepts of making mistakes and losing are not often seen as an option for elite athletes. However, Guardiola possibly has a bigger vision. By affording the opportunity for players to make mistakes, perhaps they will then take risks and try new things to push their performance to another level, perhaps they will play with a sense of freedom. Perhaps, it was such freedom that enabled defender Vincent Kompany to shoot from 35 yards out and score an unlikely but vital winning goal for Man City vs Leicester City on their way to winning the 2018/2019 premier league title by one point over Liverpool. Perhaps without that freedom and mentality, Kompany would have never taken on that shot and Man City may not have won the title that year as a result. Such words from a coach, in such a high position of power, may offer players a sense of psychological safety.

England Football Head Coach Gareth Southgate also describes the longer-term impact of allowing players to take risks and make mistakes. As far back as the 2018 World Cup, Southgate suggested that a psychologically safe environment can offer an effective space for fostering great performances:

> *I want the team to be making mistakes because if they are making mistakes, then they are trying things. For me, all of our players, if they want to try and be as good as they can be, they have to try things and we have to accept that it might mean the odd failure; but what you then maybe get is the odd moment like they produced tonight, which is 'wow!' (McNulty, 2018)*

England has enjoyed one of the most prosperous spells in their history under his management making the Euro 2020 Final, World Cup 2018 Semi-Final and World Cup 2022 Quarter-Final.

In part, due to Google's Project Aristotle where Google conducted 200+ interviews with their employees and identified psychological safety as the most important characteristic of an effective Google team (Rozovsky, 2015), the concept of psychological safety has become more widely known and featured strongly in organizational literature in recent years, especially in the context of work teams (Edmondson, 2018). However, the construct holds a relatively limited understanding and evidence base in a sport context. Notwithstanding this point, a growing body of research has emerged focussing on how psychological safety manifests in the world of sport (see Fransen et al., 2020; Gosai et al., 2023; Jowett et al., 2022; Kinoshita & Sato, 2022; McClaren & Spink, 2021; Rice et al., 2022; Saxe et al., 2022; Smittick et al., 2019; Taylor et al., 2022a, 2022b; Vella et al., 2022). Much of this previous research suggests that improved psychological safety may offer a range of benefits for sport teams and athletes. Reflecting the embryonic nature of this literature, a lack of conceptual clarity on the construct still exists within the sport domain (Vella et al., 2022; Fransen et al., 2020), perhaps questioning the universal transferability from business to sport environments (Abrahams & Sarkar, 2021; Taylor et al., 2022a).

This lack of conceptual clarity has led to a less-than-ideal understanding of how psychological safety manifests in a sport context, leaving both researchers and practitioners keen to explore the contextual nature of psychological safety. This chapter aims to provide some context to psychological safety's current standing within the sport domain and dispel a range of perceived myths that currently exist around the construct. These myths include:

Myth 1: Psychological safety equates to being comfortable
Myth 2: Psychological safety cannot exist within a high-performance sport environment
Myth 3: Psychological safety holds universal transferability from business to sport

What is psychological safety?

Much of the recent work on psychological safety stems from the work of Edmondson (1999) which depicts psychological safety as the belief that one will not be punished or humiliated for speaking up with ideas, questions, concerns or mistakes and that the team is safe for interpersonal risk-taking. Research with business and work teams has demonstrated that psychologically safe teams can improve learning, creativity and performance, while enabling the willing contribution of oneself to collective work in relation to ideas and actions (Edmondson, 2018; O'Donovan & McAuliffe, 2020). It has been recognized that team environments characterized by psychological safety have contributed to improved personal engagement, trust, stronger relationships, mutual respect, positive intentions towards teammates and a reframing of how groups view failure and learning (Edmondson, 1999; Edmondson et al., 2004; Kahn, 1990; Newman et al., 2017; Schein, 1993). It is unsurprising these positive outcomes are also sought by sports coaches and administrators in an athletic context, hence the recent interest within the field of sport in this concept.

Psychological safety in sport

Building on a relatively limited evidence base, literature on psychological safety in sport has started to grow (see Fransen et al., 2020; Gosai et al., 2023; Jowett et al., 2022; Kinoshita & Sato, 2022; McClaren & Spink, 2021; Rice et al., 2022; Saxe et al., 2022; Smittick et al., 2019; Taylor et al., 2022a, 2022b; Vella et al., 2022). As noted previously, however, the concept of psychological safety in sport still lacks conceptual clarity (Vella et al., 2022). Ambiguous use of the term has, at times, strayed from Edmondson's (1999) original definition (Vella et al., 2022). The universal applicability and relevance of psychological safety within the high-performance sport setting have also been debated (Taylor et al., 2022a).

Sport, especially elite sport, is often deemed inherently unsafe (Abrahams & Sarkar, 2021; Portch, 2021; Taylor et al., 2022b). With this consideration, it may be particularly difficult to ensure that every sport environment is characterized by psychological safety and that every athlete will experience high levels of psychological safety. However, the notion that positive sport environments can help athletes increase their levels of psychological safety from whatever their current standpoint is, maybe a more practical concept. Rather than seeing psychological safety as black and white, something that is switched on or off, one could view psychological safety as a notion that exists on a continuum (Bowers et al., 2014).

One also needs to consider the individual aspects of psychological safety in sport. Psychological safety is often related to one's perception or beliefs and hence is inherently subjective by nature. That is, each individual may have different thresholds for when they feel safe or unsafe. The same events and experiences that greatly influence one athlete's perception of psychological safety may barely register with another. Each individual athlete will have contributing factors which influence their individual levels of psychological safety. Literature has however demonstrated that several antecedents may contribute towards feelings of psychological safety for all athletes. Such phenomena include appropriate programme design, organizational culture and values, social interactions, the absence of negative parent and coaching behaviours and positive relationships (Vella et al., 2022).

Due to the nascent nature of the literature, areas within psychological safety have not been fully explored from a sport perspective. For example, how safe is too safe? At which point does too much safety begin to offer a negative outcome? Additionally, it may be unwise to suggest that psychological safety exhibits the same outcomes across a range of different competitive sporting levels (e.g. grassroots sport, performance pathway, elite/high performance). Is striving for psychological safety applicable to all of these domains? These questions are currently unanswered and therefore addressing them in future research may offer a valuable contribution towards better understanding the concept. Edmondson (2018) notes that, to better understand psychological safety, it is important to ensure clarity about what psychological safety is not. By addressing, and dispelling, a range of perceived myths which currently exist, we aim to provide conceptual clarity around psychological safety.

Myth 1: Psychological safety equates to being comfortable

Irish rugby captain Johnny Sexton looked ahead towards the 2023 World Cup in France. 'You've got to keep evolving, you've got to keep getting better', he says. Sexton follows this notion of constant evolution with a complacency warning, 'We need to build a real competition for places so that no one can get comfortable and that is exactly what the coaches are doing' (Belfast Telegraph, 2022). Sexton is speaking here of positional competition (Harenberg et al., 2021) which is inevitable and essential to guard against complacency. According to Sexton, comfort can be detrimental to progress. It is often perceived that growth occurs in uncertain dwellings outside of one's comfort zone. The experiences which challenge us most can often lead to improvement and development. These challenging experiences, while uncomfortable in the short term, may lead to longer-term prosperity. It has been seen in sport where coaches and, indeed, athletes have described their toughest days as the ones that have made the biggest difference in their career trajectory (Sarkar et al., 2015).

At a surface level, the term psychological safety may conjure up an image of comfort – an environment where the presence of 'safety' equates to the absence of accountability, where safety mitigates against any conflict and discomfort. Some research on psychological safety in an organizational setting has further reinforced a comparison between comfort and psychological safety. Deng et al. (2019) found that a psychologically safe climate improved group creativity through reduced feelings of fear of failure. The authors did however propose that psychological safety can offer a comfortable socio-emotional group context which can reduce team members' work motivation and effort exertion due to a lack of accountability.

Edmondson (2018) acknowledges that, when psychological safety is high and performance standards are low, many people enter a 'comfort zone' with a sense of apathy. It is when both psychological safety and expected standards are high that learning and high performance occur (Edmondson, 2018). Athletes can be challenged and held highly accountable for performance and behaviours while still feeling a strong sense of psychological safety. The very nature of sport, especially high-performance sport, encourages accountability and/or consequences. Having permission to try new things, make errors on the field of play or voice an opinion is not permission to lower standards or adopt an 'anything goes' approach in training or competition.

In the Leaders Performance Institute Special Report on psychological safety (Portch, 2021), Dr David Fletcher reinforced this notion. 'When we talk about performance environments, particularly at the elite level, a lot of the growth that can come about, actually comes from being a little uncomfortable at times', he says.

> *When you have that trust, and you have leaders that can take feedback, then you can get into a position where you can get uncomfortable in certain scenarios, but*

you know that it's being done for a good reason. That's the hard place to operate not just as coaches but as a collective, striking that balance between psychological safety where you can express yourself but also being in safe elements of discomfort. (Portch, 2021, p. 18)

To suggest that all psychologically safe environments encourage being in a comfort zone is a myth. Skilled coaches can ensure that their athletes feel challenged but also psychologically safe to meet their challenges.

Myth 2: Psychological safety cannot exist within a high-performance sport environment

Harvey Elliot has firmly cemented his place with Jurgen Klopp's squad at Liverpool FC. The head coach undoubtedly trusts the young player to perform a key role. In an interview with the club's official media channels (Liverpool Football Club, 2022), Elliot described the freedom he was afforded by those around him in senior positions of power during his assimilation into the first-team environment. He said,

The one thing about this club is everyone tells you to go out there and show who you are. You're coming up against people like Milly (James Milner), who has been in the game for years now and you sort of look up to them and don't want to make mistakes. But having people around us [youngsters] to give us that confidence to go and express yourself, play with freedom, helps me a lot.

Elliot's description of his experiences links strongly to one of the features of psychological safety in a (high-performance) sport context – the promotion of risk-taking behaviours. Playing with freedom, as he puts it, can offer the opportunity to be innovative and creative and ultimately enhance performance.

The nature of high-performance sport is inherently unsafe (Abrahams & Sarkar, 2021; Portch, 2021; Taylor et al., 2022b). So much is on the line. Major stressors often accompany the world of high-performance sport – the highs and lows of competition, negative chance events (i.e. injury, illness), travel, funding, juggling a dual-career, non-selection, self-perceived poor performance, losses, relegation and the impact of social media (Burns et al., 2019). With such immense constant challenges, it would be easy to contend that high-performance sport does not have the capacity to afford psychological safety. Indeed, it has been acknowledged that psychological safety may be more difficult to foster in the high-performance sphere as opposed to other domains, grassroots or recreational sport for example (Abrahams & Sarkar, 2021); however, it remains possible. The relevant questions may be when and how psychological safety can be developed within high-performance sport?

Taylor et al. (2022a) questioned the contextual alignment of psychological safety within the high-performance sport environment, noting that certain scenarios may be more favourable than others to create psychological safety. The authors illustrated this point via the clear contrast between the experience of an athlete approaching a funding/contract decision or competing in a major final and an athlete coach pairing experimenting with a technical adjustment 12 months into a quadrennial cycle. Creating psychological safety in this instance is dependent on a range of factors and situations. While a high-performance coach may not want their athletes to take risks in the final of a major competition, they may have encouraged their athletes to have taken many risks in the prior months and years to refine and improve performance, via learning through errors and adjustments. However, most scenarios of how psychological safety unfolds in high-performance sport environments are largely anecdotal at present, thus research needs to be advanced to address these gaps and fully capture the nuances of psychological safety in high-performance sport. However, the anecdotal examples presented at the start of the chapter suggest it is a worthwhile area of study and that it does seem to exist in high-performance sport and should not be dismissed.

Much of the current sport research has explored the potential benefits and impacts of psychologically safe sport climates. However, Watcham-Roy (2022) explored the effect of psychological safety's absence within the high-performance sport domain. The purpose of that research was to provide a national sport organization (Rugby Canada) with actionable recommendations to ensure their athletes have a psychologically safe environment in pursuit of successful outcomes. The study found that a hierarchical and power-over culture influenced the organization and that athletes were subject to psychological maltreatment. The athletes wanted a high-performance environment where they are safe to be themselves and learn from mistakes, and the athletes desired the organization and coaches to provide a humanistic approach to performance. The author noted that a priority for psychological safety needs to be present in high-performance sport to ensure optimal performance and experience. Such findings suggest that psychological safety can, and indeed should, be a consideration for those operating within the high-performance sport domain. Rather than dismissing the construct all together without proper attempts to research and understand the nuances and intricacies of psychological safety, researchers, practitioners, coaches, athletes and administrators can work together to better understand the construct and work towards making psychological safety become a normalized reality in the world of elite level sport.

Myth 3: Psychological safety holds universal transferability from business to sport

The standing of psychological safety within the organizational literature is well founded (Edmondson, 2018); however, its under-developed status in sport (Vella et al., 2022) means many of its intricacies are still yet to be explored. To illustrate, the need for clear conceptualization and operationalization of the construct is apparent (Fransen et al., 2020). Taylor et al. (2022a) warn against psychological safety being considered as universally applicable or necessarily positive for high-performance sport, suggesting the term is redefined for applicability, emphasis on performance consequence should be removed and that psychological safety may be more relevant for certain roles or contexts. Undoubtedly, work and sport environments possess similar characteristics, however important differences also exist, which suggests continued endeavours to better understand psychological safety as it applies specifically to sport are warranted (Abrahams & Sarkar, 2021; McClaren & Spink, 2021). Such research poses the challenge to be more critical as to how psychological safety manifests in sport.

One aspect of the construct's transferability which needs to be considered is the current ability to measure psychological safety specifically related to the sport environment. The most prominent measurement tool presently used is Edmonson's (1999) seven-item questionnaire. The following items are scored to capture the level of psychological safety experienced within the group climate:

1. If you make a mistake on this team, it is often held against you.
2. Members of this team are able to bring up problems and tough issues.
3. People on this team sometimes reject others for being different.
4. It is safe to take a risk on this team.
5. It is difficult to ask other members of this team for help.
6. No one on this team would deliberately act in a way that undermines my efforts.
7. Working with members of this team, my unique skills and talents are valued and utilized.

Although this questionnaire has been utilized by many empirical studies within the organizational literature (Newman et al., 2017), both theoretical considerations on the wording of the items and data-driven issues on the structural validity of the measure need to be further assessed in the context of sport (Fransen et al., 2020).

Rice et al. (2022) attempted to develop a bespoke scale for assessing perceived psychological safety within high-performance sport environments. However, one of the limitations of this measure is that the definition of psychological safety adopted varied greatly from Edmonson's (1999) original definition and focussed heavily on mental health and well-being. Although the latter may represent an outcome from a psychologically safe environment, it is perhaps not measuring the nature of psychological safety per se, again reinforcing the requirement for improved conceptual clarity (Vella et al., 2022). In addition, the fact that Fransen et al. (2020) adopted a modified six-item version of Edmondson's (1999) measure gives further credence to the (lack of) applicability of the current measure within a sport context and may suggest that greater nuance and careful consideration is required without assuming universal applicability (Taylor et al., 2022a).

Another aspect which challenges the notion of psychological safety transferring neatly from business to sport is the idea that athletes may experience psychological safety differently in alternative settings within the wider sport environment. To illustrate, Cooke et al. (2022) identified that psychological safety was experienced both on and off the 'field of play'. Athletes viewed one of the facets of psychological safety as the freedom to take risks during training and competition, while the same athletes also perceived psychological safety as a freedom to ask questions and to raise issues away from the training or competition, for example, during team meetings or a one-to-one conversation with coaches or teammates. In this instance, the player who feels safe to take a risk on the field of play may not necessarily feel safe to ask a question away from the competition and training arena, and vice versa. This nuanced example further highlights that psychological safety, based on its original conception (Edmondson, 1999), requires greater critique and further study as to how it manifests in the sport environment. Notwithstanding this critique and the need for nuance, it is worth noting that endeavouring to improve psychological safety within athletes and the wider sport environment still offers much value to sport research and practice.

Practical implications for coaches, sports practitioners and administrators

Presuming psychological safety does offer positive group and individual outcomes (Vella et al., 2022) that current research suggests, coaches and sport administrators may take an interest in how this could benefit their sport climate and those situated within it. From a practical perspective, sport administrators and national governing bodies may consider evaluating team climates through the lens of psychological safety (Saxe et al., 2022). Portch (2021) highlights seven key items which may prove as useful considerations: (i) social skills as opposed to mental skills, (ii) value in conversation turn-taking, (iii) safe doesn't mean comfortable, (iv) promote calculated risks, (v) take collective responsibility for errors, (vi) let people be themselves and (vii) can psychological safety be linked to performance outcomes?

Until recently, psychological safety has gained scant attention in the world of coach development and coach education; however, Watcham-Roy (2022) demonstrated how a national sport association can place psychological safety at the forefront of priorities to assist with challenging toxic sport climates. Watcham-Roy's (2022) report put forward a series of recommendations to Rugby Canada based on the organization's gaps. Such recommendations were identified as necessary to support athletes feeling psychologically safe: (i) new member onboarding, (ii) clear selection guidelines, (iii) support in forming a healthy coach–athlete partnership and (iv) providing athletes with a safe platform to share feedback and complete a yearly audit of the environment. Such aspects are important to consider for any coach interested in creating a sense of psychological safety with their athletes. Coach education and coach development programmes could provide an opportunity for coaches to learn more about psychological safety and discuss if and how they can improve it in their athletes.

While much of the research has currently focussed on the psychological safety of athletes, Saxe et al. (2022) suggest that further research is needed to understand if coaches and wider sports practitioners feel psychologically safe in their roles and sporting climates. This could have implications for national governing bodies. Should they wish to ensure their coaches feel a sense of psychological safety, it may be useful to explore how they can create such an environment for their coaches both in their coaching practice and their coach education programmes. As the concept grows and gains more awareness, it is important that the concept does not manifest as a 'buzzword' (Portch, 2021). Improved conceptual clarity will support this (Fransen et al., 2020; Vella et al., 2022) as will increased focus within coach education programmes exploring the concept in the specific sport context via a critical lens (Taylor et al., 2022a).

Summary and conclusion

This chapter has endeavoured to 'dispel' some of the myths that currently surround psychological safety in sport with the hope of providing some conceptual clarity in this area. First, we proposed that psychological safety does not necessarily equate to being comfortable. The main rationale to dispel this myth is that psychological safety is not concurrent with the avoidance of accountability or the lowering of performance standards (Edmondson, 2018; Portch, 2021). Second, we challenged the myth that psychological safety cannot exist within the high-performance sport environment. Granted, it may be more difficult to establish psychological safety in high-performance sport than in a grassroots environment, for example, due to the extensive performance pressures present within a high-performance setting (Burns et al., 2019); however, the examples provided in this chapter demonstrated that it is possible. Indeed, we have seen the detrimental impact that has the potential to occur when psychological safety is absent from high-performance sport environments (Watcham-Roy, 2022). Third, and finally, we refuted the myth that psychological safety is universally transferable from its origins within the organizational (business) literature to sport. We suggest that developing psychological safety within athletes (and coaches) can have a profoundly positive impact on a number of group and individual factors (Vella et al., 2022). However, we need to be mindful of the intricacies and nuances of the concept as to how it manifests in the sport environment (Abrahams & Sarkar, 2021; Taylor et al., 2022a). The notion that psychological safety can play out within different settings in sport – 'on-field' and 'off-field' (Cooke et al., 2022) – suggests there are differences that may need to be contextualized. Measuring psychological safety within sport has also found challenges, again suggesting the need for critical consideration of theoretical and psychometric issues with Edmondson's (1999) original measure from business (Fransen et al., 2020) and Rice et al.'s (2022) sport-specific measure focussing heavily on mental health and well-being and not necessarily measuring the nature of psychological safety per se.

While the growing body of research has demonstrated a positive contribution to better understanding psychological safety in a sport context, it is felt that the surface has only been scratched when it comes to coaching practice. Supporting coaches to explore if, how and when certain interventions can be utilized to increase psychological safety may be a fruitful endeavour to bring a currently underdeveloped concept to life in a practical sense. Rather than completely dismissing an emerging construct without giving it the due process of rigorous research, finding exactly how psychological safety manifests within a range of sport environments will be an exciting challenge for both researchers and practitioners alike.

References

Abrahams, D., & Sarkar, M. (Host and contributor). (2021, November). How to create a psychologically safe environment (No. 167) [Audio podcast episode]. In *The Sport Psych Show*. https://thesportpsychshow.libsyn.com/167-dr-mustafa-sarkar-how-to-create-a-psychologically-safe-environment

Belfast Telegraph: (Elliot, E. 2022, Nov 02): https://m.belfasttelegraph.co.uk/sport/rugby/johnny-sexton-ireland-building-real-competition-for-places-ahead-ofworld-cup/42112846.html

Bowers, M. T., Green, B. C., Hemme, F., & Chalip, L. (2014). Assessing the relationship between youth sport participation settings and creativity in adulthood. *Creativity Research Journal*, 26(3), 314–327.

Burns, L., Weissensteiner, J. R., & Cohen, M. (2019). Supportive interpersonal relationships: A key component to high-performance sport. *British Journal of Sports Medicine*, 53(22), 1386–1389.

Cooke, M., Paradis, K., Sharp, L., Woods, D., & Sarkar M. (2022, November). A qualitative assessment of psychological safety in high-performance pathway coaches and athletes. Paper presented at British Psychologial Society-Division of Sport and Exercise Psychology Conference, Swansea, UK.

Deng, H., Leung, K., Lam, C. K., & Huang, X. (2019). Slacking off in comfort: A dual-pathway model for psychological safety climate. *Journal of Management*, 45(3), 1114–1144.

Edmondson, A. (1999). Psychological safety and learning behaviour in work teams. *Administrative Science Quarterly*, 44(2), 350–383.

Edmondson, A. C. (2018). *The fearless organization: Creating psychological safety in the workplace for learning, innovation, and growth*. John Wiley & Sons.

Edmondson, A. C., Kramer, R. M., & Cook, K. S. (2004). Psychological safety, trust, and learning in organizations: A group-level lens. *Trust and Distrust in Organizations: Dilemmas and Approaches*, 12, 239–272.

Fransen, K., McEwan, D., & Sarkar, M. (2020). The impact of identity leadership on team functioning and well-being in team sport: Is psychological safety the missing link? *Psychology of Sport and Exercise*, 51, 101763.

Gosai, J., Jowett, S., & Nascimento-Júnior, J. R. A. D. (2023). When leadership, relationships and psychological safety promote flourishing in sport and life. *Sports Coaching Review*, 12(2), 1–21.

Harenberg, S., Riemer, H. A., Dorsch, K. D., Karreman, E., & Paradis, K. F. (2021). Advancement of a conceptual framework for positional competition in sport: Development and validation of the positional competition in team sports questionnaire. *Journal of Applied Sport Psychology*, 33(3), 321–342.

Jowett, S., Do Nascimento-Junior, J. R. A., Zhao, C., & Gosai, J. (2022). Creating conditions for psychological safety and its impact on quality coach-athlete relationships. *Psychology of Sport and Exercise*, 102363.

Kahn, W. A. (1990). Psychological conditions of personal engagement and disengagement at work. *Academy of Management Journal*, 33(4), 692–724.

Kinoshita, K., & Sato, S. (2022). Incivility and psychological safety in youth sport: The reciprocal effects and its impact on well-being and social outcomes. *Sport Management Review*, 1–25.

Liverpool Football Club. (2022). https://www.liverpoolfc.com/news/first-team/406476-harvey-elliott-austria-feature-interview

McLaren, C. D., & Spink, K. S. (2021). Testing boundary conditions in the communication–cohesion relationship in team sport: The case for psychological safety. *Group Dynamics: Theory, Research, and Practice, 26*(1), 12–23.

McNulty, P. (2018, June). World Cup 2018: "England head for Russia with a rare sense of serenity". https://www.bbc.co.uk/sport/football/44402945

Newman, A., Donohue, R., & Eva, N. (2017). Psychological safety: A systematic review of the literature. *Human Resource Management Review, 27*(3), 521–535.

O'Donovan, R., & McAuliffe, E. (2020). Exploring psychological safety in healthcare teams to inform the development of interventions: Combining observational, survey and interview data. *BMC Health Services Research, 20*(1), 1–16.

Portch, J. (2021, March). Psychological safety: The origins, reality and shelf life of an evolving high performance concept. *Leaders Performance Institute Special Report*.

Rice, S., Walton, C. C., Pilkington, V., Gwyther, K., Olive, L. S., Lloyd, M., Kountouris, A., Butterworth, M., Clements, M., & Purcell, R. (2022). Psychological safety in elite sport settings: A psychometric study of the Sport Psychological Safety Inventory. *BMJ Open Sport & Exercise Medicine, 8*(2), e001251.

Rozovsky, J. (2015). The five keys to a successful Google team. re:Work. http://rework.withgoogle.com/blog/five-keys-to-a-successful-google team

Sarkar, M., Fletcher, D., & Brown, D. J. (2015). What doesn't kill me…: Adversity-related experiences are vital in the development of superior Olympic performance. *Journal of Science and Medicine in Sport, 18*(4), 475–479.

Saxe, K., & Hardin, R. (2022). Psychological safety in athletic team environments. *Journal of Sport Behavior, 45*(2), 203–216.

Schein, E. H. (1993). How can organizations learn faster?: The problem of entering the Green Room. *Sloan Management Review, 34*, 85–92.

Smittick, A. L., Miner, K. N., & Cunningham, G. B. (2019). The "I" in team: Coach incivility, coach gender, and team performance in women's basketball teams. *Sport Management Review, 22*(3), 419–433.

Taylor, J., Collins, D., & Ashford, M. (2022a). Psychological safety in high-performance sport: Contextually applicable? *Frontiers in Sports and Active Living*, 169.

Taylor, J., Ashford, M., & Collins, D. (2022b). Tough love - Impactful, caring coaching in psychologically unsafe environments. *Sports, 10*(6), 83.

Vella, S. A., Mayland, E., Schweickle, M. J., Sutcliffe, J. T., McEwan, D., & Swann, C. (2022). Psychological safety in sport: A systematic review and concept analysis. *International Review of Sport and Exercise Psychology*, 1–24.

Watcham-Roy, N. (2022). Psychological safety in high-performance sport. [Doctoral Dissertation], Royal Roads University, Canada.

13 Harnessing the Power of Attention

Exploring 'Focus of Attention' Theories, Practice and Myths

Marianne Davies, Robin Owen, Victoria M. Gottwald, and Harjiv Singh

Introduction

Where are we directing an athlete's attention when giving verbal instructions? This extract from a conversation with Olympic Canoe Slalom coach Craig Morris gives a valuable and interesting insight into the influence of instructions on the focus of attention.

> In the end I came to thinking that if the athlete's intentionality is to win, then how a performance looks is largely irrelevant. What's important is that it's functional and it's stable. A few heavy jolts led me to that, mostly from athlete feedback. I remember at a big event I was doing a video review of a run with one of the athletes. When I paused the video, the athlete said to me 'When I went around that gate, I thought, Craig's gonna hate that stroke, the shape of it, the position under the chin etc'.
>
> I recall initially being pleased and thinking, 'Oh, I'm getting through to my athletes, nice! They are listening to my coaching'. The subsequent athlete response however, had a profoundly lasting effect on my coaching, 'Effective though, wasn't it?'
>
> The thing is, it was undeniably 'effective'. So if it's effective then how important is it for them to focus on their body position and hands when negotiating gates on an Olympic slalom course amidst very dynamic and turbulent water? I've come to realise that we must be very careful about having too narrow a, or even any, significant technical model. Because if

you have it as a coach, it'll inevitably become an information constraint for the athlete. A boundary on their attention, their interaction. So for example, when paddling, the athletes were often evaluating their action against information I had predetermined for how something should look rather than paying attention to, and actually seeing and feeling, the task-relevant information in the environment. The information of what a wave is or is not inviting them to do, or what the wind's effect on a pole means for action, thus restricting their ability to interact with these things more freely as they emerge. So effectively, I was overly constraining what information they picked up by guiding their attention to something that wasn't conducive with what I have come to view as skilled performance.

The myth: Every instruction is a good instruction

If you immerse yourself in any environment where physical movements are being practised under the supervision of an instructor or coach, you will no doubt hear endless verbal instructions that reference body movements. Whether in a Physical Education setting with a teacher directing an adolescent to *bend their knees* to support a softer landing when jumping, a sports coach instructing an elite athlete to *snap the wrist* when shooting a basketball or a medical doctor teaching a trainee how to *grip a needle with the fingers* when learning to suture.

Some scientists believe that these verbal instructions are fundamental to skill learning, and it is our job as coaches and educators to use them effectively to help guide individuals towards a predetermined technique or technical model. This concept of using instructions to hone in on an optimal technique is supported by what is termed the 'cognitive' or 'information processing' account of skill learning, where learning is a result of 'computer-like' processing, and movements are pre-planned, stored in memory and drawn upon when needed (Broadbent, 1958; Schmidt, 2003). However, others believe that contrary to skilled movements being pre-programmed via the brain, movement is instead more spontaneous and continuously (re)organized based on the ever-changing relationship between the individual, the task and what is happening in the environment (Davids et al., 2008; Kelso, 1995). Within this 'ecological dynamics' model of skill learning, there is not one correct way to move, but instead, skilful movement is conceptualized as the ability to be adaptive and repeat successful outcomes (repetition without repetition), rather than repeat exactly the same movement techniques. The focus is on biomechanical flexibility, rather than biomechanical correctness. The role of the coach is to facilitate what scientists term 'self-organization' of the motor system by cultivating environments that support movement exploration. Instructions are used to influence what an individual pays attention to and will subsequently either help or hinder dynamic self-organized performance.

But whichever side of the fence you sit on, verbal instructions are commonplace in teaching and coaching, and unlikely to lose their value any time soon. Regardless of the mechanisms at play underpinning the role of instructions to support learning, what many do not realize is that sometimes the instructions we provide can actually do more harm than good if we do not consider the language being used and where the learner's attention is likely to be focussed. Not all instruction is good instruction, and the literature would suggest that even in a relatively simple task such as balancing, instructing a rehabilitation patient to 'keep their feet level' while balancing on a balance board has been shown to constrain actions and inhibit performance (for a review, see Park et al., 2015). Fascinatingly, just slight alterations to the language, which instead directs the patient to 'keep the board level' can improve performance (e.g. smaller and more frequent movements, both indicative of enhanced balance performance).

Focus of attention definitions

External focus	Directing attention towards the effects of our body movements on the environment (e.g. typically this would be towards a bat, racket, club or ball). This might also include perceptual information relevant to the task (e.g. the movement of an opposition player in a hockey game). External focus of attention can be proximal (i.e. aspects in the environment nearer to the body) or distal (i.e. aspects in the environment further away from the body).
Internal focus	Paying attention to our body movements (e.g. the pendulum motion of the arms during a golf putt or the raized position of the leg during an arabesque – a one-legged pose).
Somaesthetic	A somaesthetic focus of attention is a subset of the internal focus of attention. It is what is being experienced or 'felt' in the body. There are four main types: nociception (pain), equilibrioception

	(balance), mechanoreception (vibration, touch and pressure) and proprioception (positioning and movement).
Holistic focus of attention	Focus on the quality of a movement (e.g. being 'explosive' during an athletics triple jump or rebound in basketball).

The origins of this topic of interest

It was Dr Gabriella (Gaby) Wulf who first noticed the consequences of changing focus of attention while she was learning to windsurf. When she focussed externally on moving the board to turn, she found that her movements were more effective compared to when she focussed her attention internally towards moving her feet to make the turn (Wulf, 2007). In the first scientific study of this nature, Wulf et al. (1998) tested this phenomenon in two different tasks: (1) a ski-simulator task where participants were instructed to focus on the slalom motion of either their feet (internal focus) or the ski-simulator wheels (external focus) and (2) a balance board task where participants had to focus on keeping either their feet level (internal focus) or the board level (external focus). In both instances, the external focus of attention (i.e. on the simulator wheels or balance board) led to better performance outcomes (in this case, movement amplitude and balance, respectively).

Since these early studies, we now understand far more about the mechanisms that underlie the impact of focus of attention on performance and learning. The most prominent theory is an information processing theory, the *constrained action hypothesis* (Wulf et al., 2001), which proposes that directing attention internally to the bodily mechanics of a movement can disrupt what is usually automatic movement planning/execution. Just like if you were to walk down the stairs (a skill you probably do every day without thinking about it), while consciously thinking about what you were doing with your feet, you might find that your movements become quite 'constrained' and awkward. More recently, scientists have begun to consider these attentional mechanisms together with psychological factors such as confidence and motivation. This is based on the idea that the processing that goes on to organize our movements is also likely affected by an individual's psychological state. Specifically, Wulf and Lewthwaite's (2016, 2021) *OPTIMAL theory* (optimizing performance through intrinsic motivation and attention for learning) suggests that practice environments that provide individuals with greater autonomy (i.e. choice) and stronger beliefs that practise will benefit performance (i.e. enhanced expectancies) will lead to better performance outcomes when combined with an external focus of attention. Wulf and Lewthwaite explain this with the idea that enhanced performance when adopting an external focus of attention will increase our self-confidence to continue to perform a skill and subsequently provide us with greater expectancies for future performance. For example, in a standing long-jump task, placing physical markers such as cones on the floor to 'target' (i.e. an external focus of attention), combined with enhanced autonomy (e.g. providing the participants or athletes the choice over where to place the cones), can enhance jump distance and subsequently self-efficacy, with this relationship continuing in a cyclic fashion.

The benefits of an external attentional focus are now well established within academic research circles (see Chua et al., 2021; Gottwald et al., 2023; and Wulf, 2007, 2013), with positive outcomes including movement accuracy, movement efficiency, strength, power and movement form (for a review, see Wulf, 2013). Similarly, the attentional focus phenomenon has been tested in many domains, including sport (for reviews, see Wulf, 2007, 2013), strength and conditioning (see Grgic et al., 2021), clinical rehabilitation settings (see Park et al., 2015) and the military (e.g. Amini & Vaezmousavi, 2020).

Current scientific directions

While early evidence demonstrated overwhelming support for an external focus of attention, more recent literature has begun to question the rigidity of the constrained action hypothesis (Wulf et al., 2001) and OPTIMAL theory (Wulf & Lewthwaite, 2016, 2021). For example, scientific papers (Toner & Moran, 2015, 2016; Wulf, 2015) have sparked interest in what we should focus on if we have to relearn a skill or correct a technical error (e.g. an athlete not following through sufficiently on a golf swing or forehand tennis drive). One example of this is scientists' debate surrounding the reasons for Tiger Woods' performance slump in 2015, around the time he was adjusting his swing pattern. While Toner and Moran argued that this process was a necessary phase in technique refinement, Wulf was doubtful that Tiger Woods would ever return to form once his attention was directed to his body movements in this reflective manner. Toner and Moran propose that there may indeed be a time and a place to pay attention to the body via what they term a 'somaesthetic awareness' based on Shusterman's (2011) view that reflective body consciousness has pragmatic value when re-learning movements or correcting errors. This would also be consistent with Carson and Collins' (2011, 2014, 2016) non-linear Five-A model of technical refinement, which presents a practical approach to skill refinement, involving stages of analysis, awareness, adjustment, (re)automation and assurance.

In line with debate surrounding the benefits of somaesthetic awareness, Gottwald et al. (2023) present a useful critique of the attentional focus literature, highlighting instances where an internal focus, which promotes somaesthetic awareness, has been identified as having potential value. This includes: in more real/naturalistic (less-artificial) environments (e.g. Anderson et al., 2022), when focussing on body movements is more aligned with criteria for successful skill execution (e.g. Gottwald et al., 2020 suggest that focussing on the body would be more aligned with important proprioceptive information to perform well in an artistic gymnastics routine) or for use in retraining movement form (e.g. Moore et al., 2019 used internal focus prompts to correct the gait of rear-foot striking runners).

An alternative explanation for the attentional focus effect

With existing theoretical approaches lacking the flexibility required to fit complex practical environments and ecological dynamics approaches gaining prominence in the literature, a more recent Ecological Dynamics Account of Attentional Focus (Gottwald et al., 2023) is timely. The authors propose a more flexible approach to explain the varying functions of attentional focus (see Figure 13.1). In this manner, directing attentional resources towards relevant information in the environment can support a participant or athlete to identify more opportunities for action, improving decision-making and allowing the self-organization of more accurate and efficient movement. For example, in a far aiming task such as golf, this might be the target hole and changing surface conditions leading up to it. In a team sport it might be scanning to become aware of, and influence, the movements of team and opposition players. In a proprioceptive task, this might be the arm motion relative to the torso in an artistic gymnastics floor routine. These nuances cannot be explained by either the constrained action hypothesis (Wulf et al., 2001) or OPTIMAL theory (Wulf & Lewthwaite, 2016, 2021) alone.

So what: Practical recommendations for coaching

The myth that any instruction is a good instruction is likely false. This means that coaches should carefully consider what attentional focus is promoted by

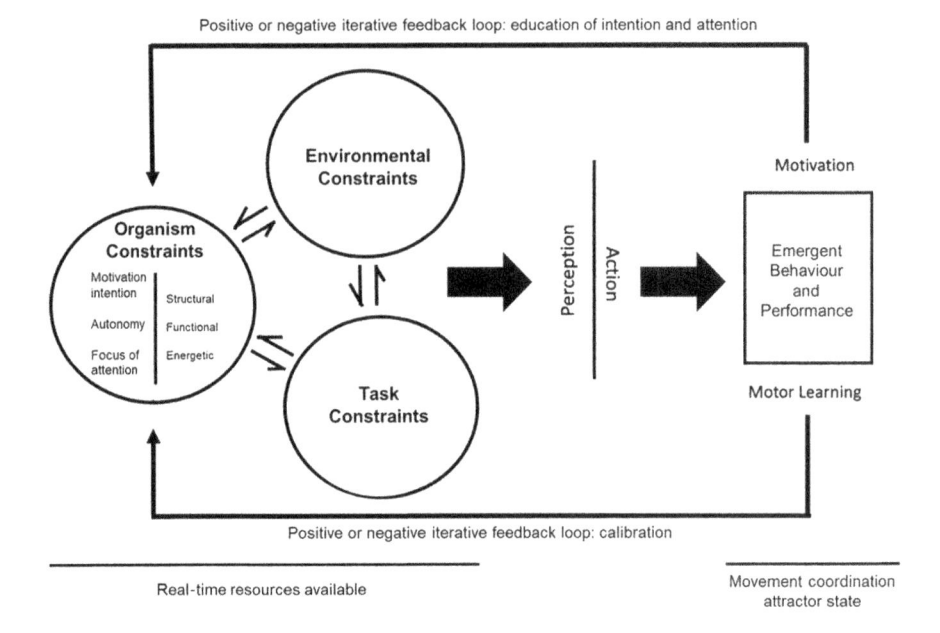

Figure 13.1. An ecological account of focus of attention (Davies and Davies, 2018).

the instructions they give. The aim of any instruction may need to be twofold to ensure it is 'good' instruction. First, and in line with established convention, coaches may need to provide corrective information to help address technical/performance issues. Second, but perhaps equally importantly, coaches need to provide instructions which are worded in a way where they direct athletes' attentional focus to task-relevant information. This latter aim is supported by an increasingly large body of research which advocates for task-specific focus of attention prescription (Gottwald et al., 2023). The matching of attentional focus and task-relevant factors should benefit self-organization for movement by prioritizing perceptual information, which is easier to detect as well as contextually relevant (i.e. key body and/or environment constraints).

Performance in aiming tasks

If a 'task' constitutes an athlete performing successful shots at a target, the most relevant information would be the target (e.g. hoop for a basketball shot). In such instances, and in line with seminal work by Wulf and colleagues (for review see Wulf, 2013), coach instructions should advise athletes to adopt an external focus towards the centre of the hoop. Based on the proposals of the Ecological

Account of Attentional Focus (Gottwald et al., 2023), such an attentional focus should enable athletes to identify the most relevant environmental information for movement self-organization (e.g. appropriate ball force, angle and release parameters) as well as efficiency, by directing valuable cognitive resources further away from less-relevant internal bodily information. Plentiful evidence has been observed to support the adoption of an external focus for optimal performance in aiming-type motor tasks (Chua et al., 2021).

Performance in form tasks

If a 'task' constitutes an athlete performing aesthetic/form aspects with high precision, the most relevant information would be the body (e.g. having the back leg higher than the head during a spiral in figure skating). In these instances, coaches may need to advise athletes to adopt an internal focus of attention towards their leg position relative to their head. Based on the proposals of the Ecological Account of Attentional Focus (Gottwald et al., 2023), such an internal attentional focus should enable athletes to identify the most relevant bodily information for movement self-organization (e.g. leg in relation to head location) as well as efficiency, by directing cognitive resources away from less-relevant external environmental information. The evidence-base in support of internal foci for form-based tasks has received less exhaustive investigation compared to pairings of external foci with aiming tasks but is rapidly growing (see, Gottwald et al., 2020, 2023; Lawrence et al., 2011; McKay et al., 2023).

Performance in endurance, strength and power tasks

If a 'task' primarily comprises endurance (e.g. distance running), strength (e.g. weightlifting 1 rep max) or power (e.g. high jump) components, the adoption of either external (e.g. 'shortest path through the environment' or 'upward motion of the dumbbell') or holistic foci of attention (i.e. 'feeling of the movement as a whole') may be desirable for optimal performance (Schücker & Parrington, 2019; Freudenheim et al., 2010). Specifically, external foci may facilitate movement self-organization and efficiency relative to the environment. This can ultimately benefit time/speed/force. Holistic foci may offer a practical alternative with similar benefits when a skill does not feature a clear 'external' component to focus on (Zhuravleva et al., 2023). However, if a strength or power task wishes to ultimately achieve muscle growth as its measure of performance (e.g. bodybuilding), then an internal focus of attention (e.g. 'focus on the squeezing of your biceps while doing your biceps curls') may be desirable to increase mind-muscle connections (Grgic & Mikulic, 2021); this internal focus-instigated neural drive directed to desired muscles would produce overall less-efficient movement with lower peak strength/power outputs but result in overall greater muscle activation which should benefit muscle growth in the long term.

Modification of technique and long-term development

Contrary to common 'either-or' approaches to focus attention, modification of technique should be seen as a process in terms of the attentional foci adopted. The focus of attention which produces the change in technique may be different from the usual focus adopted for optimal performance. First, in instances where a task usually performs optimally with an external focus (i.e. aiming, endurance, strength and power tasks) but communicating the required technical changes to an athlete without referring internally to the body is impractical or impossible, somaesthetic awareness of kinaesthetic/kinetic body processes elicited via internal focus instructions should help athletes quickly identify task-relevant changes to their technique. Importantly, once the desired technical changes are beginning to take place, coaches should endeavour to move away from the temporary internal focus used to achieve change and gradually guide athletes towards an external focus which would produce optimal performance (Moore et al., 2019; Singh & Wulf, 2020). Second, if it is possible to achieve the initial technique change within external-favouring tasks (aiming/endurance/strength/power) via externally focussed instructions or task/environmental constraints manipulation in practice design, then this may be optimal given the plentiful evidence suggesting that the skill learning of individuals at lower skill levels benefit from external foci similarly to experts (Chua et al., 2021). Lastly, tasks that usually perform optimally with internal or holistic foci (i.e. form tasks) may have similar internal attentional foci during technique modification and subsequent performance when competing.

Conclusion

Subtleties in the language that coaches use to give instructions can have a significant effect on a participant's performance and learning. Using language that supports a focus of attention towards the effects of a movement or towards task-relevant information is more effective for learning. Like most principles, although the use of an external focus of attention is most often more effective, it is not as absolute as suggested by early motor learning research. There are times when an internal focus is needed.

Have a go

1. What is the intention of the practice session?

When planning your coaching sessions, think about what the *intention* is for the participants or athletes. Is it to score a goal or is it to achieve desired form? Then think about where they might find the information that supports them to solve that movement skill. Where and on what might you need to direct their *focus of attention?*

2. Do you need to give instructions? Less is often more.

Could you use practice design principles such as Constraints-Led Approach (CLA) or Space, Time/Task, Environment, People (STEP)? For example, in aiming tasks you could make the target bigger or brightly coloured and encourage your participants to choose the distance and challenge level. Practice design can work well for disrupting poor technique if you can design the practice so that the poor technique will not be effective.

Would cues and analogies be more effective? For developing a holistic focus of attention these work well, especially if the participant can choose the cues and analogies that work for them. For example 'exploding past the line'.

Could you use questioning? Ask the participants what they think they might need to pay attention to. For example, an ice climber might need to listen to the sound the ice makes when they hit it with an axe to become aware of how stable and strong the ice is before pulling on it.

Of course, instructions are important and you will need to use them. Below are some ideas for how you can become more aware of how you are using instructions and where your participant's (and your) focus of attention is.

3. Gathering information about where you and your participants are focussing attention.

As a coach, you could ask your participants to 'think aloud' and tell you what they are noticing during a practice activity. You can ask your participants to use a smartphone and headphones to record as they are active, then listen back to them (ideally with a video of the same activity).

You can use your smartphone and headphones to record *your coaching* during the session and listen back to the instructions you give. When you give instructions, where are you trying to focus *your participants'* attention? Are you using internal technique-based instructions or promoting an external focus of attention? Could you be more clear and more intentional with which focus of attention you are encouraging with your instructions?

It is also useful to become more aware of where *your* focus of attention is as a coach. If you find that you are giving predominantly internal focus, form/technique-based instructions, it may be because of where you are focussing your attention in your observations. Using your smartphone and earphones, you can record what you are paying attention to by '*thinking aloud*' either while observing or before you give instructions. When you listen back, pay attention to where your focus of attention was. Was it on the participant's body/technique, their interaction with the task, other participants, the environment or towards task-relevant information that they may be paying attention to? Challenge yourself to become more intentional about where you place your attention as well as the language that you use to support your participant's focus of attention.

References

Amini, A., & Vaezmousavi, M. (2020). The effect of differential attentional focus strategies on the performance of military elite shooters. *Behavioural Neurology, 2020.*

Anderson, D. N. J., Gottwald, V. M., & Lawrence, G. P. (2022). Capturing the holistic profile of high performance Olympic weightlifting development. *Frontiers in Sports and Active Living, 4*, 986134.

Broadbent, D. (1958). *Perception and communication.* London: Pergamon Press.

Carson, H. J., & Collins, D. (2011). Refining and regaining skills in fixation/diversification stage performers: The Five-A Model. *International Review of Sport and Exercise Psychology, 4*(2), 146–167.

Carson, H. J., & Collins, D. (2014). Effective skill refinement: Focusing on process to ensure outcome. *Central European Journal of Sport Sciences and Medicine, 7*(3), 5–21.

Carson, H. J., & Collins, D. (2016). Implementing the Five-A Model of technical refinement: Key roles of the sport psychologist. *Journal of Applied Sport Psychology, 28*(4), 392–409.

Chua, L.-K., Jimenez-Diaz, J., Lewthwaite, R., Kim, T., & Wulf, G. (2021). Superiority of external attentional focus for motor performance and learning: Systematic reviews and meta-analyses. *Psychological Bulletin, 147,* 618–645. https://doi.org/10.1037/bul0000335

Davids, K., Button, C., & Bennett, S. (2008). *Dynamics of skill acquisition: A constraints-led approach.* Human Kinetics.

Davies, M.J. & Davies, R.S. (2018). Beyond Below-Ground Geological Complexity: Developing Adaptive Expertise in Exploration Decision- Making. In *Proceedings of the Complex Orebodies Conference*, Brisbane, Australia, 19–21 November 2018.

Freudenheim, A. M., Wulf, G., Madureira, F., Pasetto, S. C., & Corrêa, U. C. (2010). An external focus of attention results in greater swimming speed. *International Journal of Sports Science & Coaching, 5*(4), 533–542.

Gottwald, V., Davies, M., & Owen, R. (2023). Every story has two sides: Evaluating information processing and ecological dynamics perspectives of focus of attention in skill acquisition. *Frontiers in Sports and Active Living, 5*, 167.

Gottwald, V. M., Owen, R., Lawrence, G. P., & McNevin, N. (2020). An internal focus of attention is optimal when congruent with afferent proprioceptive task information. *Psychology of Sport and Exercise, 47*, 101634.

Grgic, J., & Mikulic, P. (2021). Effects of attentional focus on muscular endurance: A meta-analysis. *International Journal of Environmental Research and Public Health, 19*(1), 89.

Grgic, J., Mikulic, I., & Mikulic, P. (2021). Acute and long-term effects of attentional focus strategies on muscular strength: A meta-analysis. *Sports, 9*(11), 153.

Kelso, J. S. (1995). *Dynamic patterns: The self-organization of brain and behavior.* Cambridge, MA: MIT Press.

Lawrence, G. P., Gottwald, V. M., Hardy, J., & Khan, M. A. (2011). Internal and external focus of attention in a novice form sport. *Research Quarterly for Exercise and Sport, 82*(3), 431–441.

McKay, B., Bacelar, M. F., Parma, J. O., Miller, M. W., & Carter, M. J. (2023). The combination of reporting bias and underpowered study designs has substantially exaggerated the motor learning benefits of self-controlled practice and enhanced expectancies: A meta-analysis. *International Review of Sport and Exercise Psychology*, 1–21.

Moore, I. S., Phillips, D. J., Ashford, K. J., Mullen, R., Goom, T., & Gittoes, M. R. (2019). An interdisciplinary examination of attentional focus strategies used during running gait retraining. *Scandinavian Journal of Medicine & Science in Sports, 29*(10), 1572–1582.

Park, S. H., Yi, C. W., Shin, J. Y., & Ryu, Y. U. (2015). Effects of external focus of attention on balance: A short review. *Journal of Physical Therapy Science, 27*(12), 3929–3931.

Schmidt, R. A. (2003). Motor schema theory after 27 years: Reflections and implications for a new theory. *Research Quarterly for Exercise and Sport, 74*(4), 366–375. https://doi.org/10.1080/02701367.2003.10609106

Schücker, L., & Parrington, L. (2019). Thinking about your running movement makes you less efficient: Attentional focus effects on running economy and kinematics. *Journal of Sports Sciences, 37*(6), 638–646.

Shusterman, R. (2011). "Somaesthetic awareness, proprioceptive perception, and performance," in consciousness, perception, and behavior: Conceptual, theoretical, and methodological issues. In E. R. Iñesta, & J. E. Burgos (Eds.), *Proceedings of the 11th Biannual Symposium on the Science of Behavior*, Guadalajara, México, February 2010. New Orleans: University Press of the South.

Singh, H., & Wulf, G. (2020). The distance effect and level of expertise: Is the optimal external focus different for low-skilled and high-skilled performers?. *Human Movement Science, 73*, 102663.

Toner, J., & Moran, A. (2015). Enhancing performance proficiency at the expert level: Considering the role of 'somaesthetic awareness'. *Psychology of Sport and Exercise, 16*, 110–117. https://doi.org/10.1016/j.psychsport.2014.07.006

Toner, J., & Moran, A. (2016). On the importance of critical thinking: A response to Wulf's (2015). Commentary. *Psychology of Sport and Exercise, 22*, 339–340. https://doi.org/10.1016/j.psychsport.2015.05.007

Wulf, G. (2007). *Attention and motor skill learning.* Human Kinetics.

Wulf, G. (2013). Attentional focus and motor learning: A review of 15 years. *International Review of Sport and Exercise Psychology, 6*, 77–104. https://doi.org/10.1080/1750984X.2012.723728

Wulf, G. (2015). Why did Tiger Woods shoot 82? A commentary on Toner and Moran (2015). *Psychology of Sport and Exercise, 22*, 337–338. https://doi.org/10.1016/j.psychsport.2015.05.006

Wulf, G., Höß, M., & Prinz, W. (1998). Instructions for motor learning. Differential effects of internal versus external focus of attention. *Journal of Motor Behaviour, 30*, 169–179. https://doi.org/10.1080/00222899809601334

Wulf, G., & Lewthwaite, R. (2016). Optimizing performance through intrinsic motivation and attention for learning: The OPTIMAL theory of motor learning. *Psychonomic Bulletin and Review, 23*(5), 1382–1414. https://doi.org/10.3758/s13423-015-0999-9

Wulf, G., & Lewthwaite, R. (2021). Translating thoughts into action: Optimizing motor performance and learning through brief motivational and attentional influences. *Current Directions in Psychological Science, 30*(6), 535–541. https://doi.org/10.1177/09637214211046199

Wulf, G., McNevin, N. H., & Shea, C. H. (2001). The automaticity of complex motor skill learning as a function of attentional focus. *Quarterly Journal of Experimental Psychology, 54*, 1143–1154. https://doi.org/10.1080/713756012

Zhuravleva, T., Aiken, C. A., Becker, K. A., Lin, P. C., & Sampson, J. J. (2023). The use of a holistic focus of attention to improve standing long jump performance among NCAA track and field athletes. *International Journal of Sports Science & Coaching*, 17479541231178981.

14 Menstrual Cycle Myths

Jacky J. Forsyth

The myths explored in this chapter include the following:

- The menstrual cycle is not important for athletes to consider.
- The menstrual cycle is all about negative symptoms that need to be managed.
- Tracking the menstrual cycle can't be done in a team setting.
- Phase-based training improves muscle strength and power.
- Men always outperform women in sport.
- Loss of menstruation (bleeding) is a sign of an effective training response.
- Pain, related to the menstrual cycle, is normal.

Introduction

In this chapter, the myths around menstrual cycle and its effects on physiological performance, exercise and training will be explored. The rationale for focussing on menstrual cycle is threefold. First, there has been some recent growth, albeit minor, in research on menstrual cycle and its effects on performance, as evidenced in systematic reviews (Blagrove et al., 2020; Meignié et al., 2021; Thompson et al., 2020). Second, there has been some recent media attention about the effects of menstrual cycle on athletic performance, because of well-known athletes talking about their concerns. For instance, Dina-Asher Smith, British sprinter, reported 'girl-stuff issues' on underperforming at the 2022 European Championships in Munich, calling for more research on menstrual cycle (Ronald, 2022). Amongst stakeholders (such as coaches, managers and practitioners), a need has also been expressed for further research on menstrual cycle (Antero, 2023; Heyward, Emmonds et al., 2022). Third, when the focus is on the physiological discrepancies between the sexes, one of the key differences that underpin variations is the sex steroid hormones (oestrogens, progestins and androgens) (Blair, 2007). Because of recent research and media attention and because variations in sex steroid hormones underpin physiological response and training adaptation, coaches' knowledge and experiences of the menstrual cycle have been explored (Brown & Knight, 2022). It is important to attempt to dispel any myths and misunderstandings regarding the effect of endogenous ovarian hormones on exercise performance, training and health, as well as dispelling myths around how exercise, training and performance may impact a eumenorrhoeic (regular) menstrual cycle.

Overview of the menstrual cycle

The menstrual cycle can be broken up into phases according to the levels of the two hormones, oestrogen and progesterone. There is some discrepancy in the literature as to the number of phases the menstrual cycle can be divided into, from two phases (luteal and follicular) (Reed & Carr, 2000) to as many as eight phases (Bisdee et al., 1989) having been identified, as well as all number of phases in between. This variation in the number of identified phases causes difficulties when trying to compare the effects of the menstrual cycle on physical performance through meta-analysis (McNulty et al., 2020). For the coach, it might be more straightforward to consider four phases, since this is common practice in menstrual cycle tracking apps, such as the Fitrwoman app (https://www.fitrwoman.com/post/fitrwoman-guide) or Flo (https://floliving.com/blog/menstrual-phase). These four phases are shown in Figure 14.1. It could be argued, however, that a much better approach is to focus on the individual day-to-day fluctuations that are experienced and to monitor these fluctuations through menstrual cycle tracking apps (Bruinvels et al., 2022).

A 'textbook' regular menstrual cycle lasts 28 days with ovulation occurring around day 14, but there is high variability in length, with durations between 26 and 34 days being typical (Harlow et al., 2013). The cycle starts by using the term 'day one', which is the first day of the bleed or menses. Bleeding, in terms of duration and amount of blood loss, is also highly variable between and within women, but generally menses continues for around four days (Bull et al., 2019) and usual blood loss is around 30 mL (Hallberg et al., 1966). This first phase is characterized by low levels of the hormones, oestrogen and progesterone, but because there are symptoms associated with menses, such as

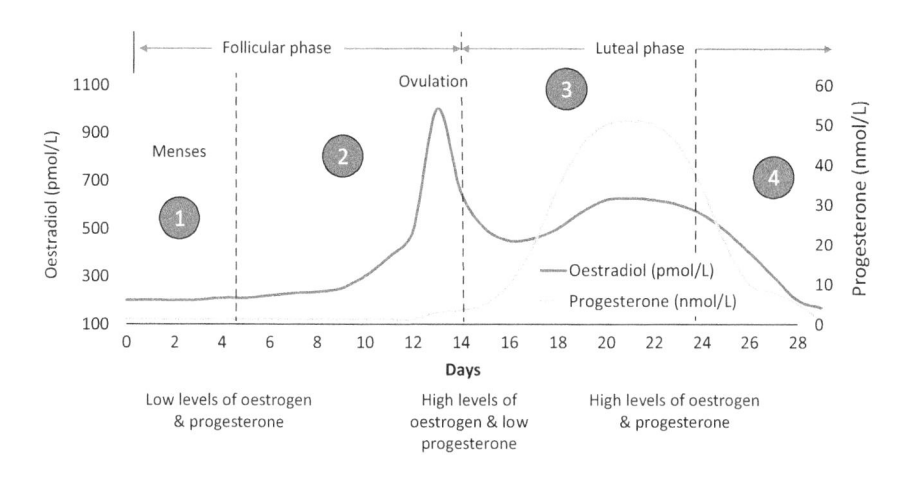

Figure 14.1. Variations in oestrogen and progesterone across a hypothetical, 28-day eumenorrhoeic menstrual cycle.

dysmenorrhoea (painful periods) and menorrhagia [blood loss > 80 mL (Hallberg et al., 1966)], then this phase is usually considered separately from the subsequent phase, which also consists of low levels of oestrogen and progesterone but without the bleed. Oestrogen levels begin to rise during this second phase, culminating in a peak just prior to ovulation. Following ovulation, oestrogen drops initially, then increases again, concurrently with progesterone. A final phase can be distinguished, where progesterone and oestrogen start to decline, and symptoms of pre-menstrual syndrome can be experienced. Symptoms occurring in this final phase have been reported by athletes to include stomach cramps or abdominal pain, headache/migraine, bloating, increased appetite, breast pain and mood disturbances (Brown et al., 2021; Bruinvels et al., 2021). There are, therefore, changes that occur across the menstrual cycle, in terms of relative levels of oestrogen and progesterone, which are perceived to have a profound effect on the athlete's training (Brown et al., 2021). The effect of the menstrual cycle on performance should, therefore, not be dismissed as being irrelevant or insignificant.

The menstrual cycle – is it all negative?

In an applied setting, when athletes and coaches are asked about the menstrual cycle, focus is often on the negative symptoms that are experienced. There is a plethora of research that has been carried out on athletes, in which the negative symptoms of the menstrual cycle have been the focus (Brown et al., 2021; Ekenros et al., 2022; Findlay et al., 2020; Martin et al., 2018). These negative side effects have been perceived to affect performance and training. It is perhaps not surprising that the emphasis is on the undesirable aspects of having a menstrual cycle, perpetuated perhaps by media messages that focus on the negative, such as the pain experienced in response to menstrual cramp simulation. In Westernized society, menstruation is often represented as something that is undesirable, and pre-menstrual women are defined by their irritability, mood swings and irrational, even violent, behaviour (King et al., 2014). Coaches and their athletes, therefore, may hold notions that the menstrual cycle can have a debilitating influence on exercise performance, with these messages reinforced by the media, a lack of education and general miscommunicated folklore. Understanding negative symptomology and trying to prevent symptoms is of course necessary to improve performance and training, but often the positive aspects of having a normal, regular menstrual cycle are overlooked or not even considered (Chrisler et al., 1994). The myth is perpetuated in sporting domains that the menstrual cycle has negative connotations for the athlete.

Variations in hormones associated with the menstrual cycle have the potential to optimize performance and training in sport. For instance, there is research evidence to suggest that there may be beneficial effects of menstrual cycle-related hormonal perturbations regarding muscle strength and adaptation (Kissow et al., 2022; Thompson et al., 2020), muscle injury incidence, especially anterior crucial ligament (ACL) injury (Herzberg et al., 2017), and energy metabolism (Oosthuyse et al., 2022). Even though the performance consequences may not always be discernible in the research (McNulty et al., 2020), owing to inter- and intra-individual differences and a lack of hormone testing to confirm status (Elliott-Sale et al., 2021), the mechanisms to explain the effects of oestrogen and progesterone are well understood (Oosthuyse et al., 2022), which suggests that hormonal variations can have an important individual impact on athletes. Instead of focussing on symptoms and managing symptoms, which although important to ensure effective training and performance, the coach could focus on how performance, training and health can be optimized by appreciating the individual variations in ovarian hormones across the cycle. The myth needs to be changed that the menstrual cycle is 'bad' or is associated with negative symptoms that need to be 'managed'. We need to reframe the discussion and talk about how performance, training and health can be optimized in relation to positive menstrual health.

Methodological considerations in the research

Before a more in-depth consideration of the positive aspects of ovarian hormone variation on exercise performance, an understanding of the limits of the research should be considered. Often, coaches may talk about there not being enough good quality research on the menstrual cycle, or that there is confusion over what to change and adapt as the research is not considered sufficient to support a change. For instance, in a survey on oral contraceptive use in elite women's rugby union, lack of supporting evidence was identified as a barrier for athletes speaking to coaching staff about their menstrual cycle (Heyward et al., 2022). This opinion about the lack of research is, to some extent, justified, as research on the effect of menstrual cycle on performance is complex. A sample of eumenorrhoeic women athletes needs to be initially sought. Already, this sample excludes a large proportion of women – women who are using some form of hormonal contraception [in an athletic population, this figure is around 40–60% (Brown et al., 2023; Cheng et al., 2021; Heyward et al., 2022), depending on the sport, country and athletic status of the athlete] and women who have any type of menstrual dysfunction or disorder, again with these being highly prevalent in athletic populations (Gimunová et al., 2022; Taim et al., 2023). Having obtained this unique sample of women, eumenorrhoea needs to be established, first by the athlete recording the duration of their cycle over several months, then checking whether they ovulate using urine ovulation test kits, followed by a verification of their oestrogen and progesterone levels at different phases of the menstrual cycle through lab-based blood or salivary analysis (Hirschberg, 2022; Janse De Jonge et al., 2019). By this time, the researcher is left with such an unrealistic subsample of women that, even if differences in a performance variable are ascertained, this result would only apply to less than half of an athletic population. Because of the exclusions, the sample size also tends to be very small, and hence the test is underpowered, which has led to researchers concluding that the quality of the research is 'low' (McNulty et al., 2020; Meignié et al., 2021; Thompson et al., 2020). Quality of the research is also deemed low if the measures described above to verify menstrual cycle status are not performed. On top of the difficulties in obtaining good quality research, there is also a lack of research about the physiological responses throughout the menstrual cycle. The intricacies of having to monitor and control for fluctuations in ovarian hormones are often a deterrent when it comes to even carrying out research on women (Blair, 2007), leading to low number of females included in sport and exercise medicine and science research (Costello et al., 2014; Cowley et al., 2021). This lack of research and of purportedly low-quality research filters to coaches, who then may hold the myth that the menstrual cycle is not worth considering.

Inferences can be made from the literature, and from applied work and anecdotal experiences of athletes, despite the limitations of the research. In an applied setting, it is acknowledged that many athletes perceive their menstrual cycle as influencing their performance and training (Brown et al., 2021; Paludo et al., 2022). There is likely to be some aspect of performance, training and health that is affected by the variation in levels of ovarian hormones, although it will be very individualistic (Burden et al., 2021). Hence, because women's cycles differ so much, the coach needs to consider the day-to-day variation of the individual. There is still research to be done on menstrual cycle, so that specific conclusions can be reached and recommendations can be given, but it is clear that menstrual cycle, in some form or other, plays a role in an athlete's performance and training, especially at an individual level.

Physiological responses to exercise and adaptations to training across the menstrual cycle

Monitoring of physiological responses – what could be done?

Changes in ovarian hormones across the menstrual cycle cause changes in physiological responses of the body to exercise, although these changes have not always been detectable in the research and do not necessarily translate into improved performance (McNulty et al., 2020). There are some performance and training aspects that may alter across the menstrual cycle that the coach might, however, consider. For instance, around ovulation, there is a peak in core body temperature, and body temperature remains elevated throughout the second half of the cycle, the luteal phase, with this rise being detectable before, during and after exercise (Giersch et al., 2020). There have also been reports, by some researchers, of variations across the menstrual cycle in terms of exercising heart rate (Hessemer & Bruck, 1985), breathing response to exercise (Schoene et al., 1981), ratings of perceived exertion (Paludo et al., 2022), the threshold for sweating onset (Stachenfeld et al., 2000) and blood lactate concentration during exercise (Forsyth & Reilly, 2005). These responses have typically been found to be elevated in the mid-luteal phase of the menstrual cycle of eumenorrhoeic females. If monitoring training using such parameters, which are typical parameters to measure training load, then there may be variation across the menstrual cycle for some women. Because of these distinct variations in physiological responses at rest and during exercise, we should dispel the myth that menstrual cycle does not need to be considered. The coach should, therefore, be mindful of individual differences in training response, which could be accounted for by the menstrual cycle.

Phase-based training?

Coaches may have heard that muscular training around the late follicular phase and around ovulation may be beneficial, owing to improved muscle-related responses and adaptation. Follicular phase-based training, or menstrual cycle-based training, has therefore gained some momentum, although unfortunately there are very few studies in which follicular phase-based training has been empirically researched (Reis et al., 1995; Sung et al., 2014; Wikström-Frisén et al., 2017). Mechanistically, this idea does seem to make sense, since high levels of oestrogen are associated with increased protein synthesis, inhibition of protein catabolism and improved muscle quality and fibre-type distribution (Oosthuyse et al., 2022). Oestrogen may also interact with other hormones such as growth hormone, insulin-like growth factor 1 and insulin, which in turn could trigger muscle anabolic processes (Knowles et al., 2019). Around ovulation, there is an increase in androgens, including testosterone, as well as an increase in the growth hormone, which could contribute to muscle development. It, therefore, seems correct from a physiological perspective that strength and power performance could be better and lead to more growth in muscle tissue during the late follicular phase (Kissow et al., 2022). There have been, however, conflicting findings in the research, again due to the suggestion that the research from which the reviews have been drawn is of low quality (Blagrove et al., 2020; Thompson et al., 2020), but also because, in an applied setting, progesterone may be antagonizing the response. It was recently concluded, based on an umbrella review of systematic studies to date, that the menstrual cycle had limited effects on strength performance (Colenso-Semple et al., 2023). Despite this conclusion, oestrogen will affect the muscle but in an applied setting, it might be really difficult to target resistance training according to menstrual cycle phase. That said, in a rehabilitation setting, where a single athlete is being rehabilitated after injury, this type of targeted training might be useful (O'Loughlin et al., 2022). In addition, high oestrogen levels may help prevent exercise-induced muscle damage, since oestrogen activates satellite cells and contributes to phospholipid membrane stability and integrity (Enns & Tiidus, 2010; Oosthuyse et al., 2022). Scheduling resistance training according to menstrual cycle phase might be too much of a gamble, but perhaps rehabilitation training and scheduling high-intensity, unusual eccentric training (that may cause muscle damage) to coincide with peaks in oestrogen may work for some athletes.

Injury prevention

When coaches and athletes are asked about their knowledge of how the menstrual cycle might impact performance and training, musculoskeletal injuries are often cited, particularly incidence of ACL injuries (Forsyth et al., 2022). This is not a myth, since hormonal variations across the menstrual cycle alter joint laxity and lower tendon collagen synthesis (Dos'Santos et al., 2023; Hansen, 2018); the ovulatory phase has been found to be associated with a trend for increased risk of injury (Martínez-Fortuny et al., 2023), but again, as with previous research, it is not possible to establish causality. Musculoskeletal injuries, including ACL injuries, are multifactorial, involving biomechanical, anatomical, environmental, genetic, nutritional and socio-psychological factors. In addition, pinpointing the exact time of elevated oestrogen-related effects in each athlete is difficult, with much variability found (Dos'Santos et al., 2023; Hansen, 2018). The coach should not dismiss hormone-related causes of injury but should be advised to monitor injury in relation to menstrual cycle, so that patterns in individual data may be ascertained.

Hormone-mediated optimization of performance

There is the notion that women perform worse than men in all aspects of sport requiring physical exertion or physical prowess. This could be considered a myth, as there are individual examples of women performing better than men in ultradistance events. For instance, from Gertrude Ederle being the first woman to swim across the English Channel in 1926, we now have examples of other women achieving amazing feats, such as Sarah Thompson, who holds the record for swimming across the English Channel non-stop four times, and Diana Nyad, who holds the record for swimming from Cuba to Florida. Based on statistics from race times, the performance gap between men and women becomes narrow with increased distance, especially in swimming (Knechtle et al., 2020; Tiller et al., 2021). Hence, women do particularly well in ultradistance events. Higher rates of lipid oxidation in women that are oestrogen-mediated may contribute to this better ultradistance endurance performance in women compared to that of men (Tarnopolsky et al., 1990). In the luteal phase of the menstrual cycle, when oestrogen levels are elevated, there is a significant reliance on fat for fuel during exercise, and a concomitant reduction in carbohydrate oxidation (Oosthuyse & Bosch, 2010; Zderic et al., 1998). These changes in energetics ultimately mean that long-duration exercise may be better and feel easier in the luteal phase of the cycle. The myth that men always outperform women can be dispelled, since oestrogen contributes to women's success in ultradistance events.

Menstrual dysfunction and pain should not be ignored

The myth about the menstrual cycle not being relevant for the coach and athlete could be dispelled by thinking about what the athlete is like when they don't have a regular menstrual cycle. It is perhaps only when a woman has a problem, such as becoming amenorrhoeic (a loss of menstrual bleed for three months or more) that the negative consequences of not having appropriate levels of oestrogen and progesterone are realized. Menstrual dysfunction consists of a spectrum of disorders ranging from a short luteal phase to functional hypothalamic amenorrhoea (Gibbs et al., 2013) (Figure 14.2). Dysfunction in athletes can occur when energy expenditure is not matched by energy intake, which may be both inadvertent and advertent. Low energy availability can have long-lasting health and clinical consequences, including infertility, osteoporosis, increased musculoskeletal injury risk, dyslipidaemia, impaired endothelial function and decrements in performance (Mountjoy et al., 2014; VanHeest et al., 2014). These negative consequences have been extensively researched, as part of the

Eumenorrhoea	Luteal phase defects	Anovulation	Oligomenorrhoea	Amenorrhoea
• Consistent, regular cycle, with ovulation • Menstrual bleed every approx. 26 to 36 days	• Short luteal phase • Low progesterone in luteal phase • Ovulation occurs	• No ovulation • Low progesterone in luteal phase • Cycle still seems regular	• Irregular, inconsistent cycles • Cycles >36 days • Ovulation or no ovulation	• No menstrual bleed for 3 months or more • Low levels of oestrogen and progesterone

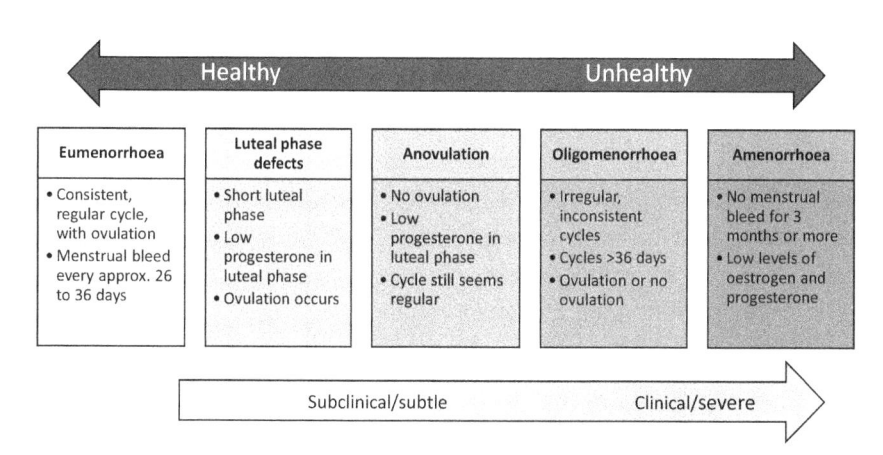

Healthy ←→ Unhealthy

Subclinical/subtle → Clinical/severe

Figure 14.2. Healthy, eumenorrhoic menstrual cycle symptoms to unhealthy menorrhoeic cycle symptoms.

female athlete triad (De Souza et al., 2014), now renamed relative energy deficiency in sport or RED-S (Mountjoy et al., 2014). Menstrual dysfunction may also lead to some athletes leaving the sport or not pursuing the sport at a higher level, especially if concerns about their future health and well-being take priority (Calthorpe et al., 2019). Knowledge, awareness and understanding of the menstrual cycle, variations in hormones and RED-S are, therefore, paramount to ensure that the athlete's well-being, performance and training are maintained.

Unfortunately, there is the myth that a lack of menstruation can be indicative of an effective training response. For instance, elite athletes from various sports were asked about their reasons for not seeking help in the absence of menses and said that they felt not having a period was normalized or not perceived as a problem (Verhoef et al., 2021). More knowledge and understanding are needed regarding what constitutes a healthy menstrual cycle. Menstrual health is not a topic typically covered as part of coaching courses; based on research, there is a lack of awareness and knowledge about the menstrual cycle amongst coaches (Brown & Knight, 2022; Clarke et al., 2021; Höök et al., 2021), especially with regard to menstrual dysfunction (Kroshus et al., 2014). A lack of knowledge on menstrual cycle could be a barrier to communication between the athlete and coach (Höök et al., 2021). Knowledge about the menstrual cycle and menstrual dysfunction, therefore, needs to be improved to help maximize performance and incite open conversations between the athlete and coach (Forsyth et al., 2022).

The coach needs knowledge of other menstrual-related issues, such as endometriosis severe dysmenorrhoea, polycystic ovary syndrome (PCOS), menorrhagia, hysterectomy, premature menopause and how these impact the athlete's performance, training and health. There is the myth that pain should be tolerated, but often severe or persistent pain is a sign that there is something wrong. The athlete may be told to endure the pain and to continue with training, with the myth that exercise can make the pain go away. For instance, athletes have been reported to 'endure' or tolerate negative symptoms associated with the menstrual cycle when competing (Armour et al., 2020; Findlay et al., 2020). Pain and menstrual dysfunction are, therefore, not normal and should not be ignored by the coach.

Summary recommendations

The effects of the menstrual cycle have been, at times, taken out of context, mainly because there are limitations in the research and hence limitations in how research is interpreted in an applied setting. Key take-home messages, however, include the following:

- The menstrual cycle differs from one cycle to the next and between females, so tracking the menstrual cycle should be the first step to understanding how variations may affect the individual athlete's performance, training and health.
- If women and girls can track their menstrual cycle and their perceptions of both positive and negative daily variations (easily done through an app), then the coach should be able to adapt and change the training to suit the individual, regardless of the setting – individual or team sport.
- The menstrual cycle is not all negative. Although negative symptoms experienced typically during pre-menses and menses are important for the coach to acknowledge, there are optimal times in the menstrual cycle when performance might be at a peak. Adapting training to coincide with the individual's peaks should be considered.
- Menstrual dysfunction, especially an absence of bleeding, and menstrual disorders like severe pain and heavy bleeding should not be considered normal and therefore should not be ignored. Coaches should be striving for positive menstrual health in their athletes.
- The relationship between the athlete and coach needs to be one of trust and empowerment, so that positive and negative issues relating to the menstrual cycle and hormonal contraceptive use and their association with athletic performance can be openly and unambiguously discussed.

References

Antero, J. (2023). *Empow'her.* Laboratoires de recherche de l'INSEP. Retrieved July 27, 2023, from https://labos-recherche.insep.fr/fr

Armour, M., Parry, K. A., Steel, K., & Smith, C. A. (2020). Australian female athlete perceptions of the challenges associated with training and competing when menstrual symptoms are present. *International Journal of Sports Science and Coaching, 15*(3), 316–323. https://10.1177/1747954120916073

Bisdee, J. T., Garlick, P. J., & James, W. P. T. (1989). Metabolic changes during the menstrual cycle. *British Journal of Nutrition, 61*(3), 641–650. https://10.1079/BJN19890151

Blagrove, R. C., Bruinvels, G., & Pedlar, C. R. (2020). Variations in strength-related measures during the menstrual cycle in eumenorrheic women: A systematic review and meta-analysis. *Journal of Science and Medicine in Sport, 23*(12), 1220–1227. https://10.1016/J.JSAMS.2020.04.022

Blair, M. L. (2007). Sex-based differences in physiology: What should we teach in the medical curriculum? *Advances in Physiology Education, 31*(1), 23–25. https://10.1152/advan.00118.2006

Brown, N., & Knight, C. J. (2022). Understanding female coaches' and practitioners' experience and support provision in relation to the menstrual cycle. *International Journal of Sports Science & Coaching, 17*(2), 235–243. https://10.1177/17479541211058579

Brown, N., Knight, C. J., & Forrest (née Whyte), L. J. (2021). Elite female athletes' experiences and perceptions of the menstrual cycle on training and sport performance. *Scandinavian Journal of Medicine & Science in Sports, 31*(1), 52–69. https://10.1111/sms.13818

Brown, N., Roldan-Reoyo, O., Williams, G. K. R., Stodter, A., Moore, I. S., Mackintosh, K. A., McNarry, M. A., & Williams, E. M. P. (2023). Profiling hormonal contraceptive use and perceived impact on training and performance in a global sample of women rugby players. *International Journal of Sports Physiology and Performance, 18*, 1–7. https://10.1123/ijspp.2023-0137

Bruinvels, G., Goldsmith, E., Blagrove, R., Simpkin, A., Lewis, N., Morton, K., Suppiah, A., Rogers, J. P., Ackerman, K. E., Newell, J., & Pedlar, C. (2021). Prevalence and frequency of menstrual cycle symptoms are associated with availability to train and compete: A study of 6812 exercising women recruited using the Strava exercise app. *British Journal of Sports Medicine, 55*(8), 438–443. https://10.1136/BJSPORTS-2020-102792

Bruinvels, G., Hackney, A. C., & Pedlar, C. R. (2022). Menstrual cycle: The importance of both the phases and the transitions between phases on training and performance. *Sports Medicine (Auckland), 52*(7), 1457–1460. https://10.1007/s40279-022-01691-2

Bull, J. R., Rowland, S. P., Scherwitzl, E. B., Scherwitzl, R., Danielsson, K. G., & Harper, J. (2019). Real-world menstrual cycle characteristics of more than 600,000 menstrual cycles. *NPJ Digital Medicine, 2*(1), 83. https://10.1038/s41746-019-0152-7

Burden, R. J., Shill, A. L., & Bishop, N. C. (2021). Elite female athlete research: Stop searching for the 'magic P'. *Experimental Physiology, 106*(10), 2029–2030. https://10.1113/EP089884

Calthorpe, L., Brage, S., & Ong, K. K. (2019). Systematic review and meta-analysis of the association between childhood physical activity and age at menarche. *Acta Paediatrica, 108*(6), 1008–1015.

Cheng, J., Santiago, K. A., Abutalib, Z., Temme, K. E., Hulme, A., Goolsby, M. A., Esopenko, C. L., & Casey, E. K. (2021). Menstrual irregularity, hormonal contraceptive use, and bone stress injuries in collegiate female athletes in the United States. *Pm & R, 13*(11), 1207–1215. https://10.1002/pmrj.12539

Chrisler, J. C., Johnston, I. K., Champagne, N. M., & Preston, K. E. (1994). Menstrual joy: The construct and its consequences. *Psychology of Women Quarterly, 18*(3), 375–387. https://10.1111/j.1471-6402.1994.tb004

Clarke, A., Govus, A., & Donaldson, A. (2021). What male coaches want to know about the menstrual cycle in women's team sports: Performance, health, and communication. *International Journal of Sports Science & Coaching, 16*(3), 544–553. https://10.1177/1747954121989237

Colenso-Semple, L. M., D'Souza, A. C., Elliott-Sale, K. J., & Phillips, S. M. (2023). Current evidence shows no influence of women's menstrual cycle phase on acute strength performance or adaptations to resistance exercise training. *Frontiers in Sports and Active Living, 5*, 1054542. https://10.3389/fspor.2023.1054542

Costello, J. T., Bieuzen, F., & Bleakley, C. M. (2014). Where are all the female participants in sports and exercise medicine research? *European Journal of Sport Science, 14*(8), 847–851. https://10.1080/17461391.2014.911354

Cowley, E. S., Olenick, A. A., McNulty, K. L., & Ross, E. Z. (2021). "Invisible sportswomen": The sex data gap in sport and exercise science research. *Women in Sport and Physical Activity Journal, 29*(2), 146–151. https://10.1123/wspaj.2021-0028

De Souza, M. J, Nattiv, A, Joy, E, Misra, M, Williams, N. I., Mallinson, R.J., Gibbs, J. C., Olmsted, M., Goolsby, M, Matheson, G. et al. (2014). Female athlete triad coalition consensus statement on treatment and return to play of the female athlete triad: 1st International Conference held in San Francisco, California, May 2012 and 2nd International Conference held in Indianapolis, Indiana, May 2013. *Br J Sports Med, 48*, 289.

Dos'Santos, T., Stebbings, G. K., Morse, C., Shashidharan, M., Daniels, K. A. J., & Sanderson, A. (2023). Effects of the menstrual cycle phase on anterior cruciate ligament neuromuscular and biomechanical injury risk surrogates in eumenorrheic and naturally menstruating women: A systematic review. *PloS One, 18*(1), e0280800. https://10.1371/journal.pone.0280800

Ekenros, L., von Rosen, P., Solli, G. S., Sandbakk, Ø, Holmberg, H., Hirschberg, A. L., & Fridén, C. (2022). Perceived impact of the menstrual cycle and hormonal contraceptives on physical exercise and performance in 1,086 athletes from 57 sports. *Frontiers in Physiology, 13*, 954760. https://10.3389/fphys.2022.954760

Elliott-Sale, K. J., Minahan, C. L., de Jonge, X. A. K. J., Ackerman, K. E., Sipilä, S., Constantini, N. W., Lebrun, C. M., & Hackney, A. C. (2021). Methodological considerations for studies in sport and exercise science with women as participants: A working guide for standards of practice for research on women. *Sports Medicine, 51*(5), 843–861. https://10.1007/s40279-021-01435-8

Enns, D. L., & Tiidus, P. M. (2010). The influence of estrogen on skeletal muscle: Sex matters. *Sports Medicine, 40*(1), 41–58. https://10.2165/11319760-000000000-00000

Findlay, R. J., MacRae, E. H. R., Whyte, I. Y., Easton, C., & Forrest, L. J. (2020). How the menstrual cycle and menstruation affect sporting performance: Experiences and perceptions of elite female rugby players. *British Journal of Sports Medicine, 54*(18), 1108–1113. https://10.1136/bjsports-2019-101486

Forsyth, J. J., & Reilly, T. (2005). The combined effect of time of day and menstrual cycle on lactate threshold. *Medicine & Science in Sports & Exercise, 37*(12), 2046–2053. https://10.1249/01.mss.0000179094.47765.d0

Forsyth, J. J., Sams, L., Blackett, A. D., Ellis, N., & Abouna, M. (2022). Menstrual cycle, hormonal contraception and pregnancy in women's football: Perceptions of players, coaches and managers. *Sport in Society, 26*(7), 1280–1295. https://10.1080/17430437.2022.2125385

Gibbs, J. C., Williams, N. I., & De Souza, M. J. (2013). Prevalence of individual and combined components of the female athlete triad. *Med Sci Sports Exerc, 45*(5), 985–996.

Giersch, G. E. W., Charkoudian, N., Stearns, R. L., & Casa, D. J. (2020). Fluid balance and hydration considerations for women: Review and future directions. *Sports Medicine, 50*(2), 253–261. https://10.1007/S40279-019-01206-6

Gimunová, M., Paulínyová, A., Bernaciková, M., & Paludo, A. C. (2022). The prevalence of menstrual cycle disorders in female athletes from different sports disciplines: A rapid review. *International Journal of Environmental Research and Public Health, 19*(21), 14243. https://10.3390/ijerph192114243

Hallberg, L., Hôgdahl, A., Nilsson, L., & Rybo, G. (1966). Menstrual blood loss-A population study: Variation at different ages and attempts to define normality. *Acta Obstetricia Et Gynecologica Scandinavica, 45*(3), 320–351. https://10.3109/00016346609158455

Hansen, M. (2018). Female hormones: Do they influence muscle and tendon protein metabolism? *Proceedings of the Nutrition Society, 77*(1), 32–41. https://10.1017/S0029665117001951

Harlow, S. D., Windham, G. C., & Paramsothy, P. (2013). Chapter 12 – Menstruation and menstrual disorders: The epidemiology of menstruation and menstrual dysfunction. *Women and Health* (Second Edition ed., pp. 163–177). Elsevier Inc. https://10.1016/B978-0-12-384978-6.00012-1

Herzberg, S. D., Motu'apuaka, M. L., Lambert, W., Fu, R., Brady, J., & Guise, J. (2017). The effect of menstrual cycle and contraceptives on ACL injuries and laxity: A systematic review and meta-analysis. *Orthopaedic Journal of Sports Medicine, 5*(7), 232596711771878. https://10.1177/2325967117718781

Hessemer, V., & Bruck, K. (1985). Influence of menstrual cycle on thermoregulatory, metabolic, and heart rate responses to exercise at night. *Journal of Applied Physiology, 59*(6), 1911–1917. https://10.1152/jappl.1985.59.6.1911

Heyward, O., Elliott-Sale, K. J., Roe, G., Emmonds, S., Hornby, K., Stokes, K. A., & Jones, B. (2022). Oral contraceptive use in Premiership and Championship women's rugby union: Perceived symptomology, management strategies, and performance and wellness effects. *Science and Medicine in Football,* 1–8. https://10.1080/24733938.2022.2156588

Heyward, O., Emmonds, S., Roe, G., Scantlebury, S., Stokes, K., & Jones, B. (2022). Applied sports science and sports medicine in women's rugby: Systematic scoping review and Delphi study to establish future research priorities. *BMJ Open Sport & Exercise Medicine, 8*(3), e001287. https://10.1136/bmjsem-2021-001287

Hirschberg, A. L. (2022). Challenging aspects of research on the influence of the menstrual cycle and oral contraceptives on physical performance. *Sports Medicine (Auckland), 52*(7), 1453–1456. https://10.1007/s40279-021-01616-5

Höök, M., Bergström, M., Sæther, S. A., & McGawley, K. (2021). "Do elite sport first, get your period back later." Are barriers to communication hindering female athletes? *International Journal of Environmental Research and Public Health, 18*(22), 12075. https://10.3390/IJERPH182212075

Janse De Jonge, X., Thompson, B., & Han, A. (2019). Methodological recommendations for menstrual cycle research in sports and exercise. *Medicine & Science in Sports & Exercise, 51*(12), 2610–2617. https://10.1249/MSS.0000000000002073

King, M., Ussher, J. M., & Perz, J. (2014). Representations of PMS and premenstrual women in men's accounts: An analysis of online posts from PMSBuddy.com. *Women's Reproductive Health, 1*(1), 3–20. https://10.1080/23293691.2014.901796

Kissow, J., Jacobsen, K. J., Gunnarsson, T. P., Jessen, S., & Hostrup, M. (2022). Effects of follicular and luteal phase-based menstrual cycle resistance training on muscle strength and mass. *Sports Medicine (Auckland, N.Z.).* https://10.1007/s40279-022-01679-y

Knechtle, B., Dalamitros, A. A., Barbosa, T. M., Sousa, C. V., Rosemann, T., & Nikolaidis, P. T. (2020). Sex differences in swimming disciplines-can women outperform men in swimming? *17*(10), 3651. https://10.3390/ijerph17103651

Knowles, O. E., Aisbett, B., Main, L. C., Drinkwater, E. J., Orellana, L., & Lamon, S. (2019). Resistance training and skeletal muscle protein metabolism in eumenorrheic females: Implications for researchers and practitioners. *Sports Medicine (Auckland), 49*(11), 1637–1650. https://10.1007/s40279-019-01132-7

Kroshus, E., Sherman, R. T., Thompson, R. A., Sossin, K., & Austin, S. B. (2014). Gender differences in high school coaches' knowledge, attitudes, and communication about the female athlete triad. *Eating Disorders, 22*(3), 193–208. https://10.1080/10640266.2013.874827

Martin, D., Sale, C., Cooper, S. B., & Elliott-Sale, K. J. (2018). Period prevalence and perceived side effects of hormonal contraceptive use and the menstrual cycle in elite athletes. *International Journal of Sports Physiology and Performance, 13*(7), 926–932. https://10.1123/ijspp.2017-0330

Martínez-Fortuny, N., Alonso-Calvete, A., Da Cuña-Carrera, I., & Abalo-Núñez, R. (2023). Menstrual cycle and sport injuries: A systematic review. *International Journal of Environmental Research and Public Health, 20*(4), 3264. https://10.3390/ijerph20043264

McNulty, K. L., Elliott-Sale, K. J., Dolan, E., Swinton, P. A., Ansdell, P., Goodall, S., Thomas, K., & Hicks, K. M. (2020). The effects of menstrual cycle phase on exercise performance in eumenorrheic women: A systematic review and meta-analysis. *Sports Medicine, 50*(10), 1813–1827. https://10.1007/s40279-020-01319-3

Meignié, A., Duclos, M., Carling, C., Orhant, E., Provost, P., Toussaint, J., & Antero, J. (2021). The effects of menstrual cycle phase on elite athlete performance: A critical and systematic review. *Frontiers in Physiology, 12*. https://10.3389/fphys.2021.654585

Mountjoy, M., Sundgot-Borgen, J., Burke, L., Carter, S., Constantini, N., Lebrun, C., ... & Ljungqvist, A. (2014). The IOC consensus statement: beyond the female athlete triad—relative energy deficiency in sport (RED-S). *British journal of sports medicine, 48*(7), 491–497.

O'Loughlin, E., Reid, D., & Sims, S. (2022). Is there a role for menstrual cycle phased resistance training programmes for women post anterior cruciate ligament reconstruction? A scoping review protocol. *Physical Therapy Reviews, 27*(3), 176–180. https://10.1080/108331 96.2021.2017613

Oosthuyse, T., & Bosch, A. N. (2010). The effect of the menstrual cycle on exercise metabolism: Implications for exercise performance in eumenorrhoeic women. *Sports Medicine, 40*(3), 207–227. https://10.2165/11317090-000000000-00000

Oosthuyse, T., Strauss, J. A., & Hackney, A. C. (2022). Understanding the female athlete: Molecular mechanisms underpinning menstrual phase differences in exercise metabolism. *European Journal of Applied Physiology*. https://10.1007/s00421-022-05090-3

Paludo, A. C., Paravlic, A., Dvořáková, K., & Gimunová, M. (2022). The effect of menstrual cycle on perceptual responses in athletes: A systematic review with meta-analysis. *Frontiers in Psychology, 13*, 926854. https://10.3389/fpsyg.2022.926854

Reed, B. G., & Carr, B. R. (2000). *The normal menstrual cycle and the control of ovulation*. MDText.com, Inc., South Dartmouth (MA).

Reis, E., Frick, U., & Schmidtbleicher, D. (1995). Frequency variations of strength training sessions triggered by the phases of the menstrual cycle. *International Journal of Sports Medicine, 16*(8), 545–550. https://10.1055/s-2007-973052

Ronald, I. (2022, August 19). Olympic medalist Dina Asher-Smith calls for more research into how periods affect athletic performance. *CNN Wire Service*. https://search.proquest.com/docview/2703837251

Schoene, R. B., Robertson, H. T., Pierson, D. J., & Peterson, A. P. (1981). Respiratory drives and exercise in menstrual cycles of athletic and nonathletic women. *Journal of Applied Physiology, 50*(6), 1300–1305. https://10.1152/jappl.1981.50.6.1300

Stachenfeld, N. S., Silva, C., & Keefe, D. L. (2000). Estrogen modifies the temperature effects of progesterone. *Journal of Applied Physiology, 88*(5), 1643–1649. https://10.1152/jappl.2000.88.5.1643

Sung, E., Han, A., Hinrichs, T., Vorgerd, M., Manchado, C., & Platen, P. (2014). Effects of follicular versus luteal phase-based strength training in young women. *SpringerPlus, 3*(1), 668. https://10.1186/2193-1801-3-668

Taim, B. C., Ó Catháin, C., Renard, M., Elliott-Sale, K. J., Madigan, S., & Ní Chéilleachair, N. (2023). The prevalence of menstrual cycle disorders and menstrual cycle-related symptoms in female athletes: A systematic literature review. *Sports Medicine (Auckland)*. https://10.1007/s40279-023-01871-8

Tarnopolsky, L. J., MacDougall, J. D., Atkinson, S. A., Tarnopolsky, M. A., & Sutton, J. R. (1990). Gender differences in substrate for endurance exercise. *Journal of Applied Physiology, 68*(1), 302–308.

Thompson, B., Almarjawi, A., Sculley, D., & Janse de Jonge, X. (2020). Effect of the menstrual cycle and oral contraceptives on acute responses and chronic adaptations to resistance training: A systematic review of the literature. *Sports Medicine, 50*(1), 171–185. https://10.1007/s40279-019-01219-1

Tiller, N. B., Elliott-Sale, K. J., Knechtle, B., Wilson, P. B., Roberts, J. D., & Millet, G. Y. (2021). Do sex differences in physiology confer a female advantage in ultra-endurance sport? *Sports Medicine (Auckland), 51*(5), 895–915. https://10.1007/s40279-020-01417-2

VanHeest, J. L., Rodgers, C. D., Mahoney, C. E., & De Souza, M. J. (2014). Ovarian suppression impairs sport performance in junior elite female swimmers. *Med Sci Sports Exerc, 46*(1), 156–66.

Verhoef, S. J., Wielink, M. C., Achterberg, E. A., Bongers, M. Y., & Goossens, S. M. T. A. (2021). Absence of menstruation in female athletes: Why they do not seek help. *BMC Sports Science, Medicine and Rehabilitation, 13*(1), 146. https://10.1186/S13102-021-00372-3

Wikström-Frisén, L., Boraxbekk, C. J., & Henriksson-Larsén, K. (2017). Effects on power, strength and lean body mass of menstrual/oral contraceptive cycle based resistance training. *Journal of Sports Medicine and Physical Fitness, 57*(1–2), 43–52. https://10.23736/S0022-4707.16.05848-5

Zderic, T. W., Coggan, A. R., Sharkey, B. J., & Ruby, B. C. (1998). Glucose kinetics and substrate oxidation during exercise in the follicular and luteal phases. *Medicine & Science in Sports & Exercise, 30*(Supplement), 258. https://10.1097/00005768-199805001-01469

15 Challenging the Myths of High Performance in Esports

Laura Swettenham, Kabir Bubna and Matthew Watson

Introduction

The world of esports is a rapidly growing domain that has caught the attention of academics across varying domains (i.e. business, sport psychology, law; Reitman et al., 2020 for a review). This chapter will follow the definition of esports proposed by Pedraza-Ramirez et al. (2020): 'Esports is the casual or organised competitive activity of playing specific video games. ... These games are established by ranking systems and competitions and are regulated by official leagues' (p. 6). Briefly, esports is the competitive play of certain videos and spans across a variety of genres including first-person shooters, multiplayer online battle arenas, real-time strategy, fighting games and sports games. Each genre has distinct aspects of gameplay and performance that make them unique. These distinctions are similar to those made in sports (i.e. invasion games, racquet sports, bat-and-ball games). Similarly, to sports, esports can be individual player-based or team-based.

The purpose of this chapter is to explore a few prevalent myths about esports coaching and performance that largely emerge from stereotypes placed on gaming and gamers. The myths include that esports is just playing video games, e'athletes are unhealthy and e'athletes don't need a coach. Of course, there may be some truth in the myths that we present, rather than claiming falsehood towards these myths, we wish to delve deeper into their assumptions and provide information to show there is more than meets the eye when it comes to the unique and complex world of esports performance.

Myth 1: Esports is just playing video games

Much like having a kick about in the park isn't Premier League football, esports is not simply playing video games. In the definition of esports by Pedraza-Ramirez et al. (2020), we see that there's more to it, such as the need for some organization (e.g. a competitive structure) around the game itself. This distinction is important to highlight in order to challenge some of the stereotypes that come along with the identity of a 'gamer'. The authors of this chapter have themselves encountered criticisms such as esports encouraging isolated sedentary behaviour, screen time and even 'basement dwelling'. The negative gamer stereotype shouldn't carry over to esports because esports is, by definition, an activity that requires interaction with at least one other human being (e.g. an opponent or teammates). Current approaches to esports training reflect this, emphasizing the need for effective communication (Nagorsky & Wiemeyer, 2020), team cohesion (Swettenham & Whitehead, 2022) and health and well-being (Hong & Connelly, 2022) to support individual mastery and performance. This is not necessarily the case for casual gaming.

A useful principle to bear in mind when considering the nature of esports is that all esports games are video games but not all video games are esports games (2020). This delineation between gaming and esports can be seen in the competitive nature and intention of participation in games. Video games such as League of Legends (LoL), Counter Strike: Global Offensive (CS:GO), FIFA, Rocket League and Fortnite are prime examples of prominent esports as they are highly competitive (playing against other players with the objective to win) and adhere to ranking systems which align with the definition posited above. Other video games are typically played for leisure and appeal to the hobbyist. Games such as Skyrim, Super Mario and Grand Theft Auto are not commonly seen as esports games due to the lack of robust ranking systems and official competitions. In many esports, professional e'athletes are no longer competing from the comfort of their own homes and instead are presented in front of vast numbers of fans who either live at the event or online.

To summarize this section, there is much more to being a professional e'athlete than simply playing a video game, much like competitive football is more than just kicking a ball in a park. There can be intense external and internal performance demands that affect performance and well-being. This section will continue to explore this myth by detailing the performance structures and demands within professional esports.

Performance demands in esports

To illustrate the difference in the individual's experience between gaming and esports, allow us to first extend from our football analogy. Imagine two individuals, one walking out onto a local park to go and take a few freekicks into an empty goal and the other walking out onto a freshly lined pitch, accompanied by teammates, a referee and opponents, with a small group of spectators on the sidelines. Both individuals are going to play football; neither is paid to do so; the physical tasks are fairly similar; but their internal/psychological experiences are likely to be quite different. For the individual, this difference is in large part the essence of the difference between gaming and esports (at least at the amateur level before financial incentives come into play) and reflects a number of additional demands on the performer – playing in front of a crowd, executing what was rehearsed in training, the need to work with teammates, awareness of a consequential score. Efforts to *improve* performance in the face of these demands in esports commonly take the form of those that we see in sport, primarily training, coaching and taking care of one's health and well-being, which we would argue are worthwhile pursuits.

Recognizing that esports participation involves the aforementioned demands, researchers have turned their attention to examining these demands in more detail (Leis et al., 2022; Poulus et al., 2022; Smith et al., 2019). Research has posited that the most common stressors arise from performance expectations. For e'athletes, an inability to cope with the demands and stressors placed on them can result in serious negative consequences such as mental ill-health (e.g. Smith et al., 2019), injury (e.g. McGee & Ho, 2021) and early career retirement (e.g. Ward & Harmon, 2019).

To overcome these demands, e'athletes need to develop technical (e.g. game-specific skills and fine motor control), tactical (e.g. strategy and anticipation), psychological (e.g. motivation, attentional control and adaptive coping) and social skills (e.g. communication and feedback reciprocity; Himmelstein et al., 2017; Nagorsky & Wiemeyer, 2020). Esports performance is driven by cognitive capability (Campbell et al., 2018), and recent research has identified that e'athletes may utilize mental strategies to regulate their emotions and sustain focus (Poulus et al., 2020). This helps e'athletes to experience high levels of confidence, longer durations of focus and even enter flow states, all of which can enhance performance outcomes.

The esports performance environment

Performance environments are messy, and human interaction is key for a successful team. Despite the act of esports being, typically, an online interaction between two teams or individuals, the development, learning and heart of esports lie in the interpersonal relationships held within the performance environment. Nielsen and Hanghøj's (2019) research highlights that esports skills are people skills, with communication skills being vital both inside and outside of the game. This may include team cohesion and the relationships built between e'athletes and staff members. To understand more about the demands placed on e'athletes, we can turn to their performance environment (see Figure 15.1) (e.g. Reid et al., 2004). When looking at Figure 15.1, it is important to note that some esports organizations will not have multidisciplinary teams (MDTs) to this level of depth, and the staff members present will vary from organization to organization.

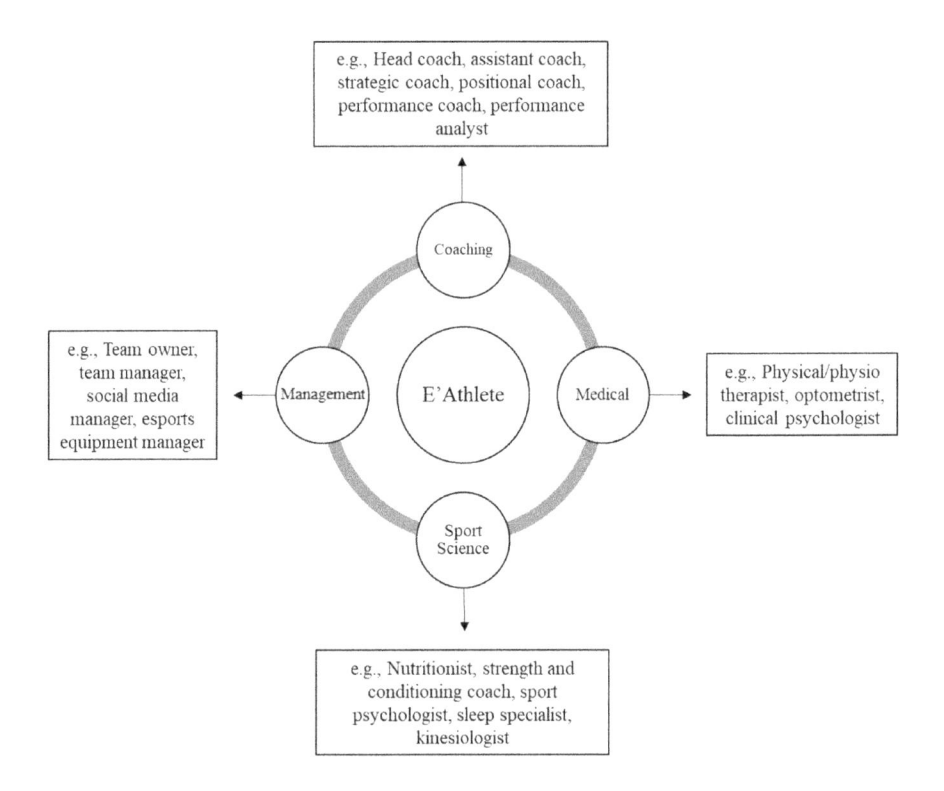

Figure 15.1. Examples of staff members within an esports multidisciplinary team.

Despite some professionals entering esports MDTs, there is still a paucity of qualified practitioners working with teams and individuals to provide advice on topics such as nutrition, sleep and mental health. Esports teams often bring in a single staff member to cover multiple roles. For example, a 'performance coach' may provide support surrounding physical activity, strength and conditioning, nutrition, sport psychology and coaching (Watson et al., 2021). From the authors' experiences, this individual will not be qualified in each of these areas. This is an ethical concern and is an area that esports can advance within in order to provide ethical, high-quality, context-specific support within the performance environment.

To zoom in on the role of the sport psychologist in esports, Ramaker and Pedraza-Ramirez (2023) state that 'everyone is figuring it out along the way'. There are no set guidelines or structures for sport psychologists (or other staff members) within esports. Instead, practice is influenced by scientific literature from sport and the growing research base within esports. It is vital that esports staff members engage in reflective practice, peer support and co-create support within the team to provide high-quality, context-specific support. When transitioning from traditional sport to esports, the challenges faced by sport psychologists may include a lack of qualified professionals to provide feedback, learning the 'language' and culture of the esports title and learning to work effectively online (Ramaker & Pedraza-Remirez, 2023).

To conclude, high performance in esports, much like traditional sport, is a challenging and complex world to navigate and requires teams bolstered by professionals rallying around teams of e'athletes to support performance and well-being demands. It requires not just game-specific, professional knowledge but also interpersonal and intrapersonal skills to allow the environment and people within it to thrive.

Myth 2: E'athletes are unhealthy

A prevalent myth is the poor health of e'athletes in terms of nutrition, sleep, well-being and physical activity (e.g. McNulty et al., 2023, Trotter et al., 2020). The stereotypical view of a gamer is of an individual who is sedentary in their room playing video games late into the night, drinking energy drinks and not interacting socially. Though some of these stereotypes may hold true in some cases and may carry across to some e'athletes, with the growing professionalism in the industry there is certainly more complexity to the argument. Notably, as we'll discuss below, the research presents ambiguous results concerning the relationship between esports, physical activity and obesity that requires attention. We will discuss the current research into the health and well-being of e'athletes, specifically physical activity and mental health, to show that there is more to consider than the stereotypes placed upon e'athletes.

Physical activity

Esports is a sedentary activity, and one account reports e'athletes to be sedentary for 4.2 hours per day during training (Kari & Karhulahti, 2016). One reason for this time spent sitting is due to 'grind culture' within esports (Abbott et al., 2023), which encourages e'athletes to play for hours at a time as they attempt to climb game ranks. Increased time sitting can lead to health-related issues such as increased injury risk, neck and back dysfunction, shoulder pain and poor posture and vascular health (Zwibel et al., 2019). Gaming more generally has been associated with higher levels of obesity and unhealthy lifestyle behaviours in adults (Turel et al., 2016). However, Marker et al (2019) concluded the link between gaming and obesity is small and does not support the assumption of a strong link between video gaming and body mass. Additionally, it's important to highlight that these associations were mostly observed amongst the adult population, with those who play esports titles mostly falling within the 24–27-year-old age bracket (Heggem, 2016).

Trotter et al. (2020) found that e'athletes met the physical activity guidelines less than the general population; however, the top-ranked e'athletes in the sample were 10% more physically active compared to the rest of the esports sample. Additionally, Giakoni-Ramírez et al. (2022) found 92.7% of a sample of 260 male professional e'athletes to have moderate and high levels of physical activity. This may reflect the increasing high-performance mindset amongst e'athletes within the highest leagues, who may recognize the importance of performance gains through a health and well-being lens (McNulty et al., 2023). In Trotter et al. (2020), more e'athletes were classed as a normal weight in comparison to the general population; however, e'athletes were also more likely to fall within obesity classes 2 and 3. This research shows some of the nuances between e'athletes and gamers and that physical activity behaviours may change depending on their level of play. However, it is important to recognize that the research regarding physical activity and obesity levels within esports and video gaming is still ambiguous and requires further investigation and support through physical activity initiatives, such as breaking up periods of sitting with a six-minute walk (DiFrancisco-Donoghue et al., 2021).

Mental health

Though limited, research shows the prevalence of mental ill-health is high in e'athletes (e.g. Smith et al., 2019). Mental health can be defined as 'a state of mental well-being that enables people to cope with the stresses of life, realize their abilities, learn well and work well, and contribute to their community' (WHO, 2022). As discussed earlier in the chapter, e'athletes face numerous performance demands and stressors, which can lead to mental ill-health if they feel they do not have the resources to cope with the stressors in their environment. Severe mental ill-health includes diagnosable disorders, such as depression, anxiety and attention deficit disorder. Within the media, there are reports of e'athletes struggling with their mental health, including instances of burnout (Rawat, 2021), depression (Starkey, 2020) and suicide (Wright, 2023).

Despite the potential mental health risks that e'athletes face, there is a lack of clinical support for e'athletes. Referral systems to gain access to a clinical psychologist are still rare within esports; unlike in traditional sport environments where clinical psychologists are becoming more commonplace. As such, there is a greater need to ensure that professionals working within MDTs in esports have the awareness and skills to recognize and refer e'athlete to a clinical psychologist. For example, qualified sport psychologists will have a clinical contact to refer the e'athlete to in the case that the e'athlete's needs go beyond the sport psychologist's competence (i.e. clinical diagnosis and intervention).

Though a high prevalence of mental ill-health in esports has been reported, video games have been associated with cognitive, motivational, social and health benefits (Granic et al., 2014) and even the potential to improve cognitive skills in young footballers (Boonwang et al., 2022). Esports programmes have shown a potential to develop communication, teamwork and problem-solving skills (Rothwell & Shaffner, 2019) as well as social belonging and mental health (Tjønndal & Skauge, 2020), showing esports can be a vehicle in which positive social, emotional and cognitive development can occur if implemented appropriately (Polman et al., 2018).

Though more research is required to explore the physical health and well-being of e'athletes and despite the challenges faced in terms of sedentary behaviour, we can see that many individuals participating in esports are meeting national physical activity guidelines. However, promotion of physical activity is still needed and efforts to provide physical activity initiatives are welcomed (McNulty et al., 2023). Finally, we must be aware of the concerns regarding the prevalence of mental ill-health and consider how e'athletes can be better supported, while recognizing that, when done correctly, esports has the potential to support many aspects of positive development.

Myth 3: E'athletes don't need a coach!

'Why would anyone need someone to coach them in a video game, when the game itself is designed to deliver real-time and highly personalized instruction and feedback?' 'What could a coach possibly do to improve a player who is far superior at the game than them?' These questions have been raised at times over recent years, sometimes in quite high-profile and public discussions on social media, sometimes levied directly at the authors of this chapter. For those who ask them, the belief is sometimes that coaches are not necessary in esports. For those outside of esports, it might also be hard to comprehend the idea of an esports coach, particularly if they are used to the highly physical (e.g. emphasis on physical movement skills) nature of coaching in sport. However, we contend that these questions stem from a misconception about coaching and an oversimplification of the demands of esports participation.

Although coaching is not a new concept, coaching in esports is a novel activity as the esports industry is still in its infancy compared to its sporting counterparts. One major difference at present pertains to the experience of those being coached. Many e'athletes will have begun interacting with esports for primarily social purposes (i.e. playing with friends) and their motivations may have later shifted to play in more competitive environments as they developed and refined their skills in their chosen esports title. As such, e'athletes typically encounter coach-led, structured training environments much later than their sport counterparts, who enter into such structured sport environments at a young age, often encouraged by parents or school teachers. In other words, e'athletes spend most of their early learning and formal skill development stages without consistent access to coaches. This may change in esports over the years, as esports coaches learn to differentiate coaching approaches for adults and younger people. For now, esports arguably require coaches to be more skilled 'interpersonally' and versatile 'pedagogically'.

The relative absence of coaching at the beginning of one's esports career may provide an explanation for the current myth, with e'athletes learning from the game in their early development and questioning their role or value later on. However, esports coaches are now a prominent feature of the esports landscape, commonplace in amateur, semi-professional and professional teams. Outside of these formal structures, e'athletes can hire coaches, much like hiring a tutor for a subject to help them develop their skills through feedback and review of performance. The following section will explore the role of the coach within esports, why it is necessary and what effective esports coaching may look like. With a dearth of research on esports coaching, we will draw on sport coaching research alongside esports research as the field continues to learn more about the esports coach.

The role of the esports coach

Esports coaching is largely unexplored academically and, for those active within the industry prior to the emergence of the role, coaches are often a point of contention. An early academic definition and description of the role of an esports coach highlights some similarities with the role of the coach in sport: 'A game coach has a direct effect on the team's or player's actions in preparation for or while playing the game. These coaches analyse game play, tactics, and strategies; identify the team's, players', and opponents' strengths, weaknesses, and playing styles; and develop game plans and strategies for victory based on the team's or players' abilities' (Hedlund et al., 2020, p.160).

While coaching in sport is traditionally heavily focussed on developing physical technical skills (e.g. technique to kick a ball, or serve in tennis), this aspect is less evident in esports as the game itself will develop many of these. As such, the coach's role in esports shifts to focus more on other aspects, such as strategy, interpersonal relationships, team coordination and organization and other holistic elements of performance (Watson et al., 2022). A study conducted by Sabtan et al. (2022) interviewed six participants, four head coaches, one analyst and one general manager working within LoL. Their findings reported that LoL coaches aim to achieve several key objectives, such as utilizing and integrating players' strengths, developing effective communication and trust within the team, developing the players' weaknesses through training, scouting and analysing opponents to co-create strategy with players, setting frequent (i.e. weekly) goals for players and supporting the players' motivation. However, one must be cognizant that, much like traditional sport coaching, not all esports coaches will share the same objectives and methods. For example, a coach working with a team of novice players ('rookies') may shift which objectives they focus on and the methods they use to achieve them in comparison to a coach working with a team of more established players.

Coaches focus on helping athletes grow within their games but are often said to help them grow not only as performers but as people too. This is no different in esports and may even be of greater importance to the esport coach given the relatively sedentary nature of gaming itself. Through the development of the coach–athlete relationship, as well as mentorship and role modelling, the e'athlete will pick up valuable intangible skills or 'soft' skills that can effectively transfer to their life outside of esports and after being an e'athlete. During their time as e'athletes, they will use and hopefully develop skills such as communication, teamwork and collaboration, receiving and giving feedback. All these skills can effectively translate into the personal, professional and educational aspects of their lives to further support their development and success in the future.

Effectiveness of esports coaching

A debate that periodically occupies both sporting and esports worlds is whether coaches are more effective if they've previously held high-level playing experiences. While it is common practice to hire coaches who have had extensive playing careers, it is important to understand how playing experiences can be useful and how they can be detrimental to those who make the athlete–coach transition. A former professional player turned coach will have accrued social and cultural capital that allows them to be 'fast-tracked' into high-performance contexts (Rynne, 2014). The assumption being that former e'athletes are familiar with the demands of high performance and, having had firsthand experience of being coached, are thus able to 'swap seats in the boat' and replicate the success they experienced. Furthermore, coaches who are e'athletes will possess nuanced knowledge about the game which can inform their coaching approach. Interestingly, despite being a popular belief within esports, many coaches in esports were not propelled into their coaching careers immediately following a successful playing career at the highest level. In fact, the current career path in esports is strikingly varied, primarily characterized by a lack of structure and external support (Watson et al., 2022). Unlike in sport, where coaches typically need some form of qualification (i.e. coaching badges) to assume their position, there is also a lack of standardization of coaching practice within esports (Watson et al., 2022). In the absence of structured career paths, coach education and qualifications, it could be that previous playing is taken by some as a simple metric by which to judge a coach's potential.

Conversely, coaches who transition from being an e'athlete may struggle to develop talent as they may not have the necessary skills and frameworks to inform their coaching practice. Fitts and Posners' (1974) three-phase model of skill acquisition states that learners advance through an early cognitive phase, an associative phase and end at the autonomous phase for both motor and cognitive skills. As those transitioning from e'athlete to coach have spent countless hours refining their skills within their esport, leading to automatic or habitual execution (Magill, 2004), they can struggle to explain their decision-making process as it has become autonomous in nature. This 'expert-induced amnesia' (Beilock & Carr, 2001, p. 703) may be a reason why transitioning coaches struggle to explain their decision-making process and empathize with the needs of the learner thus making them less effective in their objective of developing and nurturing talent.

As highlighted above, one of the key objectives of an esports coach is to plan training sessions that align with the developmental needs of the individual or team. Abbott et al. (2022) found the perceived effectiveness of training was lacking, and the mindset to grind (play a high volume of games in a short time) was perceived as an ineffective method for talent development, expertise and well-being (i.e. mental ill-health and burnout; DiFrancisco-Donoghue et al., 2019). More studies within esports and expertise have shown that practice quantity only explains a fraction of player expertise and performance outcomes (Pluss et al., 2021). A follow-up study in the form of a 52-week longitudinal analysis analysing practice behaviour suggested that e'athletes could invest up to 16,000+ hours over a 10-year period (Pluss et al., 2022) aligning with the popular myth that to attain expertise one must practise for 10,000 hours.

Current research advocates for athletes to engage within deliberate and purposeful practice environments (Farrow et al., 2013). Ericsson (2021) sets out five criteria that could help practitioners (i.e. esports coaches) to evaluate their training session to integrate deliberateness within their context: (1) clear session intention, (2) performer(s) can complete the task individually and will help them develop, (3) provision of immediate and actionable feedback is available, (4) performer(s) are afforded multiple attempts at the task and (5) the coach can oversee the development to appropriately develop future tasks to supplement development. The concept of deliberate practice can help shift away from ineffective practices such as grinding games and can provide an established framework for coaches looking to develop their coaching practice and talent development (Bubna et al., 2023).

Further, within Abbott et al.'s. (2022) exploration of the perceptions of effective training practice in LoL, there was a mixed reception to the effectiveness of a coach. Some participants acknowledged that the coach-provided feedback would aid in their development as individuals and as a team. However, some participants were sceptical about the effect a coach had on their development saying 'there's a lot of like posers. … And a lot of people who like, like to talk but don't really like to put in the effort' (p.9). This quote may reflect the lack of professionalization of esports coaches, without formal development of the key skills and knowledge that can help them perform within their roles. As coaching formalizes, it will be important to consider the key skills and knowledge that can help esports coaches to perform within their roles.

We can see that there may be some truth to the myth of not needing a coach, in the same way that a coach is not strictly necessary in sport. One argument being that the early stages of an esports player's development are often taught by the game itself rather than through the support of a coach. Of course, a coach may benefit the young developing player at this time; however, it is not commonplace, and the research is limited. When embarking upon the higher levels of esports, coaches can have a meaningful impact on aspects such as creating deliberate and effective training environments. There is some question as to the effectiveness of esports coaches; however, this is largely due to the lack of training pathway for prospective coaches to embark upon. In the future, clearer training pathways and research to support effective esports coaching are needed.

Conclusion

Within this chapter, we have presented a few myths about esports. We have highlighted the performance demands in esports, the challenges that e'athletes face and the support systems in place to help them thrive. We have explored the research on the physical health of e'athletes, showing that the stereotypes of an 'unhealthy' gamer do not necessarily transfer to all esports participants. However, the well-being challenges that e'athletes can face are prominent, and the field has space to grow in its understanding of how to identify, refer and intervene with mental health cases. Finally, we picked apart the role of the esports coach and recognized their role as a necessity within the field, despite the development in training and professionalization that is still to occur.

We recommend that practitioners within traditional sport settings explore the world of esports further by engaging with the esports community, tuning into official matches online and considering how their skill set may be suited to esports high performance. Further, we recommend that researchers and coach developers consider the context of esports and the professionalization of coaching practice in esports. We encourage those currently working in esports to check in with their own biases regarding esports performance, well-being and coaching and to not work in silo. By sharing knowledge and experiences with other practitioners in the field, we can create a greater collective understanding of the esports performance environment to better understand and support e'athletes, coaches and teams. Of course, we still have much to learn about coaching and performance in esports as the research base steadily grows, but we hope this chapter has added some nuance to the understanding of high performance within esports and demystified some of the assumptions and stereotypes that exist in order to promote the unique and exciting world of esports.

References

Abbott, C., Watson, M., & Birch, P. (2022). Perceptions of effective training practices in league of legends: A qualitative exploration. *Journal of Electronic Gaming and Esports, 1*(1). https://doi.org/10.1123/jege.2022-0011

Beilock, S. L., & Carr, T. H. (2001). On the fragility of skilled performance: What governs choking under pressure? *Journal of Experimental Psychology, 130*, 701–725. https://doi.org/10.1037/0096-3445.130.4.701

Boonwang, T., Namwaing, P., Srisaphonphusitti, L., Chainarong, A., Kaewwong, S. C., Kaewwong, T., ... Khamsai, S. (2022). Esports may improve cognitive skills in soccer players: A systematic review. *Asia-Pacific Journal of Science and Technology, 27*(3). https://doi.org/10.14456/apst.2022.44

Bubna, K., Trotter, M. G., Watson, M., & Polman, R. (2023). Coaching and talent development in esports: A theoretical framework and suggestions for future research. *Frontiers in Psychology, 14*, 1191801. https://doi.org/10.3389/fpsyg.2023.119180

Campbell, M. J., Toth, A. J., Moran, A. P., Kowal, M., & Exton, C. (2018). eSports: A new window on neurocognitive expertise?. *Progress in Brain Research, 240*, 161–174. https://doi.org/10.1016/bs.pbr.2018.09.006

DiFrancisco-Donoghue, J., Balentine, J., Schmidt, G., & Zwibel, H. (2019). Managing the health of the eSport athlete: an integrated health management model. *BMJ Open Sport & Exercise Medicine, 5*(1), e000467. http://dx.doi.org/10.1136/bmjsem-2018-000467

Ericsson, K. A. (2021). Given that the detailed original criteria for deliberate practice have not changed, could the understanding of this complex concept have improved over time? A response to Macnamara and Hambrick (2020). *Psychological Research, 85*(3), 1114–1120. https://doi.org/10.1007/s00426-020-01368-3

Farrow, D., Baker, J., & MacMahon, C. (Eds.). (2013). *Developing sport expertise: Researchers and coaches put theory into practice*. Routledge.

Fitts, P. M., & Posner, M. I. (1973). *Human performance*. Wadsworth Publishing Company.

Giakoni-Ramírez, F., Merellano-Navarro, E., & Duclos-Bastías, D. (2022). Professional esports players: Motivation and physical activity levels. *International Journal of Environmental Research and Public Health, 19*(4), 2256. https://doi.org/10.3390/ijerph19042256

Granic, I., Lobel, A., & Engels, R. C. (2014). The benefits of playing video games. *American Psychologist, 69*(1), 66. https://doi.org/10.1037/a0034857

Hedlund, D., Fried, G., & Smith, R. (2020). *Esports business management*. Champaign, IL: Human Kinetics.

Heggem, T. (2016). It's complicated: Analyzing the potential for esports players' unions. *Arizona State Sports and Entertainment Law Journal, 6*, 447. http://asuselj.org/wp-content/uploads/2017/08/Timothy-Its-complicated.pdf

Himmelstein, D., Liu, Y., & Shapiro, J. L. (2017). An exploration of mental skills among competitive league of legend players. *Journal International Journal of Gaming and Computer-Mediated Simulations, 9*(2), 1–21. https://doi.org/10.4018/IJGCMS.2017040101

Hong, H. J., & Connelly, J. (2022). High e-Performance: Esports players' coping skills and strategies. *International Journal of Esports, 1*(1). https://www.ijesports.org/article/93/htm

Kari, T., & Karhulahti, V. M. (2016). Do e-athletes move?: A study on training and physical exercise in elite e-sports. *International Journal of Gaming and Computer-Mediated Simulations (IJGCMS), 8*(4), 53–66. https://doi.org/10.4018/IJGCMS.2016100104

Leis, O., Lautenbach, F., Birch, P. D., & Elbe, A. M. (2022). Stressors, associated responses, and coping strategies in professional esports players: A qualitative study. *International Journal of Esports, 3*(3). https://www.ijesports.org/article/76/html

Magill, R. A. (2004). *Motor learning: Concepts and applications* (7th ed.). Boston: McGraw-Hill.

Marker, C., Gnambs, T., & Appel, M. (2022). Exploring the myth of the chubby gamer: A meta-analysis on sedentary video gaming and body mass. *Social Science & Medicine, 301*, 112325. https://doi.org/10.1016/j.socscimed.2019.05.030

McGee, C., & Ho, K. (2021). Tendinopathies in video gaming and esports. *Frontiers in Sports and Active Living, 3*, 689371. https://doi.org/10.3389/fspor.2021.689371

McNulty, C., Jenny, S. E., Leis, O., Poulus, D., Sondergeld, P., & Nicholson, M. (2023). Physical exercise and performance in esports players: An initial systematic review. *Journal of Electronic Gaming and Esports, 1*(1). https://doi.org/10.1123/jege.2022-0014

Nagorsky, E., & Wiemeyer, J. (2020). The structure of performance and training in esports. *Plos One, 15*(8), e0237584. https://doi.org/10.1371/journal.pone.0237584

Nielsen, R. K. L., & Hanghøj, T. (2019). Esports skills are people skills. *Proceedings of the 13th European Conference on Game-Based Learning* (pp. 535–542). Odense, Denmark: Academic Conferences and Publishing International. https://pure.itu.dk/en/publications/esports-skills-are-people-skills

Pedraza-Ramirez, I., Musculus, L., Raab, M., & Laborde, S. (2020). Setting the scientific stage for esports psychology: A systematic review. *International Review of Sport and Exercise Psychology, 13*(1), 319–352. https://doi.org/10.1080/1750984X.2020.1723122

Pluss, M. A., Novak, A. R., Bennett, K. J., McBride, I., Panchuk, D., Coutts, A. J., & Fransen, J. (2022). Examining the game-specific practice behaviors of professional and semi-professional esports players: A 52-week longitudinal study. *Computers in Human Behavior, 137*, 107421. https://doi.org/10.1016/j.chb.2022.107421

Pluss, M. A., Novak, A. R., Bennett, K. J., Panchuk, D., Coutts, A. J., & Fransen, J. (2021). The relationship between the quantity of practice and in-game performance during practice with tournament performance in esports: An eight-week study. *The Journal of Sport and Exercise Science, 5*(1), 69–76. https://doi.org/10.36905/jses.2021.01.09

Polman, R., Trotter, M., Poulus, D., & Borkoles, E. (2018). eSport: Friend or foe? In S. Göbel, A. Garcia-Agundez, T. Tregel, M. Ma, J. Baalsrud Hauge, M. Oliveira, et al., *Serious games* (pp. 3–8). New York, NY: Springer International Publishing.

Poulus, D., Coulter, T. J., Trotter, M. G., & Polman, R. (2020). Stress and coping in esports and the influence of mental toughness. *Frontiers in Psychology, 11*, 628. https://doi.org/10.3389/fpsyg.2020.00628

Poulus, D., Coulter, T., Trotter, M., & Polman, R. (2022). Perceived stressors experienced by competitive esports athletes. *International Journal of Esports, 3*(3). https://www.ijesports.org/article/73/html

Ramaker, B., & Pedraza-Ramirez, I. (2023). Everyone is figuring it out along the way: Diving headfirst into the world of esports. In E. Prior & T. Holder (Eds.), *Navigating applied sport and exercise psychology* (pp. 84–99). Routledge.

Rawat, A. S. (2021, December 3). Snax reveals why he is taking a break from CS:GO. *AFK Gaming*. https://afkgaming.com/csgo/news/snax-reveals-why-he-is-taking-a-break-from-csgo

Reid, C., Stewart, E., & Thorne, G. (2004). Multidisciplinary sport science teams in elite sport: Comprehensive servicing or conflict and confusion? *The Sport Psychologist, 18*(2), 204–217. https://doi.org/10.1123/tsp.18.2.204

Reitman, J. G., Anderson-Coto, M. J., Wu, M., Lee, J. S., & Steinkuehler, C. (2020). Esports research: A literature review. *Games and Culture, 15*(1), 32–50. https://doi.org/10.1177/1555412019840892

Rothwell, G., & Shaffer, M. (2019). eSports in K-12 and Post-Secondary schools. *Education Sciences, 9*(2), 105. https://doi.org/10.3390/educsci9020105

Rynne, S. (2014). 'Fast track' and 'traditional path' coaches: Affordances, agency and social capital. *Sport, Education and Society, 19*(3), 299–313.

Sabtan, B., Cao, S., & Paul, N. (2022). Current practice and challenges in coaching Esports players: An interview study with League of Legends professional team coaches. *Entertainment Computing, 100481*. https://doi.org/10.1016/j.entcom.2022.100481

Smith, M. J., Birch, P. D., & Bright, D. (2019). Identifying stressors and coping strategies of elite esports competitors. *International Journal of Gaming and Computer-Mediated Simulations (IJGCMS), 11*(2), 22–39. https://doi.org/10.4018/IJGCMS.2019040102

Starkey, B. S. (2020, May 7). Mental stress is an unspoken part of the game for esports athletes. *Andscape*. https://andscape.com/features/mental-stress-is-an-unspoken-part-of-the-game-for-esports-athletes/

Swettenham, L., & Whitehead, A. (2022). Working in esports: Developing team cohesion. *Case Studies in Sport and Exercise Psychology, 6*(1), 36–44. https://doi.org/10.1123/cssep.2021-0023

Tjønndal, A., & Skauge, M. (2020). Youth sport 2.0? The development of eSports in Norway from 2016 to 2019. *Qualitative Research in Sport, Exercise and Health, 13*(1), 166–183. https://doi.org/10.1080/2159676X.2020.1836509

Trotter, M. G., Coulter, T. J., Davis, P. A., Poulus, D. R., & Polman, R. (2020). The association between esports participation, health and physical activity behaviour. *International Journal of Environmental Research and Public Health, 17*(19), 7329. https://doi.org/10.3390/ijerph17197329

Turel, O., Romashkin, A., & Morrison, K. M. (2017). A model linking video gaming, sleep quality, sweet drinks consumption and obesity among children and youth. *Clinical Obesity, 7*(4), 191–198. https://doi.org/10.1111/cob.12191

Ward, M. R., & Harmon, A. D. (2019). ESport superstars. *Journal of Sports Economics, 20*(8), 987–1013. https://doi.org/10.1177/15270025198.59417

Watson, M., Abbott, C., & Pedraza-Ramirez, I. (2021). A parallel approach to performance and sport psychology work in esports teams. *International Journal of Esports, 1*(1). https://www.ijesports.org/article/52/html

Watson, M., Smith, D., Fenton, J., Pedraza-Ramirez, I., Laborde, S., & Cronin, C. (2022). Introducing esports coaching to sport coaching (not as sport coaching). *Sports Coaching Review*, 1–20. https://doi.org/10.1080/21640629.2022.2123960

Weiss, M. R., Moehnke, H. J., & Kipp, L. E. (2021). A united front: Coach and teammate motivational climate and team cohesion among female adolescent athletes. *International Journal of Sports Science & Coaching, 16*(4), 875–885. https://doi.org/10.1177/17479541211006905

WHO. (2022, June 17). Mental health. *World Health Organization.* https://www.who.int/news-room/fact-sheets/detail/mental-health-strengthening-our-response

Wright, A. (2023, June 8). Esports star Karel 'Twisten' Asenbrener, 19, is found dead after posting 'good night' tweet – months after he revealed he'd spent time in a mental hospital to cope with his depression. *Daily Mail.* https://www.dailymail.co.uk/news/article-12175395/Esports-star-Karel-Twisten-Asenbrener-19-dead-posting-good-night-tweet.html

Zwibel, H., DiFrancisco-Donoghue, J., DeFeo, A., & Yao, S. (2019). An osteopathic physician's approach to the Esports athlete. *Journal of Osteopathic Medicine, 119*(11), 756–762. https://doi.org/10.7556/jaoa.2019.125

16 Think Using Electronics before Bed and Only Getting Five Hours of Sleep Is OK?

We Bust These Athlete Sleep Myths

Kathleen Miles, Stephanie Shell and Dean Miller

Athlete myth 1 – 'I sleep fine even with electronic device use'

Electronic device use in bed is highly prevalent in the athletic population, especially within developing or pathways athletes (i.e., 14–18 yr). Many athletes have recounted their sleep is unaffected by electronic device use. In fact, athletes commonly report they can fall asleep quicker with use of their electronic device. Commonly used devices include TV's (use of streaming services), laptop for homework/study completion, gaming consoles, phone use (social media applications, meditation/mindfulness applications and texting/calls), and Kindle devices for e-books. Duration of use varies between individuals and sporting level; however, it is not abnormal for athletes to use their device for anywhere between 10 min and 3 h within the bed environment. Interestingly, some athlete report being unable to sleep if they don't have the opportunity to 'scroll' through social media.

The prevalence of electronic devices in our daily lives is constantly increasing. As a result, it's not uncommon for myths to arise regarding the use of such devices in bed, as seen in the practitioner excerpt mentioned above. There are two mechanisms by which an electronic device could acutely impact the sleep of an athlete – (1) delaying their bedtime to engage in behaviour (e.g. scrolling, talking to friends) and (2) the potential impact of light on the athlete's sleep–wake rhythms. Let's begin with the latter.

Blue light and sleep–wake rhythms

Melatonin is a hormone produced naturally by the body's pineal gland in response to darkness, and it plays a crucial role in regulating the sleep–wake cycle. When it is dark, melatonin production is increased, which makes us feel sleepy and helps us to fall asleep. However, exposure to light, particularly blue light, can inhibit the production of melatonin and disrupt the body's natural sleep–wake cycle (Emens & Burgess, 2015).

The suppression of melatonin production by blue light occurs because of the way that light signals are processed by the brain. The retinal ganglion cells in the eye that are responsible for detecting light send signals to the suprachiasmatic nucleus (SCN) in the brain, which serves as the body's 'master clock'. The SCN then sends signals to other parts of the brain and body to regulate the production of hormones and other physiological processes, including the production of melatonin. The phase response curve to light is a way of describing how light exposure affects the timing of melatonin secretion. Light has the most powerful impact on the body clock (Khalsa et al., 2003) with timing, duration and intensity of light determining when the body's natural sleep–wake cycle begins.

But do electronic devices emit enough light to impact athlete's sleep? Yes, they can – if the device is set to maximum brightness. Researchers from Harvard found that using e-devices before bedtime prolonged the time it took to fall asleep, delayed the body clock and suppressed melatonin levels (Chang et al., 2015). However, when researchers from Flinders University manipulated the light intensity of devices, they found no differences between a bright tablet screen (80 lux), dim screen (1 lux) and a filtered short-wavelength screen for sleep onset latency, slow-rolling eye movements, slow wave sleep (SWS) and rapid eye movement (REM) (Heath et al., 2014). Interventions for avoiding blue light, such as wearing blue blocker glasses, could effectively mitigate the impact of e-devices on sleep, particularly in individuals susceptible to sleep disturbance (Schechter et al., 2020). Unfortunately, other technological advances in blue light screen technologies, blue light filters (e.g. Apple iPhone Night Shift) and software are yet to be effective enough to have a *meaningful* impact on either melatonin levels (Calco-Sanz et al., 2020) or sleep outcomes (Duraccio et al., 2021). But, if and when we can start to manage the light with technological advances, can we continue to use our devices? This brings us to the behavioural considerations.

Behavioural factors for electronic device's impact on sleep

Aside from the biological components of sleep, the simple behaviour of delaying bedtime for engagement with electronic devices (e.g. delaying sleep to talk to family/friends or streaming services) is common amongst athletes. Given the 24/7 content stream athletes can consume on their devices, adhering to a consistent bedtime routine may be difficult. In addition, 'binge viewing' streaming services before bed has been associated with increased cognitive arousal and reduced sleep quality (Exelmans & Van den Bulck, 2017). These common athlete practices are juxtaposed with sleep hygiene recommendations (defined as behavioural and environmental factors intended to promote sleep). For example, practising good sleep hygiene involves actions such as, but not limited to, unplugging from electronics before bed, keeping a consistent routine and dimming the lights. But there is also more to consider.

It appears that individuals with higher attachment (as quantified using behavioural tests and heart rate measurements) to their mobile devices may experience behavioural and physiological stress, proximity-seeking behaviour and an attentional bias to separation-related stimuli (Konok et al., 2017). This behaviour is similar to social attachment to a person (i.e. a mobile phone becomes associated with engagement with loved ones). Therefore, engaging in sleep hygiene protocols that eliminate the use of devices in the hours leading up to sleep may elicit a stress response, potentially impacting the initiation of sleep.

Taking evidence from research into both mechanisms (i.e. light and behaviour), it is clear a nuanced approach is needed for recommendations involving electronic devices for athletes. Practical considerations for managing electronic device use are presented at the end of this chapter.

Athlete myth 2 – 'I don't need more than five hours of sleep'

Anecdotes within the applied setting can be used to inform research practice. Within the applied field, a common perception by athletes is that they do not require ≥8 h of sleep, stating they can 'get away' with less. For example, several athletes have subjectively reported only requiring 5 h of sleep per night. Following further questioning it is apparent many of these athletes hold the belief they cannot physically fall asleep any earlier as they do not feel tired, nor can they sleep in any longer as their body naturally wakes after ~5-6 h. This sleep pattern then becomes their normal routine, playing into the perception that they do not require any additional sleep as they have 'always slept this way'.

The perception that an individual can sleep less than the recommended eight hours per night and continue to successfully meet their performance goals is a prevalent myth within athletic populations (demonstrated above in a practitioner excerpt). Perhaps the justification behind this myth is a direct result of the athlete's limited sleep opportunity, in part due to their training or competition schedules. Granted, an athlete may adapt or become accustomed to performing and operating with less sleep; however, there is an array of evidence in direct contrast to this myth (Fullagar et al., 2015; Craven et al., 2022). Consequently, in this discussion, we will explore the evidence surrounding chronic sleep deficit, outlining the benefits of enhanced nocturnal sleep durations.

Sleep is essential for physiological and psychological function (Fullagar et al., 2015); however, sleep within athletic populations is often compromised due to training and competition schedules, and increased levels of fatigue or soreness (Lastella et al., 2015). Previous research has demonstrated the deleterious effects of sleep deprivation on health, productivity and general quality of life (Bonnet & Arand, 1995). An additional area for consideration within athletic populations is the decrease in performance (Belenky et al., 2003). Previous research has illustrated reductions in speed, strength, endurance, attention, motivation and skill acquisition with reduced sleep durations (varying depending on the study, but all < 8 h) (Simpson et al., 2017). This performance decrement occurs in a dose-dependent manner, meaning the greater the sleep loss, the greater the performance reduction (Simpson et al., 2017). An example of this dose–response relationship is the decline in psychomotor vigilance task (PVT) speed with decreased sleep. The PVT is used as a simple measure of athlete reaction time to a visual stimulus (Belenky et al., 2003). Belenky et al. (2003) reported substantial decreases in average PVT speed during sustained sleep loss for participants in the three- and five-hour sleep-restricted groups, as opposed to participants within the nine-hour sleep augmentation group, who showed no variation in PVT speed. This simplistic measure highlights the impact of sleep deficit on individuals.

Previous research has compared the amount of sleep athletes perceive they require versus the amount of sleep obtained, with the difference labelled as the sleep deficit index (Sargent et al., 2021). Across 175 youth and adult elite athletes from 12 individual and team-based sports, the prevalence of insufficient sleep classified through the sleep deficit index (i.e. a minimum difference of one hour self-assessed sleep need and actual habitual sleep duration) was 71%, with 38% of these athletes obtaining on average ≤ 6.5 hours of sleep per night (Sargent et al., 2021). The authors proposed the chronic sleep pattern of reduced sleep duration and increased sleep deficit index are likely to impair self-perceived exercise capacity, cognitive function and exercise performance (e.g. slowed reaction time, decreased time to fatigue, increased decision-making errors, etc.) (Sargent et al., 2021). In addition, individuals have a decreased ability to self-assess their sleep impairment level (Simpson et al., 2017), meaning they are likely unaware of the impact of their chronic sleep deficit (Simpson et al., 2017; Van Donger et al., 2003).

It is commonly accepted that sleep aids in the restoration of various physiological systems, facilitating recovery from, and adaptation to, athletic training or competition (Samuels, 2008). Within athletic populations, sleep promotes psychological recovery and maintenance of training quality, such as through enhanced skill consolidation (Doyon et al., 2009) or motivation. Sleep hygiene practices are frequently employed to promote sleep in both general populations (Baranwal et al., 2023) and athletes (Vitale et al., 2019). However, the sleep of elite athletes is often compromised because of their intense training schedules and individual life constraints (Sargent et al., 2014). As such, a vast majority of athletes frequently attain substantially less sleep hours than required, resulting in a chronic sleep deficit (Sargent et al., 2021; Gupta et al., 2017).

Where possible, athletes, coaches and practitioners should prioritize nighttime sleep to maximize training and performance outcomes. Mah et al. (2011) assessed the impact of extended nocturnal sleep duration across a five- to seven-week period on perceptual and performance indices within collegiate basketball players. Interestingly, significant reductions were seen in mean PVT reaction time and 86 m/282 ft sprint time, with significant improvements in three-point shooting accuracy and successful free throws (out of 10 shots and field goals out of 15 shots) seen (Mah et al., 2011). Additionally, participants reported improvements in daytime sleepiness as reported through the Epworth Sleepiness Scale, global mood as reported via the Profile of Mood States questionnaire, and training and game ratings of mental and physical well-being rated via a 10-point visual analogue scale (Mah et al., 2011). These results clearly demonstrate the significant benefits of nocturnal sleep extension across an extended period. With many athletes commonly obtaining ≤7 hours of sleep per night (Sargent et al., 2014), increasing sleep duration is likely to promote significant perceptual and performance improvements. Athletes, coaches and sport science practitioners should consider accommodating extended nocturnal sleep, such as through adjustments to training schedules to enable an earlier sleep, or later wake time.

It is not uncommon for sleep to be deprioritized relative to other training demands (Simpson et al., 2017); however, injury and illness are important considerations when we discuss sleep. Given athletes' high training loads, coaches and practitioners should consider every avenue possible to reduce the likelihood of injury or illness occurrence, therefore minimizing substantial time away from training or competition. One such strategy is to maximize nocturnal sleep duration. Previous research has demonstrated when athletes sleep ≥8 hours per night, they were less likely to suffer from injury (Milewski et al., 2014; Von Rosen et al., 2017) or illness (specifically colds or influenza) (Hamlin et al., 2021). As such, athletes should consider the benefits of maximizing their night-time sleep, by aiming for a sleep duration minimum of 8 hours per night.

From the evidence presented, it is apparent that reduced hours of sleep within athletic populations are likely to lead to reduced training or performance outcomes and impaired psychological responses such as mood state, motivation and perceived daytime sleepiness. Athletes, coaches and practitioners should prioritize night-time sleep where possible, to minimize the likelihood of the deleterious effects of chronic sleep deficit. Practical considerations to assist with athletic sleep are presented at the end of this chapter.

Athlete myth 3 – 'I sleep five hours at night and then nap for three hours in the day to make up my eight hours of sleep'

> Many athletes have a sleep regimen that entails approximately 5–6 hours of night-time sleep, complemented by a 2–3 hours daytime nap, resulting in a total of 8 hours of daily sleep. This approach is especially prevalent among elite athletes who often contend with additional study, work, or familial obligations, as well as athletes who frequently use electronic devices in their sleeping environment. These athletes maintain that they are unable to accumulate additional sleep hours at night and, as a result, opt for an extended daytime nap, which they subjectively perceive as promoting enhanced recovery. Athletes have additionally reported feeling more refreshed after a prolonged daytime nap than a comparable night-time sleeping period.

The idea that you can routinely make up for lost sleep by taking a nap during the day is popular within elite and sub-elite sport, as well as the general population.

It is often touted (as shown above in a practitioner excerpt) to help busy individuals catch up on the sleep they may have missed the previous night. Although napping has many beneficial impacts and can help in some instances to alleviate the effects of sleep deprivation (Ajjimaporn et al., 2020; Blanchfield et al., 2018; Boukhris et al., 2020; Brotherton et al., 2019; Romdhani et al., 2020). There is currently no conclusive evidence to suggest this strategy should be routinely used to recoup lost sleep in athletes over the long term (Mesas et al., 2023). Therefore, in this discussion, we will explore the facts surrounding this myth, followed by presenting ideas to achieve better sleep at night and nap appropriately when needed in the practical applications section of this chapter.

Normal human sleep comprises recurring cycles of non-REM and REM sleep. Non-REM sleep is further divided into three stages, representing a progression from 'light' sleep in stages 1 and 2 to 'deep' sleep in stage 3 (Carskadon & Dement, 2011; Berry et al., 2012). The duration of sleep that each person needs can vary depending on many factors, including age and lifestyle (Walsh et al., 2021). However, most elite and sub-elite athletes between the ages of 15 and 30 years require between 7 and 9 hours of sleep each night for optimal health, performance and recovery (Ohayon et al., 2004). Experiencing up to one or two weeks of partial sleep restriction, as one would when sleeping five to six hours per night, can result in impaired cognition (Belenky et al., 2003), learning and memory consolidation (Walker & Stickgold, 2005), mental well-being (Haack & Mullington, 2005), cellular growth and repair (Czeisler & Klerman, 1999), metabolism of glucose (Spiegel et al., 1999) as well as lowering the resistance to respiratory infection (Cohen et al., 2009).

A nap is a short period of sleep, typically taken during the daytime or early evening. Napping has numerous purported benefits including enhancing alertness, concentration, motor performance and mood (Milner & Cote, 2009). Athletes who cannot get sufficient night-time sleep, for example, due to early morning training times, may benefit from supplementing their sleep with a nap during the day (Blanchfield et al., 2018). Even for those athletes who typically achieve the recommended amount of night-time sleep, napping has been shown to improve their mood, alertness and cognitive performance (Milner & Cote, 2009). Despite the growing evidence suggesting naps offer similar benefits whether obtaining normal sleep durations or partial sleep deprivation during acute periods (i.e. one night) (Romyn et al., 2022), it remains unclear whether napping can fully restore measures of sports performance. Additionally, there is no conclusive evidence to support the daily use of napping as a sleep recommendation for athletes to recover lost sleep in the long term (Mesas et al., 2023).

It is no wonder the idea of routinely taking a nap during the day to make up for lost sleep at night is appealing to athletes – it does seem like an easy and convenient solution! However, despite the fundamental benefits offered by napping outlined above, there are several reasons why *relying* on daytime naps to make up for lost sleep may not be a good idea. The main two factors affecting athletes are the potential of incorrectly timed naps impacting night-time sleep and the influence of sleep inertia when waking from the nap.

The potential for napping to disrupt night-time sleep depends on various factors such as nap duration, timing and prior sleep debt (Lastella et al., 2021). Generally, longer naps lead to a greater reduction in sleep propensity (i.e. the readiness to transit from wakefulness to sleep, or the ability to stay asleep if already sleeping) (Werth et al., 1996). If an athlete takes a long nap later in the day and tries to sleep at their usual time, it may disrupt the main night-time sleep period, especially longer sleep onsets and increased awakenings (Mograss et al., 2022). Therefore, current evidence suggests the best time to nap is during the peak period of circadian sleepiness in the mid-afternoon (between 13:00 and 15:00) (Mesas et al., 2023). This timing may help prevent delays in sleep onset latency and avoid interfering with the night-time sleep period.

When athletes nap, they should also consider the notion of sleep inertia, which is a period of diminished alertness and impaired cognitive performance that follows waking (Trotti, 2017). Various factors can influence the duration and severity of sleep inertia after a nap, including prior sleep loss, waking up from slow-wave sleep, the amount of slow-wave sleep in a nap and the time of day (Tassi et al., 2006; Matchock & Mordkoff, 2014; Groeger et al., 2011). Recent evidence shows that to prevent sleep inertia from reducing the benefits of a nap on sports performance, athletes should wait at least 60 minutes after waking from a nap before training or competing (Romyn et al., 2022). To accelerate the dissipation of sleep inertia, there are other countermeasures that can be used either before or after a nap. These will be discussed in the practical applications section.

In summary, napping does have benefits for supplementing sleep in athletes during certain situations, such as busy competition periods or early morning training days. However, naps should be used carefully as there is currently no conclusive evidence to suggest napping can be routinely used to recoup lost sleep in athletes over the long term. The priority for athletes should always be to optimize night-time sleep for peak health and performance outcomes. In the practical applications section, we provide recommendations on how to nap appropriately, as well as optimize the night-time sleep experience.

Practical applications

There are an array of strategies that can assist with improving sleep duration or quality. The following recommendations are based on previous research evidence and practitioner experience in applying these strategies within elite athletic populations.

- **Minimize the duration of device use within the bed environment.**
  - Given the prevalence of electronic devices in our day-to-day lives, it is not surprising their use has infiltrated our sleep routines. Avoidance of device use within the bed environment is ideal; however, practical experience has proved it difficult to get athletes to stop using devices (particularly phones) within the bed. As such, an alternative strategy is to encourage a device usage cap, where the individual can use their device for a specified duration of time, while also ensuring this does not span hours. A common example is between 10 and 30 minutes.
- **Application of appropriate sleep hygiene practices, including**
  - Bedroom environment: ensure your room is cool (i.e. 19–21°C), dark, quiet and comfortable.
  - Pre-sleep routine: create a sleep routine that suits you and perform this each night before bed. This can be as simple as completing stretching pre-bed, reading a book or listening to a mindfulness track.
  - Electronic device checklist: create a checklist of the tasks you want to complete on your electronic device prior to bedtime (e.g. check in with friends, check emails, time-limited social media check). Remember, if you wouldn't wake up early to do a task you shouldn't stay up late to do it either!
  - Consistent sleep schedule: aim to go to sleep and wake up at the same time each day.
  - Relaxation: investigate breathing techniques, mindfulness or meditation, write down your thoughts from the day or use a to-do list to help with organization. Aim to designate time away from technology each day (e.g. a 15-minute walk without a phone).
  - Example sleep blueprint: (1) complete your personal hygiene needs, (2) set your alarm, write down any last-minute reminders, (3)

consider reading a book, using mindfulness or breathing techniques, or stretching, etc., prior to sleep to help you relax.
- **Light exposure or avoidance**
  - If possible, view morning and evening sunlight (i.e. when the sun is not directly overhead) to 'anchor' the body clock.
  - Avoid viewing light after the sunlight has dissipated in the evening. Keep house lights to a minimum (e.g. use lamps instead of overhead LED lights) and have electronic devices on low-intensity light modes.
  - If environmental light cannot be controlled at night, blue blocker glasses may help limit the impact of light.
- **Napping smartly**
  - Athletes can use a 'coffee-nap' or 'nappucino' as a useful method to minimize mid-afternoon drowsiness. This approach entails ingesting 150-200 mg of caffeine and then taking a nap that lasts ~15-20 min.
  - As part of a nap routine, athletes can benefit from exposure to bright light and washing their face upon waking.
  - It is recommended to set an alarm for 10 extra minutes beyond the planned nap duration to account for the time needed to doze off. Athletes can also use relaxation and breathing methods to facilitate sleep.
  - Those who struggle to fall asleep at night should refrain from napping.
- **Implement effective recovery strategies**
  - If training or competing late at night, athletes and coaches should ensure appropriate time is prioritized to complete a recovery session. The use of cold water immersion (CWI) is one strategy that may assist with increasing perceived sleep quality (Nedelec et al., 2015). However, further empirical research is required to support objective changes in sleep quality.
- **Responsible tracking of sleep using wearable technology**
  - If athletes are interested in measuring and tracking their sleep ensure that the device they utilize is validated against gold-standard polysomnography.
  - Focus on the total amount of sleep obtained and track any deviations from the athlete's mean. Do not place emphasis on specific 'sleep stage' metrics.
  - Aim to collect concurrent subjective data related to sleepiness, sleep quality and fatigue to supplement data obtained from the wearable.

It is worth acknowledging the considerations external to athlete training schedules, such as full- or part-time work or study (i.e. school, Tafe, University) and family or relationship commitments. The unfortunate reality for many athletes, as demonstrated through the reduced hours of sleep above, is they will often compromise on the duration of night-time sleep in order to meet these commitments, as opposed to making adjustments within their training schedules. Coaches and sport science practitioners are encouraged to consider the implications of this imbalance and collaborate with their athletes to alleviate some of this sleep deficit.

Conflict of interest

Dean Miller is a member of a research group at Central Queensland University that receives support for research (i.e. funding, equipment) from wearable technology companies. Kathleen Miles and Stephanie Shell report no conflicts of interest.

References

Ajjimaporn, A., Ramyarangsi, P., & Siripornpanich, V. (2020). Effects of a 20-min nap after sleep deprivation on brain activity and soccer performance. *International Journal of Sports Medicine*, *41*(14), 1009–1016.

Baranwal, N., Phoebe, K. Y., & Siegel, N. S. (2023). Sleep physiology, pathophysiology, and sleep hygiene. *Progress in Cardiovascular Diseases*, *77*, 59–69.

Belenky, G., Wesensten, N. J., Thorne, D. R., Thomas, M. L., Sing, H. C., Redmond, D. P., ... Balkin, T. J. (2003). Patterns of performance degradation and restoration during sleep restriction and subsequent recovery: A sleep dose-response study. *Journal of Sleep Research*, *12*(1), 1–12.

Berry, R. B., Brooks, R., Gamaldo, C. E., Harding, S. M., Marcus, C., & Vaughn, B. V. (2012). The AASM manual for the scoring of sleep and associated events. *Rules, Terminology and Technical Specifications, Darien, Illinois, American Academy of Sleep Medicine*, *176*, 2012.

Blanchfield, A. W., Lewis-Jones, T. M., Wignall, J. R., Roberts, J. B., & Oliver, S. J. (2018). The influence of an afternoon nap on the endurance performance of trained runners. *European Journal of Sport Science*, *18*(9), 1177–1184.

Bonnet, M. H., & Arand, D. L. (1995). We are chronically sleep deprived. *Sleep*, *18*(10), 908–911.

Boukhris, O., Trabelsi, K., Ammar, A., Abdessalem, R., Hsouna, H., Glenn, J. M., ... Chtourou, H. (2020). A 90 min daytime nap opportunity is better than 40 min for cognitive and physical performance. *International Journal of Environmental Research and Public Health*, *17*(13), 4650.

Brotherton, E. J., Moseley, S. E., Langan-Evans, C., Pullinger, S. A., Robertson, C. M., Burniston, J. G., & Edwards, B. J. (2019). Effects of two nights partial sleep deprivation on an evening submaximal weightlifting performance; are 1 h powernaps useful on the day of competition?. *Chronobiology International*, *36*(3), 407–426.

Calvo-Sanz, J. A., & Tapia-Ayuga, C. E. (2020). Blue light emission spectra of popular mobile devices: The extent of user protection against melatonin suppression by built-in screen technology and light filtering software systems. *Chronobiology International*, *37*(7), 1016–1022.

Carskadon, M. A., & Dement, W. C. (2011). Monitoring and staging human sleep. In M. H. Kryger, T. Roth, & W. C. Dement (Eds.), *Principles and practice of sleep medicine* (pp. 16–26). St. Louis, MO: Elsevier Saunders.

Chang, A. M., Aeschbach, D., Duffy, J. F., & Czeisler, C. A. (2015). Evening use of light-emitting eReaders negatively affects sleep, circadian timing, and next-morning alertness. *Proceedings of the National Academy of Sciences*, *112*(4), 1232–1237.

Cohen, S., Doyle, W. J., Alper, C. M., Janicki-Deverts, D., & Turner, R. B. (2009). Sleep habits and susceptibility to the common cold. *Archives of Internal Medicine*, *169*(1), 62–67.

Craven, J., McCartney, D., Desbrow, B., Sabapathy, S., Bellinger, P., Roberts, L., & Irwin, C. (2022). Effects of acute sleep loss on physical performance: A systematic and meta-analytical review. *Sports Medicine*, *52*(11), 2669–2690.

Czeisler, C. A., & Klerman, E. B. (1999). Circadian and sleep-dependent regulation of hormone release in humans. *Recent Progress in Hormone Research*, *54*, 97–130.

Doyon, J., Korman, M., Morin, A., Dostie, V., Tahar, A. H., Benali, H., ... Carrier, J. (2009). Contribution of night and day sleep vs. simple passage of time to the consolidation of motor sequence and visuomotor adaptation learning. *Experimental Brain Research*, *195*, 15–26.

Duraccio, K. M., Zaugg, K. K., Blackburn, R. C., & Jensen, C. D. (2021). Does iPhone night shift mitigate negative effects of smartphone use on sleep outcomes in emerging adults?. *Sleep Health*, *7*(4), 478–484.

Emens, J. S., & Burgess, H. J. (2015). Effect of light and melatonin and other melatonin receptor agonists on human circadian physiology. *Sleep Medicine Clinics*, *10*(4), 435–453.

Exelmans, L., & Van den Bulck, J. (2017). Binge viewing, sleep, and the role of pre-sleep arousal. *Journal of Clinical Sleep Medicine*, *13*(8), 1001–1008.

Fullagar, H. H., Skorski, S., Duffield, R., Hammes, D., Coutts, A. J., & Meyer, T. (2015). Sleep and athletic performance: The effects of sleep loss on exercise performance, and physiological and cognitive responses to exercise. *Sports Medicine*, *45*(2), 161–186.

Groeger, J. A., Lo, J. C., Burns, C. G., & Dijk, D. J. (2011). Effects of sleep inertia after daytime naps vary with executive load and time of day. *Behavioral Neuroscience*, *125*(2), 252.

Gupta, L., Morgan, K., & Gilchrist, S. (2017). Does elite sport degrade sleep quality? A systematic review. *Sports Medicine*, *47*, 1317–1333.

Haack, M., & Mullington, J. M. (2005). Sustained sleep restriction reduces emotional and physical well-being. *Pain*, *119*(1–3), 56–64.

Hamlin, M. J., Deuchrass, R. W., Olsen, P. D., Choukri, M. A., Marshall, H. C., Lizamore, C. A., ... Elliot, C. A. (2021). The effect of sleep quality and quantity on athlete's health and perceived training quality. *Frontiers in Sports and Active Living*, *3*, 705650.

Heath, M., Sutherland, C., Bartel, K., Gradisar, M., Williamson, P., Lovato, N., & Micic, G. (2014). Does one hour of bright or short-wavelength filtered tablet screenlight have a meaningful effect on adolescents' pre-bedtime alertness, sleep, and daytime functioning?. *Chronobiology International*, *31*(4), 496–505.

Khalsa, S. B. S., Jewett, M. E., Cajochen, C., & Czeisler, C. A. (2003). A phase response curve to single bright light pulses in human subjects. *The Journal of Physiology*, *549*(3), 945–952.

Konok, V., Pogány, Á., & Miklósi, Á. (2017). Mobile attachment: Separation from the mobile phone induces physiological and behavioural stress and attentional bias to separation-related stimuli. *Computers in Human Behavior*, *71*, 228–239.

Lastella, M., Roach, G. D., Halson, S. L., & Sargent, C. (2015). Sleep/wake behaviours of elite athletes from individual and team sports. *European Journal of Sport Science, 15*(2), 94–100.

Lastella, M., Halson, S. L., Vitale, J. A., Memon, A. R., & Vincent, G. E. (2021). To nap or not to nap? A systematic review evaluating napping behavior in athletes and the impact on various measures of athletic performance. *Nature and Science of Sleep*, 841–862.

Mah, C. D., Mah, K. E., Kezirian, E. J., & Dement, W. C. (2011). The effects of sleep extension on the athletic performance of collegiate basketball players. *Sleep, 34*(7), 943–950.

Matchock, R. I., & Mordkoff, J. T. (2014). Effects of sleep stage and sleep episode length on the alerting, orienting, and conflict components of attention. *Experimental Brain Research, 232*, 811–820.

Mesas, A. E., de Arenas-Arroyo, S. N., Martinez-Vizcaino, V., Garrido-Miguel, M., Fernández-Rodríguez, R., Bizzozero-Peroni, B., & Torres-Costoso, A. I. (2023). Is daytime napping an effective strategy to improve sport-related cognitive and physical performance and reduce fatigue? A systematic review and meta-analysis of randomised controlled trials. *British Journal of Sports Medicine, 57*(7), 417–426.

Milewski, M. D., Skaggs, D. L., Bishop, G. A., Pace, J. L., Ibrahim, D. A., Wren, T. A., & Barzdukas, A. (2014). Chronic lack of sleep is associated with increased sports injuries in adolescent athletes. *Journal of Pediatric Orthopaedics, 34*(2), 129–133.

Milner, C. E., & Cote, K. A. (2009). Benefits of napping in healthy adults: Impact of nap length, time of day, age, and experience with napping. *Journal of Sleep Research, 18*(2), 272–281.

Mograss, M., Abi-Jaoude, J., Frimpong, E., Chalati, D., Moretto, U., Tarelli, L., ... Dang-Vu, T. T. (2022). The effects of napping on night-time sleep in healthy young adults. *Journal of Sleep Research, 31*(5), e13578.

Nédélec, M., Halson, S., Delecroix, B., Abaidia, A. E., Ahmaidi, S., & Dupont, G. (2015). Sleep hygiene and recovery strategies in elite soccer players. *Sports Medicine, 45*, 1547–1559.

Ohayon, M. M., Carskadon, M. A., Guilleminault, C., & Vitiello, M. V. (2004). Meta-analysis of quantitative sleep parameters from childhood to old age in healthy individuals: Developing normative sleep values across the human lifespan. *Sleep, 27*(7), 1255–1273.

Romdhani, M., Souissi, N., Chaabouni, Y., Mahdouani, K., Driss, T., Chamari, K., & Hammouda, O. (2020). Improved physical performance and decreased muscular and oxidative damage with postlunch napping after partial sleep deprivation in athletes. *International Journal of Sports Physiology and Performance, 15*(6), 874–883.

Romyn, G., Roach, G. D., Lastella, M., Miller, D. J., Versey, N. G., & Sargent, C. (2022). The impact of sleep inertia on physical, cognitive, and subjective performance following a 1-or 2-hour afternoon nap in semiprofessional athletes. *International Journal of Sports Physiology and Performance, 17*(7), 1140–1150.

Samuels, C. (2008). Sleep, recovery, and performance: The new frontier in high-performance athletics. *Neurologic Clinics, 26*(1), 169–180.

Sargent, C., Lastella, M., Halson, S. L., & Roach, G. D. (2014). The impact of training schedules on the sleep and fatigue of elite athletes. *Chronobiology International, 31*(10), 1160–1168.

Sargent, C., Lastella, M., Halson, S. L., & Roach, G. D. (2021). How much sleep does an elite athlete need?. *International Journal of Sports Physiology and Performance, 16*(12), 1746–1757.

Shechter, A., Quispe, K. A., Mizhquiri Barbecho, J. S., Slater, C., & Falzon, L. (2020). Interventions to reduce short-wavelength ("blue") light exposure at night and their effects on sleep: A systematic review and meta-analysis. *Sleep Advances, 1*(1), zpaa002.

Simpson, N. S., Gibbs, E. L., & Matheson, G. O. (2017). Optimizing sleep to maximize performance: Implications and recommendations for elite athletes. *Scandinavian Journal of Medicine & Science in Sports, 27*(3), 266–274.

Spiegel, K., Leproult, R., & Van Cauter, E. (1999). Impact of sleep debt on metabolic and endocrine function. *The Lancet, 354*(9188), 1435–1439.

Tassi, P., Bonnefond, A., Engasser, O., Hoeft, A., Eschenlauer, R., & Muzet, A. (2006). EEG spectral power and cognitive performance during sleep inertia: The effect of normal sleep duration and partial sleep deprivation. *Physiology & Behavior, 87*(1), 177–184.

Trotti, L. M. (2017). Waking up is the hardest thing I do all day: Sleep inertia and sleep drunkenness. *Sleep Medicine Reviews, 35*, 76–84.

Van Dongen, H. P., Maislin, G., Mullington, J. M., & Dinges, D. F. (2003). The cumulative cost of additional wakefulness: Dose-response effects on neurobehavioral functions and sleep physiology from chronic sleep restriction and total sleep deprivation. *Sleep, 26*(2), 117–126.

Vitale, K. C., Owens, R., Hopkins, S. R., & Malhotra, A. (2019). Sleep hygiene for optimizing recovery in athletes: Review and recommendations. *International Journal of Sports Medicine, 40*(08), 535–543.

Von Rosen, P., Frohm, A., Kottorp, A., Fridén, C., & Heijne, A. (2017). Too little sleep and an unhealthy diet could increase the risk of sustaining a new injury in adolescent elite athletes. *Scandinavian Journal of Medicine & Science in Sports, 27*(11), 1364–1371.

Walker, M. P., & Stickgold, R. (2005). It's practice, with sleep, that makes perfect: Implications of sleep-dependent learning and plasticity for skill performance. *Clinics in Sports Medicine, 24*(2), 301–317.

Walsh, N. P., Halson, S. L., Sargent, C., Roach, G. D., Nédélec, M., Gupta, L., ... Samuels, C. H. (2021). Sleep and the athlete: Narrative review and 2021 expert consensus recommendations. *British Journal of Sports Medicine, 55*(7), 356–368.

Werth, E., Dijk, D. J., Achermann, P., & Borbely, A. A. (1996). Dynamics of the sleep EEG after an early evening nap: Experimental data and simulations. *American Journal of Physiology-Regulatory, Integrative and Comparative Physiology, 271*(3), R501–R510.

17 Leadership

A Title Bestowed from Above; a Position of Awarded Power. Truth or Myth?

Jane Booth

For me, the answer is simple. It is undoubtedly, unequivocally, unquestionably a myth. Yet, how many of us working in sport actually think of leadership in terms of our CEOs, the Board, the senior leadership team, our committees or our captains? How many of us wait for someone to appoint us as 'the leader' or give us permission to take a lead? How many of us associate leadership with the power of those above us and feel that often we are power-less?

Perhaps we do have a sense of 'taking the lead' on certain areas of work, strategy or function, but how often do we, as coaches, athletes, administrators, sport scientists, psychologists, development staff, coach educators, assessors or analysts, really stop to think of ourselves as leaders or people having a significant leadership responsibility? Unless, of course, we have actually been given a leadership title by someone, or we have been employed as a 'leader'. And, how many of us inwardly (or perhaps even externally and more vocally) distance ourselves from 'the leadership' and blame 'them' when things go wrong or results don't go our way?

But what really is leadership?

When reviewing the literature on change and 'leading change', it becomes apparent that there are many differing views of leadership and the role of the leader. Bennis (2007, p. 2) reflected that 'it is almost a cliché of the leadership literature that a single definition of leadership is lacking', and O'Connell (2014, p. 183) recognized that 'the quest to explain leadership as a concept and practice has generated a complex web of theories and frameworks'. The quest to define leadership appears to be ongoing and, as noted by Dinh *et al.* (2014, p. 36), 'scholarly research on the topic of leadership has witnessed a dramatic increase over the last decade, resulting in the development of diverse leadership theories'. So rather than narrowing the definition and enabling the 'field' to be clearer about what leadership really is, continued research actually appears to be broadening the scope of definitions and widening the platform for debates on leadership. What an exciting (if a little confusing) place to be!

For me, this lack of any singular definition for leadership opens up huge possibilities and potential. It tells me that there is scope for adding alternative perspectives to the existing body of work; space to challenge current thinking and offer new perspectives. I love the idea of nothing being definitive; that everything is up for debate; that the academic field of leadership is open to alternative proposals. It feels like it allows us to 'play' and explore new ways of answering the age-old question of 'what is a leader?'.

Despite the lack of a singular definition, however, there does at least appear to be agreement amongst scholars that effective leadership is a common factor within successful organizational and societal change. The role of leadership in driving change has been highlighted as crucial by numerous researchers and writers since initial interest arose in the late 1980s; for example, Nadler and Tushman (1989), Dunphy and Stace (1993) and Strebel (1994). Strebel (1994) referred to leaders of change as 'change agents' with Robbins, (2001, p. 543) defining the change agent as 'persons who act as catalysts and assume the responsibility for managing the change activities'.

So, are you a leader?

Do you see yourself as a 'change agent' or 'catalyst for change'? Do you take responsibility for leading change, or do you wait for someone else to lead, or task you with that role?

My aim in this chapter, as the introductory paragraphs suggest, is to challenge the belief that leadership is a title or something bestowed on us. I seek to bust this myth and to offer an alternative lens through which we can view the concept of leadership and what it therefore means to be a 'leader'. I believe leadership is a 'way of being' or a set of behaviours that we all have the ability to develop and, as long as we see ourselves as people who have the potential to lead, then we are more than capable of creating change, influencing others and doing great things, even when our job title feels like it is telling us otherwise. I believe in the concept of authentic leadership as originally defined by Walumbwa *et al.* (2008, p. 94) as 'a pattern of leader behaviour that draws upon and promotes both positive psychological capacities and a positive ethical climate, to foster greater self-awareness, an internalised moral perspective, balanced processing of information, and relational transparency on the part of leaders working with followers, fostering positive self-development'. To me, this is what leadership is really all about.

> Change will not come if we wait for some other person or some other time. We are the ones we've been waiting for. We are the change that we seek.
>
> President Barack Obama, 2005

Great people make amazing things happen

Mr Wylie was my form teacher in my third year at middle school. He had a bit of a mullet haircut, played electric guitar in a band, wore the coolest Hi-tech Silver Shadow trainers (and yes, I know how much that ages me) and had a passion for sport. He made PE fun, gave us handy hints for getting rid of stitches (I am still not entirely sure that any of them actually work, but I do remember them!) and generally made time spent in his classroom – in his presence – enjoyable and entertaining. I remember his enthusiasm when playing and singing 'Chain Reaction' on his guitar on a school trip away in York (I can still remember all the words to that song); his encouragement when taking a bunch of us on a cross-country training run before a county competition; and his energy every single morning when he welcomed us into his classroom.

I don't remember everything that Mr Wylie said or did, but I absolutely remember that he made me (and I am pretty sure most of the others in my class) feel excited to be at school. Excited to be learning. Excited to see what would come next. I also remember the total awe I felt when seeing his band play for the first time. I am sure that I learnt to play the guitar because of him, and I am completely certain that I ended up working in sport because he helped me to fall in love with it, and not just because of his Hi-Tech Silver Shadows! For me, Mr Wylie was absolutely a leader; a great leader, not simply because his job title of 'teacher' gave him the status or power to influence. To me, he was a leader because of the tiny things he did every day; the way he listened, responded, engaged. It was his care, compassion and kindness from one human to another that brings him to mind when I think of inspirational leaders in my life.

Who are the great people in your life? Are THEY leaders?

So I begin this chapter with an invitation. An invitation for you to think back over your life and reflect upon individuals who have been influential in your development, growth and passion – and perhaps still are. Formally or informally, in work or at play, as a child or as an adult, as a coach or simply as a human being. People who were, or are, inspiring, motivational, caring, supportive or consistently there when you need them. Whoever they are, I am curious; who are your 'Mr Wylie's'?

Picture those people. All of them.

Now, I invite you to focus on just one of those people. Concentrate on one of these amazing humans who had (or still has) a big impact upon you and your development. Maybe it was a parent, coach, teacher, mentor, boss, colleague, friend or even a team-mate. Ask yourself 'why do I remember them?' and 'what did they do?'. Spend a few minutes really thinking about these questions. Jot down or voice record your thoughts (go on, give it a go)! This perhaps isn't quite what you were expecting in this chapter, but I challenge you, I urge you, I gently nudge you. Immerse yourself and really think about that wonderful person who has stuck in your memory for all this time.

When you are ready and have a few notes, switch your reflections to thinking about how you felt, or feel, in their presence. What words come to mind? Don't think too deeply about this, trust your instincts and write what is on your heart and what first comes into your head as you focus on this person. Now have a look at this word cloud below. Compare your words to the words in this image. What feels similar? What is different? What do you notice?

[Word cloud featuring words including: Safe, Supportive, Valued, Believed in me, Confident, Encouraged, Loved, Kind, Happy, Strong, Challenged, Patient, Brave, Cared-for, Calm, Caring, Honest, Respected, Trusted, Comfortable, Inspiring, Understood, Proud, Supported, Passionate, Friend, Open, Helpful, Connected, Grateful, Goal-setter, Relaxed, Confidence, Focussed, Vision, Seen, Amazing, Always there, Funny, Fun, Trustworthy, Mentor, Belonged, Friendly, Empowered, Achieved, Innovative, Guided, Balanced, Listened, An example, Respectful, Pillar, Clear vision, Communicative, Smart, Successful, Sounding board, I am OK, Allowed me to be myself, Changed my mindset, Changed my life]

The above words were all shared by high-performing female coaches[1] (n = 99) when asked the same reflective questions I posed above. I wonder how many of the words they identified connect with you and the person/people you held in your mind? I wonder, too, how many of the people you thought about would realize the significance of their role and impact on your life? Would they realize that they had played such an influential role in shaping your work, your career, your life? Have you ever told them? And arguably most significantly for this chapter; would they consider themselves to be a leader?

Defining 'great people'

The term 'great people', to which I referred in the above paragraph, is an important theme constructed within my PhD research on effective change leaders in sport coaching.[2] Each leader I interviewed talked about a number of such influential people throughout their lives and careers; people who had challenged and supported them in their growth. Interestingly, these leaders had arguably then become 'great people' for others because of these experiences and influences. I therefore offer this definition of 'great people' from my qualitative, narrative-directed study:

> Great people are ... caring and compassionate people who make me feel safe and believe in, inspire, trust and support me to learn, grow and become the person they know I can be.
>
> Supporting me ... so I can support others.
>
> **Walters, 2020, p. 259**

Whether recalling the support of parents and guardians, the teacher who inspired a love of sport, the coach who went out of his/her way to help or the manager who trusted them with something new – each participant in my study[2] acknowledged the crucial role that 'great people' played in their development over time. Often these 'great people' were behind the scenes and made little direct input into tasks taken on by the participant. Rather, these were people who created safe spaces for individuals to learn and 'give things a go'. Now that, to me, sounds like leadership. As one participant reflected:

> They gave me that, you know, room to explore and experiment and it meant so much. (***ibid.***)

Reflecting on the introduction to this chapter and to my 'Mr Wylie' story, it does feel important to acknowledge here that the research participants in my study[2] were not all leaders by name or title, nor were the 'great people' to whom they continually referred. While each was, and continues to be, influential in their field and acknowledged by others as making a real difference in their own particular arena, they are not individuals who you would immediately label as a 'leader', nor would they necessarily refer to themselves as leaders. Importantly, they were not selected for my research because of their position or title, they were invited to participate because of who they are, the recognition from others of the positive influence they have, the innovative approaches they take and the effective changes they influence in their particular 'world'.

Relationships matter for great people – now for some theory

So far in this chapter, I have introduced and explored the idea of leaders being 'great people' who help others to develop and grow as my challenge to the myth that leadership (the act or art of leading) is something bestowed on us or a title we are given. Now, in order to really build up a robust rationale for this challenge, we need to delve into some relevant theories to support this challenge. The theory I introduce below is a theory that can help us to appreciate why the relationships we build as humans have such relevance to our abilities and capabilities as leaders. So, are you ready? Let's go!

I begin by looking at psychological attachment theory (originating from the work of Bowlby in the late 1950s and 1960s and Ainsworth in the late 1960s and 1970s), which is based on studies of the interactions between children and their parents. Bowlby defined attachment as a 'lasting psychological connectedness between human beings' (1969, p. 194) and believed that 'humans evolved to form strong emotional bonds with their primary care-givers because doing so increased the probability of survival, especially in childhood' (Finkel and Simpson, 2015, p. 6). One of the underpinning tenets of attachment theory is that the provision of a 'secure-base' by the primary care-giver 'affords the child a haven of safety and provides the confidence necessary to explore and master ordinary environments' (Waters and Cummings, 2000, p. 167).

While this early work from Bowlby (1958) and Ainsworth (1969) focussed on parent–child relationships, research into adult attachments has revealed similar secure-base dynamics in other aspects of life. Authors such as Hazan and Shaver (1987) and Rom and Mikulincer (2003) explored Bowlby's attachment theory in the context of adult relationships and uncovered similarities in the emotional bond between parents and their children and the development of emotional bonds between partners in romantic relationships. A central theme to findings from adult-based studies is the feeling of safety generated through the relationship and the belief that each provides the other with a secure-base from which to grow (Gillath *et al.*, 2018).

I find it fascinating that, despite academic criticism over the years, attachment theory has remained relevant and been explored across a number of fields, including leadership; particularly around 'leader-follower' dynamics (Eldad and Benatov, 2018; Mayseless and Popper, 2019). Within this field, there is growing empirical support for a 'perspective of leadership based on attachment theory' (Wu and Parker, 2017, p. 1043), where the heart of this approach is the belief that 'leaders, like parents, are figures whose role includes guiding, directing, taking charge, and taking care of others less powerful than they and whose fate is highly dependent on them' (Popper and Mayseless, 2003, p. 42). Given the closing part of this sentence '… whose fate depended on them', it is interesting to note a number of research papers in recent years that have considered leadership styles and/or effectiveness during the COVID-19 global pandemic, (e.g. Hinojosa *et al.*, 2020; Kagan and Hirschfeld, 2023; Wilson, 2020). Indeed, Hinojosa *et al.* (2020) looked specifically at attachment theory and the importance, for leaders, of maintaining secure-base relationships with followers during times of immense pressure, such as the COVID-19 pandemic.

Research in the field of leadership also reports links between leaders who create a secure-base environment and positive outcomes for the career development of followers (Crawshaw and Game, 2015), engagement (Byrne *et al.*, 2017) and self-efficacy (Parker *et al.*, 2010). Harms *et al.* (2016) suggested that having 'a secure-base to fall back on leads individuals to be more willing to engage in exploratory behaviours such as meeting new people [and] exploring new ideas' (p. 1855). This perspective has also been adopted in the applied literature with Kohlrieser *et al.* (2012) coining the term 'Secure-Base Leadership' whereby a secure-base is 'a person … that provides a sense of protection, safety and caring and offers a source of inspiration and energy for daring, exploration, risk taking and seeking challenge' (p. 8).

Similar conclusions are being reached in the sport coaching literature in terms of secure-base attachments and coach–athlete relationships (Davis and Jowett, 2014; Felton and Jowett, 2015). Emerging evidence suggests a positive link between relationships built on a secure-base and success for the athlete in terms of performance gain, personal outlook and unleashing potential. It is particularly interesting to note the Jowett and Shanmugam (2016, p. 472) suggestion that an athlete's hidden potential can be released when 'coaches and athletes start to form a genuine working relationship, where they trust, respect, believe, commit and work together toward one goal'.

So ... am I a leader?

As you continue to read this chapter, I invite you to keep asking yourself this question. As you do so, I urge you to also contemplate the connections you have with other people. Do you work with people on a regular basis? Does your role require you to support other people in their development, growth and learning? Are you in a position where your interactions and communication with others have the potential to influence their thinking, their actions, their behaviour, their performance? Do other people look to you for support? Do other people consider you to be a 'great person'? Also, who do you look to as a 'great leader'? Are you solely focussed on the 'big names' in your sport or context who immediately come to mind as you think of 'leaders'? Or are you looking more closely to home at those 'great people' surrounding you as you develop and grow in your role/chosen career path? How will you determine whether, or not, you feel like a leader?

Connecting leadership and change – do you lead from the top or influence from within?

To explore the connection between leadership and change, it is helpful to reflect on various models of and for change that have been developed over the years (since the early 1940s and the 'godfather of change', Kurt Lewin). When reviewing such models, it becomes evident that a thread of leadership weaves through and across the 'change' landscape (Walters, 2020, pp. 25–47). Regardless of their approach or perspective, each of the models in my PhD study (*ibid.*) acknowledged the significance of effective leadership for change; albeit with contrasting views. For example, the Lippitt *et al.* (1958) and Waterman *et al.* (1980) models believed change to be led through a 'top-down' approach and directed by 'managers' and 'change agents' working to implement a new strategy in line with a planned change. Whether the end aim is behaviour change, social engineering or organizational development, these models give us a sense that planned change is led from the top.

This approach is reflective of the views of more traditional change theorists, for example, Haberberg and Rieple (2005, p. 569), who reported that significant change in an organization was usually instigated by the chief executive, managing director or equivalent. Traditional views of change adopt this 'top-down' approach and encourage us to believe that the most effective changes are driven by top-level managers or people at the 'top' with the power and influence to 'make change happen'. This perspective effectively argues that the strategic leader establishes the direction for change, the high-level management team leads the implementation of that change and everyone else then follows. I wonder how familiar this approach feels for the UK sporting context? Think about how new strategies for sport and physical activity are implemented by a Home Country sports council; or how a new sports partnership initiative is introduced; or even how new players are acquired for high-profile sports teams. Generally speaking, and from my experience in sport in the UK over the last 25+ years, change is decided on, driven and led from the top by people at the top.

There is a contrasting view, though. Johnson and Scholes (1999, p. 530) suggested that individuals actually responsible for organizational development are not necessarily those who lead the implementation of strategic change, with Vickers (2008, p. 560) agreeing that 'strategy can be diverted or altered by managers lower down the organisation'. Greiner (1967) advocated this approach with his notion of 'shared power' for change, and, despite their initial focus on planned change being managed from the 'top down', it is possible to see some elements of this more layered approach reflected in the Lewin and McKinsey models.

For example, Lewin recognized that individual behaviour influences overall group dynamic, and Waterman *et al.* (1980) believed that all staff have a role to play in creating change. Interestingly, Kotter (1996) went so far as to argue that 'top-down' leadership was a 'very dangerous belief' (1996, p. 51). This note of caution was also issued by Nadler and Tushman (1989, p. 200) and Fullan (2001, p. 1) who argued that such leaders 'inadvertently often do more harm than good because, at best, they provide episodic improvement followed by frustrated or despondent dependency'.

Despite Kotter's warning over a 'top-down' approach to leadership, it does not appear that he fully embraced the notion that leadership takes place at every level of the organization. Kotter proposed that change must be led by a 'powerful coalition that can act as a team' (1996, p. 56) and argued that members of such teams should possess the four characteristics of *position power*, *expertise*, *credibility* and *leadership* (*ibid.*, p. 57). Kotter believed that these four characteristics were necessary as leaders required a certain level of influence and authority within an organization for change to be managed and sustained.

I have to admit that I struggle to accept this view of leadership and change. I find the suggestion that only people with position power, expertise, credibility and authority can lead change to be in complete contrast with what I witnessed and explored in my research. I also feel it conflicts with what I see happening in everyday life in terms of the influence of 'great people' on the growth and development of people everywhere. (Think back to your 'Mr Wylie'). I do, however, recognize that this 'top-down', power-based view of leadership is prevalent within the sport sector in the UK and remains the predominant story of leadership throughout governing bodies, organizations, clubs, coaching systems and beyond.

It is noticeable that the few references to leadership in even the most recent sport policy and strategy documents within the UK are in line with the more traditional 'top-down' approach to leadership. For example, while there is recognition in the 2018 England Workforce Development strategy that 'leadership takes place at all levels in the workplace, not just at the senior executive level' (Sport England, 2018, p. 15), the associated key actions directly correlate leadership with management. Note a specific reference to 'leaders and managers' through actions such as 'implement a cutting-edge programme of support for leaders and managers in prioritised organisations' (*ibid.*). Plus, the 2022–2025 Sport England 'Uniting the Movement' Implementation Plan (Sport England, 2022, online) references 'leaders and decision-makers' in strategic partners organizations in the section of their strategy on 'Leading for Renewal', as well as focussing learning interventions towards 'senior decision-makers' in the same section. The emphasis of investment in leadership again arguably towards those with the *position power*, *expertise*, *credibility* and *leadership* referenced by Kotter (1996, p. 57).

Redefining leadership in sport

But what if, in sport, leadership was considered differently? What if leadership was viewed as something required at every level of an organization in order for change (at a behavioural, individual, organizational, strategic or systemic level) to occur? What if, in sport, we considered leadership through the lens offered by Meyerson (2001, p. 13)? Meyerson argued that change agents are 'not just those characterised by bold visions and strategic savvy, but also those characterised by patience, persistence and resourcefulness'. She identified change agents as 'sensitive improvisers who are able to recognise and act on opportunities as they arise'. Adopting the term 'tempered radical', Meyerson described how such individuals are often not the chief executive, president or senior manager of an organization (*ibid.*, p. 16), rather the 'everyday leader', (*ibid.*, p. 17), who makes a significant contribution to organizational change despite their lack of authority or power.

So while Meyerson does acknowledge that traditional, senior leaders do have a role to play in initiating and sustaining change, she also embraces what I now refer to as the 'everyday leader' (Walters, 2020). I find it refreshing to think of the 'tempered radical' as a leader who pursues change in line with their own values and beliefs on an everyday basis and whenever an opportunity arises. They also consistently act in line with these values and beliefs, particularly when they feel these are being questioned or under pressure, which feels so aligned to research like Cassidy *et al.*, 2009; Jenkins, 2010; Carless and Douglas, 2013.

Such studies argue that coaches need to understand that what they 'do' in practice is directly shaped by their personal values and beliefs (Carless and Douglas, 2011, p. 1), and that coaching effectiveness is linked to the degree to which coaches can articulate their own coaching philosophy (Cassidy *et al.*, 2009). I argue, therefore, that great coaches (and athletes, administrators, sport scientists, psychologists, development staff, coach educators, assessors or analysts) who understand their personal philosophy and know that this consistently influences and guides their behaviour are brilliant examples of the 'tempered radicals' that Meyerson describes. Effective practitioners (in my mind at least) are therefore also effective leaders – whether they embrace and realize this or not.

'I am the change I seek ... I am a leader'

If you view leadership in the same way as perhaps Lippitt *et al.* (1958), Waterman *et al.* (1980), Kotter (1996) or Haberberg and Rieple (2005), then it is likely you believe leadership to be something that is bestowed upon you by someone else; someone with power, influence or authority. A role that you need to wait to be given, or a title that you need to earn by applying for a job or proving yourself to be 'worthy' of such a position. In these cases, you must wait for someone else to view you as a leader, or to see your leadership potential before you can ever fulfil such a role.

What, though, if you see leadership in similar ways to Johnson and Scholes (1999), Meyerson (2001) or Vickers (2008)? What if you believe that anyone has the potential to lead and influence change at any level? What if you see leadership as an action, a behaviour, a way of being, in which you create ripples of change for yourself and others simply by living out your life in complete line with your values and beliefs? What if you, like me, can see the obvious correlation between an effective sport coach and a 'tempered radical'? What could this mean for how you see yourself in your current role? What could this mean for others who aspire to lead and yet don't believe it is in their control or gift to make this happen?

Day and Harrison (2007, p. 365) proposed that leader identity needs to be considered as a critical component of leader development because 'how one thinks of oneself as a leader' is crucial. Van Knippenberg *et al.* (2004), Day *et al.* (2009) and Day and Dragoni (2015) also recognized the 'important role that identity processes play in motivating and supporting leaders' personal growth' (Miscenko *et al.*, 2017, p. 617). In other words, how we see ourself in leadership terms really matters. The idea that we can view or define ourselves as a leader rather than waiting for leadership to be assigned to us is really in contrast with the traditional notion of 'top-down' leadership that arguably pervades our sporting landscape.

Of notable interest in helping us to 'bust the myth' of traditional leadership role assignment is the proposition made by Day and Sin (2011, p. 547) that 'if one does not think of oneself as a leader, or aspire to lead, then there is little motivation to develop or serve as a leader'. This perspective was further supported by Day and Dragoni (2015, p. 139) who stressed that while 'leader identity can be formed through social and/or personal factors, [a critical] facet is that pertaining to how and to what extent a person views him – or herself – as a leader'. Arguably, therefore, the first step in becoming a leader is to view oneself as such, or at the very least as someone with the potential to lead.

Changing the narrative; 'I lead therefore I am'

I started this chapter with an invitation and I am going to end with another. I firmly and fundamentally believe that the traditional view of leadership and what it means to be a leader need to be challenged. I reject the idea that leadership is a title reserved for those with position power, expertise, credibility and a leadership title (Kotter, 1996). I challenge the traditional view that the change is led most effectively in a 'top-down' manner, and I want to shake our cultural acceptance that those with 'power' are only the chief executives, senior managers and executive officers within the system. If we continue to accept these ideas we will, as Byrne *et al.* (2018, p. 272), continue to reinforce our collective 'preconceived ideas about what a typical leader should look like' and 'top-down' leadership will remain our pervading culture.

On the other hand, I love the potential offered by Meyerson's notion of the 'tempered radical' and the connection with great coaches driven by a sound understanding of their coaching philosophy and how this plays out in their everyday actions. I get excited by the suggestion that leadership is not a title to be bestowed, but rather a way of thinking about ourselves, with the first step in becoming a leader linked to simply seeing yourself as a leader or someone with the potential to lead.

So what if, as Crossnan *et al.* (2013, p. 291) propose, 'our view of leadership is not focused on power or position, but rather on the capacity of individuals to bring the best of themselves to support and enable others, ensure the organisations they work with achieve at the highest level, and in doing so, contribute to society'? What if we collectively adopt a 'different conceptualisation of leadership' (Byrne *et al.*, 2018, p. 271) that enables us all to challenge our preconceived ideas of what this looks like for us in sport, coaching and beyond. To achieve this, I argue that we need to start this shift by changing how leadership is viewed by both existing leaders and those who have aspirations and potential to effectively lead in future – whatever their level, starting with us.

Starting with you.

So for my final invitation to you, I am going to revisit the Barack Obama quote shared at the start of this chapter.

> Change will not come if we wait for some other person or some other time. We are the ones we've been waiting for. We are the change that we seek.
> **President Barack Obama, 2005**

And then …

- Don't wait for change; don't wait for someone to bestow on you the title of 'leader'.
- See yourself as a leader (or at the very least as someone with the potential to lead).
- Believe that you already lead change in everything you do.
- You are the change we seek.

So, are you a leader or 'just' a …?

In my eyes, you are not 'just' an anything. If you know your values, consistently bring your values to life through everything you do and believe you lead, are a leader or have the potential to lead, then you are already one. Don't wait for someone else to give you the title or a role. In the words of a famous sporting goods brand, 'just do it'. Lead.

Notes

1. Female coaches participating in the Women into Sport High Performance Pathway (WISH) programme between August 2022 and August 2023.
2. Walters, J.L. (2020). **'I am what I am': Narratives of effective change leadership in UK sport coaching systems**. Unpublished PhD Thesis. University of Birmingham.

References

Ainsworth, M.D.S. (1969) Object relations, dependency, and attachment: A theoretical review of the infant- mother relationship. *Child Development.* 40: 969–1025.

Bennis, W. (2007) The challenges of leadership in the modern world: Introduction to the special issue. *American Psychologist.* 62 (1): 2–5.

Bowlby, J. (1958) The nature of the child's tie to his mother. *International Journal of Psychoanalysis.* 39: 350–371.

Bowlby J. (1969) *Attachment. Attachment and loss: Vol. 1. Loss.* New York: Basic Books.

Byrne, Z., Albert, L., Manning, S. and Desir, R. (2017) Relational models and engagement: An attachment theory perspective. *Journal of Managerial Psychology.* 32 (1): 30–44.

Byrne, A., Crossan, M. and Seijts, G. (2018) The development of leader character through crucible moments. *Journal of Management Education.* 42 (2): 265–293.

Carless, D. and Douglas, K. (2013) Living, resisting, and playing the part of athlete: Narrative tensions in elite sport. *Psychology of Sport and Exercise.* 14: 701–708.

Cassidy, T., Jones, R.L. and Potrac, P. (2009) *Understanding sports coaching: the social, cultural and pedagogical foundations of coaching practice.* 2nd ed. New York: Routledge.

Crawshaw, J.R. and Game, A. (2015) The role of line managers in employee career management: An attachment theory perspective. *The International Journal of Human Resource Management.* 26 (9): 1182–1203.

Crossan, M., Mazutis, D., Seijts, G. and Gandz, J. (2013) Developing leader character in business programmes. *Academy of Management Learning and Education.* 12 (2): 285–305.

Davis, L. and Jowett, S. (2014) Coach-athlete attachment and the quality of the coach-athlete relationship: Implications for athlete's well-being. *Journal of Sports Sciences.* 32 (15): 1454–1464.

Day, D.V. and Harrison, M.M. (2007) A multilevel, identity-based approach to leadership development. *Human Resource Management Review.* 17: 360–373.

Day, D.V., Harrison, M.M. and Halpin, S.M. (2009) *An integrative approach to leader development: Connecting adult development, identity and expertise.* New York: Psychology Press

Day, D.V. and Sin, H-P. (2011) Longitudinal tests of an integrative model of leader development: Charting and understanding developmental trajectories. *The Leadership Quarterly.* 22: 545–560.

Day, D.V. and Dragoni, L. (2015) Leadership development: An outcome-oriented review based on time and levels of analysis. *Annual Review of Organisational Psychology and Organisational Behaviour.* 2 (1): 133–156.

Dinh, J.E., Lord, R.G., Gardner, W.L., Meuser, J.D., Liden, R.C. and Hu, J. (2014) Leadership theory and research in the new millennium: Current theoretical trends and changing perspectives. *The Leadership Quarterly.* 25: 36–62.

Dunphy, D. and Stace, D. (1993) The strategic management of corporate change. *Human Relations.* 46 (8): 905–920.

Eldad, R. and Benatov, J. (2018) Adult attachment and perceived parental style may shape leadership behaviours. *Leadership and Organisation Development Journal.* 39 (2): 261–275.

Felton, L. and Jowett, S. (2015) On understanding the role of need thwarting in the association between athlete attachment and well/ill-being. *Scandinavian Journal of Medicine and Sports Sciences.* 25: 289–298.

Finkel, E.J. and Simpson, J.A. (2015) Editorial overview: Relationship science. *Current Opinion in Psychology.* 1: 5–9.

Fullan, M. (2001) *Leading in a culture of change.* San Francisco: Jossey-Bass.

Gillath, O., Karantzas, G.C. and Fraley, C. (2018) *Adult attachment: a concise introduction to theory and research.* London: Elsevier.

Greiner, L.E. (1967) Patterns of organisation change. *Harvard Business Review.* May-June: 119–130.

Haberberg, A. and Rieple, A. (2001) *The strategic management of organisations.* Harlow: Pearson Education Limited.

Harms, P.D., Bai, Y. and Han, G.H. (2016) How leader and follower attachment styles are mediated by trust. *Human Relations.* 69 (9): 1853–1976.

Hazan, C. and Shaver, P.R. (1987) Romantic love conceptualised as an attachment process. *Journal of Personality and Social Psychology.* 52: 511–524.

Hinojosa, A.S., Shaine, M.J.D. and McCauley, K.D. (2020) A strange situation indeed: Fostering leader–follower attachment security during unprecedented crisis. *Management Decision.* 58 (10): 2099–2115. https://doi.org/10.1108/MD-08-2020-1142

Jenkins, S. (2010) Coaching philosophy. In Lyle, J. and Cushion, C. (Eds.) *Sports coaching: Professionalisation and practice* (pp. 233–242). London: Churchill Livingstone Elsevier.

Johnson, G. and Scholes, K. (1999) *Exploring corporate strategy.* 5th ed. Hemel Hempstead, Hertfordshire: Prentice Hall Europe.

Jowett, S. and Shanmugam, V. (2016) Relational coaching in sport: It's psychological underpinnings and practical effectiveness. In Schinke, R., McGannon, K.R. and Smith, B. (Eds.) *Routledge international handbook of sport psychology.* London: Routledge.

Kagan, I. and Hirschfeld, M.J. (2023) Nursing leadership in drawing policy lessons from major events such as a COVID-19 pandemic. *Journal of Nursing Scholarship.* 55 (1): 5–7. https://doi.org/10.1111/jnu.12865.

Kohlrieser, G., Goldsworthy, S. and Coombe, D. (2012) *Care to dare: Unleashing astonishing potential through secure base leadership.* San Francisco, CA: Jossey-Bass.

Kotter, J.P. (1996) *Leading change.* Boston, Massachusetts: Harvard Business School Press.

Lippitt, R., Watson, J. and Westley, B. (1958) *The dynamics of planned change.* New York: Harcourt, Brace and World.

Mayseless, O. and Popper, M. (2019) Attachment and leadership: Review and new insights. *Current Opinion in Psychology.* 25: 157–161.

Meyerson, D.E. (2001) *Tempered radicals: How people use difference to inspire change at work.* Boston, Massachusetts: Harvard Business School Press.

Miscenko, D., Guenter, H. and Day, D.V. (2017) Am I a leader? Examining leader identity development over time. *The Leadership Quarterly.* 26: 605–620.

Nadler, D.A. and Tushman, M.L. (1989) Organisational frame bending: principles for managing re-orientation. *The Academy of Management Executive.* III (3): 194–204.

O'Connell, P.K. (2014) A simplified framework for 21st century leader development. *The Leadership Quarterly.* 25: 183–203.

Parker, S.K., Bindl, U.K. and Strauss, K. (2010) Making things happen: A model of proactive motivation. *Journal of Management.* 36: 827–856.

Popper, M. and Mayseless, O. (2003) Back to basics: Applying a parenting perspective to transformational leadership. *Leadership Quarterly.* 14: 41–65.

Rom, E. and Mikulincer, M. (2003) Attachment theory in group context: The association between attachment style and group representations, goals, memories and functioning. *Journal of Personality and Social Psychology.* 84 (1): 1220–1235.

Robbins, S.P. (2001) *Organisational behaviour.* 9th ed. New Jersey: Prentice Hall Inc.

Sport England. (2018) *Working in an active nation: The professional workforce strategy for England.* London: Sport England.

Sport England. (N.D.) *Uniting the movement: Our 10-year vision to transform lives and communities through sport and physical activity.* London: Sport England. Accessed online at https://www.sportengland.org/about-us/uniting-movement on 15/01/2024.

Strebel, P. (1994) Choosing the right change path. *California Management Review.* Winter: 29–51.

Van Knippenberg, D., Van Knippenberg, B., De Cremer, D. and Hogg, M.A. (2004) Leadership, self and identity: A review and research agenda. *The Leadership Quarterly.* 15: 825–856.

Vickers, D. (2008) Beyond the hegemonic narrative – a study of managers. *Journal of Organisational Change Management.* 21 (5): 560–573.

Walters, J.L. (2020) *'I am what I am': Narratives of effective change leadership in UK sport coaching systems.* Unpublished PhD Thesis. University of Birmingham.

Walumbwa, F.O., Avolio, B.J., Gardner, W.L., Wernsing, T.S. and Peterson, S.J. (2008) Authentic leadership: Development and validation of a theory-based measure? *Journal of Management.* 34: 89–126.

Waterman Jnr., R.H., Peters, T.J. and Phillips, J.R. (1980) Structure is not organisation. *Business Horizons.* 23 (3): 14–26.

Waters, E. and Cummings, E.M. (2000) A secure base from which to explore close relationships. *Child Development.* 71 (1): 164–172.

Wilson, S. (2020) Nursing leadership in drawing policy lessons from major events such as a COVID-19 pandemic. *Leadership.* 16 (3): 279–293.

Wu, C.-H. and Parker, S. (2017) The role of leader support in facilitating proactive work behaviour: A perspective from attachment theory. *Journal of Management.* 43 (4): 1025–1049.

18 'If You Want to Go Fast Go Alone. If You Want to Go Far, Go Together' – Engaging Productively with a Coach Developer

Andrew Bradshaw

This African proverb provides a good stimulus to thinking about coach development work and the rationale behind this chapter. Coaching is often a lonely endeavour, and this can lead to coaches developing without much support. Where coaches' learning and development is predominantly self-directed and self-reliant, progress can be perceived as fast-paced, yet coaching research points towards positive perceptions of learning being a poor proxy for developing knowledge, skills and behaviour. Short-term 'performances', such as those needed to pass assessments in formal coach education programmes, can be conflated with meaningful and lasting change, and coaches may overestimate what they have learnt from these development situations. In addition, some coaches' self-awareness and insights into their own coaching can be poor: often not matching up to what they are observed doing 'in the field' (Stodter, 2022). These factors combined can lead towards perceptions of progress, confidence and certainty of 'the way' of coaching – a position that can present as the top of the peak on Dunning-Kruger's graph (Figure 18.1) (Kruger, & Dunning, D, 1999).

In contrast, over the last decade, the value of coaches embarking on and exploring learning journeys *together* with a Coach Developer has become more established and recognized. The broader ICCE umbrella description of a Coach Developer that included coach educators, assessors, learning facilitators, presenters and mentors (ICCE, 2014) did not accurately represent the work that skilled practitioners were undertaking with coaches. The journey towards defining a much more focussed role in the UK began in 2017 and

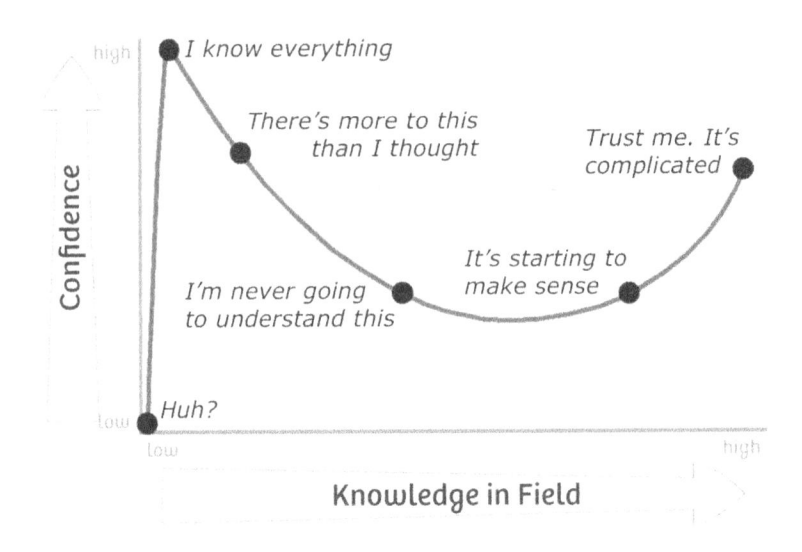

Figure 18.1. Dunning-Kruger effect graphic.

concluded with the creation of the CIMSPA Professional Standard: Coach Developer – 'expert support practitioners who plan for, implement, and sustain strategies and interventions in support of skilled performance in sport coaching' (CIMSPA Professional Standard: Coach Developer, P4, 2021). The importance of the Coach Developer role, working with coaches in context, was reinforced in the Pathway Coaching Position Statement (UK Sport and EIS Pathways Team, 2020).

> *The coach developer's work is educational, developmental, caring and support oriented: interventions may include the development of technical skills, enhancing interpersonal relationships, evolving effective strategies to manage specific challenges and constraints, or a combination of these.*
>
> *Whatever the specific nature of a coach developer's work might be, it will always be characterised by prioritising the health and wellbeing of the coach. It will also be collaborative, contextually situated, and concerned with helping coaches to develop active, critical knowledge and skills.*
> (CIMSPA, 2021)

Key themes that stand out from the description above include caring, wellbeing, collaborative and contextually situated. The learning journey of coach and Coach Developer together over time will be typified by these ways of working.

This chapter addresses some of the myths that perpetuate around how coach development support might currently be experienced or perceived and provides examples that bring to life the descriptor above and illustrate the value of emergent and ongoing learning and development journeys.

> *'I keep **six** honest serving men (they taught me all I knew); Theirs names are What and Why and When and How and Where and Who.' – Rudyard Kipling*

Rudyard Kipling's six teachers provide a useful framing for each myth.

'What?' myth – Isn't it a little like being assessed, being judged by the Coach Developer?

Experiences and reflections shared by numerous coaches involved in coach development programmes in both talent development and high-performance contexts (UK Coaching & UK Sport, Coach Development Programmes 2015–2020) centre around uncertainty and perhaps some fear when initially engaging with a Coach Developer. 'Is it because I'm not good enough?', 'How do I use a Coach Developer?', 'Will they tell me what I'm doing wrong and how to fix it?' and 'Will it be like my assessment?' are questions that have been shared in reflective conversations. While careful framing and initial contracting can help quell these reservations, coaches' expectations will be strongly shaped by what they have experienced before.

It is well established that the sum of a coach's previous experiences, knowledge, values, beliefs and practices – known as their 'biography' – has a big influence on what they learn and how they think about learning and development (Cushion et al., 2010). If prior learning activity has been through formal coach education programmes, most 'support' will have been positioned around competencies, curriculum and assessment. The experience of this tutor, educator or assessor role is more 'out-to-in' rather than the coaches' experiences, intentions, reasons, strategies and actions providing the focal point for the coach development experience – working 'in-to-out' (Muir & North, 2023).

Meeting learners/coaches where they are is a way of working that helps shape these initial and ongoing support experiences, being driven by building a thorough understanding of the coach, their environment and context and how these change over time and how things came to be. This will be typified by the Coach Developer employing the approach of seeking first to understand, rather than to be understood (Covey, 2004). This approach tends to open up valuable opportunities to establish and build meaningful relationships on genuine curiosity, rather than responses based on evaluating, judging and advising. It also enables a Coach Developer to work with agility and to flex the 'How?' of their work depending upon what the coach is experiencing.

> *Coaches could benefit from having someone who sits objectively on the side not someone who'll explain how to do this or that, someone who will ask questions and help coaches to find their own strength (Olusoga et al., 2017)*

'Why?' myth – If you want to go fast, go alone

We return to the initial proverb in this chapter highlighting the value of working together with a Coach Developer over a longer and more collaborative learning journey.

Supporting coaches to become more aware of, and acknowledge, the limitations of their own perspectives and recognize that their judgements and decisions may be influenced by various factors is a crucial role of the Coach Developer and creates room for growth and improvement (Collins & Collins, 2016). As Stodter (2022) further details, without embracing this complexity and recognizing the value of privileging different perspectives, there is a danger that coaches merely reinforce their own ideas with 'people like me' in 'echo-chambers'.

The support of a Coach Developer in exploring the potential to consider and make sense of different perspectives requires coaches to embrace uncertainty and critically reflect on their learning journeys to date. Danny Kerry (coach to the 2016 Gold-medal-winning GB Women's Hockey team) described the idea of '*maintaining your relationship with doubt*' in a conversation about performance planning. At times this may require unlearning, generating new understanding, more refined insight, slight adjustments in a process or a shift in approach (Wenger-Trayner – https://www.wenger-trayner.com/social-learning-spaces/). This uncertainty might feel quite uncomfortable and challenging in the initial stages (and possibly beyond) and having support, challenge, stretch and re-assurance throughout this journey is where Coach Developer support has significant value.

> *'I found coaching conversations with my Coach Developer really useful, as in a relatively short time I felt I discovered things about my coaching / processes that I wasn't consciously aware of.'*
> Rowing Coach on Performance Foundation programme,
> UK Coaching, 2019

The value of reflective conversations is not new. Gilbert and Trudel highlighted their utility for facilitating coaches' reflective practice back in 2001 in particular illustrating the additional value of the Coach Developer as a condition for reflective practice. In their more recent work, Downham and Cushion (2022) developed an empirically grounded understanding *of* reflection that is specific to coaching. This understanding was presented as a heuristic device enabling coaches and support Coach Developers to explore both the types of thinking and the content of reflection. By mapping where reflection is focussed offers the coach and Coach Developer the opportunity to step into the 'blank' areas, where reflective practice was not happening.

Stotder's 'coffee filter/making' analogy (2022) also illustrates the productive and transformational function of reflective conversations and that they are more than just discussions, drawing on Schön's work (1987). They are typified by repeating cycles of setting the problem (appreciation), generating ideas/experimenting/evaluating (action) and then re-appreciation. Questions that might emerge in these conversations could include the following:

- How well did that new idea or strategy work in practice?
- How do we know?
- Could it be adapted, if so, how?

Coaching conversations that enable the coach to reflect on and explore their practice while also having the ability to articulate what, how and why an approach is selected and applied create reflective spaces where criticality and adaptability are valued (Nash, Ashford & Collins, 2023). These spaces and discussions are intended to be thought-provoking and challenging, and this is where the utility and value of a Coach Developer as a collaborative and supportive part of the process is a significant enabler within ongoing learning journeys.

It is also important to note that we make sense of, and reflect upon, information that we consider to be important, that we are aware of and that we are drawn to re-examine. Supporting learners involves helping them to pay attention to a broader set of things than they have previously. A Coach Developer can play the valuable role of a *'second set of eyes'* (Royle, 2023), helping coaches notice things in their coaching and their environment that they may not have been aware of. Through reflective conversations, observations might be offered in order to generate greater understanding and help sense-making such as *'I noticed this, can you tell me more?'* or *'I observed this, I'm curious why?'*

'When?' myth – I don't have enough time to work with a coach developer

There is a strong connection to the *Coaching is a 24 hour a day job* chapter in the original myths book (Cropley, Hanton & Baldock, 2021). The authors detail how there is a pervasive narrative across coaching that it is a consuming experience that encompasses long working hours (Olusoga & Thelwell, 2017). Often being 'first in and last out' or 'putting in the extra hours' is perceived as a badge of honour, proof if it was needed of their motivation, persistence and passion for the job. Cody Royle labels this behaviour as 'chronic individualism', a condition marked by workaholism and sacrificing too much of their personal life for a job with no boundaries (Royle, 2023).

> *You lose clarity in the role because the pressure is so great. You are away so much the game consumes you and you lose perspective. You are trying to keep so many people happy and engaged you have no time for yourself.*
> Darren Lehman, ex-Australian Cricket Coach

While the additional pressures that Lehman describes above are inherent in high-performance sport, the challenges that coaches face right across the coaching landscape are complex and demanding. Grassroots coaches, mostly volunteer in nature, will be dealing with selection issues, parent relationships, player welfare, fundraising and many more all in their own time. Many coaches report experiencing mental illness (44%) (Smith et al., 2020), a variety of individual, interpersonal and organizational stressors (Norris, Didymus & Kaiseler, 2017) and challenges such as facility access, interaction with athletes and limits on their own skills (North, Piggott, Rankin-Wright & Ashford, 2020).

The response as to how coaches attempt to cope with these inevitable demands can lead to some crucial outcomes. Coaches may struggle to manage the demands that they encounter and as a consequence, the stressors experienced by coaches are likely to not only negatively affect themselves (their effectiveness) but may also affect the athletes with whom they work (Thelwell et al., 2017).

Reframing the responses to these demands as a ***performance strategy*** for the coach positions, coach development support is a key piece in the jigsaw towards *integrating well-being* into coaches' lives. Self-care is part of the solution, but building self-awareness is often helped with the support of a Coach Developer. This reflection from Troy (below) came after engaging with a coach development programme.

> *It's made me realise the importance of boundaries, the environment I work in, my well being and the well being of others, because they all contribute and underpin what we're doing. England Basketball Age Group Coach, 2020*

This connects to Colum Cronin's work on Care in Coaching (e.g. Cronin & Armour, 2017, 2018; Cronin, 2021), the challenges coaches face position them as a carer who understands and meets the sporting and personal needs of athletes. For this to be sustainable, however, coaches should not only be caregivers but they themselves should be well cared for (Cronin & Armour, 2018). Coach Developers can play an important role in supporting coaches to appreciate how they balance meeting the needs of others, with caring for themselves and their own needs while ensuring that the responsibility for care and attention to well-being does not just lie with the coach. To return to the Coach Developer standards – *whatever the specific nature of a coach developer's work might be, it will always be characterised by prioritising the health and well-being of the coach.*

'How?' myth – Won't the Coach Developer just watch me coach and tell me how to improve?

When Coach Developer work is described as being in-situ or in context, it means that coaching observation is absolutely a crucial way of working, building an understanding of the coaches' practice and their environment.

> *'working alongside coaches, supporting them to identify and resolve questions meaningful to their practice that generate opportunities for personal and professional growth' (Muir, 2018).*

The framework above illustrates how a Coach Developer would approach work with a coach. The Coach Developer's practice is the central feature creating connections across and between all other elements. The three black circles represent three areas of knowledge (Figure 18.2):

- **Who** is being developed – the coach. This would include their experiences, background, learning journey to date, age, demography.
- **How** learning is being supported – the ways in which the Coach Developer works with the coach to create meaningful learning opportunities.
- **What** are you working with them on – this can fall into two categories:
  - The what of the coaching role, for example, inter-relationships or care and well-being

Figure 18.2. Adapted from The role of the Coach Developer: A conceptual framework. P7. CIMSPA Professional Standard: Coach Developer, 2021 Source: Kruger, J., & Dunning, D. (1999).

- The what of the game/activity, for example, skill refinement or performance planning

The grey hexagons illustrate how the professional skills of the Coach Developer create unique ways of working with each coach based on them and their context. Building a deep understanding of *who* the coach is will support decisions about *how* to work with them most effectively. Discussions about what the coach might want some support to explore would then in turn link to further decisions about what learning opportunities to design together. The interconnections between the who, how and the what evolve as the work progresses and the relationship develops.

> Example: A coach wanting to explore their interactions with performers in a session might focus on their use of questions. An audio recording of the session could offer a good entry point for a coaching conversation. How the questions were phrased, when they were used, who they were directed at would be some of the areas to explore linked to the goals and intentions of the session. If the aim of the session was to promote performer thinking and problem-solving, then the way in which questions or reflections were shared would be an area to explore with the coach, possibly uncovering some contradictions between what they intended to do and how the coaching reality actually played out.

A point of note here is the skill of deciding the how, shaping the most effective learning opportunity. The use of audio capture (and perhaps even video) might generate really productive sources of feedback for some coaches, yet for others this approach may be challenging and perceived as too disruptive. Exploring more subtle approaches at times, being agile and flexible in ways of working enables Coach Developers to better meet coaches where they are.

'Where?' myth – Coach Development only happens track-side, pool-side or on the pitch

Considering the question 'where does coaching happen?' is the starting point. Of course, coaching takes place on the field/arena of play but also in so many other environments and contexts. From planning meetings with other coaches and support staff, debriefs and reviews with athletes/players to conversations with parents or others within the sport/club/organization. Exploring the coach's lived coaching experience enables the Coach Developer to learn about the coach's ideas and practices through building an understanding of the coach in their day-to-day coaching (Muir & North, 2023). The example below illustrates how an 'in-situ' visit to observe a coach could be planned to enable the Coach Developer to see, hear and feel things across a range of their coaching interactions.

> Coach Developer interaction with a Rowing coach (an example workflow):
> - Initial discussion with the coach in their office space – observing interactions with other staff and leaders getting a sense of the dynamics and relationships
> - Coaching conversation over lunch – initial conversations about coaching journey, biography, current wants and needs. Frame the fieldwork experience in the afternoon, exploring intentions
> - Visit to boat house – opportunity to see the training environment, chat with some of the athletes and other coaches
> - Out on the water – observe the coach in action and experience all the other sources of relevant coaching 'data', not just seeing but also hearing and feeling (over a series of visits this included video recording)
> - Generating feedback with the coach – both immediately afterwards and in time; both virtually and in person. A point to note here is the word 'generating', not simply offering feedback in a one-directional manner, but more working with the coach to explore the different potential sources of useful and relevant feedback together

'Who?' myth – I need to find someone to share all their knowledge

> *Learning and development is not something 'done' to coaches by the Coach Developer with the latter for example sharing his/her ideas and 'wisdom'; rather it is about working alongside coaches by supporting them to identify and resolve questions meaningful to their practice that generate opportunities for personal and professional growth (Muir, 2018).*

This view of a hierarchical relationship typified by a one-directional flow of knowledge is often rooted in more traditional mentoring roles where experienced coaches share their 'wisdom'. As we have explored in this chapter, the approach of a skilled Coach Developer is to work with the coach, alongside their learning and development journey providing support, stretch, care and challenge as identified and required. Another concept to consider here is 'questions before answers, problems before solutions'. If answers and solutions are what is being offered, then the sense of collaboration and co-creation is lost. Working through the questions that are current, helping the coach make sense of them and explore the problems they face – entering into a thriving relationship with the Coach Developer, where growth, well-being and striving for performance improvement happen at the same time (Newell, 2022).

So, how might I find a Coach Developer? The Coach Developer workforce is growing in the UK; and although full-time roles are still mainly positioned in high-performance contexts, there are a number of sports exploring deploying these roles across Talent Pathways and into participation spaces. Those involved in supporting coach learning and development need to understand the key processes of learning in order to help coaches learn. The demands on those who develop coaches and how they work with any dual role as mentors, tutors, educators or assessors are progressing alongside ever more 'learner-centred' online and blended learning formats (Stodter, 2022). The development of a more defined training pathway is still evolving in the UK, but initial contact with your NGB or local Sports Partnership would be a useful first step. For those keen on finding out more, the free Open University online 'Coaching Others to Coach' programme is a good introduction.

Concluding thoughts to consider

What might a learning journey in collaboration look like for you? Could it help promote a thriving onward route and support longevity in your role? How could you access the support of a Coach Developer or explore other options to become more curious about your coaching? This may simply start with committing to have a go at one or more of the following:

To try

- Ask someone you trust to come and watch you coach. Ask them to pay attention to what they see, hear and feel. Use this as a starting point for a coaching conversation afterwards.

- Switch roles and go and watch another coach. Be really curious about the environment, coaching and athlete–player interactions.
- Record yourself in a coaching session and listen back to it with a curious ear (use the mic in your phone earphones and the voice-recorded app).
- Map out your network and consider whom you need to connect with more – consider those that might offer useful points of difference.
- Identify a Coach Developer who can go on this coaching journey with you.

And finally, do prioritize energy and enthusiasm to create your personal performance strategy – make time and space for personal learning, development and care for yourself. Seek support from others, broaden your network of those able to offer different perspectives and be really curious about what they can offer.

Acknowledgements

This chapter includes concepts and ideas that have been utilized within the UK Sport *Supporting Coaching in High-Performance Sport* learning and development journey for Coach Developers and those supporting coaching in high-performance environments over the last three years. Dr Andrew Gillott (previously UK Sport, now University of Stirling) and Dr Bob Muir (Leeds Beckett University) were the architects of this programme and have supported my thinking in this space.

References

Chartered Institute for Management of Sport and Physical Activity (CIMSPA). (2021). CIMSPA professional standard: Coach developer. Loughborough: The Chartered Institute for the Management of Sport and Physical Activity. Available online: cimspa-ps-coach-developer-v1.0.pdf

Covey, S. (2004). *The 7 habits of highly effective people: Powerful lessons in personal change.* Rosetta Books LLC.

Cushion, C., Nelson, L., Armour, K., Lyle, J., Jones, R., Sandford, R., & O'Callaghan, C. (2010). *Coach learning and development: A review of literature.* Leeds: UK Coaching.

Cronin, C. (2021). Caring coaching: Examining the notion of 'cruel to be kind' and other caring myths. In A. Whitehead & J. Coe (Eds.), *Myths of sport coaching.* London: Sequoia Books.

Cronin, C., & Armour, K. (Eds.). (2018). *Care in sport coaching: Pedagogical cases* (1st ed.). Routledge. https://doi.org/10.4324/9781351109314

Cronin, C., & Armour, K. M. (2017). 'Being' in the coaching world: New insights on youth performance coaching from an interpretative phenomenological approach. *Sport, Education and Society, 22*(8), 919–931. https://doi.org/10.1080/13573322.2015.1108912

Cropley, B., Hanton, S., & Baldock, L. (2021). Coaching is a 24 hour-a-day job: A myth. In A. Whitehead, & J. Coe (Eds.), *Myths of sports coaching* Sequoia Books Ltd.

Downham, L., & Cushion, C. (2022). Reflection and reflective practice in high-performance sport coaching: A heuristic device. *Physical Education and Sport Pedagogy*, 1–20. https://doi.org/10.1080/17408989.2022.2136369

International Council for Coaching Excellence. (2014). International coach developer framework, version 1.1. Leeds: International Council for Coaching Excellence.

Kruger, J., & Dunning, D. (1999). Unskilled and unaware of it: How difficulties in recognizing one's own incompetence lead to inflated self-assessments. *Journal of Personality and Social Psychology, 77*(6), 1121.

Muir, B. (2018). *Coach learning and development in the performance domain: An embedded, relational and emergent intervention strategy* PhD thesis. Leeds Beckett University.

Muir, B., & North, J. (2023). Supporting coaches to learn through and from their everyday experiences: A 1:1 coach development workflow for performance sport. *International Sport Coaching Journal* (published online ahead of print 2023).

Nash, C., Ashford, M., & Collins, L. (2023). Expertise in coach development: The need for clarity. *Behavioral Sciences, 13*(11), 924.

Newell, E. (2022). Understanding thriving environments. Leeds: UK Coaching. Available online: Understanding Thriving Environments - UK Coaching.

Norris, L. A., Didymus, F. F., & Kaiseler, M. (2017). Stressors, coping, and well-being among sports coaches: A systematic review. *Psychology of Sport and Exercise, 33*, 93–112. https://doi.org/10.1016/j.psychsport.2017.08.005

North, J., Piggott, D., Rankin-Wright, A. J., & Ashford, M. (2020). An empirical examination of UK coaches' issues and problems, and their support and advice networks. *International Sport Coaching Journal / ISCJ*. ISSN 2328-918X. https://doi.org/10.1123/iscj.2019-0049

Olusoga, P., & Thelwell, R. (2017). Coach stress and associated implications. In R. Thelwell, C. Harwood, & I. Greenlees (Eds.), *The psychology of sports coaching. Research and practice* (pp. 128–141). Routledge.

Royle, C. (2023). Second set of eyes: How great coaches become champions. Independently published.

Schön, D. A. (1987). *Educating the reflective practitioner*. San Francisco: Jossey-Bass.

Smith, A., Haycock, D., Jones, J., Greenough, K., Wilcock, R., & Braid, I. (2020). Exploring mental health and illness in the UK sports coaching workforce. *International Journal of Environmental Research and Public Health, 17*.

Stodter, A. (2022). *Ten things I've learned from ten years of coach learning research*. Leeds: UK Coaching. Available online: Ten Things I've Learned From Ten Years of Coach Learning Research - UK Coaching.

Thelwell, R. C., Wagstaff, C. R. D., Rayner, A., Chapman, M., & Barker, J. (2017). Exploring athletes' perceptions of coach stress in elite sport environments. *Journal of Sports Sciences, 35*(1), 44–55. https://doi.org/10.1080/02640414.2016.1154979

Wenger Trayner, B., & Wenger Trayner, E. Social learning spaces. Available online: Social learning spaces - wenger-trayner

UK Sport Coach Development Team & English Institute of Sport Performance Pathways. (2020). Pathway coaching position statement. https://www.uksport.gov.uk/-/media/files/resources/uk-sport-eis-coaching-positioning-statement.ashx